The Letters of Gertrude Stein
and Virgil Thomson

Photograph of Virgil Thomson and Gertrude Stein looking at a copy of *Four Saints in Three Acts*

THE LETTERS OF GERTRUDE STEIN AND VIRGIL THOMSON

Composition as Conversation

Edited by Susan Holbrook and Thomas Dilworth

2010

OXFORD
UNIVERSITY PRESS

Oxford University Press, Inc., publishes works that further
Oxford University's objective of excellence
in research, scholarship, and education.

Oxford New York
Auckland Cape Town Dar es Salaam Hong Kong Karachi
Kuala Lumpur Madrid Melbourne Mexico City Nairobi
New Delhi Shanghai Taipei Toronto

With offices in
Argentina Austria Brazil Chile Czech Republic France Greece
Guatemala Hungary Italy Japan Poland Portugal Singapore
South Korea Switzerland Thailand Turkey Ukraine Vietnam

The letters of Gertrude Stein are reprinted courtesy of the
Estate of Gertrude Stein, through its Literary Executor,
Mr. Stanford Gann, Jr. of Levin & Gann, P.A.

The letters of Virgil Thomson are reprinted by permission of
The Virgil Thomson Foundation, Ltd., copyright owner.

Introduction and editorial matter Copyright © 2010
by Oxford University Press, Inc.

Published by Oxford University Press, Inc.
198 Madison Avenue, New York, New York 10016
www.oup.com

Oxford is a registered trademark of Oxford University Press

All rights reserved. No part of this publication may be reproduced,
stored in a retrieval system, or transmitted, in any form or by any means,
electronic, mechanical, photocopying, recording, or otherwise,
without the prior permission of Oxford University Press.

Library of Congress Cataloging-in-Publication Data
[Correspondence. Selections]
The letters of Gertrude Stein and Virgil Thomson : composition as
conversation / edited by Susan Holbrook and Thomas Dilworth.
p. cm.
Includes bibliographical references and index.
ISBN 978-0-19-538663-9
1. Stein, Gertrude, 1874–1946—Correspondence. 2. Authors,
American—20th century—Correspondence. 3. Thomson, Virgil,
1896–1989—Correspondence. 4. Composers—United States—Correspondence.
5. Authors and artists. I. Thomson, Virgil, 1896–1989. II. Holbrook,
Susan. III. Dilworth, Thomas.
PS3537.T323Z4977 2009
818'.5209—dc22
[B]   2009009556

1 3 5 7 9 8 6 4 2
Printed in the United States of America
on acid-free paper

Concerted music is greater than any solo performance, teamwork for the production of something beautiful being, if not the highest end of man, at least symbolic of nearly all we consider good.
—Virgil Thomson, "Maxims for a Modernist" (1925)

Collaborators tell how in union there is strength.
—Gertrude Stein, "Regular Regularly in Narrative" (1927)

Acknowledgments

The estate of Gertrude Stein granted permission to publish Stein's letters through its literary executor, Stanford Gann, Jr. of Levin & Gann, P.A. The estate of Virgil Thomson gave permission to publish Thomson's letters through James M. Kendrick. Edward Burns gave permission to publish the letters of Alice B. Toklas. Jack Larson permitted us to quote his typescript and remarks. Copyright holders also granted us permission to publish Georges Hugnet and Walter Leigh. Ulla Dydo gave generous, abiding, invaluable counsel, as did her recently published *Gertrude Stein: The Language That Rises 1923-1934*, an indispensable work in Stein studies. Edward Burns gave wise advice, provided Larson's memoir, and solved stubborn annotative problems. Logan Esdale shared clarifying information on Laura Riding. Steven Watson sent us his remarkable videotape, *Prepare for Saints*. His book *Prepare for Saints: Gertrude Stein, Virgil Thomson, and the Mainstreaming of American Modernism* was an important resource, as was Anthony Tommasini's biography *Virgil Thomson: Composer on the Aisle*. The letters of Stein and Thomson, Thomson's pocket diary and, unless otherwise specified, all letters cited in the Introduction and notes are from the Yale Collection of American Literature, Beinecke Rare Book and Manuscript Library and the Irving S. Gilmore Music Library. Thomson's tape recorded conversations with Thomas Dilworth are in Yale's Gilmore Music Library. Stein's and Thomson's exchanges with William Aspenwall Bradley and Jenny Bradley are from the Harry Ransom Humanities Research Centre at the University of Texas, Austin. Librarians greatly helped us: Tara Wegner at the Harry Ransom Humanities Research Centre; at Yale University, the librarians at the Beinecke: Jane Bik, Leigh Golden, Jill Haines, Cliff Johnson, Steve Jones, Todd Kennedy, Ngadi Kponou, Anna Marie Menta, Taran Schindler, Timothy Young, the above-and-beyond Nancy Kuhl; at the Gilmore Music Library: Kendall Crilly, Richard Boursy, and the wonderful Suzanne Eggleton Lovejoy, who continued helping with annotation; Barry Edwards at the Toronto Reference Library; and at the University of Windsor library, Johanna Foster, and again and again Graham Staffen. We received assistance from Richard Kostelanetz, Gregory Bossler, Joan Chapman, Jim Carruthers C.S.B, Lucette Dausque, Michaela Giesenkirchen, Kai Hildebrand and Susan Wendt-Hildebrand, Barrie Ruth Strauss, Christina Simmons, and James McConica C.S.B. Graduate student assistants Jasmine Elliott Shereen Inayatulla and Michael Murphy were assiduous and careful problem-solvers. Most translations from French to English (and some help with annotation) are by Basil Kingstone, idiomatically graceful in both languages. Important edits at the proofing stage could not have been completed without the assistance of Lori Kennedy. The Social Science and Humanities Research Council of Canada and the Beinecke Library gave us fellowships that made possible our research. At Oxford University Press we had helpful and discerning editors in Shannon McLachlan, Christina Gibson, Brendan O'Neill, Gwen Colvin, and Lynn Kauppi. We thank them all.

Contents

Illustrations   xi

Introduction   3

Letters with Notes   23

Epilogue: Thomson and Toklas   279

Appendix A. "Virgil Thomson"   303
by Georges Hugnet
translated by Basil Kingstone

Appendix B. Miss Gertrude Stein as a Young Girl for Violin Alone   305
by Virgil Thomson

Appendix C. "Virgil Thomson"   307
by Gertrude Stein

Appendix D. Life of Gertrude Stein   309
by Georges Hugnet
translated by Basil Kingstone

Appendix E. The Contract for *Four Saints in Three Acts*   313

Sources Cited   317

Index   321

Illustrations

Frontispiece Photograph of Virgil Thomson and Gertrude Stein looking at a copy of *Four Saints in Three Acts*

1. Page of a letter by Gertrude Stein, 26 March 1927

2. Page 306 of the manuscript score of *Four Saints in Three Acts*, "pigeon on the grass, alas . . . Lucy Lily"

3. Photograph of the original production of *Four Saints in Three Acts* (1934): Act One, second tableau, "Saint Teresa could be photographed"

4. First page of the manuscript score of *The Mother of Us All*

5. Manuscript score of Virgil Thomson's portrait, "Miss Gertrude Stein as a Young Girl"

The Letters of Gertrude Stein
and Virgil Thomson

Introduction

Gertrude Stein and Virgil Thomson are known for their contributions to twentieth-century arts and for their formidable egos. That either could collaborate intimately with anyone is surprising. Yet Stein and Thomson did work together magnificently on several projects, most notably the operas *Four Saints in Three Acts* and *The Mother of Us All*, among the most important collaborative works of the modern period. Territoriality in Stein and Thomson was ameliorated by their working in complementary métiers. There was no reason to feel competitive; indeed the ascendancy of one could only promote the other. Their one serious falling out was occasioned by Thomson's perceived misstep in mediating the doomed negotiations between Stein and a literary collaborator, the young French poet Georges Hugnet.

The drama of this quarrel and of the later ego-driven debates over production contracts partly explains recent interest in the correspondence collected here. There is undeniable entertainment value in reading the more vexed exchanges: in turns haughty, cajoling, manipulative. But overwhelming this feature of the letters are far more positive energies. The spirit of collaboration is palpable in their mutual excitement over evolving projects. Each writes about individual compositional ventures as well, so that their letters tell us much about their respective careers. The letters document sociohistorical context: indexing a web of mutual friendships and artistic community, referencing political events major and minor, and offering observations about daily life that involve cars, dogs, and food. Stylistically the correspondence is, we think, fascinating. Stein is arguably the most influential innovative literary modernist, and Thomson is an author of crisp, insightful, irreverent music criticism, the most quoted of his century and since. Her letters feature syntactical indeterminacy, charming non sequiturs and run-on constructions. His are wry and economical. Both are sometimes witty. She writes: "you nor I nor nobody knows how everything else and barley grows" and, referring to Thomson's patronage woes, "I was about to suffer as much as you although as the small boy remarked to an admonishing father not in the same place." He writes: "no amount of luxury can alleviate the state of Massachusetts," a visitor is "here and departing daily for Germany," and, about their first opera, "Act II operates." In the letters of each, style changes subtly. It is careful and forceful when the relationship is strained, but most often it is relaxed and affectionate. As a record of friendship the letters are particularly compelling, replete with love, support, and mutual fascination. In Thomson's autobiography, he comments on their correspondence:

> As I reread the letters written at that time, I am struck by the intensity with which Miss Stein and I took each other up. From the fall of 1926, in fact, till her death in July of 1946 we were forever loving being together, whether talking and walking, writing to each other, or at work. Once for a four-year period we did not speak, having quarreled for reasons we both knew to be foolish; but for the last two years of even that time we wrote constantly, our pretext being business. (97)

Recent attention to the archived correspondence has attended a revival of critical interest in *Four Saints in Three Acts* and the recent discovery of dramatic interest and popular appeal in the relationship recorded by the letters. Georg Osterman and Lola Pashalinski of the Ridiculous Theatrical Company performed an exchange of the Thomson-Stein letters in New York in 1992. Development of this project led to the successful play *Gertrude and Alice: A Likeness to Loving* (premiered in St. Louis, 1999). In 2000 The San Francisco Chamber Singers (now Volti) produced "Gertrude, Virgil & Four Saints: From Vision to Verity," in which readings from the letters alternate with scenes from the opera. The letters are widely cited in Steven Watson's *Prepare for Saints: Gertrude Stein, Virgil Thomson, and the Mainstreaming of American Modernism* (1998), and are mentioned also in his documentary film *Prepare for Saints* (1998). Our edition establishes the correct chronology of the correspondence and makes more accessible an exchange for which a growing number of artists and scholars share enthusiasm and affection.

Although Stein announced that since she started writing plays she had "practically never been inside of any kind of theatre" ("Plays" 111), her compositions were informed by the great amount of theatre and opera she was exposed to in her youth. Not surprising for a girl who worried that she might at some point "have read everything and there would be nothing unread to read" (*Autobiography* 82), she consumed a great many plays, including all of Shakespeare. In California, she attended plays and the twenty-five cent opera, and writes of seeing works as various as *Uncle Tom's Cabin*, *Faust*, Buffalo Bill's Wild West show, *Lohengrin*, and *Hamlet*. The performances she recalls most vividly were by Sarah Bernhardt, who visited San Francisco for two months when Stein was an adolescent. Of Bernhardt's performances, she recalls "it was all so foreign and her voice being so varied and it all being so french I could rest in it untroubled" (115). For some, an imperfect understanding of language would provoke anxiety, but for Stein the strangeness of the foreign afforded relief from the linear grinds of plot, speech, line. As content slipped into the background, the concrete aural qualities of words emerged, transporting her out of story and into a kind of continuous present. Her attraction to dramatic form is evident in her 1934 statement: "In the poetry of plays words are more lively words than in any other kind of poetry" ("Plays" 111).

The foreign always attracted the young Stein, possibly because her earliest childhood years were spent living in Vienna and Paris. She attended Harvard Annex (later Radcliffe) and Johns Hopkins Medical School but lost interest in her courses. She was more engaged by her summer travels; she and her brother Leo toured Italy, France, Morocco, Spain and England. In 1903, the year she started writing *The Making of Americans* and *Q.E.D.*, she and Leo moved to 27 rue de Fleurus in Paris, where they lived together for several years, cultivating a mutual interest in modern art and collecting paintings by now-renowned artists, including Cezanne, Renoir, Matisse, and Picasso. They held weekly salons, which quickly became famous, attended by cultural luminaries resident in or visiting Paris. Leo became increasingly dismissive of both Cubism and his sister's writing and, within a few years, moved to Italy. He was replaced by a woman Stein had met in 1907, Alice Babette Toklas, her lover, secretary, and homemaker. Stein and Toklas lived in France for the rest of their lives.

Stein is often quoted as saying about her chosen home, "It was not what Paris gave to you but what it did not take away from you which was important." In other words, Paris was secure in its identity and therefore tolerant of the activities of foreigners. In *Paris, France* she conveys the character of France in whimsical terms: "There are two things that french animals do not do, cats do not fight much and do not howl much and chickens do not get flustered running across the road, if they start to cross the road they keep on going which is what french people do too." Unflappable France is "exciting and peaceful" (1), its insular calm the perfect setting for the challenges to both conventional arts and conventional lifestyles engaged in by expatriates of the '20s. In Paris she and Toklas could enjoy, without harassment, a kind of marriage. In fact, their relationship was quite discreet compared to the polyamorous court of Natalie Barney on the rue Jacob. Another distinguishing feature of France for Stein was respect for the arts held by people from every walk of life: "Even in a garage an academician and a woman of letters takes precedence even of millionaires or politicians, they do, it is quite incredible but they do" (21).

Apart from French tolerance and respect for the arts, France was important for her because it was not the United States. In 1928, a survey for *transition* asked, "Why do Americans Live in Europe?" and she responded:

> The United States is just now the oldest country in the world, there always is an oldest country and she is it, it is she who is the mother of the twentieth century civilization. She began to feel herself as it just after the Civil War. And so it is a country the right age to have been born in and the wrong age to live in.

> She is the mother of modern civilization and one wants to have been born in the country that has attained and live in the countries that are attaining or going to be attaining. This is perfectly natural if you only look at facts as they are. America is now early Victorian very early Victorian, she is a rich and well nourished home but not a place to work. Your parent's home is never a place to work it is a nice place to be brought up in. Later on there will be place enough to get away from home in the United States, it is beginning, then there will be creators who live at home. A country this the oldest and therefore the most important country in the world quite naturally produces the creators, and so naturally it is I an American who was and is thinking in writing was born in America and lives in Paris. This has been and probably will be the history of the world. That it is always going to be like that makes the monotony and variety of life that and that we are after all of us ourselves. (*transition* 14 [1928]: 97–98)

Her answer illuminates her thinking behind the choice of American setting for her second opera with Thomson, *The Mother of Us All*.

In Paris, in the twenty years after meeting Alice B. Toklas, Stein completed such innovative works as *The Making of Americans*, *Tender Buttons*, *Useful Knowledge*, and *Geography and Plays*. In Paris, she met artists, composers and other writers who inspired and were inspired by her. Among these were Ernest Hemingway, Mildred Aldrich, Tristan Tzara, Sherwood Anderson, F. Scott Fitzgerald, Jacques Lipchitz, Jean Cocteau, Pablo Picasso, Jo Davidson, Man Ray and, of course, Virgil Thomson, who shared both her American patriotism and her enthusiasm for the social and aesthetic liberation that Paris offered.

During what he and Stein used to call "our war," Thomson served in the armed forces for sixteen months without leaving the United States. At twenty-two, in 1919, he began studying music at Harvard, where a graduate student in literature, S. Foster Damon, mentored him, introducing him to Erik Satie's piano music and Stein's *Tender Buttons*. Thomson told one of us, "He used to bring Satie pieces round to the house, stacks of music, and I would play them, and once he brought me a tiny book called *Tender Buttons*, and I thought it was the nicest and funniest book I'd ever read. It was a library copy. I carried it around in my pocket and I used to read it aloud to all the friends for fun" (to Dilworth, recorded conversations 2–3 Feb. 1981). Satie would be for Thomson a shield against fashionable dissonant modernist complexity and a continuing influence as he suggests when later writing about Satie:

> By using all the musical materials, melodic, rhythmic, and harmonic, for their common rather than their uncommon associations, he has made it possible to use formulas from folklore, from popular commercial music, from the classical masters, and from yesterday's little masters right along side of invented material, and without any vulgarity. (*The New York Herald Tribune*, 7 Jan. 1946)

Thomson said, "Satie used very few notes but they were all in the right place" (to Dilworth, 3 Feb. 1981). As Anthony Tommasini puts it, Thomson "didn't waste words and in his music he didn't waste notes" (Watson, *Prepare for Saints* videotape). While still an undergraduate, he went to France with the Harvard Glee Club. Financed by a traveling fellowship, he stayed on in Paris for most of 1921, studying counterpoint and harmony with thirty-four-year-old Nadia Boulanger. Choosing a female teacher was then, he said, a daring act, "disapproved of at Harvard." Among the friends he made this year were another of Boulanger's American students, Aaron Copland, and Bernard Faÿ, "ultra Catholic and royalist," a professor of eighteenth-century history and American studies (to Dilworth, 3 Feb. 1981). At the Faÿ family flat, Thomson met Cocteau, Picasso, and the young composers known as "Les Six" (Darius Milhaud, Francis Poulenc, Georges Auric, Arthur Honegger, Louis Durey, and Germaine Tailleferre) and the composer they revered, fifty-six-year-old Satie.

After his months in Paris, he returned to Harvard, where he became acquainted with people whose names appear in his correspondence with Stein. These include undergraduate friends: Maurice Grosser, a painter; Henry-Russell Hitchcock, a student of architectural history; and Sherry Mangan, a student of classics. In the winter of 1925, he played the organ weekly for a church in Whitinsville, lunching after the service with the family of Jessie and Chester Lasell, the latter the financial backer for the literary magazine *The Dial*. Thomson had earlier met and become friends with their nephew Philip Lasell and their daughter Hildegarde Watson. At this time he was publishing articles on music in *The American Mercury*, *The Boston Transcript*, and *Vanity Fair*. He read Stein's *Geography and Plays* soon after its publication and began thinking about setting her words to music.

In September 1925, he returned to Paris to stay indefinitely, sharing a berth and then, for a while, a room with Sherry Mangan. Bernard Faÿ enabled him to become Parisian, giving him access to Paris salons. Dada was then the dominant avant-garde aesthetic. Faÿ's younger brother Emmanuel explained its meaning to him, that everything is convention and all conventions have equal or no value, and that an artist is consequently free to do whatever he or she likes. Being American meant having affinity with Dada, Thomson thought, and the proof of that for him was Gertrude Stein, who had written as she did before Dada existed.

He resumed studying with Boulanger, but now found her insistences stifling and quit. In a borrowed apartment in Saint-Cloud, he was joined by Maurice Grosser, who became his principal lover. Frequenting Sylvia Beach's Shakespeare and Company bookstore, he met Ernest Hemingway, Ford Madox Ford, Ezra Pound and James Joyce, and became friends with the New Jersey born composer George Antheil, whom Pound was then promoting. Thomson and Antheil shared concerts at which works by each of them were performed. One reason for frequenting Beach's bookstore was to meet Stein, but she had stopped coming, owing to Beach's publishing *Ulysses* by Joyce, whom she considered her main literary rival.

Thomson thought it was in January 1926 that he and Stein met (to Dilworth, recorded conversations 2–3 Feb. 1981). She invited George Antheil, then considered by some a musical genius, to visit her at 27 rue de Fleurus. Anxious for intellectual support, he told Thomson falsely that they were both invited. They went together to her house. Nothing Antheil said interested Stein, but Thomson was confident, brilliant, down-to-earth, and spoke about her writing and his attempts to set some of it to music. At the end of the evening, she said goodbye to Antheil but to Thomson, "We'll be seeing each other." He was twenty-nine; she fifty-one. Their meeting opened new chapters in their social and creative lives.

He remembered,

> Gertrude was entertaining every number of ways. We were very close friends. You could hardly be closer friends, although there were nearly twenty-five years between us in age. We had things in common. Harvard was one and we used to talk about World War I. And we talked about all our friends. But we talked about all those things in our Harvard and doughboy ways. And we got very thick about it, and Alice did not mind. Alice used to get rid of people sometimes if she was jealous of their close friendship with Gertrude but she didn't seem to mind.

Actually, Alice Toklas initially disliked him, but she deferred to Stein in this case and she admired his music and eventually warmed to him. Being gay was an advantage to him in this friendship. He said,

> Gertrude was warm and she had an aura of sex around her. It worked on men, women, children, and dogs. And Gertrude liked young men. She didn't go to bed with them but she was attracted to them, and Alice was always afraid it might happen. (to Dilworth, 3 Feb. 1981)

Thomson seems to have won Toklas over by inviting them to his apartment in the spring of 1927 and playing for them Satie's thirty-minute piano version of *Socrate* (Toklas to Thomson, 20 April 1947).

Friendship with Stein began in earnest when he played for them his arrangement of her "Susie Asado." About composing to her words, he writes,

> My hope . . . had been to break, crack open, and solve for all time anything still waiting to be solved, which was almost everything, about English musical declamation. My theory was that if a text is set correctly for the sound of it, the meaning will take care of itself. And the Stein texts, for prosodizing in this way, were manna. With meanings already abstracted, or absent, or so multiplied that choice among them was impossible, there was no temptation toward tonal illustration, say of birdie babbling by the brook or heavy heavy hangs my heart. You could make a setting for sound and syntax only, then

add, if needed, an accompaniment equally functional. I had no sooner put to music after this recipe one short Stein text than I knew I had opened a door. I had never had any doubts about Stein's poetry; from then on I had none about my ability to handle it in music. (*Virgil Thomson* 90)

Soon after playing and singing "Susie Asado" for her, he suggested that they write an opera together, and she agreed to initiate the process by writing a libretto. Long a solitary writer of difficult, hard-to-publish texts, Stein had never before considered collaborating, and she was now doing so in a genre she had never before attempted.

From Thomson's point of view as a composer, the opera originated in the history of music. He said,

> I didn't think it was a good idea to try to renovate the opera, that is to say, to import it into the English language by imitating more recent and decadent forms. The Wagnerian opera was overblown in that sense, and the Italian opera in my youth—dominated by Puccini and Leoncavallo—was a popularized and degraded art form, and I thought that to do anything serious about the opera in a new language, one needed to go back to the more primitive and strong forms. I thought Italian opera seria of the seventeenth and eighteenth centuries was exactly the sort of form one could do something with. And the general principles of that were a serious mythological subject with a tragic ending, in which the commerce of the play, so to speak, takes place in rapid recitative, and the emotional moments are formalized and concentrated into set pieces strung out along this recitative. I thought that was a healthy form one could do something with. (to Dilworth, 3 Feb. 1981)

Given Stein's seniority and fame, he was in no position to dictate subject and form, as composers usually do with librettists, but together they discussed subject matter, scenes, and details.

Knowing, Thomson said, "nothing about musical forms," Stein was initially interested only in the mythological subject. He remembered, "We talked about that. I said, 'Obviously we are not going into classical mythology. That's been overdone by the Duncan family right in our own time. German mythology is patented by Richard Wagner—I'm not going to compete with that. But,' I said, 'history and religion are sources of mythology.' She said, 'What about George Washington.'" (Stein identified with Washington—she and he were both born in February, and her brother used to tell her as a child that she was very like Washington, "impulsive and slow-minded" [*Autobiography* 243].) Thomson objected: "He's an eighteenth-century character, and they all wore wigs, and on stage I can't tell one from another. Besides, he's the father of his country; it's a little hard to demythologize him" (to Dilworth, 3 Feb. 1981). In Stein's atelier, where they were talking, were many porcelain statuettes of saints placed about. Possibly inspired by these, they then began to consider the lives of saints. Stein credits a porcelain soldier in a window on the rue de Rennes with making Saint Ignatius "actual" for her ("Plays" 130). (In her libretto, Stein indicates the influence of porcelain figures for she uses the word "porcelain" five times, including "Saint Ignatius could be in porcelain actually while he was young and standing".... "Who makes it be what they had as porcelain" [*Four Saints* 20, 47].) They agreed that, in Thomson's words,

> The Italians—dominated in current usage by St. Francis, of course—were overdone, and one couldn't touch them. There were no German saints. The French saints were all kind of theological and stiff. But Gertrude had been a great deal to Spain, and she loved Spanish saints, and she said, "What about that?" I said, "It's ok by me. I've never been to Spain, but you find any saints you like." So she started work with that idea, and turned out a Spanish landscape, peopled with Spanish saints with whom she had, so to speak, geographical contact. I didn't select the saints. I agreed to the landscape and subject. (to Dilworth, 3 Feb. 1981)

The principal saints Stein chose were Teresa of Avila and Ignatius of Loyola—Teresa being a heroine of her youth; she and Ignatius, along with Francis of Assisi, had long been her favourite saints.

The decision for saints was not whimsical. Thomson writes that in the lives of saints he and Stein saw "a parallel to the life we were leading, in which consecrated artists were practicing their art . . . needing to learn the terrible disciplines of truth and spontaneity, of channeling their skills without loss of inspiration. That was our theme" (*Reader* 277). Near its conclusion, the opera expresses affinity between art and religion by associating itself with the Catholic Mass. As Teresa and Ignatius come together, a large golden chalice appears with, above it, a golden circle evoking the consecrated host. Their appearance on stage is specified in the scenario written by Maurice Grosser, following cues in the libretto where Stein writes: "Remembered as new" (46), "it is very nearly ended with bread" (47), and "When this you see remember me" (47)—this last statement echoing the words of Jesus used at the consecration of the Mass, "Do this in memory of me." Artists are concerned, if only metaphorically, with transubstantiation, and both art and religion are largely gratuitous. Thomson and Stein believed that aesthetic "inspiration and sanctity are as common phenomena as housekeeping" and that "pseudo-naiveté and pseudo-unintelligibility" in both the literary and musical structures of their opera "come from a wish to convey these major disciplines in familiar terms" (Thomson to Carolyn P. Cady, 30 Oct. 1941). The alliance between artists and saints also includes friends and lovers. Stein's two principal saints evoke, for her, Alice Toklas, whom she sometimes called Thérèse, and herself. Stein also had in mind her long friendships with two Spanish painters, Pablo Picasso and Juan Gris. One saint in her libretto is

St. Paul, in Spanish, Pablo. Another is St. Fernande, named after Picasso's first important mistress, Fernande Olivier. Gris had recently died and was, therefore, hopefully a saint (Dydo 195). For Stein, these two painters help to make the Spanish landscape evocative at once of traditional religion and artistic modernism. Thomson later concluded a synopsis of the opera by writing that if "something is evoked of the inner gayety and the strength of lives consecrated to a non-material end, the authors will consider their labors rewarded" (*Reader* 277).

Stein's libretto was unlike any other. By breaking with conventional dramatic form and literary expression, she determined that *Four Saints* would be the only opera of its kind. She thought that the temporality of theatre traditionally doomed it to exist "in syncopated time in relation to the emotion of anybody in the audience" (94). Unlike a book, a play proceeds at a rate and in a sequence not determined by its viewers, creating a kind of "nervousness." To erase this disjunction, she avoided linear narrative and aimed "to tell what happened without telling stories" (121). Her motive was akin to that driving her written portraits, which showed who someone was without description. In her early plays, she had undermined conventional crisis-centered dramatic schema and focused on the defamiliarization of language. Her efforts culminated in what she called her landscape plays, of which she would consider *Four Saints in Three Acts* the most successful. In choosing landscape as a guiding figure for drama, she made clear her desire to spatialize a temporal medium; declaring that "story is not the thing," she preferred "landscape not moving but always in relation, the trees to the hills the hills to the fields the trees to each other any piece of it to any sky and then any detail to any other detail" ("Plays" 125).

To constitute a landscape, her subjects would have to act as elements in relation through space rather than characters in development through time. Saints were the perfect choice, she decided, because

> A saint a real saint never does anything, a martyr does something but a really good saint does nothing and so I wanted to have Four Saints that did nothing and I wrote Four Saints in Three Acts and they did nothing and that was everything.
>
> Generally speaking anybody is more interesting doing nothing than doing anything. (*Everybody's Autobiography* 112)

At the level of content, Stein thematizes her landscape model throughout the opera. During the prelude, we are told "It is very easy to be land. / Imagine four benches separately" (12). Those for whom "being land" is "very easy" are likely the titular four saints, a possibility confirmed by the subsequent "four benches," which suggest the saints can be arranged concretely like furniture. Soon after, indeed, we come upon "Four saints. . . . Saint saint saint saint" (14), mapped physically on the page. The page is a kind of landscape upon which the elements of the script are arranged and rearranged. Note the words "and" and "in" switching places (bench-like) in the lines

> Saint Therese and conversation. In one.
> Saint Therese in conversation. And one. (21)

Another shuffle occurs at the micro level, as the letters in "scene one" are rearranged to produce "Scene once seen once seen once seen" (*Four Saints* 24), drawing attention to both the visual and aural elements of language, revealing that linguistic concretization is effected with equal force on stage. The line can be sung to highlight the homophonic rendering of "one scene one" and "once seen one" through repetition.

There is no recognizable character development in *Four Saints*, but rather a shifting arrangement of figures; Stein claims that "all these saints together made my landscape" and that the movement in the opera "was like a movement in and out with which anybody looking on can keep time" (*Everybody's Autobiography* 129, 131). The audience "can keep time" with characters who don't experience crises or epiphanies, and in this respect maintain correspondence with their porcelain prototypes. Our acquaintance is made with Therese in cumulative fashion, as her insistent and shifting appearance gradually bespeaks a larger-than-life saint. In "Plays," Stein recounts her inspiration for the figuration of Saint Therese:

> While I was writing the Four Saints I wanted one always does want the saints to be actually saints before them as well as inside them, I had to see them as well as feel them. As it happened there is on the Boulevard Raspail a place where they make photographs that have always held my attention. They take a photograph of a young girl dressed in the costume of her ordinary life and little by little in successive photographs they change it into a nun. These photographs are small and the thing takes four or five changes but at the end it is a nun and this is done for the family when the nun is dead and in memoriam. (130)

She memorializes this occasion of inspiration in her libretto: "Saint Therese could be photographed having been dressed like a lady and then they taking out her head changed it to a nun and a nun a saint and a saint so" and "Saint Therese had a father photographically" (*Four Saints* 17, 26). Stein's model for the character of Saint Therese is driven by the engine of repetition with change. Saint Therese emerges as the central figure of *Four Saints*, appearing as the repetitive subject of many scenes and having more lines to deliver than any other character. The importance of Saint Therese may imply a literary-autobiographical statement—according to Virgil Thomson's original suggestion that the opera feature "both male and female leads with second leads and choruses surrounding them, for all the world like Joyce and Stein themselves holding court in the rue de l'Odeon and the rue de Fleurus" (*Virgil Thomson* 90–91). That Stein and

Thomson thought so at the time is suggested by Thomson referring to Saint Ignatius as Saint Teresa's "rival" (Tues. [April 1927]). St. Ignatius founded the Jesuits, and the Jesuits educated Joyce.

Thomson did more than merely set the libretto to music. Although Stein rarely acceded to requests for changes in text, she was so impressed with Thomson's sense of what voices could do in performance that she let him make textual changes. The excessive "solo" material assigned to Saint Therese, while textually compelling, posed a challenge to staging. To meet this challenge, he split the character into St. Teresa I and St. Teresa II so they could sing duets. (In this he seems to have taken his cue from the text: "Can two saints be one" [18]; "One at a time makes two at a time" [45]; "There can be two Saint Annes if you like" [47]; "Saint Therese and Saint Therese too" [47].) He renamed them Teresa to provide a third syllable. Much of *Four Saints* is comprised of text not assigned to speakers; yet to relegate this rich material to the category of unvoiced stage direction would be to excise more than half the work. Thomson's solution to this problem was to assign lines to various characters, including two he created himself. The Commère and Compère act as commentators who mediate between the saints and the audience. Not only did he provide speakers for the unassigned lines, he provided them for the mechanical aspects of the text as well. In no other play would you hear the words "Scene V" verbalized. But if they weren't sung here, you might miss there being nine Scene V's in Act II (of which there are two). He capitalizes on the following opportunity in the libretto:

> Who settles a private life.
> Saint Therese. Who settles a private life.
> Saint Therese. Who settles a private life.
> Saint Therese. Who settles a private life. (17)

by assigning speakers in the score

> Compère. Who settles a private life
> All (spoken). Saint Teresa.
> Chorus I, II. Who settles a private life.
> Compère. Saint Teresa.
> Chorus I, II. Who settles a private life.
> Compère. Saint Teresa. (31)

Because Saint Therese's lines (among her first) are interrogative, Thomson can readily transpose the conventionally silent speech prefix "Saint Therese" into an answer to what was originally her own question. This interpretation preserves in sonic form the repetitive visual pattern in the libretto. Stein translates the formal scaffolding of drama into primary textual material, a translation Thomson makes musical. As a collaborator, Thomson contributes to making parts of the theatrical machine concrete, and thereby contributes also to exposing generic performativity of drama

Introduction 13

itself: Stein and Thomson's creative collaboration unsettles the traditional organization of textual elements and players, and unsettles, too, assumptions about the rapport between libretto and score, resulting in a defamiliarization of opera that is both celebratory and transgressive.

Maurice Grosser joined the collaboration by writing the scenario, in which he contributes action consonant with the aesthetic of the opera. Act Two opens with the Commère and Compère downstage, watching the play from an opera box. During the course of the act, they are, in turns, one with the audience, participants in dramatic action, and constituents of primary spectacle—sometimes becoming the entire spectacle, while saints watch them. After the act ends, as the audience is leaving their seats for intermission, the lights go up on the opera box, now revealed to be positioned in front of the curtain. The commentators leave their seats in tandem with audience members. This thread of the scenario throws into relief the usual divisions between stage and audience, extends and blurs the parameters of spectacle and spectator. Grosser's staging here contributes to solving the problem of syncopation. Stein allegorized this problem through the figure of the curtain, stating, "The emotion of you on one side of the curtain and what is on the other side of the curtain are not going to be going on together. One will always be behind or in front of the other" ("Plays" 95). Placing two characters on our side of the curtain has the effect of dissolving the power of the curtain to render actors and viewers out of sync.

Thomson's musical score was innovative for its prosody. In composing, he concentrated not on meaning but on the rhythm of the "word-groups" and their specific Anglo-American sound, taking care never to truncate or distort pronunciation in order to accommodate music. This had not before been done in opera and, so, is an important accomplishment, establishing *Four Saints* as a milestone in the history of music. Stein certainly appreciated this. Referring to the scoring of words in the classical canon—not to popular music—she said, he "is the only one who knows what words are about in music. Nobody else has done it except in early church music. The music should not accompany the words. Music and words should be one" (quoted in *The New York Herald Tribune* and *New York Sun*, 17 Nov. 1934). Thomson explained how Stein's writing helped him do this:

> with meanings jumbled and syntax violated, but with the words themselves all the more shockingly present, I could put those texts to music with a minimum of temptation toward the emotional conventions, spend my whole effort on the rhythm of the language, and its specific Anglo-American sound, adding shape, where that seemed to be needed, and it usually was, from music's own devices. (*Reader* 212)

Thomas Beecham told him that the opera is "the finest vocal music in English since Elizabethan times" (*Reader 254*).

Thomson writes that musically he was not attempting "a historical reconstruction when my librettist had assumed no such obligation. So

I took my musical freedom following her poetic freedom, and what came out was virtually total recall of my Southern Baptist childhood in Missouri" (*Reader* 277). The tonality of the music is traditional, retrospective, simple, naïve, religious, and American, suggesting but not quoting familiar melodies. It evokes Baptist and Anglican hymns, children's songs, marches, dances, and Gilbert and Sullivan—associations that emerge in turns through simple harmony, hymnbook cadences, melodic line, and plain choral accompaniment. It is music influenced by the principles of composition announced in Stein's "Composition as Explanation": "using everything," establishing "a continuous present . . . beginning again and again and again" (499). What he calls Stein's "expressive obscurity" precluded his adopting the prevalent dissonant mode of 'serious' modern music. Dissonance added to literary abstraction would have rendered the opera socially inaccessible. Just as Stein subverted all theatrical expectation, therefore, Thomson subverted both popular and avante garde expectations for operatic and modern music.

His light, vigorous score nudges the "great obscurity" of her libretto (*Reader* 212) towards the causality, direction, and continuity that tonal music can suggest, including feelings momentous, tender, boisterous, devout, and above all joyous. In drawing out such theatrical and narrative feeling, latent in her language, his music compensates for its obscurity even as it emphasizes that obscurity (Bucknell 184). Forced to adapt to the continuous present she generates, he begins again and again, making time for the place of her landscape. But the musical ordering is largely unmotivated, unnecessary, arbitrary, playful. As a result, and because this opera is so melodically rich, it resembles an oratorio, stooping little, if at all, to recitative, which Thomson, in later years at least, called "reshitative." The music orders language that neither endorses nor resists its musical ordering. Since the language remains enigmatic, the implied meanings of Thomson's tonalities remain, Bucknell writes, "adjacent to" it, "facilitating its enunciation, and its enactment, but never breaking its surface" (9). Aaron Copland made a similar observation when he wrote that Thomson "draws a frame of music around" Stein's words (see note to Thomson, 7 juin [1929]). Although Stein thought the words and music became one, the score and the libretto dance together, resisting synthesis in which each loses identity in something else. In *The Autobiography of Alice B. Toklas*, Stein adopts Copland's metaphor, "She delighted in listening to her words framed by his music" (246).

The opera was a huge popular success. On opening night, the audience roared approval through a half-hour of curtain calls. Many wept, as some said, to see anything so beautiful done in America (Watson 280). The novelist Winifred Bryher thought it "heavenly" (to Stein, 10 Feb. 1934). The poet Wallace Stevens wrote to Harriet Monroe that it was "a delicate and joyous work all around" (267). Gershwin thought it "refreshing as a new dessert" (Watson 286), the music "a happy inspiration" making the libretto "quite entertaining" (Kendall, 143). He was encouraged and influenced by it in producing his *Porgy and Bess* the following year, using the director

Thomson had chosen, Alexander Smallens, as his director and many of the same cast. In fact, he first approached Smallens backstage, immediately after the performers took their applause. The critic Henry McBride wrote to Stein that all those involved in the presentation were inspired: "the word miracle is the only one that describes what happened" (Watson 280). The *New York Times* reported that the discerning audience at the Broadway opening deemed it "a perfect masterpiece" (Downes 22). With five performances in Hartford and six weeks on Broadway, it had the longest run for an opera in North America. Arturo Toscanini attended twice, Henry McBride four times, Dorothy Parker five times. *Four Saints* was the most celebrated event in New York. It received more press than any show in the preceding decade. In the worst winter of the Depression, weekly gross receipts averaged $13,000 and total attendance approached 80,000.

Reviews varied, some reacting against the libretto, others against the music, the latter disliked by the intellectual devotees of complex atonal music. But dance critic John Martin praised the opera as a rare "synthesis of the theatrical arts," and theatre critic Stark Young wrote, "it lives in itself" like "a thing in nature . . . and is in essence a constant surprise" (Watson 289). Today, it is widely regarded as among the best of American operas, but it is seldom performed because, like the operas of Philip Glass, it contains few arias for solo singing, which advertise operas and musicals, and it lacks intrinsic narrative that facilitates staging. It has never been performed by the New York Metropolitan Opera. Yet it has exerted influence for decades. In *The Queer Composition of America's Sound: Gay Modernists, American Music, and National Identity* (2004), Nadine Hubbs writes about its foundational role in the development of American musical idiom. Robert Wilson and Philip Glass both acknowledge the indebtedness to the opera of their multimedia opera *Einstein on the Beach* (1976), and in 1996 Wilson staged *Four Saints* in Houston, New York, and Edinburgh (Watson 305).

The first production of *Four Saints* precipitated social change. While Negro chic was not new, this was the first casting of blacks in a public performance not depicting the life of the Southern Negro. Thomas Anderson, who played the original St. Giuseppe, recalls, "There was a time when Negro singers went down on their knees and sang the spirituals and waved their hands back and forth, but with the coming of *Four Saints in Three Acts* it took us off our knees and out of our overalls and mammy dresses" (Watson, *Prepare*, videotape). Thomson's casting choice was not politically uncomplicated; his laudatory comments about Negro enunciation, disposition, and aesthetic value are often essentializing and exoticizing (see note to Bradley, 15 May 1933). Nevertheless, his decision initiated the movement of gifted blacks to the opera stage, a movement accelerated in the 1952 Broadway revival of *Four Saints* in which twenty-five-year-old Leontyne Price was cast in the role of St. Cecilia (Tommasini 420).

Much of the importance of *Four Saints* in the history of literary modernism lies in its bridging between Stein's most hermetic writing and a large audience, making the writing emotionally widely accessible. In doing so, the opera brought modernism at its most arcane as close as it has ever come to mainstream culture, fulfilling, in the United States, what began in the Armory Show of 1913. Furthermore, what began then solely in visual art culminated now in the combined arts of literature (Stein), music (Thomson), visual art (setting and costumes by Florine Stettheimer), drama (scenes by Grosser, direction by John Houseman), orchestral direction (Smallens), and dance (choreography by Frederick Ashton). It was a culmination but not, for Stein, a completion. With the passing of time, her work attracted many more devotees, notably among contemporary poets, who see her work as inspiriting their own language-focused practice. One of these is bpNichol, whose experimental long poem, *The Martyrology*, is propelled by a speculative genealogy of saints discovered in words beginning with 'st' (st. orm, st. ranglehold, etc.)—the poem opens with an epigraph by his greatest influence, St. Ein.

Several years after the success of *Four Saints* and the break in and partial repair of their friendship—it never fully recovered its former ease and completeness—Thomson and Stein collaborated again, on a second opera, *The Mother of Us All*. Since their last collaboration, she had experienced the pleasures and pitfalls of fame arising from the reception of the *Autobiography*, *Four Saints*, and her American speaking tour. She had also published a number of books, among them *The Geographical History of America*, *Ida*, *Paris France*, and another memoir, *Everybody's Autobiography*. Thomson had worked in theatre for the WPA and on Broadway, had written musical scores for two films and a ballet, and had become the chief music critic for *The New York Herald Tribune*.

In writing the libretto for their second opera, Stein composed differently. This text is not so much a landscape. The characters populating it are not so originally imagined. And the style is not so resolutely obscure. Thomson said,

> *The Mother of Us All* is about nineteenth-century American history, which Gertrude had read devotedly for years. And born in 1874, she was a nineteenth-century character herself. She put into that libretto all those things that she knew not only from having read about them—Grant, Daniel Webster, and Susan B. Anthony—but the nineteenth-century America that she was brought up in. I didn't select the characters. I actually suggested the nineteenth-century political life of America, and the use of deliberate, either altered or unaltered quotations, which she did a great deal of. But I wasn't telling her how to write poetry, and she wasn't telling me how to write music. (to Dilworth, 3 Feb. 1981)

When he proposed the second opera, he told her he wanted something set between the Missouri Compromise and the impeachment of Andrew Johnson, and "let's not have any foolishness about putting Abraham Lincoln onstage. That can't be done" (Tommasini 382). She decided on Susan B. Anthony as heroine. In a letter dated 15 April 1946, he wrote to Stein, "certainly Susan B. comes out as a noble one. She is practically

St. Paul when she says 'let them marry'." A reference back to the saints of their first opera, the statement also highlights the magnetic presence of Susan B., who emerges triumphant in the crisis of gender and authority at the forefront of *The Mother*.

While the feminist impulse of much of Stein's work operates more covertly, through innovation at the fundamental level of language, this opera about the struggle for women's suffrage is overtly feminist. Stein's targets range from nineteenth-century gender socialization to sexist tactics still apparent after her death. The kind of doublespeak at work in contemporary rhetoric against "special interest groups" can be discerned in Thaddeus Stevens' plea, "Dear lady remember humanity comes first." "You mean men come first" (77) retorts Susan B., incisively debunking the notional inclusiveness of the term "humanity." Indiana Elliot refuses to conform to the tradition of changing her name upon marrying Jo the Loiterer, proposing that instead, "he will have to change his name, he must be Jo Elliot" (82). In the universe of *The Mother of Us All*, the androcentric logic of the patronym is thrown into question and the link between name and authority loosens. Ulysses S. Grant, whose name is synonymous with command, is reduced to impotence. He tries to stop the wedding ceremony by commanding "Everybody be silent." His order is ignored, and ultimately "he is silent" (75). As the opera concludes after the victory of suffrage, Grant has one similarly ineffectual line: "Vote the vote, the army does not vote, the general generals, there is no vote, bah vote" (87). After assuming the power to authorize marriage through her performative speech act, "Let them marry," Susan B. quickly parlays her clout into the realm of feminist activism, declaring the right of women to vote: "They are married all married and their children women as well as men will have the vote, they will they will, they will have the vote" (*Mother* 76). In 1947, Thomson received a letter that would have gratified Stein from Susan B. Anthony, the grand niece of her namesake. She writes to say that the members of the family have seen and love the opera, including her Aunt Anna, who had known the original Susan B. She praises the characterization by Dorothy Dow as having the strength, warmth, and humour of her Aunt Susan. And she writes that the opera is the most fitting commemoration of the centenary, in 1948, of the American women's movement (17 May).

The operatic Susan B. also reflects Stein. Thomson noted that when, while she was writing, she showed Susan B. "in a scene of domesticity that might as well have been herself and Alice Toklas conversing about Gertrude's career, I knew that she had got inside that theme and that the work would now be moving rapidly" (*Virgil Thomson* 366). And Stein's life, like that of her heroine, was devoted "not to what I won but to what was done" (88).

While things are "done" in *The Mother*, this opera shares with its predecessor the disruption of linear story and an evasion of catharsis. The defining moment of the victory of women's suffrage, for example, is not dramatized. The opera begins with a prologue sung by "Virgil T.", an homage to Stein's musical collaborator. (She had commemorated him more subtly in *Four Saints* : "They can remain latin latin there and Virgil Virgil Virgil virgin virgin latin there" [*Four Saints* 21].) The somewhat tautological prologue is followed by stage directions indicating that "Virgil T. after he has sung his prelude begins to sit." That he "begins to sit" rather than "sits" illustrates Stein's tendency to distend even the most minute events on stage. Stretching the moment further, Virgil T. narrates his own infinitesimal movement:

> Virgil T. Begin to sit.
>> Begins to sit.
>> He begins to sit.
>> That's why.
>> Begins to sit.
>> He begins to sit.
>> And that is the reason why. (52)

Here the lines function in relation to each other as much as, if not more than, to the "sitting" or the "reason" referred to.

The music Thomson wrote for this opera suits its rural nineteenth-century setting by incorporating recognizable hymns, ballads, waltzes, marches. It was the popular repertory of his Missouri childhood, consisting, he said, of "the basic idiom of our country because" these musical forms "are the oldest vernacular still remembered here and used" (*New York Times*, 15 April 1956). "The Americans of *The Mother*" are, he writes, "group-controlled . . . by their own spontaneity, are addicted to gospel hymns, darn-fool ditties, inspirational oratory, and parades." He writes,

> My having earlier worked on texts without much overt meaning had been of value. It had forced me to hear the sounds that the American language really makes when sung, and to eliminate all those European emotions that are automatically brought forth when European musicians get involved with dramatic poetry, with the stage. European historic models, music's old masters, . . . are not easy to escape from. And if any such evasion, however minor, takes place in *The Mother*, that is due, I think, to both Miss Stein and myself having for so long, in our work, avoided customary ways and attitudes [so] that when we got around to embracing them we could do so with a certain freshness. (*Reader* 212)

Wayne Koesternbaum's remark about *Four Saints* remains true of *The Mother* and acquires thematic relevance: "The cheerfulness one feels in hearing this opera and the patriotism is that within this commonwealth every syllable belongs, every syllable has a right to vote" (Watson, *Prepare*, videotape).

With the passing of years, it has become increasingly apparent that *Four Saints* and *The Mother of Us All* are among the preeminent collaborative works of modern art. Late in life, Thomson said he wished that he and

Stein had written an opera together every year they had known each other (to Dilworth, 3 Feb. 1981).

Their correspondence and the story it tells includes, as it does here, letters and parts of letters by Alice B. Toklas and Stein's literary agent in Paris, William Aspenwell Bradley. Toklas was for Thomson virtually an extension of Stein. Both Toklas and Bradley acted as intermediaries, so that without their letters the record of communication between Stein and Thomson would be incomplete. Moreover, Toklas and Bradley also influenced the Stein-Thomson relationship. It was tolerated and then probably broken by Toklas and healed by Bradley, who subsequently contributed to its later strained condition. Letters from Toklas are identified as such at the start of each letter. After Stein's death, Thomson and Toklas continued to write one another about the operas and Stein. Largely a prolonged wake of the creative friendship of Stein and Thomson, this correspondence is the subject of our Epilogue.

A Note on the Manuscripts and Editing

Until now, scholarly and creative work involving the Stein-Thomson exchange has been hindered by misdating and unreliable sequencing of the letters, and by undocumented details about relationships with friends and colleagues of Stein and Thomson. Letters attached to the wrong envelopes, misread and misquoted references, and incorrect transcription of difficult handwriting have led to misinterpretations of events and statements in their work and that of their friends. Some of their personal interactions, travels, work, and performances have been misdated and misinterpreted. Our edition provides the complete correspondence in a more accurate chronology than has previously been available, carefully transcribed (with scholarly consultation) and annotated.

Stein's handwriting is notoriously indistinct. Anyone who has worked with her manuscripts knows the difficulty of deciphering it. Embarking on an apprenticeship to her hand was one of the challenges facing us in editing this collection of correspondence. Another challenge was establishing the chronology of letters. In the Yale archive, several of Stein's letters are misdated. Thomson's letters are often missing dates altogether, their postmarked envelopes having been destroyed before cataloguing. Tentative dating was attempted by curators, notably Donald Gallup, and by Virgil Thomson late in his life. We were able to improve on these attempts through the close reading of both sides of the correspondence. In fact, attempting to solve concurrently the puzzles of handwriting and dating often resulted in a dovetailing solution. Transcribing a letter dated 8 Sept. 1930, we had Stein writing that her dog "Basket has had fleas but no almonds." "Almonds" was surely, we thought, a misreading of her barely legible hand. Attempting to establish the year of a Thomson letter dated simply 4 Sept., in which he writes of dreaming that Basket "instead of fur had almonds stuck in him," we found confirmation of our dubious transcription and could also establish the correct placement of Thomson's letter.

All dates outside square brackets were written by the correspondent at the time of composition. All dates inside square brackets are from postmarks or later additions (as by a librarian who may have had access to envelopes), including our own. Where date of composition can be determined, we favor that over postmarks (an important distinction in the case of envelopes forwarded or returned, or when only the arrival postmark is visible). When we establish or correct the date of a letter, we indicate that by italicizing the date or portion of the date. Where the second digit of a number is unclear in a postmark, that digit is represented by a lower case x.

Where inconsistent, spelling is sometimes regularized, but characteristic spellings are retained. Stein, for example, routinely writes simply "x" at the beginning of words starting with "ex". With Thomson, who usually punctuates to indicate the end of a sentence, we sometimes supply punctuation when he does not. Otherwise we do not regularize or correct punctuation. Thomson habitually omits apostrophes in contractions. Stein's punctuation is idiosyncratic, in accord with her statements in "Poetry and Grammar" that, for instance, a question mark is redundant, uninteresting unless employed "as a brand on cattle" (214), and "a comma by helping you along holding your coat for you and putting on your shoes keeps you from living your life as actively as you should lead it" (220). Alice Toklas punctuates mostly with dashes, some of which she may intend as periods. In our transcription, we retain their appearance as dashes unless clearly otherwise. Where a writer in haste omits a word, we supply the probable omission in square brackets. A word followed by a question mark in square brackets indicates our best guess at an illegible word. Names are also completed in square brackets where identification may not be immediately evident. Authors' footnotes are asterisked and enclosed in parentheses in the body of the text of their letters. All French words are translated in notes except the most commonly understood by non-francophone readers. Postscripts, whether added at the top, bottom or in the margin of manuscript pages, are here placed after the letter.

The correspondence is incomplete. Clearly some of Thomson's later letters to Stein were either not saved or deliberately thrown out, possibly owing to souring of relations. Fortunately, he kept copies of most of these. Stein's famous calling card terminating relations with Thomson in mid-January 1930 is not in the Beinecke files, though we reproduce its message from other sources.

At the start of each letter, where we can, we indicate the address to which it is sent. If a postcard, we describe it. Where addresses or Stein's famous circular "Rose" device appear in capitals, this is to indicate printed stationery. We do not indicate when a letter is sent as a *carte pneumatique* or *petit bleu*, though many are. These are short letters sent by the pneumatic dispatch system in Paris, a comprehensive structure of underground suction tubes linking all Parisian post offices and allowing an express letter to reach its destination in the city within hours. They are as close as a pre-twenty-first century postal system has come to the ease and speed of emails. The blue or green express letter is small, light-weight, pre-stamped, and pre-glued to be folded into its own envelope, resembling the later, larger aerogramme.

Three brief messages cannot be dated or placed in sequence. We reproduce them after the letters in sequence.

There are several undatable small cards exchanged between Stein/Toklas and Thomson: sometimes birthday or New Years greetings, his cards often accompanying flowers, theirs sometimes accompanying cakes. All of them express good wishes. In most cases they are inscribed with "love."

All letters cited in the introduction and notes are in the Yale archives (YCAL) unless otherwise specified.

As with Stein and Thomson, we exclude Toklas from the index as being too much part of the story narrated by the letters and too often mentioned in them.

Sources that do not receive full bibliographical identification in the text of the introduction and notes do so after the appendices in a list of sources cited. Articles in magazines and newspapers are not listed in Sources Cited.

Thomas Dilworth and Susan Holbrook

University of Windsor

Letters with Notes

*****

To "Miss Gertrude Stein / 27 rue de Fleurus / Paris VI"

20, rue de Berne
2 December [1926]

Dear Miss Stein

I've heard nothing of you since the summer. Are you in Paris? And may I come to see you sometime soon? I dont go out much lately. Have seen none of your friends for news of you.

Very sincerely
Virgil Thomson

*****

To "M. Virgil Thomson / 20 rue de Berne / Paris."

ROSE IS A ROSE IS A ROSE IS A ROSE [circular]
27 RUE DE FLEURUS

[3 Jan. 1927]

My dear Virgil,

Thanks so much I am delighted, I like its looks immensely and want to frame it and Miss Toklas who knows more than looks says the things in it please her a lot and when can I know a little other than its looks but I am completely satisfied with its looks, the sad part was that we were at home but we were denying ourselves to every one having been xhausted by the weeks activities but you would have been the xception you and the Susie, you or the Susie, do come in soon we will certainly be in Thursday afternoon any other time it is luck but may luck always be with you and a happy New Year to you

Alwys
Gtrde Stein.

I like its looks: On New Year's Day, Thomson took Stein the musical manuscript of his setting of "Susie Asado" for soprano and piano, accompanied by a note "Here is a New Year greeting from my own mechanical bird. . . . It is a beginning." In her notebook-diary for that day she writes, "It is very nice to have words and music and to see them at the same time when by accident it is where they need it best. Most and best" (quoted in Watson 40).
the weeks activities: Among other events, a Christmas Eve party she and Alice threw in honor of her visiting friend Sherwood Anderson, to which Thomson was invited. He writes that it involved "carols and a tree and a great Xmas cake with ribbon and candles on it" *(Virgil Thomson* 89).
denying ourselves to everyone: On New Year's Day, they were refusing visitors because all day Toklas was slowly cutting Stein's hair short, layer by layer. Inspired by the newly-bobbed head of her friend the Duchess of Clermont-Tonnerre, Stein instructed Toklas to cut off her braids, ushering in the trademark look that will inspire Sherwood Anderson to liken her to a "monk" (Mellow 334) and many to liken her to a Roman emperor.

*****

20 rue de Berne
Thursday [early 1927]

Dear Miss Stein

This telegram comes today from the young man I sent the *Water Pipe* to. If it isnt too great a bother, could you send him another copy? He is

Mr. John Sherry Mangan
12 Baker Street
Lynn, Massachusetts

I am sorry, and I apologize for his accident.

Very sincerely
Virgil

Water Pipe: Stein's piece will appear in the first number of Sherry Mangan's little magazine, *larus, the celestial visitor* (February 1927), published out of Lynn, Massachusetts, of which Thomson is European editor.
John Sherry Mangan graduated with honors in Latin and Greek Literature in 1925 from Harvard, where he and Thomson were members of the Liberal Club—once a leftist political organization but by then merely a place to eat and enjoy intelligent conversation. Mangan travelled with Thomson to Paris in 1925 and returned home in 1926 to care for his ailing father.

*****

To "M. Virgil Thomson / 20 rue de Berne / Paris."

27 RUE DE FLEURUS
[25 March 1927]

My dear Virgil,

I am asking Avery Hopwood who announces that he is in our midst to lunch on Wednesday 12:30. Will you come too if he says yes. And how are you. We did have a pleasant evening chez vous and it has left nice memories,

Alwys
Gtrde Stein.

Avery Hopwood: Forty-four-year-old American playwright, the most commercially successful of his day, having composed thirty-five works for Broadway. He was the first of many visitors to Stein sent by American friend and promoter Carl Van Vechten and the one she likes most. When in Paris, Hopwood regularly asks Stein and Toklas to dine with him. **a pleasant evening chez vous**: This is probably the evening when, at his flat in the rue de Berne, he played for them Erik Satie's *Socrate*, which, Toklas would recall, Stein and she often spoke about (20 April 1947). *Socrate* was written in 1918 for voice and small orchestra but also concurrently in a reduced version for voice and piano. It was commissioned by musical patron Winnaretta Singer, Princess Edmond de Polignac, a lesbian who requested that vocal parts be set for female voices only.

*****

20 rue de Berne
Friday [25 March 1927]

Dear Gertrude

I shall be delighted to come on Wednesday. Reading lately in encyclopedia about saints. Teresa & Ignatius Loyola might make a good Spanish pair. I fancy best plan would be fictitious names, using as much of real character and history as suits the needs, but avoiding the pretense of historical drama.

Love
Virgil

Teresa & Ignatius Loyola: the two greatest sixteenth-century Catholic reformers. Teresa of Avila (1515–1582), a Carmelite nun, influenced by Dominicans, by Thomism, and by the Jesuits, her confessors. She experienced visions, founded convents of "discalced" or reformed Carmelite nuns and friars, and wrote about these foundations and her spiritual experiences in her *Interior Castle*, *Life of St Teresa of Jesus* (autobiography), and *Way of Perfection*. Ignatius Loyola (1491–1556) was a nobleman and officer in the Spanish army, inspired by chivalric romances before becoming devout while convalescing from a wound. He subsequently earned his MA in theology in Paris, where he founded the Society of Jesus (or Jesuits), and wrote his *Spiritual Exercises*.

*****

To "M. Virgil Thomson / 20 rue de Berne / Paris."

27 RUE DE FLEURUS
[26 March 1927]

My dear Virgil,

Avery does not eat lunch so I guess it will be Wednesday dinner 7.30, that will suit you as well will it not. And I have lots of ideas and even

1. Page of a letter by Gertrude Stein, 26 March 1927

some experiments. I have begun Beginning of Studies for an opera to be sung. I think it should be late eighteenth century or early nineteenth century saints. Four saints in three acts. And others. Make it pastoral. In hills and gardens. All four and then additions. We must invent them. But next time you come I will show you a little bit and we will talk some scenes over.

Alwys
Gtrde.

Beginning of Studies for an opera to be sung: the words heading Stein's manuscript of *Four Saints*.

*****

To "M. Virgil Thomson / 20 rue de Berne / Paris."

27 RUE DE FLEURUS
[26 March 1927]

My dear Virgil

I just wrote you that it was Wednesday and another petit bleu from Avery it is to be Thursday, Thursday evening 7.30 and the saints still enjoying themselves.

Alwys
Gtrde.

petit bleu: See introduction.

*****

To "M. Virgil Thomson / 20 rue de Berne / Paris"

27 RUE DE FLEURUS
[30 March 1927]

My dear Virgil,

Come in about six Thursday, I think I have got St. Therese onto the stage, it has been an awful struggle and I think I can keep her on and gradually by the second act get St. Ignatius on and then they will both be on together but not at once in the third act. I want you to read it as far as it has gone before you go so come in about six Thursday.

Gtrde Stn.

A pneumatique just came from Avery. he is leaving town for a few days and so we must put it off till later but come in to supper 7. o'clock. just with us. G.

pneumatique: See introduction.

*****

Postcard of "Ile de Port-Cros--Le Manoir. Château de Jean d'Agrève," to "Miss Gertrude Stein / 27 rue de Fleurus / Paris VI"

[*11 April 1927*]

Dear Gertrude.

I am at Hyères for the moment. It is hot & sunny. Bum beach. Swell mountains. Incredible food. Incredible & inedible. The Capitals marches. I shall move on myself about the end of the week. Dont know where but not far. Marseille was grand. Nearly stayed on. Spent a night on the island of Port Cros. Windy, pretty, harmless, & hopeless. Geographical equivalent of a tea-room. Multiply my love by two for yourself & Alice.

Virgil

Capitals: Thomson is setting to music Stein's play *Capital Capitals* (1923) as a twenty-minute cantata for four men's voices and piano. This early collaborative work—it would be their first to be performed publicly—is imagined as a conversation among the four capital cities of Provence: Aix [-en-Provence], Arles, Avignon, and Beaux [Les Baux-de-Provence].

*****

Villefranche-s-mer
Hôtel de la Colline
Tuesday [April 1927]

Dear Gertrude

Sherry wants something more of yours to print. Send anything you like. He would especially have, if possible "something from the period which produced *The Making of Americans*, for which I conceive a belated fondness." Naturally, that's what they all want, I suppose, because it's the easiest. So send him whatever you like. Villefranche is pleasant. *Capitals* finishes. I am with Mary Butts. May be back in a week. May be in three. You and Alice, love and love.

Virgil

Send it to him.
12 Baker Street
Lynn, Mass.

I have an awful suspicion that the real difficulty in getting Teresa & Loyola on the stage together is a mistake of 100 years in their dates. What is the truth of this? Were they contemporary? If not let's scrap Loyola and find a real rival.

Villefranche: Thomson went to the south of France to join Philip Lasell, a gay friend who lived beside him at 20 rue de Berne and whom Thomson loved but found emotionally fatiguing "like anybody with whom one ought to make love but doesn't" (quoted in Tommasini 164). Thomson subsequently writes of him "(whom I love, but who has lived for three months now on my vitality) satisfactorily finished off by a sort of ethereal Proustian quarrel (a marvellous quarrel conducted with the greatest dignity on both sides and the nearest to an open display of affection that we have ever allowed ourselves . . .)" (to Briggs Buchanan 27 Dec. 1926).
Capitals: See Thomson, [11 *April 1927*].

Mary Butts: Philip Lasell introduced her to Thomson, who spent most of his time at Villefranche with her. The granddaughter of William Blake's patron Thomas Butts and former wife of the poet John Rodker, she is an English novelist, poet, and hard drinking opium addict. About her, Thomson writes, "She was . . . quite handsome, with her white skin and carrot-gold hair. . . . I used to call her 'the storm goddess,' because she was at her best surrounded by cataclysm. She could stir up others with drink and drugs and magic incantations, and then when the cyclone was at its most intense, sit down at calm center and glow. . . . There was no evil in her; her magic was all tied up to religion and great poetry. But she was strong medicine, calling herself in joke my 'unrest cure.' And she was sovereign against my juvenile reserves, my middle-class hypochondrias" (*Virgil Thomson* 87–88). Many assume at this time that she and Thomson are lovers, a misapprehension he encourages.

a mistake of a hundred years: Though they neither met nor corresponded and he was twenty-four years older, Teresa (1515–1582) and Ignatius (1491–1556) were contemporaries, he dying at the age of sixty-five when she was forty-one. This issue is subsequently reflected with fictionalizing liberty in the libretto: "Four saints were not born at one time although they knew each other. One of them had a birthday before the mother of the other one the father" (14); and: "When they were forty five and thirty five" (*Four Saints* 44).

*****

To "M. Virgil Thomson / Hotel de la Colline / Villefranche-sur-mer / A. Maritimes"

ROSE IS A ROSE IS A ROSE IS A ROSE [circular]
27 RUE DE FLEURUS

[29 April 1927]

My dear Virgil,

Did you get Three Lives I sent it to you registered via your bank, Easter Monday I think, will you find out so I can have it traced, and are you going to be there long enough there where you are to eat a piece of your most xcellent cake, Alice wants to know, and I had a charming letter from Larus, and from Mme Langlois and I will send Larus something. I would like to show you some narratives I am doing now, Felicity in Moon Light and Love a delight, may send one of them to Larus unless he really suffers for the ancient but perhaps that later, and far from being troubled about discrepancy of dates far from it Therese and Ignatius are in and out just like anything the second act which may be the first act and the third act and lots of scenes and I have a nice idea that Alice says you won't like at all, probably you won't, like it, at all. Anyway best to you always

Gtrde.

Three Lives: New York: Grafton, 1909, repr. New York: Albert and Charles Boni, 1927.

Larus: Among those published in the seven issues of Mangan's short-lived literary magazine (1927–1928) are Hart Crane, Yvor Winters, and R. P. Blackmur (none of these then well known) and—procured by Thomson—Stein, Mary Butts, Bernard Faÿ, Robert McAlmon, Pierre de Massot, and Henry de Montherlant (*Virgil Thomson* 161).

Mme Langlois: Thomson met Louise Langlois (née Philibert), a wealthy widow over forty years his senior, while vacationing in the summer of 1926. They became fast friends and—with her companion, a Russian woman physician—took sight-seeing trips, exchanged books, played bridge. He and Mme Langlois, as he always addressed her, are "as chummy as a child and its grandmother." She is slender with short gray hair, a chain smoker. He will remember, "Just as Roman Catholicism was her faith and France her country, moral elegance and personal bravery were her habit, affection and friendship her daily rite and virtually sole occupation" (*Virgil Thomson* 84–6).

Felicity . . . delight: "Felicity in Moon-light" and "Love a Delight" will be published posthumously in *Painted Lace And Other Pieces (1914–1933)*, vol. 5 of *The Yale Edition of the Unpublished Writings of Gertrude Stein* (New Haven: Yale University Press, 1955).

second act: In the finished libretto, acts and scenes are ambiguously designated in that they may follow one another in sequence or one or more may include a number of those following. This rich ambiguity especially characterizes "Act Two," which follows "Act One" and "Repeat First Act" but also contains (or is followed by) an " Act II," another "Act One," dozens of scenes (but not numbered singly in sequence—they include, for example, two "Scene One"s and ten "Scene V"s), and conceivably an "Act III."

*****

Villefranche
2 May [1927]

Dear Gertrude

I received nothing registered from you. Inquire at the bank. They'll have a record. Why not send Sherry something ancient and the new also. He will use both eventually. I move today to Juan-les-Pins. Dont send cake. It wont arrive. In a hurry. Love Alice and both

Virgil

*****

Pension Montont
Juan-les-Pins
6 May [1927]

Dear Gertrude

I inquired at Villefranche for your registered mail. Nothing doing. What was it you sent? I couldnt read the word. Thought it was mss. Was it about our saints? I love it here. I swim. Life is cheap. We have pine trees and nightingales and everything cooked in butter. I shall return to Paris the 16th or 17th. Rather against my will. Tell Alice not to bother about the fruit-cake. Send a little piece, if she likes, but only a little piece. *Capitals* amuses everybody I sing it for. I have a room in a garden on the sea. The big house is haunted but not the garden-rooms. The garden is full of live animals and the house of dead ones. Stuffed beasts & birds look from all the walls and move if you return their looks. The animals in the garden are chickens, a dog, a cat, and two donkeys named Butterfly. Keep an eye peeled for millionaires and love me always

Virgil.

The donkeys have the room just below mine.

millionaires: Stein is trying to acquaint Thomson with rich elderly women who might become his patrons, supporting him while he composes *Four Saints*.

*****

To "M. Virgil Thomson / ~~aux [words?] de Hottinger et Cie. / 38 rue de Provence. / Paris.~~ Pension Montont / Juan les Pins / [A.M]"

27 RUE DE FLEURUS
PARIS

[6 May 1927]

My dear Virgil,

I was just told that they are going to talk about me at Nathalie Barney the third of June. Mina Loy is to do so and it occurred to me to diversify it it might be nice to give one of the three, Capitals or Susie Asado or Preciosilla or anyhow Nathalie Barney was enthusiastic about the idea and so will you write to her and to me her address is 20 rue Jacob about the voice or voices and I have only the one ms. you know, Paul never gave the other back. I also saw George Antheil and wife, they looked rather sad, also Miss Flanner and she didn't.

Alwys,
Gtrde.

Nathalie Barney: Natalie Clifford Barney, Left-Bank personality notorious for flouting convention (she is openly lesbian), has held renowned literary salons at her Rue Jacob home for two decades and will continue to do so for four more decades, her "Fridays" including such guests as Ezra Pound, Rainer Marie Rilke, Colette, William Carlos Williams, James Joyce, Edna St. Vincent Millay, T. S. Eliot, Isadora Duncan, and Scott and Zelda Fitzgerald.
Mina Loy: Forty-four-year-old English-born Dadaist and now Surrealist artist and avant-garde poet, whose writing Ezra Pound and William Carlos Williams admire. In her poem "Gertrude Stein," first published as part of her long letter on Stein in the *Transatlantic Review*, Loy famously dubs Stein "Curie / of the laboratory / of vocabulary" (*Transatlantic Review* 2 (1924): 305–309, 427–30).
Preciosilla: Like "Susie Asado," "Preciosilla" was written in Spain fourteen years earlier. Thomson inscribed his setting of "Preciosilla" to Stein in February 1927.
Paul: Elliot Paul, journalist writing for the Paris *Herald Tribune*, novelist, poet, co-editor with Eugene Jolas of *transition*.
George Antheil: Stein met Thomson through Antheil (see introduction). A young American composer in Paris, Antheil was wildly popular there for a time, celebrated for his famously modernist *Ballet mécanique* (1924), composed for sixteen player pianos, two regular pianos, four bass drums, three xylophones, a tam-tam, seven electric bells, a siren, and three airplane propellers. It will never be performed with all this instrumentation in his lifetime, but a modified score was performed in April 1927 at Carnegie Hall, where it was met with ridicule and disdain—which may be why he and his wife, Böske, "looked rather sad." He will go on to enjoy a productive career but will lose his cachet as a serious artist.
Miss Flanner: Janet Flanner, author, translator, and Paris correspondent for the *New Yorker* since September 1925, writing under the pen name Genêt. Stein is reported to have said that Janet Flanner looks "like the buffalo side of an Indian-head nickel." She is a regular visitor, reveres Stein, likes her talking "with the greatest sense, coherency, simplicity, and precision" and is reminded by the more reserved, cagey Alice of a "praying mantis among strawberry leaves" (Wineapple 77–8).

*****

Monday [9 May 1927]

Dear Gertrude

Go to it. Let's do the *Capitals*. Also the others if there is time. Capitals needs four men who know English. 1 Tenor, 1 Bass, 2 High Baritones or Low Tenors. I'll play piano if necessary. For Susie & Preciosilla I'd like a lady (soprano) with a real voice. If necessary the tenor could sing them. I reenter Monday the 16th

Love both
Virgil

My bank writes they have your package.
I've found a good summer house in mountains above Antibes.

*****

To "M. Virgil Thomson / Pension Montot / Juan le Pins / Alpes Maritimes"

27 RUE DE FLEURUS
[19 May 1927]

My dear Virgil,

Thats alright your bank has the registered package and they are holding it at your disposition and it was only the new edition of Three Lives so as long as it is not lost there is nothing to worry about and since then I have written you another letter perhaps you have it by now and that is to say and I repeat not for repetition but in case the other one which is on the way has not got there that Nathalie Barney on her Friday afternoons which is or at least one of them is of June the third. Mina Loy is to discourse shortly on my work in French and then they want to illustrate now I would rather have them illustrate with your songs and it might be a chance to hear them. I have only the Preciosilla here. Will you communicate with her 20 rue Jacob and suggest what you want and if it is the Capitals possibly well any way communicate with her. She wanted to know how many voices and what voices and I imagine also how long and anyway would you like it Alice will send you the cake she has it on her mind as well as in her tummy and the Saints, Alice says the Saints are satisfactory, just at this moment I am interested in a funny thing but the Saints persist. I have gotten to scene VIII Act II I sent Larus the old thing he wanted and when you come we will send him Felicity in moon-light or Love a delight, whichever you like. But first Nathalie Barney. and how do you feel about it

Lots of love
Gtrde.

Letters with Notes

disposition: arrangement, convenience.

*****

To "M. Virgil Thomson / Hotel Jacob / rue Jacob / Paris"

ROSE IS A ROSE IS A ROSE IS A ROSE [circular]
27 RUE DE FLEURUS

[20 May 1927]

My dear Virgil

We forgot that we have to go to the Fords Thursday so shall we say Wednesday. If that suit alright I will write to Mme. Langlois. We are happy about your music, and it means a lot to me that I like the variations and the children as much as the Capitals. We are both happy about it that is Alice and I are. Have finished the second Act of the Saints. Will go easy on the third as it is important as it is not the last.

Alwys
Gtrde.

the Fords: Ford Madox Ford, English novelist and editor of *The Transatlantic Review*, in which *The Making of Americans* was published serially in 1924. Stein and Toklas visit often with him, his mistress Stella Bowen, and their daughter Julie. According to Bravig Imbs, Stein likes Ford because he published her. She told Imbs, "I never could read anything he wrote, but his chronicles. His little articles on what he is seeing and hearing in Paris are often masterpieces" (173).
variations and the children: *Variations and Fugues on Sunday School Hymns*, a piece for organ written concurrently with *Capitals*.

*****

To "Miss Stein / 27, rue des Fleurs / E.V. [En Ville, i.e. In Town] (6)"

[28 May 1927]

Dear Gertrude

Can I bring Miss Newell to see you on Monday afternoon?

Toujours
Virgil

Miss Newell: Gertrude Newell, a New York decorator traveling in literary and theatrical circles.

*****

Letters with Notes 33

To "M. Virgil Thomson / Hotel Jacob / rue Jacob / Paris"

27 RUE DE FLEURUS
[28 May 1927]

My dear Virgil,

Encore et encore. The Sitwells are here and we are giving a party an early tea Monday and you can get here any time after half past three preferably about that time. They are much xcited about the Opera and like the sound of your name. Bring [Philip] Laselle [sic] who is a personable young man and can make himself useful and also let us have Miss Gertrude Newell at the same time, that will be distinguished and give us a day off do you see. Life is too strenuous I have not even been able to write in a diary let alone a saint, we must go away but at any rate Monday about after half past three and Miss Newell and Lasalle or selle. We like Mme Langlois a lot

Alwys
Gtrde.

Encore et encore: Yet more news.
The Sitwells: Edith and Sacheverell but not their brother Osbert, as Thomson will remember: "I met her brother Sacheverell at Gertrude's house once. I met Osbert sometime later" (to Dilworth, 3 Feb. 1981). English poet Edith Sitwell met Stein in 1925 and was instrumental in organizing Stein's lectures at Oxford and Cambridge in 1926. She is in Paris to see Sacheverell's pantomime-ballet, *The Triumph of Neptune*, which was commissioned by Diaghilev and premiered in London in 1926. Thomson later remembers, "Edith Sitwell was around. Gertrude used to say that in the three Sitwells there was enough talent to make one first-class English man of letters. But Edith she rather liked, and didn't want to drop her or be rude to her, so she suggested that Edith have her portrait painted by Pavel Tchelitcheff.... The first time she went to pose he told her that she looked like Queen Elizabeth. She couldn't resist that, so they became very close friends" (*Reader* 208).

*****

To "Miss Stein / 27, rue des Fleurus / E.V. VI"

[28 May 1927]

Dear Gertrude

I have sent out the commands. Mary Butts is arriving tomorrow and I shall bring her too if you dont mind.

I am glad you like my friends.

Love
Virgil

The cake is swell.

*****

To "M. Virgil Thomson / Hotel Jacob / rue Jacob / Paris"

27 RUE DE FLEURUS
Sunday [29 May 1927]

No Virgil not Mary Butts this time we are alas not suffering for any xtra ladies alright to-morrow then. We have just had a nice quiet day in the country,

Alwys
Gtrde.

---

not Mary Butts: Relations between Stein and Butts are tense over Thomson's allegiance to Stein. In June 1927, Butts writes in her journal, "Real row with Virgil because he has spoilt or broken or violated the magical secret between us. I don't want him to be an old lady's tame musician, just a salon composer. A wide cast of the net brought strange information about Gertrude. I can only repeat & repeat & repeat that a real relation is worth the effort to retain" (254).

*****

To "M. Virgil Thomson / Hotel Jacob / rue Jacob, / Paris."

ROSE IS A ROSE IS A ROSE IS A ROSE [circular]
27 RUE DE FLEURUS

[31 *May* 1927]

My dear Virgil,

I seem to pass my days writing you letters. It would appear that Alice told Miss Flanner to come in Friday evening and Friday evening well not Friday evening but Saturday evening, the Fords are to be here etc. Will you let her know we have not her address and come with her if you like and bring the Saints and I'll correct it in the next few days.
Alors Friday,

Alwys
Gtrde.

Alors Friday: Till Friday, June 3, the date of Barney's soirée, where Thomson will play and sing "Preciosilla" and "Susie Asado."

*****

To "Miss Gertrude Stein / 27, rue de Fleurus / Paris VI"

Tuesday [7 *June* 1927]

Dear Gertrude

Janet Flanner pursues us with notes about you. I dont quite understand what I have to do with the matter, but anyway I seem to be appointed as liaison officer. For the promised interview she is ready & eager any time this week afternoon or evening except Wednesday evening. To avoid note writing, let's say Thursday evening sauf contraire. Otherwise, you appoint a time, write us, and we'll be there. If I cant come it is of no matter, though I shall because I always like to.

Love Virgil

I copy Capitals fast.

---

pursues us with notes about you: In 1927, Flanner plans to write a profile of Stein—though she will later deny this, claiming she never writes about friends—a profile never completed or which the *New Yorker* did not accept (Wineapple 78).
sauf contraire: unless otherwise.

*****

To "M. Virgil Thomson / Hotel Jacob & Angleterre / 44 rue Jacob / Paris."

27 RUE DE FLEURUS
[7 June 1927]

My dear Virgil,

It has been Alice's intention to calm Miss Flanner any time these last three days but she is still uncalmed incidentally she ought to use petit bleu paper that don't weigh too heavy for obvious financial reasons but anyhow Alice is writing her to come in Wednesday afternoon that seeming for the moment to be most convenient and do you come too and I will give you back the corrected saints which I would have you know is an opera not any funny business but just an opera, owing to a complication of things I have not gone further but there is still some untyped and soon I will,

Alwys
Gtrde.

---

calm Miss Flanner: Letters from Janet Flanner to Stein and Toklas suggest she is "uncalmed" in her attempts to set up an interview (her underscorings indicate anxiety): "Dear Miss Toklas: I could not wait until after Virgil's singing to speak to Miss Stein as I had an article to do before midnight—I have received a cable to cover the <u>Wednesday</u> night instead of the <u>Tuesday</u> night ballet, so may it be <u>any other night at all</u>?" (Flanner to Toklas, n.d.).

*****

27 RUE DE FLEURUS
[*June 1927*]

My dear Virgil.

Here it is and they will have their names on their halos. I liked doing it all it is also nice to pass the buck good luck

Gtrde.

It is (any one to tease a saint seriously) you will see.

Here it is: The manuscript of the near complete libretto of *Four Saints*, to which this note is attached.
any one to tease a saint seriously: She quotes her libretto (*Four Saints* 15).

*****

To "Miss Stein / 27, rue des Fleurus / E.V. VI"

[17 June 1927]

Dear Gertrude

Thank you for the saints. For each and every and all. Bébé will do décors. He's full of swell ideas. Also wants to give you a picture. You can argue him out of that, I think. Wants me to bring him again to your house. I suggested Tuesday afternoon. Rehearsal Sunday evening at 8.30 at the Duchesse's house 67, rue Raynouard. You might let her know in advance that you are coming. And do come. I need your moral effect on the singers.
Love Virgil

Bébé: The painter Christian Bérard, one of Thomson's painter-comrades. Early in discussions about the opera, Stein offered the services of Picasso as stage designer, but Thomson preferred, he writes, "to remain, except for her, within my age group" and asked Bérard "to consider designing an eventual production . . . and he said yes with joy, began instantly giving off ideas" (99). Stein writes in the persona of Toklas, "Virgil had in his room a great many pictures by Christian Bérard and Gertrude Stein used to look at them a great deal. She could not find out at all what she thought about them. She and Virgil Thomson used to talk about them endlessly. . . . She used to say of Bérard's pictures, they are almost something and then they are just not" (*Autobiography* 246).
Rehearsal: *Capital Capitals* is being rehearsed, and will be sung during a 21 June Grande Semaine costume party at the house of elizabeth de Gramont, Duchesse de Clermont-Tonnerre, a writer, descendent of Henry IV, formerly a close friend of Proust, and a member of the feminist literary group led by Natalie Barney called "l'Académie des Femmes." The Duchess's house is an eighteenth-century gatehouse on the right bank across from the Eiffel Tower. The success of this concert and the local fame it gives Stein will incline her to allow Thomson to make changes in the newly completed libretto of *Four Saints*.

*****

To "M. Virgil Thomson / Hotel Jacob / rue Jacob / Paris."
    ROSE IS A ROSE IS A ROSE IS A ROSE [circular]
              27 RUE DE FLEURUS

[*18 June* 1927]

My dear Virgil,

Tuesday afternoon suits very well as we are then giving a farewell tea party and Fania Marinoff will be here and she is a good advance agent for reclame and Covarrubias and some others. About Sunday we won't be able to manage it got to see Mildred Aldrich and anyway it is not practicable but be a brave young man and remember our hearts are with you. The opera has given me lots of ideas for a novel I want to write and

Alwys
Gtrde.

If Mme Langlois should be in town on Tuesday it would give us a lot of pleasure if she came and if she is to be I will write her a note too.

Fania Marinoff: Actress and wife of Carl Van Vechten, Stein's lifelong friend and publicist. For Van Vechten, see note to Stein, [21 Aug. 1928].
reclame: *réclame*, publicity.
Covarrubias: Miguel Covarrubias, twenty-two-year-old self-taught Mexican artist now studying in Paris, already famous in the U.S. for caricatures published in *Vanity Fair, Vogue, Life*, and on Alfred A. Knopf book jackets. A close friend of Diego Rivera, a friend also of Marinoff and Carl Van Vechten, who has been his promoter since they met in 1923.
Mildred Aldrich: Seventy-four-year-old American editor, writer, journalist and critic who is spending her last years in France. She lived in a farmhouse in Huiry on the Marne throughout World War I, even as neighbouring villages were evacuated, witnessing battles firsthand and billeting French and British soldiers. The peak of her fame was occasioned by her bestselling 1915 account of these experiences, *A Hilltop on the Marne*, composed in part of letters she wrote to Stein. From the time they met in 1904 until her death in 1928, Aldrich and Stein remain close friends. Stein and Toklas campaigned successfully to have her awarded the Legion of Honour and to establish a fund for her living expenses.
novel I want to write: *Lucy Church Amiably*, 1927, to be published in 1930 as the first title in the Plain Edition, Stein's publishing venture, designed to print all Stein's unpublished works. Like the opera, *Lucy Church Amiably* is pastoral, and features the name Therese. Its constellation of names also includes Lucy, of course, and Lily, perhaps born of the opera's lyrical riff: "Let Lucy Lily Lily Lucy Lucy let Lucy Lucy Lily Lily Lily Lily let Lily Lucy Lucy let Lily. Let Lucy Lily" (*Four Saints* 36).

*****

To "Miss Gertrude Stein / 27, rue de Fleurus / Paris VI"

Hotel Jacob
[20 June 1927]

Dear Gertrude

Must inform you that the Capitals sounds like exactly one million dollars, one full twelfth of a dozen, no less.
Duchesse completely *enthousiaste*. Even the singers somewhat convinced. Madame Langlois reenters tomorrow. Whether for five o'clock I don't know, though I fancy yes. End of opera is swell.
Histories about your tomorrow party. Which I will explain tonight. Be sure to come before 11.30. We perform promptly at that moment.

Love   Virgil

*****

Sunday [*3 July* 1927]

Dear Gertrude

The Cones have just left. Heavily impressed. Enthusiastic. Moved. Touched. Pleased. Flattered. No mention of money. They cagily brought along a companion. So I just played and was nice. The invalid has done her bit. You, I suppose, have left. All is lost. Barring the possibility of your going in person to the Lutetia and making a request. And that I don't count on. Elsa Maxwell excellent. Lunch with Polignac next Saturday. Maxwell offers performance of opera at Monte Carlo in spring of 1929. Sounds big but God knows. Bon voyage

                                          Love
                                          Virgil

38, rue de Provence

The Cones: Etta and Claribel Cone, the latter a physician, American art collectors, staying at the Hotel Lutetia, 45 Boulevard Raspail. Etta Cone typed Stein's manuscript of *Three Lives* and, induced by Stein, began collecting art by occasionally buying drawings from Picasso when he was impoverished. Stein wrote portraits of both of them. She arranged the meeting between the Cone sisters and Thomson, one of her many attempts to secure patronage for Thomson while he composes the music for the opera.
The invalid: Mrs. Chester Whitin (Jessie) Lasell, Philip's aunt. She and her rich Republican family befriended Thomson in 1924 when he was weekend church-organist in Whitinsville, Massachusetts (see introduction). Thomson has postponed setting Stein's libretto to music in order to take a motor trip through Brittany and Normandy with Mrs. Lasell and her granddaughter, Nancy Clare Verdi. Mrs. Lasell contracted mastoiditis, a potentially deadly inflammation of the area behind the ear. Her illness stopped the tour in Rouen, from which Thomson is visiting Paris and to which he will return to care for her. The trip is to become two months of caring for the invalid.
Elsa Maxwell: whose life work is, Thomson writes, "showing people how to spend money." Through the sculptor Jo Davidson, Stein arranged for Thomson to meet her. He recalls:
> Miss Maxwell immediately invited me to lunch at the Ritz, where at a table of twelve I sat between her (Oh, yes, at her right) and a Roman principessa and where, between cocktails and bridge, she outlined for me in detail a custom-made career, which she herself was to take in hand right off. The first item of this was to be a commission from the Princesse Edmond de Polignac for a work to be performed the next season at one of this lady's regular musical receptions. The last item was to be a production of my opera at Monte Carlo in the spring of 1929, two years thence. And we were both to lunch with the princesse the next Saturday. The Monte Carlo deal appeared to me more credible than the other, because Miss Maxwell was employed at that time by the principality of Monaco as a promoter of its gambling casinos, hotels, and beach. (*Virgil Thomson* 96)

Lutetia: Hotel Lutetia, 45 Boulevard Raspail, where the Cone sisters are staying.

                                          *****

To "M. Virgil Thomson / c/o Hottinger Freres / 38 rue de Provence / Paris. Hotel Jacob / 44 rue Jacob / 7 Gd Hotel de la Poste / Rouen"

HOTEL PERNOLLET   [9 July 1927]
    BELLEY
      (AIN)

My dear Virgil.

Where are you and how are you and what has happened to you something good I hope and how are you liking it very well I hope. As for us it is not Alice's fault that the copies of the opera have not been made but I did kind of want to enjoy our buttered nightingales peacefully for awhile and we will be doing it next week the two copies and and what. Well tell Baby Berard M. Christian Berard to keep an eye out for scare crows they are most saintish. We saw a white shirt on a cross, a petticoat tied top and bottom very good and a bird with wing outstretched on a stick and we are going to see others as the grain ripens but he knows. Anyway it is peaceful and belleyish and everything makes us think happily of dear distant Paris. Tell us your news and remember us to everybody. I had an invitation for you to Romaine Brooks but it came too late to do any good you may have gotten there anyway. Love to anybody and yourself principally.

> Alwys
> Gtrde.

Belley: a town of about 5000 people in the valley of the Rhône, which Stein and Toklas first visited during the war and where at that time, Stein writes, "she began writing a great deal.... The landscape, the strange life stimulated her" (*Autobiography* 201).
buttered nightingales: Joking reference to Thomson's letter of 6 May, 1927: "We have pine trees and nightingales and everything cooked in butter." This turn of phrase made an impression on Stein and Toklas, who mentions it in a letter years after Stein's death: "Everything has come—it is all beautiful—your book and Maurice's—the opera and the snow—and all cooked in butter as you once said" (to Thomson, 26 Feb. 1948, see epilogue).
Romaine Brooks: Wealthy, fifty-three-year-old expatriate portrait painter awarded the Legion of Honour in 1920. Since 1915 a long-time lover of Natalie Barney and member of her salon, she and Barney recently built near Beauvallon their "Villa Trait d'Union" or hyphenated-villa, two distinct houses joined by a common dining room.

*****

Postcard of "Avila- Iglesia de San Pedro" in Spain, to "M. Virgil Thomson / Hotel Jacob / rue Jacob / Paris. Gd. Hotel de la Poste / Rouen"

Hotel Pernolet [sic]   [12? July 1927]
Belley
Ain.

My dear Virgil.

Where are you, the copies are ready but you have not let me know where to send them.

> G.S.

*****

Postcard of "Segovia—El Parral—Puerta de la Sacristia—LL," to "M. Virgil Thomson ~~Hottinger & Co. / 38 rue de Provence / Paris~~ Grand Hotel de la Poste/ Rouen."

Hotel Pernolet [sic] [16 July 1927]
Belley
Ain

faire suive s.v.p.

Where do you want the copies sent and where are you and what are you. Answer.

G.S.

———

faire suive s.v.p: please forward.

*****

GRAND HÔTEL DE LA POSTE
ROUEN
17 July [1927]

Dear Gertrude and Alice,

    I'm stuck in Rouen with an invalid. Mrs. Lasell, Philip's aunt. And grand-daughter aged 14. We started from Cherbourg to motor some and she took to bed here with an ear abscess. I drove to Paris and brought back a specialist who operated and left her to a local one and a nurse. I lead grand-daughter into churches and occasionally hold invalid's hand. For the rest I have a room with a bath and swell food and nothing to do. Not working. Alone too much for that. Toward the end of the week I can probably take patient to Paris. Early in August I shall join Madamme Langlois somewhere.

Results of Paris projects.

1.) The Cones came across with a long history of poverty and a gift of 1000 francs.
2.) Elsa Maxwell did nothing. Posed me six lapins in three days and then left word she had quitted Paris.
3.) Cocteau came and was conquered (apparently). He has talked much and even wrote a letter to the Princesse. But since the Maxwell never arranged the promised meeting, nothing can come of that at the moment. I wrote Cocteau the story (he had told me similar ones about the Maxwell) and I shall see him again in Paris. Also probably at Chantilly in September.
4.) Send me the *Saints* copies to the bank in about a week. I'll be in Paris then. Mark the envelope "Please Hold".
5.) For the moment I am housed and fed and cigaretted. Hoping grateful invalid may make a contribution later.

Letters with Notes   41

6.) Please write the Maxwell story to Jo Davidson.

I am glad of the scarecrow idea. "The night-shirt on the cross" would make a grand scene. Too bad you didnt put words for it but it doesnt really make any difference. We can use it for the funeral.

Getting away from Paris was hard. American visitors. Quarrels with Mary. Friends attacked with illness. One Russian had a heart-failure. Another, an American visitor, got hysterical, had illusions of persecution, & had to be handed over to American hospital. I had a hell of a bronchial cold myself and an American boy-friend who came in late every night to weep over his heart-matters and early every morning to make me go to fittings with his tailor.

Now it's hard getting back there. I hate Rouen. Except Saint Maclou church. Thanks church Avila.

Love both.   Virgil

Maxwell did nothing: Not knowing whether her "plans encountered resistance" or she was bluffing from the start, Thomson writes, "the lunch in the avenue Henri Martin never came off and . . . within a week after the one at the Ritz, Miss Maxwell made six engagements with me in three days and failed to appear at any of them, leaving word the last time that she had quit Paris. Jean Cocteau, to whom I told the story, offered to write the princess himself explaining that I was not to be judged from my acquaintances in café society. But I discouraged this, doubting she had ever heard of me" (*Virgil Thomson* 99, 97). According to Thomson's letter, Cocteau did write to her, apparently to no avail.
Posed me six lapins: Anglicization of *elle me pose un lapin*, "she stood me up."
Jo Davidson: American sculptor, famous for his busts of prominent figures. Of his 1923 sculpture of Stein, he recalls, "To do a head of Gertrude was not enough—there was so much more to her than that. So I did a seated figure of her—a sort of modern Buddha." Their mutual portraits were published in *Vanity Fair* (February 1923). Davidson remembers that Stein would read to him at his studio, noting "I never felt any sense of mystification. 'A rose is a rose is a rose,' took on a different meaning with each inflection. When she read aloud, I got the humor of it. We both laughed, and her laughter was something to hear. There was an eternal quality about her—she somehow symbolized wisdom" (*Between Sittings* 174–75).
Quarrels with Mary: Thomson is establishing emotional distance from Butts owing to tension with her over his relationship with Stein, and to demands by Butts for attention and money. He later writes that he could not "take on for long a greedy and determined femme de lettres some seven years older. The mental powers were too imposing, the ways inflexible. We had lovely times together, warmths, clarities, and laughter. Then bickering began." By the end of 1927 they will no longer be meeting (*Virgil Thomson* 88).
Thanks church Avila: Stein's postcard of 12 [?] July features the Iglesia de San Pedro at Avila

*****

To "M. Virgil Thomson / of Hottinger & Co. / 38 rue de Provence / Paris."

[2x July 1927]

    HOTEL PERNOLLET
        BELLEY
        (AIN)

My dear Virgil.

You seem to be having what one of the ladies of the American Fund for French Wounded used to describe as a busy and successful day. They were just that kind. Sorry the Cones were poor and now I am making one more effort in your behalf. I have just written Emily Chadbourne all about it and given her your address. Nothing may come of it it mostly does not of course but if she should write to you don't have it in your head that she is stupid because she isn't and if she interests herself and she has in many she is very generous. Beside I am not very sure of her address. But anyhow. About Jo call him up and tell him about it but do not be too Virgilian just tell him. He probably is [primed?] by George Middleton anyway George Middleton always [primes?] him but just tell him about it nicely perhaps he will think of something else. It is so easy to think. Otherwise peace. I am progressing with my novel. There are times even when it is going to be a historical novel a geographical novel etc. I hope eventually to get the habit of conversation. Am sending the saints registered mail to-morrow. Let's hear when you get it. and otherwise that's all.

    Alwys
    Gtrde.

American ... Wounded: In 1917 Stein and Toklas drove their first Ford, "Auntie," as a supply truck for the American Fund for French Wounded.
Emily Chadbourne: Emily Chadbourne Crane, Chicago millionaire, erstwhile leader of the anti-opium campaign in China, friend of Stein, proposed by her as a patron for Thomson.
tell him about it: "The Maxwell story." See Thomson, 17 July [1927].
George Middleton: New York playwright, author of eleven Broadway plays.

*****

[From Toklas]

To "Virgil Thomson Esquire / aux Louis d'Hottinger et Cie. / 38 rue de Provence / Paris / Seine"

[25 July 1927]

HOTEL PERNOLLET
 BELLEY
 (AIN)

Dear Virgil

The dragées of the Caby gourmand are delicious and it was sweet of you to know they are our favourite sweets. They're the prettiest pink hues & tones to any summer day I've ever known. We do have summer weather here—the rain gets here for a day a week and keeps the country a brilliant green which is pleasant and not at all an annoyance. We have revisited our most cherished spots and have been advised to investigate precipices and altitudes with extended views and perilous descents but we prefer everything to be "very nice and quiet I thank you" as an uncle of mine said when he was asked how his nerves were getting on at a moment when assessments and taxes were beyond him—It's a peaceful country and lives happily in and on the memory of Brillat Savarin's recipes—I'm so pleased you liked Saint Maclou—it's delicious—Isn't it there that we saw some Louis Phillipeish windows with the [dancers?] in crinolines and pantalettes? I think it was there and did you get to Madame Bovary's? If not—the next time you must

With ever so many thanks and a very fond remembrance

Yours ever
Alice Toklas

2. Page 306 of the manuscript score of *Four Saints in Three Acts*, "pigeon on the grass, alas . . . Lucy Lily"

dragées: sugared almonds
Brillat Savarin: Jean Anthelme Brillat-Savarin (1755-1826), French politician and gourmet born in Belley, author of seminal work on gastronomy, *Physiologie de Goût* (*The Physiology of Taste*).

*****

To "M. Virgil Thomson Hottinger & Co. / 38 rue de Provence / Paris Hotel Jacob / 44 rue Jacob / Paris."

[27 July 1927]

HOTEL PERNOLLET
    BELLEY
    (AIN)

My dear Virgil.

This is what I just got this morning from Emily Chadbourne. I do hope to God she likes you when she sees you because as I told you she is generous continuous and uninterfering if she once begins and not without a certain delicacy of impression. I told her that you needed $150 a month occasional concerts and perhaps the opera. God bless you both and may you live long and prosper.

Otherwise nothing but we are enjoying it. Let us know what happens to you and that you have received this.

Alwys
Gtrde.

*****

HOTEL JACOB & D'ANGLETERRE
44, RUE JACOB -- PARIS
J. BERTHIER, PROP[re]   31 July, 1927

Dear Gertrude

Thank you for many letters, kind offices, faith hope and charity. Copied saints received. Many thanks.
Things are in the air and many plans. Grateful invalid on the verge of making a nice gift. Offers me a trip to America. I want her to make it money. Mrs. Chadbourne will be received as charmingly as I can (which is not bad) when she appears. I have not telephoned Jo. I suppose I should and shall. No work done. Occupied with invalid. That's all right, because I'm earning good money. She sails 24th. I shall come to Jura to pass a few days with Madame Langlois and unless you find it inconvenient I should like to do the same to you at Belley around 1st September.

My hunch is that something nice will come of my meeting with Mrs. Chadbourne. Something pretty nice is also sure to come out of Mrs. Lasell. On the whole, things are looking up. Cocteau much impressed by the music. "Voila une table qui se tient debout. Voila une porte qui s'ouvre et qui se ferme." And much much more of the same sort. To me and to others. Bébé sends you love. I send you love. Paris thinks about you. You think about us and send us your love (plus good offices) and Alice writes me a charming letter. And really everything is doing very nicely for us all just now it seems. And I had a nice visit last night from the Saint Pigeon. Love Virgil

---

Mrs. Chadbourne will be received . . . charmingly: In a letter dated "Sunday," Chadbourne cancels the anticipated meeting to go to Berlin and writes that she must postpone hearing his music.
Voila une porte . . . ferme: "At last a table that stands on four legs, a door that really opens and shuts." Accompanying himself on the piano, Thomson sang *Capital Capitals*, all four voices, in his narrow room in the Hotel Jacob to Jean Cocteau and others, including Mary Butts, who invited Cocteau, an acquaintance of Thomson since their first meeting in 1921.
Saint Pigeon: The Holy Spirit, who appears in the Gospels in the form of a dove. "The pigeon on the grass" is celebrated in Stein's libretto (*Four Saints* 36). In the same passage of the opera, moreover, the "magpies in the sky" recall, Stein said, the magpies in Avila, which "hold themselves up and down and look flat against the sky. . . . exactly like the birds in the Annunciation pictures the bird which is the Holy Ghost and rests flat against the sky very high" ("Plays" 129). Thomson will say, "The Holy Spirit composes my music" (to Dilworth, 2 Feb. 1981). Reference to Saint Pigeon in this letter and that of [June or July 1929] suggest that he thinks this now.

*****

To "M. Virgil Thomson / Hotel Jacob & D'Angleterre / 44 rue Jacob / Paris"

HOTEL PERNOLLET   [4 Aug. 1927]
    BELLEY
     (AIN)

My dear Virgil,

May all news continue to be good news, we are religious here we have had a [word?] fête it does not sound religious but it was very and they were ideas but vague ideas. Anyway we will be awfully pleased to have you the first of September. Sorry about not asking Mrs. Langlois to join us I like her very much but I don't like to be burdened in the summer and you are never a burden well it is just like that and in summer. Let us know when you want to come it makes no difference really as we just eat chicken and cake in the landscape anyway. Had a letter from Jo poor Yvonne is ill again and so they are in Paris just now and I know he will be glad to hear the sound of your voice. And Emily Chadbourne I imagine you might write to her not too generously you and I have a bad habit of wanting to give it all to them but just so that she has your present Paris address I only gave her the bank. Otherwise my novel is progressing, I made a historical background and now I have created Lucy Church otherwise known as Lucy

Pagoda and she is enjoying herself very likely. Have heard nothing from Larus. Is my daughter never going to paint again. She often doesn't. Anyway lots of love

Gtrde.

Yvonne: wife of Jo Davidson (see note to Thomson, 17 July [1927]), née de Kerstrat, an actress when they met, later a dressmaker and designer.
I made a historical background . . . Lucy Church: *Lucy Church Amiably* begins with "Begins the Middle of May," an introduction four chapters long, before presenting chapter 1 of "The Novel."

*****

Sunday [14 Aug. 1927]

Dear Gertrude

Did you send me nice Savoy cakes? Thank you. Mrs. Chadbourne replies as inclosed. Toujours quelque chose. Not seen Jo. Still nurse invalid. Operation pending. Daughter arrives 22nd. (Mrs. Sibley Watson.) Maybe we work her too. No news. No work. Nobody in town. Sorta bored. Got a swell new piano. I cant read what kind of a fête you had. Larus continues. But slowly. Lucy Church sounds indefatigable. People named Church always are. And with a fluttering prename like hers, no wonder she is sometimes Lucy Pagoda. Thanks again cake

Love
Virgil

Save me Mrs. Chadbourne's letter. Mustnt lose incriminating evidence.

Daughter: Mrs. Sibley (Hildegarde) Watson is Mrs. Lasell's daughter and Thomson's friend, to whom he dedicates *Five Phrases from the Song of Solomon* and who occasionally gives him money.
Mrs. E.C. Chadbourne replies as inclosed: On 10 August, she writes to Thomson from Paris that "Miss Stein" wrote her about him, saying he is away from Paris, that she (Chadbourne) is leaving the next day for the south and wants to return next month, and that she is unwilling to support him but can give $50 a month if that will help and will let him know more upon her return.
Toujours quelque chose: always something.
incriminating evidence: Thomson does not want Mrs. Lasell to know of this new patron. He later writes, "I did not tell Jessie Lasell that Gertrude's Chicago millionairess Mrs. Emily Chadbourne Crane had at Gertrude's extreme insistence also become temporarily my patron" (*Virgil Thomson* 111).

*****

To "M. Virgil Thomson / Hotel Jacob / 44 rue Jacob / Paris."

HOTEL PERNOLLET [16 Aug. 1927]
   BELLEY
   (AIN)

My dear Virgil,

Here is Emily's letter back and it is not such a bad beginning, it will keep a little of the wolf off the door a piece of him out, and then if you meet you may like each other and all will be well. You do sound a little so so from far too much Paris. When are you coming here. We really do want you to stay with us a bit of course there is nothing to do but us and cakes and patty and chicken and landscape, nothing and that we like it. Otherwise no news. Close Up is printing the thing I did last spring that I liked telling why they love me and it is quite nice. Lucy Church Pagodas as she should. She has two men John Mary and Simon Therese. It is a very pleasant society. We hear a good deal from René, we kind of feel like neighbors, he is very sad and writes sweetly in English,

And so forth   Alwys
                                Gtrde.

---

patty: A small pie or pastry.
John Mary and Simon Therese: Along with Lucy Church, these comprise the principal triad of figures in *Lucy Church Amiably*.
Close Up: Film journal edited by Kenneth MacPherson, H. D., and Winifred Bryher. They printed "Three Sitting Here" in two parts, appearing in issue nos. 3 and 4. The piece does indeed explore "why they love me," beginning, "The reason why they do not know why they love me so is because everybody has to begin a thing" (17), suggesting Stein's awareness of her appeal as an innovator.
René Crevel: Twenty-seven-year-old author of *Les Pieds dans le Plat* (1923) and *Babylon* (1927) and friend of Tristan Tzara, André Gide, and Jean Cocteau; a "devout surréaliste" described by Stein as "young and violent and ill and revolutionary and sweet and tender" (*Autobiography* 245, 256), whom she feels "tender about" and whom Alice loves (*Virgil Thomson* 175). She probably has him in mind when writing in her libretto, "very sweetly Rene very sweetly many very sweetly. They are very sweetly many very sweetly Rene very sweetly there are many very sweetly" (*Four Saints* 39).

*****

Postcard: "Burgos: Catedral, El Santo Cristo," Jesus on the Cross, to "M. Virgil Thomson / Hotel Jacob / rue Jacob / Paris."

Hotel Pernollet   [2x Aug., 1927]

Belley, Ain.

Whats the news. Lucy is doing nicely, it rained a week but now its good weather, had a letter from Mangan, he seems pleased with the Elie and with its salutary effect on compositors me too but did he send the July Larus, I haven't it and would like to see it, have you it. Otherwise pleasant little things but nothing xciting and you, less pleasant and more xciting I hope not, give us your news, and best to Bebe Berard,   Alwys

                                                                Gtrde.

Mangan . . . compositors: Sherry Mangan published Stein's "Elie Nadelman" in *Larus* 1 no. 4 (July 1927): 19–20. In a letter of 11 August, he writes, "Quite aside from its other merits, I find that your style improves the accuracy of compositors. For the man who set this last piece, though his work is usually full of errors, was this time so terrified lest he be penalized for a[n] omitted word that there was not a mistake in it. I hope this may amuse you" (Mangan to Stein, 11 Aug. 1927).

*****

Sunday [*Sept.* 1927]

Dear Gertrude

Love but no news. I have some new clothes from Lanvin. Awful swell. I am not leaving Paris for a bit. I love the Spanish Christ standing on Eggs. Send me more. I hope to hear this month from the Chadbourne. There are also other breezes stirring.

Love
Virgil

Lanvin: Jeanne Lanvin, fashionable clothing store. Grateful for his two months of attentiveness during her illness, Mrs. Lasell has become his patron, providing a monthly allowance of $125 for the next three years in addition to funding concerts and the copying of music. This fall Thomson uses the new funds to purchase a new wardrobe and his favourite Lanvin cologne.
on Eggs: He is responding to Stein's postcard, on which a large crucifix hangs behind an altar, a cluster of five ostrich eggs immediately below Jesus' feet.

*****

To "M. Virgil Thomson / Hotel Jacob / rue Jacob / Paris."

27 RUE DE FLEURUS
[*mid-Sept.* 1927]

My dear Virgil,

Here we are, what's the news,

Gtrde.

Here we are: Stein and Toklas returned to Paris from Belley.

*****

To "M. Virgil Thomson / Hotel Jacob / rue Jacob / Paris."

27 RUE DE FLEURUS
[24 Sept. 1927]

My dear Virgil,

Emily Chadbourne has just turned up and seems possibly quite interested possibly, anyhow you are to come to dinner all of us are to dine with her Monday and we meet here at seven, not too much Lanvin, otherwise just your own natural self and good luck,

Alwys
Gtrde.

---

possibly quite interested: As a result of Stein's urging and this meeting, Emily Chadbourne will give Thomson $1,000 to support him while he composes the score for *Four Saints*.
not too much Lanvin: Stein objects to the cologne Thomson bought at Lanvin.

*****

Sunday [25 Sept. 1927]

Dear Gertrude

The saints are singing. Gaily praising their maker. and trying not to be too catty to one another. Especially about what key their next pieces will be written in. Occasionally a pair indulges in a moment of duet. but no open scandal as yet.
I shall come for you tomorrow at seven. I renounce, naturally, for the evening at least, Jeanne Lanvin and all her works. Havent found no flat yet. Bébé and Mary send amitiés.

I Also love
Virgil

Eric says will you read this poem.

The saints are singing: Thomson will begin composing in earnest once ensconced in his own flat at 17 Quai Voltaire in November.
amitiés: best wishes.
Eric de Haulleville, aristocratic Belgian poet, friend of Thomson.

*****

[From Toklas]

ROSE IS A ROSE IS A ROSE IS A ROSE. [circular]
27 RUE DE FLEURUS
[*Oct.* 1927]

Dear Virgil

There's a studio with bath (I don't know how much nearer) to be free in three weeks at 17 Quai Voltaire—You can see it by making an appointment by letter with Mr James Grimeu—who has it now—Will you let him hear from you at once if you want to investigate it—if not drop me a line at once as they have some one else who will look at it.

Fond remembrance   from
Alice

*****

To "Miss Stein / 27, rue de Fleurus / Paris VI"

Monday [17 Oct. 1927]

Dear G—

Bébé is demanding to see you. I have told him we would both call on you on Tuesday afternoon. If this doesnt suit you, please let me know.

Love, Virgil

Too cold to work. I chase flats. Nothing yet. Enrhumé. Sore throat. Rotten disposition. No heat till Nov.

---

demanding: Punning on French *demandant*, "asking".
Enrhumé: I have a cold.

*****

To "M. Virgil Thomson / Hotel Jacob / 44 rue Jacob / Paris."

27 RUE DE FLEURUS
[17 Oct. 1927]

My dear Virgil,

So sorry but to-morrow is not possible, and I would like to see Bebé and you but this week is more than full, something pleasant may be happening for me but more of that when we meet which will be next week, bring Bebe and yourself then,

Alwys
Gtrde.

*****

To "M. Virgil Thomson / Hotel Jacob / rue Jacob / Paris."

    ROSE IS A ROSE IS A ROSE IS A ROSE [circular]
    27 RUE DE FLEURUS

[26 Oct. 1927]

My dear Virgil.

Thanks for the very beautiful flowers, we may look upon them both as a pleasure and a necessity.

Alwys
Gtrde.

---

flowers: Thomson sent yellow roses as an apology for misbehaving in her home the previous week. In front of the aristocratic émigré Russian painter Pavel Tchelitchev and his demure sister, he had mentioned a young woman singer having asked him to coach her. Her regular accompanist is part of the household of Tchelitchev, who suddenly regarded him as stealing a paying client. When Stein asked how Thomson had met her, he said, "Through her having slept with one of my friends." Toklas then remarked, "One doesn't say that." In a huff, Tchelitchev left with his sister. Stein then admonished Thomson for quarrelling with him in her house (*Virgil Thomson* 183).

*****

17 Quai Voltaire
Sunday [Nov. 1927]

Dear Alice

I cant thank you enough for this heavenly flat. I am very happy here. If you and Gertrude want to honour me with a visit, you have only to name the day and hour.

Love always
Virgil

---

heavenly flat: Thomson has taken possession of the furnished studio apartment Alice wrote him about in October. The apartment is five flights up, at the top of 17 Quai Voltaire in a row of eighteenth-century houses across the Seine from the Louvre. Next door is a hotel where, he likes to recall, Wagner, Baudelaire, and Wilde stayed. The day after moving in, he began composing the music for Act One of the opera on a rental piano. He remembers the process:

> With the text on my piano's music rack, I would sing and play, improvising melody to fit the words and harmony for underpinning them with shape. I did this every day, wrote down nothing. When the first act would improvise itself every day in the same way, I knew it was set. That took all of November. Then I wrote it out from memory, which took ten days. By mid-December I had a score consisting of the vocal lines and a figured bass, a score from which I could perform. (*Virgil Thomson* 104)

*****

To "M. Virgil Thomson / 17 Quai Voltaire / Paris."

ROSE IS A ROSE IS A ROSE IS A ROSE [circular]
27 RUE DE FLEURUS

[11? Nov. 1927]

My dear Virgil,

    Yes with pleasure,
        Alwys
            Gtrde.

*****

To "M. Virgil Thomson / 17 Quai Voltaire / Paris."

    ROSE IS A ROSE IS A ROSE IS A ROSE [circular]
    27 RUE DE FLEURUS

[*21* Nov. *1927*]

My dear Virgil

Janet Scudder and Countess Pecorini want to hear the opera. They go back to New York the beginning of the month and they have connections that may make the proper connections, anyway if it suits you they will come to the studio Friday at 4.30, we will be along too more or less, Let us know if that is alright. René [Crevel] writes me that Lasalle [sic] is a noble character which means I suppose that others aren't. Anyway

        Alwys
          Gtrde.

[**21 Nov. 1927**]: The dating of this and the following three letters is in dispute, with Ulla Dydo (with whom we communicated on this matter) placing the second and third in October 1928 owing to Stein's statement: "sometime there is going to be a very interesting portrait of you. it gestates" ([*22 Nov. 1927*]). Dydo has established late 1928 as the period of composition for "Virgil Thomson;" see Stein, [14 Jan. 1929]. We have decided to place the exchange in 1927, principally because: a) Letter #4, a one-piece pneumatique, bears a fairly clear 23 Nov. 1927 postmark; b) Thomson has written "Monday" on letter #2, which would indicate Nov. 21st or 28th in 1927, Nov. 26th in 1928—the postmark date on letter #1, which he refers to as "your letter of this date," is either the 21st or 24th; c) in 1928 he writes from the Ile-de-France on 2 December but there is no indication here that a trip is imminent, particularly as he is enthusiastic about a proposed concert for January, when he will still be in America; d) interest in Mrs. Chadbourne's response makes more sense in 1927, her patronage to be terminated in June of 1928; e) it would be odd for Thomson to speak of Cliquet-Pleyel in an introductory manner in 1928 and for Stein to speak then as though having been recently introduced to Bernard Faÿ. These four letters must appear as a group owing to clear interconnecting conversational threads. Stein may already be contemplating Thomson's portrait of 1928 but she is more likely planning a piece she will complete within a few months of this letter and entitle "To Virgil and Eugene." It will be published posthumously in *Painted Lace and Other Pieces* (1955), listed in the table of contents under the heading "Portraits and Figures," a heading that will be decided by Toklas. The portrait (or double portrait) refers to Thomson's birth in Missouri and quotes from *Four Saints* the words: "One two three four five six seven all good children go to heaven some are good and some are bad one two three four five six seven" (*Four Saints* 24). Here is the piece in its entirety:

    Show me I am from Missouri. How do they count out loud one two three four five six seven all good children go to heaven. Show me I am from Missouri one two three four five six seven all good children go to heaven. How do they do I do I count out loud one two three four five six seven all good children go to heaven some are good and some are bad one two three four five six seven all good children go to heaven. Certainly does kill at noon certainly does double soon a pretty name and named as so to suffer how can have it be my my might life. A cherry not a cherry a strawberry. (310–11)

Janet Scudder and Countess Pecorini: Scudder is a fifty-eight-year-old sculptor, originally from Terre Haute, Indiana, whom Stein thought "solemn" and having "all the subtlety of the doughboy and all his nice ways and all his lonesomeness" as well as "a pioneer's passion for buying useless real estate" (*Autobiography* 224–25). Margherita Pecorini is her companion and a sometime fortune teller.

*****

Monday [*21 Nov. 1927*]

Dear Gertrude

Bernard Faÿ has asked me to go with him on Friday to call on you. He is writing you to that effect. I will write him of the other emergency and ask him to come here. He is interested in the opera anyway. You and Alice and Miss Scudder and the countess are therefore expected chez moi as per your letter of this date unless you advise me elsewise. My pleasure needs no inscription.

Paragraph 2. French composer, one Henri Cliquet-Pleyel, having heard today our Capitals, is enthusiastic. Wants to give in early January a joint concert of his & my works. Also some readings for variety and fun are suggested. Would you read for ten minutes from your works? Or better still write a short perhaps *conférence sur la musique* or a ditty about *Me and Music* or about *Me and Virgil* or a soi-disant anything you like and why not? And isnt it a pleasant idea and it would be given in the salle de la Mairie du IXeme in the rue Drouot and I hope you will be inspired to collaborate and your collaboration would make it awful impressive and we would all profit and Mrs. Chadbourne would certainly be pleased and godknows maybe there and love,

Virgil

Bernard Faÿ: Ultra-Catholic royalist, "wildly reactionary" but "a most amiable man" (to Dilworth, 3 Feb. 1981), from an extremely conservative Catholic family of bankers and lawyers, professor in the University of Clermont-Ferrand, writer of books on eighteenth-century Franco-American history, a friend of Thomson since 1921 (see introduction) and soon of Stein. She first met him through René Crevel but found they "had nothing in particular to say to each other" (256). She is now remeeting him through Thomson and will write that Faÿ's is "one of the four permanent friendships of Gertrude Stein's life" (*Autobiography* 268).
Cliquet-Pleyel: See note to Thomson, 2 September [1928].
conférence sur la musique: talk on the music.
soi-disant: so-called.

*****

To "M. Virgil Thomson / 17 Quai Voltaire / Paris"

27 RUE DE FLEURUS
[*22 Nov. 1927*]

My dear Virgil,

Its alright be glad to see Bernard Fay I liked him. I also like Henri Cliquet Pleyel and the mairie of the IX arrondissement and the Hotel that is the rue Drouot is such familiar ground. As for me you scarce xpect one of my age to appear upon a mairie stage. No but sometime there is going to be a very interesting portrait of you. it gestates. Anyway Friday

Alwys
Gtrde.

---

mairie: town-hall

*****

To "Miss Stein / 27, rue de Fleurus / Paris VI"

[23 Nov. 1927]

Dear Gertrude

I am asking also for Friday a Mrs. Stoddard of Boston who was once a dispenser of largesse in my education. She has turned up suddenly after some years, eager to hear her protégé's progress. So I take this opportunity of letting her in on a hallelujah-party and she is sure to report swell in Boston and she is influential and she is also a perfectly nice person whom you will maybe like. No frills or pretense. Of course you are right about the mairie. I cant expect "one of your age" to show herself on any stage this side of New York, where you're very certain to have to bow after the curtain.

Love
Virgil

*****

17 Quai Voltaire
Tuesday 6 December [1927]

Dear Gertrude

Malheur malheur! I've made another gaff. Somewhere between your house and mine the Coates book disappeared. I've got you another one but it isnt signed. I hope you will spank me hard on Friday.

love repentant
Virgil

---

malheur: misfortune.
Coates book: *Eater of Darkness* (Paris: Contact Editions, 1926), an experimental first novel by Robert Myron Coates, a New Haven-born expatriate living in Paris, since soon

after the war a friend of Stein, to whom he gave a copy. She thought him "the one young man who had an individual rhythm, his words made a sound to the eyes" as "most people's words do not" (*Autobiography* 214). Toklas writes, "Gertrude became quite attached to Robert Coates. He had a pretty, velvety voice and gentle ways" (*What is Remembered* 111).

*****

To "M. Virgil Thomson / 17 Quai Voltaire / Paris."

ROSE IS A ROSE IS A ROSE IS A ROSE [circular]
27 RUE DE FLEURUS

[8 Dec. 1927]

My dear Virgil,

Please make a serious effort and get back Coates book, I do not like his gift to me to be permanently lost here, I may count upon you for that, we will be very pleased to come Friday but may be a little late as we have an earlier engagement, have rather an amusing book to show you of Burton Rascoe,   Awy

     Gtrde Stein

---

a serious effort: Thomson advertises for the lost, signed copy in the Paris *Herald Tribune*, but does not recover it (Toklas, *What is Remembered* 111).
amusing book: Burton Rascoe edited *Morrow's Almanack* for 1928, which includes a portrait of Carl Van Vechten by Stein.

*****

17 Quai Voltaire
Sunday [Dec. 1927]

Dear Gertrude

It seems Peter Smith would like very much to see the houses of Cook, Lipschitz, et al. So could we have cards? If you would like to see mine, I have just written Alice to say that it is entirely at your disposition. Thanks for ever for finding it. It is too lovely.

     Love
     Virgil

Peter Smith . . . Cook, Lipschitz: Smith, an architect-friend of Thomson's Harvard friend Henry-Russell Hitchcock; Jacques Lipschitz and William Cook are friends of Stein: Cook, an expatriate American, former taxi-driver who taught her how to drive; Lipschitz, a Russian sculptor who did a bust of Stein, who did a verbal portrait of him.

*****

[*Possible placement*]

To "M. Virgil Thomson / 17 Quai Voltaire / Paris."

ROSE IS A ROSE IS A ROSE IS A ROSE [circular]
27 RUE DE FLEURUS

My dear Virgil,

Have just written to William Cook 6, rue Denfert-Rochereau Boulogne sur Seine. I always believe in you but when I hear other music I believe in you a lot,

Alwys
Gtrde.

*****

To "M. Virgil Thomson / Grand Hotel Kurhaus / Engelberg / Suisse."

27 RUE DE FLEURUS
[1 Jan. 1928]

My dear Virgil

It does not sound a bad place to be sick again and even to go on being sick again but now that has been done, be all well again and try that, its nice too anyway happy new year any new year is happy though as well as that, there is no news, we are giving a party next Wednesday, Bernard Fay wants to come on Saturday but he wants to come with you and there is no you so we will wait not for the party but for Bernard Fay, it was a nice party I mean yours, and best of good luck to you alwys

Gtrde.

---

sick: See following letter.
nice party: On Christmas night, Thomson held a party for twelve at which he performed Act One of the opera. He writes, "Gertrude Stein was pleased . . . and Alice too. Everybody, in fact, seemed buoyed up by the opera's vivacity. Tristan Tzara told Hugnet he had been deeply impressed by a music at once so 'physical' and so gay. I had wondered whether a piece so drenched in Anglican chant (running from Gilbert and Sullivan to Morning Prayer and back) could rise and sail. But no one else seemed bothered by its origins. On the contrary, they had all undergone a musical and poetic experience so unfamiliar that only their faith in me (for they were chosen friends) had allowed them to be carried along, which indeed they had been, as on a magic carpet" (*Virgil Thomson* 104–105).

*****

Grand Hotel
Engelberg
1 January [1928]

Dear Gertrude

Busy day today. I got up and dressed. Fever suddenly disappeared under quinine. Went in 24 hours from 104 to 94 and up to proper and stopped. Throat improves apparently and I am officially convalescent though not allowed to go out doors. That should come shortly. Anyway I shaved and put on my clothes and went down stairs and sat in the lobby for an hour while my ankles got cold and had my first meal in the dining room in solitary state and tried to smoke a cigarette but couldnt taste it and came back to my room and went to bed as per instructions and read a whole novel by Edith Wharton all about love and Modern Life and Society and everything during which I ate a respectable tea and dinner and tried to smoke two more cigarettes but couldnt taste them either so you see it was a busy day. Edith's novel was a scream. 364 pages including 1 1/2 bright remarks and a galaxy of prize examples to illustrate bad grammar bad language bad thinking bad noise and openly bad construction. Chief character surprised and horrified twice within one week's time and fifty pages apart at learning the same piece of news. The hero is supposed to have serious literary talent but is named Nick Lansing. He never decides whether to be an archeologist or to write novels about archeology although he is sure his books will never sell. However at the end he sells an article for $200 and gets an order for more and he decides to finish a novel called The Pageant of Alexander which may sell after all. He is full of high moral scruples and offended at the more worldly ways of heroines. Eventually they both decide that if one has a great love in one's life and the possibility of a swell writing career, one can forgo the Ritz, at least for a few years. Heroine is then safely allowed to return an ill-gotten sapphire bracelet. Excuse my writing you at such length about the Wharton or anything else, but it really amused me and besides I havent anybody to talk to and I fancy you wont mind because you do a good [deal] of reading anyway. The plot is modern classic. Difficulty not of getting the opponent to begin sexual relations but to continue them. Poor but experienced society girl named Susy Branch. Ought to marry a man with a dot. But has acquired the habits of the pampered rich and must have an artist. Meets poor but well bred writer. They kiss. He offers to give himself. But she says "no you will always regret it. I will marry you." So he puts all his little income in her name and she manages to get contributions from rich friends enough for simple necessities of a honeymoon villa at Como and a "bel étage" in Venice. Naturally she doesnt bother him about business details and all is sweet and lovey-dovey and one day their joy is complete when he whispers that he thinks he is going to have a novel. So they go on to Venice and he spends his mornings quietly working and she sees that he keeps up his health and good spirits. But one day he learns that her business methods are not what he thinks honorable. A very fine point here, but he is a very tender plant from any moral point of view. So he just runs away and disappears. Gets a job as companion to other rich friends on a yacht. She is sorry. Tries to forget at various Ritzes. Nearly marries an English lord. Announces engagement and prospective divorce. Then hubby who has nobly refused his employer's rich daughter and seriously pursued archeology (plus a bit of Roman society-life) hubby returns to arrange her divorce. He doesnt cry or anything but she sees how sorry he is and after all she hasnt been really happy herself and so she suddenly cries out "Why this must be love!" And indeed it is no other. And so there is a genteel finale and the check arrives and they both forgo chinchilla and pearls for love and a career while she returns the sapphire-bracelet and promises to earn their living honestly with a new sense of her sacred responsibility. There are three side-shows of sad noble and hard-working husbands who suffer silent while wives philander or divorce or import Italian princes. Alice is right. If hero and heroine had divorced, she would have been forced to offer him alimony. He of course would have been too high-principled to accept.

    Good night.

            Love

             Virgil

---

a whole novel by Edith Wharton: *The Glimpse of the Moon* (1922).
a dot: A fortune, originally capital or property brought into a marriage (not, as suggested here by the groom but) by the bride, the annual income or interest from which was under the husband's control.
bel étage: large flat.

      *****

To "M. Virgil Thomson / [Engelberg] / Suisse 17 Quai Voltaire / Paris."

         27 RUE DE FLEURUS
         [13 Jan. 1928]

My dear Virgil,

  I am glad Angina has flapped her wings and flown away and now you can enjoy the nice spring weather. It is nice. We liked all about Edith, She is like that, Saw Tzara yesterday he has plans of having you printed in Germany, he thinks he may be able to, but just at present he is going away for a couple of weeks, when he gets back I imagine he may be going to commence to try it, he thinks it can be done and that would be nice. Otherwise no news, we have lots of flowers and the sun is shining nicely my long winded effort is progressing, sometime a short long winded something might be nice, Lafayette here we are, and I guess that's all

            Alwys
             Gtrde.

Tzara: Tristan Tzara, Romanian-born French poet, a founder of Dadaism, now thirty-one years old and a Surrealist, the one Thomson likes best, with whom he socializes, as his presence at Thomson's Christmas party suggests (see note to Stein, [1 Jan. 1928]). Thomson thinks him "chummy and witty and pleasant" (to Dilworth, 3 Feb. 1981).
plans of having you printed in Germany: Tzara may have been arranging for publication, possibly through his and Thomson's mutual friend the composer Max Deutsch, but there is no record of a publication by Thomson in Germany in 1928–1929.
my long winded effort: She is in the middle of several months' work on "Finally George A Vocabulary of Thinking," published in *How to Write* (Paris: Plain Edition, 1931).
Lafayette here we are: Stein's twist on a famous phrase from WWI, "Lafayette, we are here!" uttered in July 1917 by Army Colonel Charles E. Stanton on behalf of Gen. John

Joseph Pershing, commander of the American Expeditionary Force. The officers were paying homage at the tomb of the Marquis de Lafayette, who served the patriot cause during the American Revolution as France's liaison to George Washington.

*****

To "M. Virgil Thomson / 17 Quai Voltaire / Paris."

27 RUE DE FLEURUS
[17 Jan. 1928]

My dear Virgil

    Just communicated with Jo who got back to-day and leaves for New York a week from to-day. He will see when he can come to hear you (it) and will let you know by petit bleu, I told him you were keeping your time free till you heard. He said he would let you know to-day or to-morrow. I hope everything is the right degree of peacefulness etc,   Alwys
Gtrde.

*****

To "M. Virgil Thomson / 17 Quai Voltaire / Paris."

[25 Jan. 1928]

[Enclosure: Typed letter to Stein from Jo Davidson dated 24 January 1928 indicating that when he is in New York he will try to interest Otto Kahn, director of the Metropolitan Opera, in her opera, even though he himself has not heard it. What little he has heard of Thomson's music convinces him that it is bound to be a great success. On the bottom of Davidson's letter, Stein writes:]
Here is Jo's letter and it sounds as if he will do all he can, the chills did not do anything further did they, you are alright   Gtrde.

*****

To "Miss Stein / 27, rue de Fleurus / Paris VI"

[26 Jan. 1928]

Dear Gertrude

    Thanks Joe's letter. Madame Langlois & I think of coming in on Wednesday evening. Act II operates. If you dont want us for Wed. or prefer afternoon, say same in writing. Brisk walk chased off chills.

Love
Virgil

*****

To "Miss Stein / 27, rue de Fleurus / Paris VI"

>17 Quai Voltaire
>Tuesday [31 Jan. 1928]

Dear G—

Miss Todd not back from London. Mrs. Garland accepts. Will come with Madame Langlois & me.
I grateful about Richard Strauss and Germans in general.

>Love
>Virgil

———

Miss Todd: Dorothy Todd, editor of British *Vogue*.
Mrs. Garland: Madge Garland, fashion editor of *Vogue* under Todd.
grateful about Strauss and Germans in general: On 30 Jan., Stein sent Thomson a clipping from the Paris *Herald Tribune* of 29 Jan.:
> NEW STRAUSS WORK TO BE GIVEN FIRST BY DRESDEN OPERA
> "Egyptian Helen" Will Be Sung Later in Vienna With Jeritza DRESDEN.—The Dresden opera has come off victorious in a strenuous competition. Some time ago it was verbally arranged, as announced in THE HERALD, that the original production of Richard Strauss' new opera, "Aegyptische Helena" (the Egyptian Helen) would take place in Dresden. Afterward there arose what one critic has amusingly called a veritable Trojan war over the possession of this fair Helen, as Vienna was anxious to give the original production. Moreover, the role was written by Strauss for Vienna's famous soprano, Jeritza . . . its influence especially on the younger ones has been very marked. In Germany, I am told, they are now writing "jazz operas" and naming them as such.

(At the top of the clipping Toklas writes "Cheerio." Stein writes "American" over the word "Egyptian" in the subheadline.) Thomson's interest is sharpened by antipathy. Using various metaphors, he objects all his adult life to the stranglehold on the American concert-music scene by "central Europe's immortality machine" with Strauss and others as "tails to the kite" of Beethoven. The conservative backwardness of the Germans and their devotees leave innovation open for the French, the Americans, and Thomson, for whom Paris is a place to keep contact with European music while avoiding German decadence (*Virgil Thomson* 118).

*****

To "M Virgil Thomson / 17 Quai Voltaire / Paris"

>ROSE IS A ROSE IS A ROSE IS A ROSE [circular]
>27 RUE DE FLEURUS
>
>[6 March 1928]

My dear Virgil,

I could not in any case come to-morrow as my friend Mrs Knoblauch is in Paris just for the day and as I have not seen her for years it would not be possible not to be with her. I am sorry about the Hugnet matter it should have been left as I suggested to Bravig Imbs and then it would have been alright, Good luck,

>Gtrde.

Mrs Knoblauch: Mary (May), formerly Bookstaver, acts as Stein's unofficial literary agent in America. Stein's vexed early love affair with her is recounted in Stein's novel *Q.E.D.*

Hugnet: George, twenty-one-year-old French poet publishing his own work, whom Thomson met in 1926 and took to Stein in early 1927. He is now a favorite of hers. Thomson describes Hugnet as "small, truculent, and sentimental, a type at once tough and tender .... Self-indulgent early about food and drink ... his conversation ... outrageous and, if you like outrage, hilarious. Rarely have I heard matched the gutter-snipe wit with which he can lay out an enemy. His poetry is liltingly lyrical, pleasingly farfetched as to image, and sweet on the tongue" (*Virgil Thomson* 94).

Bravig Imbs: Twenty-three-year-old expatriate American poet, novelist, living in Paris. Stein later writes that he was one of the "young men who came to the house at the time when they came in such numbers. We liked Bravig, even though ... his aim was to please" (*Autobiography* 257). He introduced Elliot Paul to Stein and is helping Paul and Eugene and Maria Jolas edit early numbers of *transition*.

*****

To "Miss Stein / 27, rue de Fleurus / Paris VI"

[9 March 1928]

Dear Gertrude

Hugnet came and I too to bring his poetry and our homage. But you were out drinking tea. We will try again on Saturday.
Act II is on paper in a book to itself and looks very well indeed.

Love
Virgil

---

our homage: Hugnet and Thomson collaborated on a tribute to Stein, entitled "Le Berceau de Gertrude Stein ou le mystère de la rue de Fleurus / huit poêmes de Georges Hugnet mis en musique par Virgil Thomson sous le titre de Lady Godiva's Waltzes" (The Cradle of Gertrude Stein or the Mystery of the rue de Fleurus / Eight Poems of Georges Hugnet Set to Music by Virgil Thomson under the Title of Lady Godiva's Waltzes). The musical setting is marked by "the cough and tripping rhythms" of Stein's Ford car (*Virgil Thomson* 111), which she calls "Godiva".

*****

To "M. Virgil Thomson / 17 Quai Voltaire / Paris"

27 RUE DE FLEURUS
[9 March 1928]

My dear Virgil,

Yes we were drinking tea and we were sorry about the homages and to-morrow Saturday we are having a dinner party so will they the homages come Wednesday tea, that would be nice. A whole book of second act sounds very satisfactory and so do we all

Alwys
Gtrde.

Letters with Notes

*****

To "M. Virgil Thomson / 17 Quai Voltaire / Paris."

27 RUE DE FLEURUS
[13 March 1928]

My dear Virgil,

Instead of the afternoon we will come to you Friday evening half past eight, then we will hear the second act and that will be very nice,

Alwys
Gtrde.

*****

To "Miss Stein / 27 rue de Fleurus / Paris VI"

Monday [26 March 1928]

Dear Gertrude

Yvonne [Davidson] & ladies are coming tomorrow at 1 ocl to Madame Branlière's flat, 26 rue Francois Ier. I should be glad, on principle, to have you there, though I think, as you suggested, it is likely more advantageous for me to handle them alone this time. Alice Branlière will give them tea.

Undying affection
Virgil

Branlière: Alice Woodfin Branlière, wealthy, well-connected expatriate American amateur musician from Vermont. Thomson will make a musical portrait of her in Paris on 24 Oct. 1929.

*****

To "Miss Stein / 27 rue de Fleurus / Paris VI"

[28 *March* 1928]

Dear Gertrude

I dont think the nice sad Jewish lady is spending money on anything so frivolous as us. Still every body was pleased and a good time was enjoyed by most of those present

Love
Virgil

Concert the 8th May.

*****

17 Quai Voltaire
Saturday [*April* 1928]

Dear Alice

    I never had the letter you mentioned. I hope there was nothing important in it. If so, please repeat. But a curious incident has arrived. I receive a program from New York where one of my works is being played and right next to me is a real live Mexican composer named Carlos Chavez. And I thought it was a made up name and maybe it was but whichever way it was terribly nice of him to come to life.

Love
Virgil

Chavez: In *Four Saints*, Sts. Chavez and Settlement are companions to Sts. Teresa and Ignatius. The concert, on 22 April 1928 at the Edyth Totten Theatre, is the first of the Copland-Sessions Concerts, in which Thomson's *Five Phrases from the Song of Solomon* is sung by Radiana Pazmor with Aaron Copland accompanying on tam-tam, cymbals, and woodblock. Twenty-nine-year-old Carlos Chávez is conductor for Mexico's first permanent symphony orchestra, which he organized, and is director of the National Conservatory of Music. He will be preeminent among Mexican composers and one of the most influential Mexican musicians of the century.

*****

[from Toklas] Postcard from Spain, reproduction of a portion of what appears to be an Epiphany scene, showing two of the magi presenting gifts to the infant Jesus in bed with his mother. Addressed incorrectly to "M. Virgil Thomson / 19 Quai Voltaire / En Ville." Postman's note "Parti sans adresse" (i.e. no forwarding address).

[17 April [?] *1928*]

No it was not a letter with any thing important in it but just a pretty note of thanks—Chavez would appear to be a nice plain name—even in Mexico—let us consider its appearance on a programme in N.Y. as a favourable omen—Ever yours

A.B.T.—

*****

17 Quai Voltaire
Mercredi [*April 1928*]

Dear Alice

    For the séance poetique et musicale of Marcel Herrand et Madame Batheri, about which I spoke the other night, the plans are to read from three French poets (Max Jacob, Philip Soupault, and Georges Hugnet) and three Americans (V[achel]. Lindsay, Gertrude, & the third whom I persist in forgetting—It may be Sherwood [Anderson]). Also to sing works of same by Cliquet-Pleyel, Sauguet, Benoist-Mechin, and me. Can you give me copies of the French translation of *Cezanne, Water-pipe, Picasso,* and *Relieve.* I fancy the *Saint* too long to read. Will try to finish *Cocteau* and the second *Picasso.* I apply to you because the existing free copies are chez editors and Madame Langlois's pencil versions would have to be corrected by you anyway. Does the séance amuse Gertrude? And do you mind tapping these out again? Better make carbons this time.

Always devoted
Virgil

Marcel Herrand: Actor, thirty-years old, friend of Thomson's since 1921.
Soupault: Philippe, thirty-year old French poet, former Dadaist, cofounder with André Breton of Surrealism, from which he was expelled for being too literary in 1926, when the movement embraced Communism.

*****

[From Toklas]

ROSE IS A ROSE IS A ROSE IS A ROSE. [circular]   27 RUE DE FLEURUS
                                                  [*April 1928*]

Dear Virgil—

Here are the two french translations Gertrude has—the only two. The others I'll do but only after we're finished correcting proof of the new book—its just come but must be returned as soon as possible—we're fairly expert but it does take time. If it's not too late when I'm free again you may count on me. You don't say where the lady singer and gentleman reader are to sing and read our friend's literatures—
This large paper is intended for more than two lines of explanation and a warm remembrance but its envelope is all I have large enough for the already too-frequently folded enclosures—

Yours Ever
Alice

---

the new book: *Useful Knowledge* (New York: Payson and Clarke, 1928). Proofs were sent to Stein on 12 April 1928.

*****

To "Miss Stein / 27, rue de Fleurus / Paris VI"

17 Quai Voltaire
Saturday [26 May 1928]

Letters with Notes

Dear Gertrude

I am having an espèce de répétition générale chez moi on Tuesday evening at 8 ½. This is especially for the Capitals. To give them courage and to pull the piece together by means of an audience. It would be very good of you and Alice to come if you could possibly arrange it.

Love Virgil

As you see from the new programs, I've changed my lady-singer. The first one resigned, as I expected. The second is excellent. All does well, though *Capitals* still shaky.

---

espèce de répétition générale chez moi: a sort of dress rehearsal at my place. This is for his upcoming concert of 30 May. See note to Stein [29 May 1928].
changed my lady-singer: The first singer, Alice Mock, refused to be associated with the Stein texts she was to sing and quit after Thomson refused to drop them from the program. Unable to find an English-speaking singer of Mock's quality, he engaged Marthe-Marthine, "a singer of remarkable musicianship" and coached her to sing the Song of Solomon phonetically. He did decide, finally, to drop the Stein texts rather than expose Marthe "to the comedy risks of pronouncing Stein with a foreign accent" and instead gave her "a batch of songs to sing in French" (*Virgil Thomson* 109, 115).

*****

To "M. Virgil Thomson / 17 Quai Voltaire / Paris."

27 RUE DE FLEURUS
[27 May 1928]

My dear Virgil,

I am awfully sorry that we cannot come but we have not a moment free this week, if they cannot manage the Capitals you might change to the two songs, I would not like the Capitals poorly sung. I had a very nice letter of acceptance from [Holman-Black?], the Picassos cannot come their nurse is away on her vacation and since Paulo's accident they are nervous about leaving him with anyone else, Best of luck to you

Alwys
Gtrde.

The Picassos: Picasso's wife is Olga Khoklova, a former ballerina with Diaghilev's troop.
Paulo's accident: Picasso's seven-year-old son injured his finger.

*****

To "Miss Stein / 27, rue de Fleurus / Paris VI"

[28 May 1928]

Dear Gertrude

The Capitals are doing quite well, thank you. Dont be unquiet. I am sorry, all the same, that you cant arrange Tuesday.

Love
Virgil

There will be a large and brilliant audience on Wednesday, if acceptances mean anything

*****

To "M. Virgil Thomson / 17 Quai Voltaire / Paris"

27 RUE DE FLEURUS
[29 May 1928]

My dear Virgil,

Glad everything is going so nicely and do keep one of the big affiches for me for a souvenir, I have just taken Alice up to see one. So sorry we cannot come to-night but to-morrow good luck to us all. Have some interesting things to tell you about your music that will please you, but more of that anon in calm,   Alwys

Gtrde.

---

affiches: posters.

to-morrow: On Wednesday 30 May 1928 in the Salle d'Orgue of the Old Conservatory at 47 rue Blanche near the Folies-Bergére, a concert will take place of Thomson's *Variations et Fugues, Five Phrases from the Song of Solomon, Sonata d'Eglise (Sonata da Chiesa), Capital Capitals*, under the direction of Victor Prahl, and *Airs divers*, including *Valse Grégorienne*. The "brilliant audience" promised by Thomson in his letter of 28 May will include Gertrude Stein, Jean Cocteau, Marcel Jouhandeau, Charles-Albert Cingria, Roy Harris, Nadia Boulanger, and Jennie Tourel. It is a one-man show of what Thomson, Henri Sauguet, and the Neo-Romantic group believe to be the newest music. Reaction in the press will be divided and will convince Thomson that the French musical establishment—as typified by Milhaud, Honegger, Auric, and Poulenc, and represented by Cocteau—have decided against approving of his music (*Virgil Thomson* 120). He later remembers:

> Nobody said so in my presence; but I could feel it, smell it, know it for true that my music, my career, my position in the whole time-and-place setup was something the French power group did not choose to handle. I was not being suppressed . . . but certainly I was not being adopted. Nor were any of the power-circle benefits—such as a commission from the Princesse de Polignac or from Serge de Diaghilev—to be coming my way. I was clearly not grist either for the French immortality-mill or for international snob-bohemia.

The coolness of the French response would be, he later decides, "in the long run for me beneficial. It kept me an American composer." In the ensuing weeks, while enduring a flu, he will consider "the creation of an American music . . . to be a far worthier aspiration than any effort to construct a wing, a portico, even a single brick that might be fitted on to Europe's historic edifice" (*Virgil Thomson* 116-7).

*****

Postcard of "Biscuiterie de la Mere Prusse—Amezieu, pres d'Artemare (Ain)" to "M. Virgil Thomson / 17 Quai Voltaire / Paris."

[13 June 1928]

Here we are all peaceful and very pleased to be so, and you. Also have commenced something, it is nice being here, it took us six days and we ate on the way, and how are the echoes, and all,

Alwys
Gtrde.

---

commenced something: Perhaps "Arthur a Grammar," composed over the next few months, published in *How to Write* (Paris: Plain Edition, 1931). See note to Stein, [21 Aug. 1928].

*****

17 Quai Voltaire
Sunday 17 juin [1928]

Dear Gertrude

I am glad to know you had a nice trip and that you ate on the way. I remain in ville because health goes bad and music good. One week of bed and bronchitis and three days of sun-stroke plus blister have advanced Act III to what is practically the end. The enclosed is my entire press up to yet. Please return it. I wrote Mrs. Chadbourne but have no answer. I got up from bed to go to the Scudder's house and Bradley didn't come. There are no echoes. General opinion seems to be great success and let it go at that. And, I suspect, takes the music to be as highly special as the audience was. Nabachoffs *Ode* seems to have been a mess from every point of view. Latest low-down from America mentions a meeting between Lindbergh and Mr Tunney. Since Liberté and the book, Georges Hugnet is quite insupportable. My own disposition is exactly ditto (due let us hope more to illness and creative activity than to any public glory, though the ways of God *are* mysterious). The weather is bitter cold. And the Deux Magots is full of my American rivals. I have a new picture by Bébé and that is something. And Act III of course is very grand (got the tenor up to high C). But on the whole life is very sad and my neck is stiff. Belgium is favorable.

Love
Virgil

---

in ville: in town.
wrote Mrs. Chadbourne: Possibly noticing her absence at his concert on 30 May—she later apologizes for missing it—on 4 June he wrote to her but she had left for the U.S. before receiving his letter.
Scudder: Janet Scudder. See note to Stein, [*21* Nov. *1927*].
Bradley: William Aspenwall Bradley, an American social acquaintance, fifty years old, a distinguished translator and well-known literary agent for American and English

expatriates in Paris. On 13 May 1934, he writes to Stein, "Don't forget that you first sent for me five years ago because you had reasons for wanting to make *money* out of your writings."

Nabachoff . . . mess: Nicholas Nabokov, Russian émigré composer. His ballet-oratorio *Ode*, composed for Serge Diaghilev's Ballet Russes, is receiving mixed reviews.

Lindberg and Mr Tunney: Charles Lindberg, the first to fly across the Atlantic, landing in Paris's Le Bourget Airport on 21 May 1927; Gene Tunney, the world heavyweight boxing champion. The *New Yorker* (12 May 1928) reports a private meeting between them at the studio of artist Charles Baskerville in Manhattan, during which they discussed the "damned nuisance" of being a hero. They discussed the idea of wearing a disguise in public, the perils of autograph hunters, President Coolidge who "has certainly learned how to shake hands," the ordeal of having to shake hands with lots of admirers at one time, the largeness of Lindburg's hands, the larger size of Jack Dempsey's hands (16–17).

Liberté and the book: Hugnet's story "Le Journal d'Antoinette" will be published in *La Liberté* on 23 June 1928. It has just been awarded the Prix Littéraire de la Liberté for authors younger than twenty-three. "The book" is Hugnet's first, appearing pseudonymously as *40 poésies de Stanislaus Boutemer*, illustrated by Max Jacob, published in November 1928 by Théophile Briant. In this book, one poem "L'ami" is dedicated to Thomson, another, "Les îles fortunes," to Stein. Hugnet gives copies to each of them. In translation, his dedications read: "To Gertrude Stein, whose friendship is for me a refreshing spring, Georges Hugnet, 5 June 1928"; and "Dear Virgil, always love these poems otherwise I will be very unhappy. In thanks for the wonderfully fresh music of the Gregorian Waltz and the 'Cradle of Gertrude Stein.' And always keep your kind and frank friendship for me. Georges, 5 June 1928."

American rivals: One of Thomson's "rivals" at the Two Magots café is Roger Sessions, who has written for *Modern Music* a negative critique of Thomson's *Sonate d'Eglise*, performed at a concert of six composers in May 1926.

*****

To "M. Virgil Thomson / 17 Quai Voltaire / Paris."

[19 June 1928]

HOTEL PERNOLLET
    BELLEY
      (AIN)

My dear Virgil

Thanks for the clippings, they are very good on the whole and the Gaulois is alright it shows interest, is it somebody you know. If not all the better. Sorry you are all so lonesome with each other but that always does happen when the great open spaces call, and they are nice there is no doubt about that, I am trying not to work I have begun a very nice idea but I am waiting. Pavlik wrote me in full about the Ode, he does show awfully well in defeat I must say, Bebé seems to have behaved very well, my love to him and otherwise no news, Alice is practicing snapshots of me for the final number of the Little Review and we sit and we still eat and I guess that's all,

                    Alwys
                    Gtrde.

Pavlik: nickname for Pavel Tchelitchev (see note to Stein, [26 Oct. 1927]). Stein had been interested in his work: "painting colour that was no colour, he was painting blue pictures and he was painting three heads in one" (*Selected Writings* 213). He is one of the group of painters later called Neo-Romantic—the others having been introduced by Thomson to Stein: Kristians Tonny, the brothers Eugène and Léonide Berman, and Christian (Bébé) Bérard. According to Thomson, Tchelitchev falls out of Stein's favour around this time. Still miffed by Thomson's behaviour the previous October, Tchelitchev asks her to choose between him and Thomson. This irritates her, which allows Toklas, who has long been unhappy with a portrait he painted of her, to engineer a permanent break (*Virgil Thomson* 183).

Ode . . . defeat: Tchelitchev designed the sets for Nabokov's *Ode*. Already controversial for its experimental forays into lighting effects, film projection and phosphorescent costumes, the production went awry, according to Tchelitchev, because Diaghilev skimped on rehearsal and "chopped and rearranged everything to suit himself" (Tchelitchev to Stein, June 14 1928).

the Gaulois: There are four brief mentions in French newspapers of Thomson's concert, at which *The Song of Solomon* and the *Sonata d'Eglise* were performed (*Esctrait du Gutransigeun*, 10 Juin; *La Liberté*, 8 Juin; *Excelsior*, 7 Juin; and *Le Gaulois*, 3 Juin). In *Le Gaulois*, Pierre Leroi writes, in English translation:

> Mr. Virgil Thomson, a young American composer, invited us to listen to some of his compositions; hearing them left us somewhat perplexed. His art of the fugue is at present rather rudimentary; the accompanying pedal work is awkward to the point of making the tonality uncertain. On the other hand, one can hear some delicious contrapuntal details, but in general there is a harshness of tone and especially a lack of sincerity. One senses a strong desire to fabricate rather than any spontaneous inspiration.

final number in the Little Review: A photograph of Stein in her Ford appears in *The Little Review* (May 1929): 73, juxtaposed with her answers to a questionnaire:

> L[ittle].R[eview]. What should you most like to do, to know, to be? (In case you are not satisfied)
> G.S. But I am.
> L.R. Why wouldn't you change places with any other human being?
> G.S. Because I am I.
> L.R. What do you look forward to?
> G.S. More of the same.
> L.R. What do you fear most from the future?
> G.S. Anything.
> L.R. What has been the happiest moment of your life? The unhappiest? (if you dare tell).
> G.S. Birthday.
> L.R. What do you consider your weakest characteristics? Your strongest? What do you like most about yourself? Dislike most?
> G.S. 1 Weakness, 2 Nothing, 3 Everything, 4 Almost anything.
> L.R. What things do you really like? Dislike (Nature, people, ideas, objects, etc. Answer in a phrase or a page, as you will).
> G.S. 1 What I like. 2 Hardly anything.
> L.R. What is your attitude towards art today.
> G.S. I like to look at it.
> L.R. What is your world view? (Are you a reasonable being in a reasonable scheme?)
> G.S. Not very likely or often.
> L.R. Why do you go on living?
> G.S. I am.

*****

[*Possible placement*]   17 Quai Voltaire
                                                        Sunday [1928?]

Dear Gertrude

Madame Langlois in the country sends me this. It may amuse you

Love
Virgil

*****

To "M. Virgil Thomson / 17 Quai Voltaire / Paris."

[24 June 1928]

HOTEL PERNOLLET
    BELLEY
    (AIN)

My dear Virgil,

    I just had a letter from Burton Rascoe, he is going to make the next number of the Calendar even more literary and he has asked me to suggest something from Paris. I sent him your concert programme suggesting that he put in Hugnet's poem and your music to the Duchess of Rohan's Seine. I don't at all know whether this would interest you but if it should I imagine that with a little account by you of the Duchess might interest him. Anyway there you are. His address is Burton Rascoe, care of William Morrow and Co. 386 Fourth Avenue. Otherwise no news, its hot and we are still peaceable and taking care of ourselves. Henry McBride is in town and Jo Davidson is in town, have you seen them, strawberries are plentiful and very large and very agreeable, and otherwise the country is very lovely, Love to all from all,

Alwys
Gtrde.

---

letter . . . Paris: Rascoe is gathering work for the 1929 *Morrow's Almanac*. In a letter of 23 May 1928, he writes to Stein, "Not only do I want another contribution from you, but I should also like you to use your influence to get a few contributions from some of your friends in Paris, either drawings or writings." He does, as she suggested, "put in Hugnet's poem," "Le Berceau de Gertrude Stein" (206–208).

Rascoe defends Stein's work in "The Case of Gertrude Stein," *A Bookman's Daybook* (New York: Horace Liveright, 1929):

> Miss Stein has written reams of stories, so many that they line her walls in neatly arranged, ticketed typescript. She has the means wherewith to publish these experiments in expression, but she chooses not to do so . . . knowledge has come to her that her experiments are of use rather to writers than to the general public, that in dissociating words and making new patterns of verbal suggestion and imagery she cannot hope to evoke more than ridicule from the public and from the critics who are hostile to new forms. And so she continues in her earnest, honest and visionary way to labour in secret. . . .
> (42–43)

the Duchess de Rohan: "a naïve writer often unconsciously comical whom certain French compared to the naïve painter, Henri (le Douanier) Rousseau" (*Virgil Thomson* 115). "La Seine" is among three of her poems Thomson set to music.

Henry McBride: art critic for *The Dial* and *The New York Sun*, introduced to Stein by Mildred Aldrich. Toklas will remember, "Henry McBride was one of the first of the New York newspapermen, he was really an art critic, who put Gertrude's name prominently forward in connection with pictures and her work. Laugh if you like, he said to her detractors, but laugh with her and not at her" (*What is Remembered* 62).

*****

17 Quai Voltaire
28 June [1928]

Dear Gertrude

I expect to leave Sunday for St Jean de Luz. I shall write a letter soon. This is to show sign of life and to thank for B. Rascoe. I shall write him something, though I dont know just what. It seems scarcely my place to inform him who was the Duchess de Rohan. And what of E. Chadbourne? No answer to my letter nor no check. Disposition improved. Opera slightly lengthened. Invited to give concert at Harvard, expense of Music Department. Havent seen Jo [Davidson] or McBride. Read Bravig's book and had a swell time.

Love {Love Love Gertrude} Love
{Love Love Alice}
Virgil

....

Accounts are not unanimous about the [Nabokov's] *Ode*.
Mostly French disapprove, while admitting qualities, especially dancing.
Americans adored the décor, I find.
Nobody has anything to say for the music.
On the whole not a total loss. Pavlick [Tchelitchev] comes off pretty well. It's the whole show that fails to register.

....

Belgium remains friendly. I lunch today at the Ursels. I shall try to dispel the slight cloud of moral turpitude raised in their minds by our equivocal concert audience.

....

Americans confirm Lindbergh-Tunney gossip. I prefer the mecanicien story myself.

Bravig's book: *The Professor's Wife* (New York: Dial Press, 1928).
the Ursels: The Comte and Comtesse d'Ursel, Belgian friends of Stein and Thomson.
mecanicien: garage mechanic.

*****

17 Quai Voltaire

Thursday [*28 June* 1928]

Dear Gertrude

Alice was right. I have just had this from E. C. I cant think of any answer so I shant send any for the present. Later I may send a polite and gentle thanks for the past assistance. There remains Mrs L[asell]'s 3000 francs a month. In the fall I shall give up my flat and either go to a hotel or find a cheaper one. But for the present, *status quo* and who knows God may provide more luxury to His needy ones.

Love

Virgil

Saw V^{cte} de Noailles at lunch. Many protestations about you and the opera.

---

this from E. C.: a letter from Emily Chadbourne at home in New York State dated 19 June 1928 explaining that she has only just received his letter of 4 June, which followed her to America, and that she is sorry to have missed his concert. She declines further to assist him financially and says that she is chiefly interested in his collaboration with Stein, at whose urging she gave him the thousand dollars in the previous year. After seeing the first production of the opera at Hartford, she will write to Stein "The whole thing seemed to be more like music than music itself" (14 Feb. 1934).
V^{cte} de Noailles: Charles, the Vicomte, a rich patron who finances Hugnet's film *La Perle*.

*****

To "M. Virgil Thomson / 17 Quai Voltaire / Paris."

[30 June 1928]

HOTEL PERNOLLET
    BELLEY
      (AIN)

My dear Virgil,

It does not come at a black moment and I am just reading a nice novel that says it is always darkest before the dawn, so there is cheer. Bravig writes enthusiastically about the goings on of the opera. The weather here is lovely and we are almost having peace on earth with calm. I am sorry to miss Bernard Fay's sister's wedding and the Harvard concert sounds nice. Would you go over for it, that too would be nice,

Alwys

Gtrde.

Letters with Notes

we are almost having peace on earth with calm: Echoing the line in her libretto for the opera, "There can be no peace on earth with calm with calm" (*Four Saints* 21). Other allusions to this line may occur in letters of 29 May and 14 Sept 1928.

*****

    ETCHOLA
    ASCAIN   —   Basses Pyrenées
                                        5 July [1928]

Dear Gertrude

    I saw San Inacio today. By his real name, just like that. In a chapel on a mountain divide called the Col de St. Ignace. And he was handsome and thirty-five, between thirty-five and forty-five and alive and had a black beard and was singing an aria out of the Spiritual Exercises. This was in France, two miles from where I live. Not far over the border he has a monastery which I shall go and see one day. I am 6 km from St. Jean de Luz and I can go on a bicycle to swim and come back here to eat and sleep which both one does very well indeed. St. Jean is too dear and too mondain-restless. Charming town, however. Swell church with wooden balconies very New Orleans (we have same in Ascain) and a nice fishing-port and a fair pastry shop. Hendaye has a nice beach and a swell view of Spain. But it was dear too and nobody there but thousands of children. Here I pay 35 francs a day, wine included, and everything is excellent. Eventually I shall go to Spain, however. I feel that to be inevitable, money or none. Otherwise no news but

                                                love
                                              Virgil

The queer word at the head of this paper is the name of my hotel. But I havent any confidence in such a word. Better write me in Paris.
P.S. I read of Avery Hopwood's death in the newspaper. I'm sorry because he was your friend.

Ascain: On 1 July he went to the Basque village of Ascain and until mid month is composing Acts Three and Four, "not with figured bass, as with Acts One and Two, but as a complete voice-and-piano score" (*Virgil Thomson* 120).
Inacio: Misspelling of the Spanish Ignacio or playful use of Inácio, Portuguese for (in English) Ignatius.
Between thirty-five and forty-five and alive: a quotation from Stein's libretto (*Four Saints* 44).
mondain: society.
Avery Hopwood's death: at forty-six from drowning while swimming drunk on the French Riviera.

*****

Postcard of "Hotel Etchola" with 'x' by Thomson below far right, second story window, no stamp, not addressed.

                                                                [*July* 1928]

I live over the cross. I have another window around the corner. I eat in a garden. And there are magnolia-trees. I sleep after lunch. The weather is hot and bright and the nights are cool. There is soft water to wash in.

Postcard: Thomson stays at the Hotel Etchola for the next month. This postcard enclosed with one of the several letters sent, most likely the first one above, 5 July [1928].

*****

ETCHOLA
ASCAIN   8 juillet [1928]

Dear Gertrude

This from a much-read critic in New York Sun. Sunday meditations anent my trade. Well well.

Love
Virgil

Everyday I walk nearer to Spain. This is an extremely God's-country sort of country. Act III goes on paper

---

This . . . my trade: The meditations are Thomson's and practical rather than aesthetic. On 3 July 1928 under the title "New Native Music," Ward Morehouse writes in the the *New York Sun*, which does not publish on Sundays or holidays, about the Juilliard Foundation initiating annual publication of new US musical compositions, this year's selection (one of twenty-five submitted by American composers) being Arthur Shepherd's suite for orchestra entitled "Horizons." The foundation will also collaborate with the Schubert Centennial Committee for the United States in publishing Louis Gruenberg's "The Enchanted Isle." And, Morehouse writes, American scores are also now being published by the Society for the Publication of American Music and the Eastman Foundation.

*****

To "M. Virgil Thomson / ~~17 Quai Voltaire / Paris~~. Hotel Etchola / à Ascain / Basses / Pyrénées"

[13 July 1928]

HOTEL PERNOLLET
   BELLEY
   (AIN)

My dear Virgil,

I am most awfully pleased that they are beginning to sit up and take notice, Henry McBride also of the Sun & Dial has just been here with us he is much interested in the opera and he seems to think that private people can be found to put it on publicly and when they do they do it well, I don't know, but it would be nice. I am beginning to be very interested in the idea of the Capitals being sung over there. Well anyway. The Lyrical Opera is done was just before I left, but I have not looked at it since. Will pretty soon and see how it is, I think it is not impossible. But have started a new one called, Their Wills a bouquet. It begins with an introduction on the making of a bouquet. In the middle is a entreacte, Simons a bouquet, and it ought to be in six acts, and it is to have a chorus of Baltimoreans, and it has an idea, and I commenced it when I first came down, but as I was kind of tired I quit. Now if the fourteenth is not too hot, will begin again. but golly it is hot. We always thought we would like Jean de Luz, I am not surprised it is nice, we almost had the use of a garden with [immured?] sisters only we haven't but perhaps we will. Anyway Their Wills is strictly laïque.

Gtrde.

Lyrical Opera: *A Lyrical Opera Made By Two To Be Sung*, an intimate chamber opera composed for the occasions of Toklas's birthday (April 30) and the couple's unofficial wedding anniversary, likely May 2 (Dydo 227). Published in *Operas & Plays* (1932).
Their Wills a bouquet: Stein completes the opera libretto *A Bouquet. Their Wills* this summer. It will be published in *Operas & Plays* (1932), never produced.
entreacte [entracte]: interlude. The opera features an "An Interlude / Simons a Bouquet" which is longer than any of the acts.
use of a garden: If the word is "immured", perhaps they have been interested in the use of a garden in a nearby convent. In her absence, the Baroness Lucy Pierlot grants Stein and Toklas the use of her garden at the Château de Béon.
laïque: lay, secular.

*****

ETCHOLA
ASCAIN   19 July [1928]

Dear Gertrude

The opera is finished including the intermezzo and Act IV. That is to say it isnt finished by a long shot but all the composing is done. I am glad to have done the music before seeing Spain. My plan now is to go look and listen to Spain a bit because I've an idea that Spain makes a special kind of noise that will bear imitation orchestrally. Her tunes & her rhythms are too good to be interesting and there isnt anything to be done about them but I think her *timbre* may have possibilities. I shant not [sic] go immediately but maybe next month or so. In the meantime I have some violin pieces to write and that same symphony to finish. I love more and more Pyrenees country. I plan to advance slowly on Spain, a little expedition one day to the monastery of St. Ignatius at Loyola, a little glimpse of beach and finishing at Fontarabie, and then one day when nobody is looking I shall openly take a Spanish train and go somewhere. When your weather gets cooler, why dont you drive over and hear the opera. It's a swell trip. *Their Wills* has a nice sound. We shall certainly do the *Capitals* in NY next winter. I hope you get your garden. Here are some clippings.   And love.

Virgil

glad to have done the music before seeing Spain: Years later he recalls, "I refrained from going there till I had finished my score. I did not wish to encounter 20th-century Spain, so thickly overlaid musically with 19th-century gypsy ways, while trying to evoke an earlier time" (*Reader* 277).
her *timbre*: Writing about the timbre of Spanish noise, he may be thinking partly of "high-squealing" Spanish laughter he heard on the beach at St. Jean-de-Luz (*Virgil Thomson* 121).
that same symphony: *Symphony on a Hymn Tune*.

*****

ETCHOLA
ASCAIN   23 July [1928]

Dear Gertrude

I'm going to Spain tomorrow in a auto led by an American army officer & wife I've picked up. Showed music to a young (and very swell) Russian Jewish pianist (son of Madame Lubochitz, very swell Jewish violinist). You get the school. His reaction was surprising and most pleasant. Fell all over himself about Preciosilla and the Berceau. It was nice, because he didnt know anything in advance about either me or you. Simply cracked the nut and extracted the kernel whole. It made up for some disappointment about the concert.   Love, Virgil
Did a musical portrait (for violin) of a Spanish lady & her mother recognized it.

Berceau: Thomson had composed a score for Georges Hugnet's poem "Le Berceau de Gertrude Stein." See note to Thomson, [9 March 1928].
a musical portrait (for violin) of a Spanish lady & her mother: He remembers:
   A young Spanishwoman who played the violin had asked me to write her something. She had a way of entering the hotel's dining-arbor with assurance, her equally self-assured mother one step behind, that pleased me because this granting of priority to youth, in Europe uniquely Spanish, was also our American way. Otherwise the mother and daughter were not of American pattern; they were almost like sisters, happy together, discussing but not chattering, alert in repose, occupying themselves while waiting for evening, and not surprised that a particular evening should bring no mating male, though when it did they would be ready, for Spain is a timeless image of eternity. All this plus some gesture (Spanish gesture) I endeavoured to depict in music; and although the piece was written to be played without piano, I called it a *Portrait of Señorita Juanita de Medina Accompanied by Her Mother*.
Composed by Thomson in one sitting and taking only two minutes to perform, this is his first musical portrait. He knows that musical portraits have been made by Couperin, Schumann, Anton Rubinstein, and Elgar, but his model is the literary portrait invented by Stein, in which she tries spontaneously and in one sitting to express the "bottom nature" of a person. What makes portrait-composing possible for Thomson is his realization two years before that the logic and syntax of classic composers does not always make perfect sense. "My sudden awareness of their liberties," he later writes, "so firmly forced me to take up my own freedom that never again was I to feel that I must necessarily 'know what I was doing.' This meant that I could write almost automatically, cultivate the discipline of spontaneity, let it flow" (*Virgil Thomson* 123, 124). Passing from Stein to Thomson and later to Florine Stettheimer this notion of the portrait will influence the set design for *Four Saints*, see note to Thomson, 30 May [1933].

*****

Postcard of Stein and Toklas in a street, to "M. Virgil Thomson /~~17 Quai Voltaire / Paris~~ Hotel Etchola / à Ascain / Basses Pyrénées

[23 July 1928]

My dear Virgil,

Sweetly drinking water, do you know anything about who is Regis Michaud Mercure, 15 Juillet, Its nice and cool now, Bravig is with us and liking it, otherwise no news,

Alwys
Gtrde.

Regis Michaud Mercure: Stein has just read an article by Michaud, "La Littérature américaine d'Aujourd'hui. De New York à Montparnasse" *Mercure de France* 205, no 722, 39e Année (15 Juillet 1928), 310–23. Devoting two full pages to Stein (319–20), he writes that postwar European American modernists address the crisis of the present with a new freedom, involving spontaneity and parody, part of the new aesthetic implied by the car, airplane, cinema, radio, telephone—the media that has transformed the world. In poetry, this newness now receives, he says, original inspiration from Gertrude Stein's aesthetic of deliberate simplicity, her verbal and syntactical rhythms, and her Dada-like sacrifice of idea to form, logic to sound, and intention to technique.

*****

Postcard of naval fleet at Santander-La Bahía, to "Miss Alice Toklas / Hotel Pernollet / Belley –Ain / Francia"

Valladolid   27 June [sic, postmarked 28 July 1928]

Dear Alice - I saw a bull fight in Santander and a swell church in Palencia and a grand museum here of poly-chrome wood-carving and marvellous sweets in the shops which I ate. Everything is proper and I think of you and the scenery is grand like Texas.   Love Virgil

*****

ETCHOLA
ASCAIN   31 July [1928]

Dear Gertrude

Regis Michaud is a Frenchman who professes either American Civilization at the Sorbonne or French ditto at the University of California. I think the latter, in fact, I am almost certain. He has been last year in Paris and considerably in the Left Bank Notes. His article is very nice certainly. A few more of those would come in handy. Also thanks for the very sweet photograph. I am just back from Spain. It is certainly all anybody ever said about it and more. I went to San Sebastian and Bilbao and Castro-Urdiales and Santander and Palencia and Valladolid and Burgos and Logroño and

Pamplona. I was terribly impressed and came home with the diarrhoea. I saw a good bull-fight in Santander and the arrival of the N.Y. yacht race and the whole French navy and some of the American and some very hot weather and lots of sad sweet Spaniards but not so many after all because there dont seem to be very many people in Spain but it was all very impressive O very and I shall eventually go again. I leave here in a week or so and go to Brittany where I shall see Madame Langlois and Hugnet and I suppose Max and in September I am supposed to visit Peter Smith in England. Hugnet wrote a swell article about me for the Revue de Belgique. The last part of the symphony is vaguely sketched. The summer has been very nice and seems to be about to continue so. Especially the disposition is much improved. It was low that last month in town.

Best and love
Virgil

Max: Max Jacob, "the literary mentor" of the painters, later called Neo-Romantic, who are Thomson's friends. Jacob is "poet, painter, satirical storyteller, Picasso's friend from early youth, a Jew from Brittany, a penitent, a Catholic, and something of a saint" (*Virgil Thomson* 93), whose poem "Stabat Mater" Thomson will set to music in 1931. One night in 1909, Max Jacob saw Jesus on the walls of his room in Montmartre. He went to the local priest, claimed to have experienced a miracle, and requested baptism. Thomson remembered, "The priest sort of laughed it off and put him off, did nothing about it. But it worried Max because he knew it was for real, and five years later it happened again . . . on the walls of a movie house in Montparnasse. This time he knew what to do. After being turned down by the priest he had investigated such matters. So he went to the Fathers of Zion, who are a religious order with the particular assignment of converting Jews. . . . They gave him all the proper lessons, and he was baptized. At the baptism, his old and close friend Pablo Picasso was his godfather" (to Dilworth, 3 Feb. 1981). Jacob is "mean and generous, envious and kind, malicious and great-hearted," and "most important of all," he can "speak straightforwardly, whether ridiculing bourgeois ways or recounting religious experience." Stein knew him before the war but ceased receiving him, owing to "his uncleanly persona and bohemian ways, which at that time had included sniffing ether" (*Virgil Thomson* 93).
the symphony: *Symphony on a Hymn Tune.*

*****

To "M. Virgil Thomson / ~~17 Quai Voltaire / Paris~~ Hotel Etchola / à Ascain / Bsses Pyrénées"

[3 Aug. 1928]

HOTEL PERNOLLET
    BELLEY
    (AIN)

My dear Virgil,

Spain is always worth diarrhoea, I once had it bad in Seville and had a wonderful trip to Gibraltar afterwards with it, a striking and xciting story, but it is worth it. Nice place and nice people even if there aren't many. Hugnet writes that he did an article on you, do send it to me, he writes darn well that kid the little thing he did in transition was alright, strong intelligent and distinguished, lots of power, Henry McBride was quite impressed and promised to mention him in one of his Dial articles, otherwise as we were work has commenced, George Maratier sent me some charming photos of Tonny and his yacht, also Desbordes sent me his book j'adore, to my surprise it is awfully good I don't quite know why I should have been surprised because Jean Cocteau is not a bad discoverer anyway it is good, please best to Mm Langlois,

Alwys
Gtrde.

---

an article on you: By Hugnet. Thomson will get it published in *Pagany, a Native Quarterly* 1, no. 1 (Winter 1930), 37–38, by sending it to Sherry Mangan who will give it to Richard Johns, editor of *Pagany* (Mangan to Thomson, 15 October 1929). For an English translation of the article, see appendix A.

little thing he did in transition: In *transition* no. 13 (1928), Hugnet contributes to "Inquiry Among European Writers into the Spirit of America" (248–70):

> The American influences on France: the spirit of the films, jazz, advertising, the commercial attitude . . . etc., and also a certain vulgarity which is the French translation of the rudeness of the American soldiers during the war. But these are only absolutely exterior influences. The vertical life of New York does not take in Paris which is a horizontal city: New York is a big city, while Paris is only the biggest provincial town. The celebrated American speed cannot adjust itself to Paris. . . . Literary influences are even more superficial. . . . In 1928 I think there is no influence whatsoever. American literature has so little influence on French that it seems to me to be, in general, even influenced by the French. Moreover no Frenchman knows English. . . . It is quite regrettable that a state of mind and an achievement such as Gertrude Stein's should not be known in France . . . I think that all influences are good and that they are bad. It all depends on what one does with them, I am not really a partisan of influences. (265–66)

Other contributors to this "Inquiry" include Tristan Tzara and Bernard Faÿ. In this number is also published Joyce's "Continuation of a Work in Progress," W. C. Williams's "Improvisations," and Stein's "Descriptions of Literature" and "An instant answer or A hundred prominent men."

George Maratier: French artist, art dealer, works as editor at Hugnet's Editions de la Montagne.

Tonny: Kristians Tonny, twenty-one-year-old Dutch painter, handsome blue-eyed blond. See note to Stein, [19 June 1928].

Desbordes . . . j'adore: *J'adore* (Paris: B. Grasset, 1928) by Jean Desbordes is essentially a book-length love letter to his older lover, Jean Cocteau (Desbordes is twenty-three; Cocteau, forty). Cocteau is publicizing the book and will give Desbordes a role in his 1930 film *La sang d'un poète*. Desbordes will become a leader in the Resistance, will be arrested in 1944 and tortured to death by the Gestapo.

*****

ETCHOLA
ASCAIN

Tuesday
7 August [1928]

Dear G—

I havent Hugnet's article because I had to send it back to him but I asked him to send it to you if he had a copy.

I leave tomorrow, spend a few days with Mme. Langlois and then go to St. Malo where Georges and I will go from together to visit Cliquet-Pleyel and

Marthe-Marthine at Bagnoles-de-l'Orne. The symphony sketch is now finished and I have written a very sweet letter to Emily Chadbourne and the diarrhoea has quieted down and I am feeling quite sufficiently angelic although devoured by fleas (St. Jean de Puces is the local plaisantry) and rather too toned up nervously from quite enough sea-air. But all is well nevertheless and I am smoking again.

And please tell Alice she ought to be glad because she always looked rather with noble patience on my not smoking and also give her my love and keep it yourself at the same time. The friends in Holland write that "le petit Tonny plonge. Il nage avec bonheur. et G. Maratier singe, jadis, a son ardeur."

Toujours Virgil

------

le petit Tonny . . . ardeur: "Little Tonny is diving. He swims happily and G. Maratier thinks about his ardour of times past."

*****

Loctudy
Sunday [1928]

Dear Gertrude

Here is a picture Mrs. Lasell sent from America. I've made fifty pages of symphony score. I am contented. I go the end of the week to Hugnet at St Malo. This is a good country.

Love
Virgil

I sent you some cookies.
Made by my landlady.

Hugnet at St Malo: Hugnet's mother's family home is in St Malo.

*****

To "M. Virgil Thomson / ~~17 Quai Voltaire / Paris~~ Pension [Chever?] Loctudy / Finistére"

HOTEL PERNOLLET   [21 Aug. 1928]
    BELLEY
    (AIN)

My dear Virgil,

The cookies are delicious thanks so much for them, and where are you, Hugnet write[s] that he is xpecting you but that you are not there, he also sent me the article about you there are some awfully nice spots

Letters with Notes   81

in it, particularly about you making them like the old french song which doesn't xist without you he did that charmingly and then pieces of the little poem at the end are delightful. He is a sweet kid. I had a note from Bebé I did not realise that he had been raised to be a soldier you kind of don't think of it with these city boys although we are very used to it here with the country ones and Hugnet will he have to be going soon he will make an awfully cute little soldier, and be wonderfully explosive, the inclosed to go on to another subject, was a surprise as she had not given a copy to either of us, keep it if you like I will probably have another and I like you spelled with an e. still without an e is best. The Bouquet of Wills is finished rather amusing and grammar is really opening up, I can quite not be worried by sight and sound [confusion?] to any such consideration and to prove it on the ride here began a pastoral on a marsh, Geronimo on a marsh which does do some very good things so far, otherwise life continues to be leisurely, there are friends who pass through our pleasant little town, Bravig is having strange adventures in Danzig, and Carl Van Vechten is coming to Paris in September and October and the English Department of the University of Indiana is taking me on, otherwise as we were, and you lots of love to you and Georges Hugnet,   alwys

Gtrde.

tell him I am writing him very soon.___

---

french song . . . without you: In Hugnet's article (see appendix A), he suggests he cannot imagine poems put to music by Thomson without their settings "any more than I can imagine children's rhymes like 'Malbrouck' or 'Maman, les petits bateaux' without music."

I like you spelled with an e: "Vergil" is a variant of his name, presumably used in the enclosure, now lost.

grammar . . . up: Stein embarks on a meditation upon grammar, culminating in "Arthur A Grammar" (*How To Write* 37–101). Her investigations into grammar inform many of her concurrent projects, so that "Arthur" serves as "a bass line for that summer" (Dydo 235).

Geronimo: Name figuring persistently and playfully in Stein's pastoral play, *Paisieu*, published in *Last Operas and Plays* (1949).

Bravig . . . Danzig: One of Imbs's "adventures" during his trip to Eastern Europe was meeting his future wife Valeska, whom he brought back to Paris with him. From Riga, Latvia, he writes Stein that he has fallen in love with the Comtesse Balbarishky (spelled variously in his letter), detailing both the romance and its complications. He sends Stein a photograph, noting, "Really the photograph I am sending you is an amazing one for it is a record of the exact moment I fell in love. It was the first time I had ever looked directly into her eyes and then I knew. A few hours after we were speeding across the plains of Latvia and in the third class compartment of the train, crowded with peasants, I proposed to her and she accepted." Among the impediments were the objections of Valeska's family, financial constraints, Valeska's engagement to a friend of Imbs's, and Imbs's relationship with Maratier. Regarding the latter, Imbs writes, "I have told her all about Georges which is a complication in the future but I am tired of his lion taming and will prefer to be just his friend" (Imbs to Stein, ca. 1928). See note to Stein [6 March 1928].

Van Vechten is coming: Carl Van Vechten, Iowa-born graduate of the University of Chicago, music and dance critic for the *New York Times*, devotee of opera, avid visitor to Harlem, promoter of black artists and writers, close friend of Stein since 1913, now becoming one also of Thomson. Van Vechten has arranged for the publication of Stein's writings, including *Tender Buttons* in 1914. He will arrive on 11 September and be reported in the Paris *Herald Tribune* (12 Sept.) as saying of Stein, "She is like yeast . . . one of the greatest influences" on Sherwood Anderson and "important in the literary development of James Joyce, Dorothy Richardson and others."

*****

[Possible placement: enclosed with letter of 2 September]

Postcard from Thomson in "Bagnoles de L'Orne," illustration of "La Légende de Bagnoles de–l'Orne," not addressed or stamped, n.d.

People pretend they come here for phlebitis and varicose veins but there is a beauty-cure which seems to be the real reason.

*****

Bagnoles-de-l'Orne
2 September [1928]

Dear Gertrude

It has been very nice here with Georges & Cliquet & Marthe and I have done a good deal of sleeping and cracked my nose wide open on the bottom of the swimming-pool and made a portrait of Marthe for the fiddle and I am going back to Paris tomorrow. I also played on the piano Acts III & IV because I have worked all summer without a piano and I hadnt heard any of it and wasnt I surprised it is very swell and full of inspiration and variety and I can only hope it isnt as bad as my contentment would maybe indicate. I also read Desbordes's book some of it and had pleasure. St. Malo was nice too and we swam and ate cafe viennois. Your picture of Georges as an explosive little soldier reminds me that you must make him recount his military career to you because it is a good story and very him. I meditate your portrait. When do you come back to Paris because I shall be awfully glad to see you again and Alice and sing opera and tell stories. Cliquet & Marthe & I plan a concert for November. Georges writes a long poem every now and then and improves steadily. My portrait trick is developing nicely and seems to be quite new. That is, for music, because the idea of it comes obviously out of you. We had chicken today for lunch and good wine. Love, Virgil

---

Cliquet & Marthe: Henri Cliquet-Pleyel, whom Thomson will remember as:
>a pianist of unusual facility, a sight reader of renown, and a composer of wilful banality. His music was a tender parody, his life a slavery to pot-boiling jobs. Marthe-Marthine too was not ever to be prosperous; she had thrown away her singing career for marriage in Rumania, and she could not fight her way back. She and Cliquet, though attached relentlessly, did each other no good. He would go into tantrums in which he burned his manuscripts or destroyed pictures with razors . . . and she would take to red wine, quarts of it a day. Yet they remained for me gentle companions and colleagues of impeccable solidarity. (*Virgil Thomson* 109)

portrait of Marthe for the fiddle: The second of his portraits. That autumn, back in Paris, he makes the portrait he meditates here, *Miss Gertrude Stein as a Young Girl*. He later writes:

> Making portraits of people was just beginning to serve me, as it had long served Gertrude, as an exercise not only in objectivity but also in avoiding the premeditated.... And it was from her success with this (in my view) that I was led to try it in music. My first efforts came out so well, both in likenesses and as compositions, that I was sure I had discovered something. But exploring could wait. Opera and symphony were my preoccupations right then. (*Virgil Thomson* 124)

Desbordes's book: Jean Desbordes, *J'adore* (1928). See note to Stein, [3 Aug. 1928].
viennois: Viennese.

*****

Sunday 9th [*Sept. 1928*]

Dear Gertrude

Thanks for the prospectus. It is nice the blurb you wrote. Saw Tonny and Maratier happy about Holland. Put Eric [de Haulleville] on a train for Brussells. Cliquet and Marthe reenter tomorrow. Georges gone back to St. Malo. I nearly got a cheap flat and then I didn't. Baby is in Toulon preparing his exposition. Paris is warm and summery. I finish symphony and get acquainted with Acts III & IV. For the present I keep my flat and economize. Saw Fania Marinoff. It seems Carl wont be in Paris except maybe two days. I hope all is well and happy at Belley.

Love both
Virgil

prospectus ... blurb: Her advertisement for *Useful Knowledge*, also printed in published text. See note to Stein, [23 Sept. 1928].
Tonny ... Georges: Thomson, Hugnet, Cliquet-Pleyel, Marthe-Marthine, and Kristians Tonny constitute "*a petite famille* for dinners and laughter" (*Virgil Thomson* 109).
exposition: exhibition.
Fania Marinoff: See note to Stein, [*18 June* 1927].

*****

Postcard of "Avila–Vista general," to "M. Virgil Thomson / 17 Quai Voltaire / Paris,"

Hotel Pernollet [14 Sept. 1928]
Belley, Ain,

Did you like Tonny's [speech?], it was very beautiful, we do not yet languish for Paris, but remember us to every one, particularly to Marthe Marthine, whose [mot?] I liked immensely and Pleyel, Bravig is coming home surprisingly, by and by, my new book looks awfully pretty and seems to be doing nicely, has Hugnet had a review copy, otherwise fog and calm and grammar   Alwys Gtrde Stein.

mot: comment or note.
new book: *Useful Knowledge*. See Stein and note [23 Sept. 1928].

*****

17 Quai Voltaire
Friday [*Sept.* 1928]

Dear Gertrude

I do hope you will be coming along soon because I am eager to try the opera on you. I did a rendition yesterday for Marthe and Cliquet and Tonny & Maratier which apparently impressed in spite of length. Paris is pleasant as to weather. But full of departing visitors. Baby prepares his exposition. At Toulon. Quite a season there just now. Eugene and company and many "young gentlemen". I am diverted at news of Bravig's bravery. And I suppose it isnt a bad idea. He wouldnt be the kind, I fancy, to make such a step without knowing his mind. So we all offer blessings. Though up to yet nothing more substantial. I loved your Avila card and could read it mostly though there was a question about Hugnet having received a copy of something which I cant answer because I couldn't quite make out what it was about. Bernard sends me the Kansas City war monument which here is. You once asked to see it. I hope you will be coming home soon.

Best love Alice and love love
Virgil

I've been doing Isadora's *Life* which is not bad reading

---

exposition: exhibition.
Bravig's bravery: Bravig's marriage. See note to Stein, [21 Aug. 1928].
Kansas City war monument: On 3 Sept. 1928, Bernard Faÿ sent Thomson a postcard of the Liberty War Memorial in Kansas City at night, a tall tower topped by a flame and illuminated from two sides by floodlights. His message translates, "In passing through your hometown, I am sending this good symbol of virility as an encouragement and souvenir. B. F."
Isadora's *Life*: American dancer Isadora Duncan's autobiography, *My Life* (Boni & Liveright, 1927). Duncan, widely considered the mother of modern dance, had died the year before in Nice, strangled by one of her own trademark flowing scarves when it became entangled in the wheel of a car in which she was a passenger. Stein's response to the bizarre accident was to remark that "affectations can be dangerous."

*****

To "M. Virgil Thomson / 17 Quai Voltaire / Paris."

HOTEL PERNOLLET [23 Sept. 1928]
    BELLEY
    (AIN)

My dear Virgil,

Georges has just sent me the introduction for Orbes that he has just done and I like it tremendously, it pleased me profoundly, one does like to be written about but in him there is a freshness of comprehension that touches me to the heart. I am returning Bernard's postal it delighted me, it is beautiful and his remarks to you just right. He is funny alright. Bravig is a lamb, he is wonderfully literal and a child of romance, he has written perfectly delightful letters from the beginning to the culmination, I hope it will work out well, she looks very nice in a photo and very natural, beside she is Polish and one believes in Poles. The elections are funny, I follow them Hoover and all all not being Smith with great xcitement, I begin the morning with oh my and Alice says what is it who has made a speech. Useful Knowledge is nice they has gotten it up awfully prettily, I can't give you it now because the first lot is a limited first edition but there will soon be more and cheaper because it does seem to be selling and then I will, the Four Religions look awfully nice in it, I was able to run Hugnet in for a copy, as a Review Copy, at least I hope he has gotten it, I think it was that question that was illegible, I am practicing legibility, do you recognise it, it is lovely now but cold, but I am making a lot, grammar is coming on, and a play, we are looking forward to having the music of the opera, lots of love

Gtrde.

introduction for Orbes: To introduce Louise Langlois's translation of Stein's "A Saint in Seven" in the periodical *Orbes*, Hugnet wrote a preface on Steinian poetics entitled "La Vie de Gertrude Stein." These were published in the second issue, Spring 1929. For "La Vie" in translation see appendix D.
Bernard's postal: See note to preceding letter.
elections . . . Smith: Herbert Hoover is running against Democrat Alfred Smith, the first Roman Catholic to run for the presidency. Popular response to the major issues of the campaign, religion and prohibition, make it a lively election year.
Useful Knowledge: London: John Lane, Bodley Head, 1928; New York: Payson & Clarke, 1928.
Four Religions: "Lend a Hand or Four Religions," the final selection in *Useful Knowledge*.

*****

Wednesday [26 Sept. 1928]

Dear Gertrude

Your letter came as I went to post. Your legibility is excellent and I am glad Useful Knowledge is nice. Georges hasnt mentioned receiving it. But he wrote the introduction to you was good. You are not alone in enjoying the election. I have a leaning for Smith. Inherited Democraticness and just naturally agin the government anyway. And in l'Oeuvre I follow eagerly the enquête sur la poésie pure (àpropos Valéry). It is un-payable. It seems everybody in France, academicians and everybody, can explain exactly what poetry is and what every poem means and Valery is freed from any charges of not having a clear meaning. J.-E. Blanche did it today. The copyist is preparing my symphony. Do come home as soon [as] your work lets up a little.

Love & love Alice
Virgil

the introduction: See note to preceding letter on Hugnet piece in *Orbes*.
enquête sur la poésie pure: enquiry on pure poetry.
un-payable: Gallicism for priceless.
J.-E. Blanche: Jacques-Émile Blanche, successful Parisian painter, best known for portraiture. In 1884, he coorganized and exhibited at the first Salon des Indépendants at the Galerie Georges Petit in Paris.

*****

Postcard of "Environs de Belley—Les Gorges de la Balme," to "M. Virgil Thomson / 17 Quai Voltaire / Paris"

[29 Sept. 1928]

My dear Virgil,

This little autobus does so sweetly go through the gorge I am very pleased with it I also have one in glass not the gorge the autobus it was to be a prize for having bought tinned goods but we bought it all by itself, we are going vintaging to-morrow much xcited, everything is peaceful   G.S.

*****

Wednesday [*early Oct. 1928*]

Dear Gertrude

The cake is grand and many thanks it arrived just before tea-guests and was a great success and it is beautiful to look at not to speak of eat. Hugnet sent me also a round glass ball with a mirror on the lining. And my own spirits are higher. Fall having nicely arrived. With warmish cold fog overhead and diffused light and Paris is herself again. I continue trying Act III on everybody in sight and I dont know yet what to make of it. Hugnet reenters Sunday. The flower market has handsome dahlias. I was dragged to Folies Bergère by visiting Americans. René [Crevel] is working hard finishing a book. G. Maratier has sold his business and makes a trip to America on the proceeds. Tonny is sweet these days. Eugene consorts with Princesses in Marseilles and sailors in Toulon. Peter Smith turns up after a summer in England with a novel written. Nancy Cunard has bought Bill Bird's press and is about to publish something or other. The Flanner looks chipper. A few new Christians appear.

My love remains
Virgil

finishing a book: *Paul Klee* (Paris: Galimard, 1930).
Nancy Cunard has bought Bill Bird's press: Thirty-two-year-old poet and avant-garde patron Nancy Cunard founds the Hours Press, formerly U.S. journalist Bill Bird's Paris-based Three Mountains Press, which published important modernists, including Pound, Hemingway, and Williams.

*****

To "M. Virgil Thomson / 17 Quai Voltaire / Paris." Postmark 12 Oct. See note prefacing following letter.

HOTEL PERNOLLET [7 Oct. 1928]
  BELLEY
    (AIN)

My dear Virgil,

It is rather curious we have been meeting the local country people and find them good fun and strangely enough the ones we like the best are your neighbours, the Count & Countess D'aiguy who live on your second floor, they were amused that you were a friend of ours because I imagine the concierge had sung your praises, and they want to hear you etc, have given them the programme of the late concert and they were interested, we are still pleased with ourselves here and the weather is beautiful we will be staying on another couple of weeks at least, I have finished my second play the story of the Geronimos rather nice, but grammar which is slow is getting on its a good country for grammar because cooking is so admirably and simply organised, a continuous illustration of the essentials of grammar. Did you like my portrait of Hugnet, it came quite nicely, we will all come nicely sometime, and Mrs. Bravig, Bravig writes me that he is there, do gossip to us what all the news, there is also a very nice young woman here who is a friend of these people and a friend of Bernard Fay's but more of all that later, otherwise there is the vintage the wine they make is bad but the grapes this year very good and we have been cutting and eating our fill,

                                    Alwys
                                        Gtrde.

Alice is going on with Erasmus.

Count and Countess D'aiguy: François and Diane (May) d'Aiguy, whose daughter is the Rose of Stein's *The World is Round* (1939). "The D'Aiguys" appears in Stein's *Portraits and Prayers*, 108.
my second play: see note to Stein [21 Aug. 1928].
portrait of Hugnet: "George Hugnet," in *A Stein Reader*, 538.
Mrs. Bravig: Bravig Imbs's new wife, Valeska. See note to Stein, [21 Aug. 1928].
Erasmus: Thomson's copy, on loan, of *Life, Character and Influence of Desiderius Erasmus of Rotterdam Derived from a Study of his Works and Correspondence*, 2 vols. (New York: Burns, Oates & Washbourne, 1927), by John Joseph Mangan A.M., M.D., seventy-year-old father of John Sherry Mangan, who helped with research, editing, and preparation for publication. (See note to Thomson, 22 September [1929].) This is a work of original scholarship, conservative-Catholic in its assessment and corrective of the till-now conventional scholarly view of Erasmus as a forerunner of the Enlightenment.

*****

Envelope from Hotel Pernollet, to "M. Virgil Thomson / 27 Quai Voltaire / Paris", stamped "RETOUR A L'ENVOYER" and "INCONNU."

Original postmark 7 Oct. Presumably held above letter and resent in above envelope.

[12 Oct. 1928]

[Note on envelope:]

I did undoubtedly not address this correctly, are you alright Bravig said you did not look well there is nothing the matter is there, it rains but we seem happy.

G.

*****

17 Quai Voltaire
13 October [1928]

Dear Gertrude

Your nice letter arrives and is nice. Ever since I came to Paris all healthy and fine I've had a series of things all more or less the same, a congestion, a cold in head, a reappearance of congestion, and now a very painful throat and there doesnt seem to be anything to be done. Illnesses have kept me in at working so that I have completely revised last act and orchestrated end of symphony and made a piece on the Marquis de Sade for the new *Cahiers Sade*. General state excellent and disposition fair. I merely have January's throat in October. Doing it early because I shant be here to have it at the proper time. Bravig brought his countess one day. She is excellent and not *méchante* and nicely *bien élevée* and seems to like Bravig. She speaks English & German & Russian and isnt heavy like Russians. Bravig seems proud and contented, though he treats her more like a new suit than like a wife. Still, he was always careful of his clothes. And now he's got a little hotel room in Chevreuse somewhere and is putting her in it with a typewriter and she looks as if that were what she expected and really a very good idea it is seeing as she isnt a bit Latin Quarter and there isnt any money for Paris anyhow and Bravig is going to study the bassoon. We plan our concert (Marthe & Cliquet & me) for the 13th of November. Mairie du IX[eme]. Hugnet had an access of composition at the end of the summer and has produced some long poems of excellent quality with no rhythm or images in them much and sometimes nice grammar. Your piece about him is pretty and a jewel. Tonny is quarreling and making up with his family about *moeurs*. He got mad and made a profession of faith and then he retracted so all is quiet just now but Maratier is taking a flat for and with him. All seem to think it time Tonny left home. Baby is back but invisible. Also Eugene full of amours and heaviness. Bravig heard the opera and has no doubt written you of it. He said complimentary things. Madame Langlois is moving into a hotel as the only lady-like way of getting rid of her servant *Louis* who is a nuisance as old servants often are. I am having a warm winter overcoat on credit. It is red and black and very beautiful. Would it upset your plans if I blew into Belley for a few days of fresh air and serious eating? And what about heat?

Love
Virgil

---

a piece on the Marquis de Sade: *Commentaire sur Saint Jérome* (1928), for voice and piano.
méchante: nasty.
bien élevée: well mannered.
moeurs: morals.
Mairie du IXeme: The salle de la Mairie du IXeme in the rue Drouot; *mairie*, "town hall".
the only lady-like way of getting rid of her servant: The servant stole money and furniture but had shown devotion to her dying husband, so, rather than fire him, she is giving up her Saint-Germain apartment, is giving him a pension, and will live for the rest of her life in a hotel (*Virgil Thomson* 85).

*****

To "M. Virgil Thomson / 17 Quai Voltaire / Paris."

HOTEL PERNOLLET   [15 Oct. 1928]
    BELLEY
        (AIN)

My dear Virgil.

I wish you had thought of coming down earlier, we had lovely weather though cold but now the fogs have started in earnest and the sun doesn't go through them at all and won't until the first of November so we are quitting grammar is done for the present, and as soon as it is type written and corrected we leave, I wish you had thought of coming earlier, but now it is deadly damp, and I don't advise it at all, well anyway we will be seeing you soon and that will be nice because we have been away a long time. We liked all your descriptions, I think you will like grammar and a pastoral, and then there are two operas, a little light one and a heavy one, Bravig is very pleased with the opera, he says the music makes him very happy which is all to the good, we are looking forward to hearing it, I also did a portrait of our new French friends all of them as a family its a delightful bit of contrast but more of all that and the concert, and your plans and the new overcoat, and Composition & Xplanation being most respectably printed by Doubleday Doran in Hogarth Essays along with T.S. Eliot & 10 other respectables, and I was taken off in a topical song by the T.S.F. from London so Nelly Jacott writes and we are all going to be happy though glorious,

Gtrde.

Best regards to M. Marthine and Cliquet.

grammar and a pastoral: "Arthur a Grammar" and *Paisieu*. See notes to Stein [21 Aug. 1928].
two operas: *A Lyrical Opera Made By Two To Be Sung* and *A Bouquet. Their Wills*. See notes to Stein, [13 July 1928])
portrait . . . friends: "The d'Aiguys." See note to Stein [7 Oct. 1928].
Composition . . . respectables: Virginia and Leonard Woolf published "Composition as Explanation" in 1926 as part of their Hogarth Essays series. In 1928, Doubleday Doran is publishing an anthology of selected essays from the series, among them T. S. Eliot's "Homage to John Dryden," E. M. Forster's "Anonymity: an enquiry," Virginia Woolf's "Mr. Bennett and Mrs. Brown," and Robert Graves's "The Future of the Art of Poetry."
taken off . . . Jacott: In her letter of Oct. 14, Stein's friend Nellie Jacott writes that she has just heard the piece on the radio minutes before about a music critic bowing before Stein but not understanding "why the cows motive" (Jacott to Stein, 14 Oct. 1928).
T.S.F: *Télégraphie Sans Fil*, wireless radio.

*****

Thursday [*18 Oct.* 1928]

Dear Gertrude

Thanks again for the cake again which arrived again just as tea was preparing. I have done your portrait for a violin. Also *Cliquet-Pleyel in F* and *Georges Hugnet, poète et homme de lettres*. Sauguet says the opera is not tiresome. It seems Baby cant ever have another exposition, because Pierre sells his pictures as soon as they get to the store. More later and do let us see you soon.

Love
Virgil

I hear you have had snow.

your portrait for violin: Thomson's *Miss Gertrude Stein as a Young Girl*, 14 Oct. 1928, appendix B.
Sauguet: Henri, twenty-seven-year-old French Neo-Romantic composer of the ballet *La Chatte* for Diaghilev. A devotee of Satie, having cofounded the Ecole d'Arcueil, named after the suburb in which Satie lived, he is a companion of Thomson on long walks through Paris. Thomson will remember that Sauguet "dared the use both of curvilinear melody and of harmony unrelated to Stravinsky's practices, as well as the straightforward expression of sentiment (without irony)." "We showed each other music, shared adventures and addresses, bound ourselves together by an unspoken credo (based on Satie) that forbade us to be bogus either in our music or in our lives" (*Virgil Thomson* 113, 108–109).
exposition: exhibition.

*****

17 Quai Voltaire
Tuesday [*23 Oct.* 1928]

Dear Gertrude

Concert changed to Salle Majestic. 14 November. Very swell. Here are a few clippings. L'oeuvre had a good day. Your portrait pleases. Is said to resemble. I did also Mrs. Lasell. I have six now. Saturday I do Sauguet from life. The cake lasts.

Love
Virgil

Concert changed: Originally planned for the 13th in the salle du Mairie du IXeme, the concert will include music by Thomson and Cliquet-Pleyel, played by them, poems by Hugnet set to music by them and sung by Marthe-Marthine, Satie's *The Death of Socrates*, played by Thomson and sung by Marthe, two longer poems by Hugnet read by the actor Marcel Herrand, Thomson's settings of *Commentaire sur Saint Jérome* and *Les Soirées bagnolaises*, and six of his portraits played by Lucien Schwartz. Stein and Toklas attend, the latter saying afterward of Cliquet, "He's your Matisse," referring to when Matisse and Picasso exhibited together (*Virgil Thomson* 125). Janet Flanner also attends and subsequently writes, over her penname, "Genêt," in her "Paris Letter" in *The New Yorker* of 8 December 1928:

> A small advance-guard concert, featuring the briefer works of the American, Virgil Thomson, and the French composer, Cliquet-Pleyel, was given lately in the Salle Majestic. These two represent almost all that is left of the Groupe d'Accueil [sic].
>
> Certain of Mr. Thomson's pieces have already been heard in New York, notably the "Five Phrases from the Song of Solomon," for voice and percussion. His newer compositions continue his early tradition, which is melodic and scholarly, economical, and essentially sound. His "Commentaire sur Saint Jerome," text from the Marquis de Sade, and his "Six Portraits" for violin solo—including a "bust" of Gertrude Stein, a sketch of Sauget, and one of the "Señorita J. de M. Accompanied by her Mother"—were musical *croquis* which afforded the auditors high pleasure. . . .
>
> It is now only three years since Satie departed from his suburban attic where, with a hammock, a candle, an enormous collection of old umbrellas, new shoes, and derby hats which were his passions, he lived for twenty-four years and died as he had lived, in poverty; writing, though with little to laugh at, the first modern humorous French music. The Groupe d'Accueil [sic], formed by his disciples, still deserves the praise given to persistence.

L'oeuvre: the work.

six now: In addition to portraits of Marthe, Juanita de Medina, and Stein, he finished *Cliquet-Pleyel in F, Georges Hugnet, Poet and Man of Letters, Mrs C.W.L.* (Mrs Lasell, signed 18 Oct. 1928), all done from memory. With *Sauguet, from Life* he will begin composing while his subject sits (or lies reading or sleeping), finishing in a single sitting. He later recalls, "it was through practicing my spontaneities, at first in a primitive way, and through questioning Gertrude Stein about this method of work, which was her own, that I grew expert at tapping my resources" (*Virgil Thomson* 124). He is accustomed to watching his painter friends finish a drawing in one sitting, but his principal model is Stein, who applied the practice of visual artists to writing.

*****

To "M. Virgil Thomson / 17 Quai Voltaire / Paris."

GERTRUDE STEIN
27 RUE DE FLEURUS
PARIS

[25 Oct. 1928]

My dear Virgil,

Here we are, at home and house cleaning, but all will be ready Saturday and will you come in Saturday afternoon, Bravig and Valeska will be at lunch with us and I am trying to get your neighbor the very nice woman we met and who wants to meet you, it may even be good for the concert a nice concert and we are very anxious to hear all about everything,

Alwys
Gtrde.

Eric's fragments in transition are good, do please tell him so for me.

Eric's fragments: Eric de Haulleville's "Fragments" published in *transition* no. 14, 206–207.

*****

17 Quai Voltaire
Thursday [*25 Oct. 1928*]

Dear Gertrude

    Saturday with pleasure. Only Sauguet is coming for lunch and to pose for his portrait and I'll get to your house as early as possible after. Maybe three. Maybe four. May two even.

Love
Virgil

*****

17 Quai Voltaire
Saturday Morning [*27 Oct. 1928*]

Dear Gertrude

    I've a frightful head-ache and cant budge. So unless it lets up I shant be able to come this afternoon. Please excuse me. And love

And see you soon.

    Virgil

*****

To "M. Virgil Thomson / 17 Quai Voltaire / Paris."

27 RUE DE FLEURUS
[7 Nov. 1928]

My dear Virgil,

    This Mme Wertheim turned up here with some one and it would appear that she is just starting a press to print young music in New York, and that she devotes herself to printing music, she is Morgenthau's daughter if that means anything to you any way she got quite xcited about the opera and wanted to see the score as soon as you got to New York, If you would call her up. She may be nothing and may be not, you should know about that, but anyway here is her address, we are still very impressed with the third act and I have almost something to say about you perhaps, a Thursday,

Gtrde.

Mme Wertheim: Alma Morgenthau Wertheim, whose small press, Cos Cob, publishes music, mainly by Aaron Copland.
Morgenthau: Henry, seventy-two-year-old real-estate magnate and former American Ambassador to Turkey (1913–1916), who protested the Armenian massacres, appealing in vain first to the U.S. government to intervene, then to the Ottoman rulers and German military leaders. He made public the genocide in *Ambassador Morgenthau's Story* (New York: Doubleday, 1918). After the 1914–1918 war he raised money for the financial relief of Eastern European nations.
still very impressed with the third act: Upon Stein's return from the country, late in the autumn of 1928, Thomson played Acts Three and Four of *Four Saints* for her and other close friends, Sauguet, Bérard, Tonny, Imbs, Maratier, Hitchcock, Madame Langlois, John Kirkpatrick (the pianist), and the composer Roy Harris, "who kept exclaiming over and over, 'Living! Living!'" (*Virgil Thomson* 124).

*****

To "Miss Stein / 27, rue de Fleurus / E.V. VI"

17 Quai Voltaire
[10 Nov. 1928?]

Dear Gertrude

Bébé is coming to tea on Monday. Alone. Will you and Alice come too? Many thanks for the apples which are delicious and O so plentiful. Also for kind words in re music.

Love
Virgil

*****

SS. ILE DE FRANCE   2 Decembre [1928]

Dear Gertrude

The voyage to Havre was nice with the most photogeniques of movie stars in next compartments, and Mme. Langlois went on board ship and presented herself and me to the captain who has since done me all the last honors and invited me to the bridge and made me eat 1st class and showed me all the beautiful electrical devices for steering which never work and had me showed engine-rooms by 1st lieutenants and invited to aperitifs and officers messes and so I dont really go back much to third class except to dress or sleep or be sick which I was most awfully for 1 ½ days. But all is calm now and the boat is really very handsome from the toppest pink officer to the lowest Lalique port-hole of the dining hall. There are only the rarest of rare woods and the most variegated india-rubber. Cuties in red trousers run our errands, huskies from below box daily for our pleasure, domestics are of the most amiable, barbers of the most competent, and there are primeurs at table and quails in jelly and foie gras à volonté. Raymond Mortimer turns up and we eat together and my Lanvin overcoat holds up with the best England can offer. The added swank of my third class cabin gives me an edge on Britain of which all concerned are conscious and which I try not to accent. I have a nice cabin-mate too, a husky, an aviator in Canada winter postal service between Montreal and Nova Scotia where airplanes wear skis and icicles and he shows me his tattoos and his war wounds and only sleeps four hours and combs his hair over a bald spot and uses Coty's face-powder and eats with the officers and dances second-class because he doesnt like dress clothes and really all around a *chic type*.

Love
Virgil

140 East 19th Street. New York City

The voyage: Visiting Paris, Aaron Copland urged Thomson to return home. Copland wanted to perform *Capital Capitals* in one of his Copland-Sessions Concerts and asked Thomson to coach the singers and perform the piano part—so Thomson is on his way to America. He also wants—Copland urged it—to show his *Symphony on a Hymn Tune* to Serge Koussevitzky, director of the Boston Symphony Orchestra. Thomson thinks Koussevitzky a sympathetic contact, having become friendly with him in Boston in 1923–1924 after Koussevitsky obtained his directorship partly owing (both knew) to Thomson's positive review of Koussevitzky's 1921 Paris concerts in *The Boston Transcript*.
the captain has done me all the last honors: It is because Madame Langlois is sister to an admiral that her introducing herself and Thomson to the captain has resulted in Thomson receiving special treatment.
Lalique: The art-producing firm of René Lalique (1860–1945), innovative Art-Nouveau stylist in various materials.
primeurs: early produce.
Raymond Mortimer: Thirty-three-year-old writer of fiction, literary and art criticism, and reviews published in *Vogue*, the *London Mercury*, the *New Statesman*, the *Nation*, and *The Dial*. Living in both London and Paris, he is an associate of the Bloomsbury Group and friend of Cocteau, Tzara, and Louis Aragon.
140 East 19th Street: Thomson's contact address during his four-month visit to the U.S., and his residence for February and March. Hildegarde Watson's four-story town house (with garden) in Manhattan features a two-story drawing room containing a grand piano, which he uses to demonstrate his music. He recalls, "My most effective number was the singing of *Four Saints* complete, which by this time I could do from memory" (*Virgil Thomson* 134).

*****

OAKHURST
WHITINSVILLE MASSACHUSETTS

12 December [1928]

Dear Gertrude

What luxe what snow what sun and blue skies what food what o my God what a bore. The Capitals are being performed on February 24 at the Little Theatre in New York.

I go tomorrow to Boston to arrange what can be arranged there. This is just a note with love.

I have no impressions of America. It's just the same as before only the liquor is better.

Love
Virgil

What luxe ... bore: Thomson spends the month of December at Jessie Lasell's luxurious manor in Massachusetts. He later recalls the lives of her family and visitors as monotonous and hemmed in by privilege: "They read, but not advanced books or unknown ones; they owned pictures and art objects but not distinguished ones, nothing they could not explain to Worcester County; they backed causes, but not dangerous ones; they risked their lives, but only in wars, private airplanes, or polo. . . . not one of them was passionate or mystical or scholarly or aflame" (*Virgil Thomson* 129).

the liquor is better: This is the era of Prohibition in the United States (1920–1933), when the Eighteenth Amendment to the Constitution makes it illegal to make, import, transport, or sell—but not to possess or drink—alcoholic beverages.

*****

To "M. Virgil Thomson / 140 East 19th Street / New York / N.Y. / U.S.A"

GERTRUDE STEIN
27 RUE DE FLEURUS
PARIS

[*13?* Dec. 1928]

My dear Virgil,

Merry Christmas and happy New Year to you and god bless our native land and how are you liking the templed hills, we are peacefully and completely translating it goes, I go alone and then Alice goes over me and then we all do it with George and then he goes alone and really it all goes faster than any one would think. I guess we will get it done on time. Otherwise life is peaceful that is with the usual gentle xplosions, do give us your news and do take the best of holiday greetings from us

Alwys
Gtrde.

---

translating: They are translating selections from *The Making of Americans*, which will be the first publication of Hugnet's Editions de la Montagne: *Morceaux choisis de La fabrication des Américains. Histoire du progrès d'une famille*, with preface by Hugnet (1929). Hugnet began translating selections in collaboration with Thomson and is finishing in collaboration with Stein. The collaborative translation produces an interesting Steinian French; in his preface Hugnet explains (here in translation), "In this translation what is not 'French' is not French because in the text English is not 'English'."

*****

OAKHURST
WHITINSVILLE, MASACHUSSETS

29 Dec. [1928]

Dear Gertrude

All goes swell. Koussevitsky refused my symphony cold. I was a little surprised I knew it was pretty good but hadnt really imagined it that good. Opera pleases every where. Harvard Glee Club wants to sing Processional scene. I go west next week. Glad. Tired of quail and strawberries. Visit quite successful though, I suppose on the whole. America as usual

Love
Virgil

———

Koussevitsky refused: Thomson recalls the visit:
> At his house in Jamaica Plain I played it to him while he read the score. After one movement he said, 'Good!' After two he said, 'Very good!' After three he said, 'Wonderful!' After the fourth, he threw up his hands and said, 'I could never play my audience that.' He was not articulate about his troubles with the fourth movement, but he seemed to find it not serious enough for a Boston public. He besought me to salvage the work by writing another last movement. I thanked him for his graciousness and left. (*Virgil Thomson* 131)

Koussevitzsky's rejection affects Thomson more deeply than he reveals here, causing him to hold back performance of the piece for a decade. He is about to go to his home in Kansas City.

*****

To "M. Virgil Thomson / ~~140 East 19th Street / New York / N.Y. / U.S.~~ "a/c Henwar Rodakiewicz / Santa Fe, / New Mex / U.S.A."

GERTRUDE STEIN
27 RUE DE FLEURUS
PARIS

[2 Jan. 1929]

My dear Virgil,

Happy New Year at least it is happy new year here and nice sun shine, our little friends Tonny and Grge Hugnet had a happy Christmas have you heard, they had a beautiful fight Christmas eve at the Select with Vitrac purely on the subject of how they that is Hugnet did not like his play and it all ended with their being put out with contusions and our commissariat around the corner and some of the details particularly the next days newspaper [notoriously?] concerning Hugnet senior are too funny for words but it is really all too long to write. The translation is all finished, bebe's drawings of me are finished are very nice but a bit of the nose rubbed off in excess of zeal but we are reblacking that, Tonny made a nice drawing for the device of the edition and when New Year's festivities are once over I xpect printing will begin, lets see what else oh poor Gody has lost her stability owing to too many poems and music she took to dropping little pieces of herself and groaning distressfully and once had to be disgracefully rocked in front of the senate and now I am having a new Ford car and with the unfaithfulness characteristic of us all I am violently interested and dvoted to the new. It is taking a bit of time to accustom myself to the new tricks but it is coming, Alice is making tapestry in our leisure moments, I am making sentences in my leisure moments and darn good sentences they are, otherwise as we were xcept for the usual and sometimes unusual coming and going, but I will do my best to remember what I can against your return, and how are you and your prospects, do remember me most kindly to Mrs. Laselle [sic],

Alwys
Gtrde.

Vitrac: Twenty-nine-year-old Roger Vitrac, Surrealist poet and playwright, in 1927 cofounder with Antonin Artaud of the Theatre Alfred Jarry, which led to their expulsion by Breton from the Surrealist group. Author of the play *Les Mystères de l'amour* (1927) and *Victor, ou Les enfants au pouvoir* (1928).
commissariat: police station.
all too long to write: For Hugnet's account, see note to Thomson, 16 January [1929].
Gody: Godiva, Stein's Ford, a two-seated roundabout, so named because it arrived from Detroit naked of ornament and accessories (*Autobiography*, 207).
Alice is making tapestry: She began embroidering tapestries when Picasso copied one of his paintings onto tapestry canvas for her. Stein writes that Toklas has "been making tapestry of his drawings ever since," that he "is kind enough . . . to make" drawings on her "working canvas and to colour them" (*Autobiography* 202).
making sentences: See note to Stein [23 Feb. 1929].

*****

2629 Wabash Ave.
Kansas City
9 January [1929]

Dear Gertrude

I'm home at last and am I glad? All is calm and sweet and quiet and I have work to do and nature is friendly (in spite of snow and slush). I have always been unhappy in Massachusetts in spite of busy activities of guardian angel. There is an unfriendly genius loci. I conduct *Church Sonata* in Boston on 17th March. Harvard Glee Club wants to sing Processional scene from opera, as I fancy I wrote you already. I have some amusing propos about our native land but they dont write very well. One about seeing and how the eye cant rest on anything but turns inward on itself, hence the decay of handwork and the disappearance of texture. Travelling salesmen on trains get lyrical about

E. Hemingway. A lengthy study of the case of Sibley Watson has brought me new details of the story and some sympathy but no change in the main diagnosis as we discussed it once at your house long ago. Talked to Carl V[an].V[echten]. He doesnt understand why I didnt bring Tonny's drawings. Says he can sell them easy and hopes you (or Tonny) are sending them. I have no news much from Paris. Let's hope there isnt any to have. I return around 1st April. I shant come here again soon. Visiting my family is really the only nice part. No amount of luxury can alleviate the state of Massachusetts. I think it rather aggravates it, in fact. Soggy food and the elements would at least preoccupy attention.

Love and Alice
Virgil

140 East 19
    N.Y.C.

Church Sonata: The words translate the Italian *sonata da chiesa*, so the reference is to *Sonata da Chiesa (Chorale, Tango, and Fugue) for Five Instruments: Clarinet in E-flat, Horn, Trombone, Trumpet and Viola*, 1926. The chorale and fugue are quite churchy; the tango is not.
propos: words.

*****

To "M. Virgil Thomson / Oakhurst / Whitinsville / Massachusetts. / U.S.A"

GERTRUDE STEIN
27 RUE DE FLEURUS
PARIS

[14 Jan. 1929]

My dear Virgil

    I am most awfully sorry about the symphony but then how could the Russian like it, I do hope it will come off all the same and we believe in you a lot as you can see from the profundity of inclosed portrait, it has a new rhythm with sense, I am making a lot just did a portrait of Bernard, but mostly a very detailed action upon the parts of a sentence, but I am happy that you can come back and work I gather that is alright. I am pleased about the glee club, I hope they will sing it, give it my love (I mean the glee club) they were so romantic in my youth when in the moon-light they sang Here is a health to King Charles, I like to think of them [serving?] us instead. Inclosed also prospectus of the edition, we had a beautiful reunion dinner at the Hugnets in honor of the first outbreak of the edition, it looks as if it were going to be quite alright, we all spoke of you very tenderly, you are as our dear Nellie [Jacott] would say not forgotten by your little friends. Nothing more xciting than usual, Tonny is preparing his xhibition with much circumvention, we are to see the things Tuesday, we saw Hitchcock the other day but I think I told you that, he is really very nice, I have not read his thing but hope to soon what with sending out prospectuses, entertaining an American colonel and his wife writing to the absent and writing a little time does pass. What other news is there, some more of Allen Tanner's family is coming over, and perhaps but that is not likely Tonny will do a Russian ballet, Anyway lots of love

Gtrde.

---

inclosed portrait: "Virgil Thomson." See appendix C.
portrait of Bernard: This portrait of Faÿ will be included in *Dix Portraits*. It also appears in *Portraits and Prayers*.
detailed . . . sentence: "Sentences." *How to Write* (1931).
prospectus: For *Morceaux choisis*. See note to Stein [13? Dec. 1928].
Hitchcock: Henry-Russell Hitchcock (1903–1987). Harvard-educated architectural historian, soon to be, in 1930, the intellectual father of "the international style" (his phrase) in architecture. He will go on to publish twenty books defining modern architecture, including *The International Style: Architecture since 1922* (with Philip Johnson, 1932), and *In the Nature of Materials, 1887–1941: The Buildings of Frank Lloyd Wright* (1942).
his thing: probably his newly finished, soon to be published book, *Modern Architecture* (1929).
Allen Tanner: American pianist. In 1926 he and companion Pavel Tchelitchev visited Belley, and Stein composed portraits of both of them.

*****

2629 Wabash Ave.
Kansas City
16 January [1929]

Dear Alice

Here are some things you might try over on your kitchen-piano. The salmon dish I recommend especially. It makes a delicate and fluffy entrée, highly digestible, and elegant to offer.
Kansas City is charming and I enjoy home and mother though the weather is hopeless. Oceans of slush froze last week and everything is now solid ice (motors waltzing). Today it rained and froze, so that all the little bare spots are covered now with slick ice and even walking is impossible. Temperature at zero. Humidity at 100% (official reports). I write music at home and cure cold and enjoy it all. Saturday I go to Santa Fe for a week. It will be warmer there. I am invited to lecture at Rochester with illustrations from my own works. The opera continues to excite and to please. The male-chorus arrangement of the Saints' Procession (for Harvard Glee Club) is a wow. I shall be glad to get back to Paris where I am not a public character. Hugnet writes an entertaining letter about his Vildrac [sic] encounter. I write a piece (for Boston) for four clarinets. My mending is being brought up to date. And new pyjamas are being made. The score and parts of my symphony (left to be finished in Paris) have never arrived. If they do, same will likely be played in Rochester. I make observations of Missouri speech. It is curious and interesting. In its local or provincial

condition it is incredibly low and horrid. And yet it seems to lose all its horrid quality with only a very little training and to become quite beautiful when properly educated. Unlike Kansas or Illinois, which are difficult to train and almost never lose their harsh intonation. And there are marked differences between male and female speech. And as for strawberries! The town is very gay. And everybody is amused and happy over the war memorial.

             Love
             Virgil

---

an entertaining letter: In the last week of December (n.d.), Hugnet writes (here translated):
> I have a sprained ankle and I have to stay home and work. This is how I got it: last Monday, December 24, was the dress rehearsal of a play by Roger Vitrac. He had insisted on my going to the performance, since he thought I would *demonstrate* and get beaten up by the police, who had special orders. Warned by Georges Neveux, who is the secretary of the Comédie des Champs-Élysées theatre, I kept my mouth shut, but at the end of the performance I delivered a violent diatribe against Vitrac. That evening (it was Christmas Eve) I met Vitrac (I was with Tonny, Maratier, Florence, Cliquet and Marthe), we traded insults, then we had a fight, and I smashed a glass over his head. The bar owner was scared and thought I would break everything in the place (I knocked over a table in cowboy-movie style), had me thrown out by some of the waiters, and they sprained my ankle for me. The police came and I was taken to the station for an hour. And that's it. My ankle is better already, but I'd love to know what state Vitrac is in, his head must be like a squashed *coloquinte* ['bitter apple' and, colloquially, 'head']. This story will amuse Gertrude. I mention in passing the bravery of Tonny, who jumped from a great height on Vitrac's shoulders (1.90 metres) better than Douglas Fairbanks would have done.

piece . . . for four clarinets: *Portraits of Ladies: Exercise in Composition: for 4 Clarinets*, composed in Kansas City.
war memorial: Liberty War Memorial. See note to Thomson, Friday [*Sept.* 1928].

*****

To "M. Virgil Thomson / 140 East 19 Street / New York / N.Y. / U.S.A."

      GERTRUDE STEIN
      27 RUE DE FLEURUS
        PARIS

                 [? Jan. 1929]

My dear Virgil,

  Glad to hear you that Kansas city is better than New England we just have had some visitors from Boston so we can appreciate that fact, otherwise, Alice is as pleased as can be that they are doing the church sonata in Boston she has great faith in the church sonata undoubtedly would have in the symphony if she had heard it. Tonny's drawings are on the ocean so Carl will have them soon and if he can sell them it will give pleasure and relieve a necessity I gather, the show is coming off soon, otherwise everything peaceful, I am writing a lot sentences get more and more fascinating, one can amuse oneself endlessly with them, transition is printing the bibliography of all my works they look quite nice, as names, everybody is very funny, lots of stories hope I can remember at least some, very pleased with your descriptions of E. Hemingway, the French I think are going to like me in translation all thanks to you, and I do understand that you want to come back, sometime I suppose I will have to want to come back too. Jo & Yvonne, Yvonne for the first time in a long time have left these shores for those shores I imagine you will see them in New York. Continue to give us your news and good news

       Lots of love Gtrde.

---

transition . . . names: Stein's bibliography is published in *transition* no. 15 (February 1929): 47–55.

*****

Postcard, photograph untitled of long, low sod-roofed house, to "Miss Stein / 27, rue de Fleurus / Paris VI / France"

       Santa Fé (25 Jan.)[1929]

Dear Gertrude

  This is a swell country. Picture illustrates Kit Carson's house at Taos. Saw Mabel's also. She away. Had your gay letter yesterday. Condolences for Godiva. And long live the new.

     Love Virgil

Santa Fé: Although planning to stay for a month in Kansas City, Thomson has been invited to New Mexico by Henwar Rodakiewicz, a wealthy private film maker. Thomson is staying on Rodakiewicz's ranch and observing society in Taos and Santa Fé. "To see my beloved Southwest again," he will remember, "was precious for that replugging into Western things that I was finding so much more tonic than the Northeast" (*Virgil Thomson* 131).
Mabel's: The home of Stein's former friend, Mabel Dodge Luhan at 240 Morada Lane, Taos.

*****

NEW YORK CENTRAL LINES
TWILIGHT LIMITED

       2 Feb. [1929]

Dear Gertrude

  Thanks and many. The portrait is very beautiful and serious and like me too. Yes very serious and with a quite gratuitous beauty an extra beauty par dessus du marché. The train wiggles and makes it hard to write straight. I am on my way to lecture on us at Rochester. Then New York and having to find singers for Capitals. I wish it were all over. Two months is enough not to work, especially visiting. Though I arranged the Saints' Procession and wrote a Conversation for 4 Clarinets. But I bear up and am of course very well and not even a cold so far. It was nice visiting my grandfather who at 97 was full of wise political comment and people comment and questions about French life and agriculture. I am glad the Americans are finished and I shall see them when I return. All write varied letters about this Hugnet-Vildrac [sic] story. I love it.

Please write many and often

Love
Virgil

140 E. 19
New York City

The portrait: Stein's portrait of Thomson, appendix B.
par dessus du marché: into the bargain.
Conversation: see note to Thomson 16 January [1929].
the Americans: *Morceaux choisis de La fabrication des Américains. Histoire du progrès d'une famille.* See note to Stein, [*13?* Dec. 1928].

*****

[from Toklas]

ROSE IS A ROSE IS A ROSE IS A ROSE.[circular] 27 RUE DE FLEURUS
8th February 1929

Dear Virgil

Thanks so much for your letter and the recipes—Indeed it is to your very kind mother that my thanks for the recipes are addressed—They sound delicious—and quite to our so special taste—and I'm most eager to try them—we are just now being served by an astonishing beautiful young enceinte Rubens—whose gift for the kitchen is entirely in the direction of scrubbing and polishing—she's too young and too handsome to be interested in cooking—but she's not permanent and we've hopes of less looks and more cooking in the near future. G- is off driving the new Ford—its got another technique from dear Godiva's and we go into the country for the day on Sunday to see what we feel about it. G-'s news is always a Ford—happy or otherwise—its a Ford that makes her temperature rise or fall—Tonny was here last night—rather sweet—his show goes well—there are several possible purchases for large pictures at proportionate prices— and we hope for the best. Everybody was at the vernissage from the conte d' Ursel to Florence Tanner accompanied by "How do you do Eugene"— "Oh Miss Stein"—Last week Alphonse Kann bought a Tonny—this week he bought a Christian Berard—we hope he doesnt spoil the effect by buying a Tcheletchef next week—Guevara has married an English heiress whose mother does not love her—The Guevaras love each other very much—quite in the manner of the more innocent past century

I do hope your affairs are progressing in the way you wish them to—please do remember any detail of the way women live chez vous—they do do do strangely and so well—not of course that that is your affair—but whatever you see and tell us will be nice –

Good luck to you –

Ever yours

Alice

---

enceinte: pregnant.
vernissage: private viewing.
conte d'Ursel: See note to Stein, 28 June [1928]. This year the Comte collaborates with Hugnet on their film *La Perle*.
Florence Tanner: Sister of pianist Allen Tanner, will marry Georges Maratier in the summer of 1929.
Alphonse Kann: Vienna-born, Jewish art collector, from whom hundreds of works will be stolen by the Nazis during World War II.
Guevara . . . heiress: Alvaro Guevara, Chilean painter introduced to Stein by Edith Sitwell, has married painter Meraud Guinness.

*****

140 E. 19
12 fevrier [1929]

Dear Gertrude

I've been to see Mabel Dodge and I think she's swell she has a voice like a young girl. I've also been elaborately interviewed by the press and I have written a statement for publication about our work and the Capitals are in rehearsal and Carl is having a party for me tomorrow night at which I shall demonstrate sample passages of Saints and I am to give in March when I go to Boston for the Church Sonata a program of works for Harvard Musical Club. Rochester sends favorable letter about symphony but no date yet. I am home-sick for Quai Voltaire and being at work again but I am sticking it out with grit. New York is not unpleasant just now cold but sunny and I am in swell feeling and health though not too good in purse because food is so high when it is any good and I couldnt manage at all if I had to pay room rent but I dont not even telephones and I get a good many free meals, though that is tiresome spending the evening on being took to a show nevertheless New York is not unpleasant because I am alone and that is very nice except sometimes Philip [Lasell] is here and he comes in in early morning and puts on a prima donna drunk for my watching and that is tiresome as hell. Muriel's book is a best-seller with your picture in it. Bernard's book about American federalism is being badly reviewed. Somebody will probably cable for your permission to print my portrait in a newspaper as concert publicity. If you consent, you will be paid for it at regular rates. In case same is not tempting to New York papers, it may be next month to Boston Transcript and so you'd better write me your wish in the matter anyway. Mabel speaks of you with greatest admiration and faithful affection and I guess she's really a pretty grand girl especially O such a nice voice. I reread my portrait twice and find it has a very fine texture especially the long middle paragraphs and great variety of sentences and a really concentrated progress in those parts which is I suppose what we mean by profundity or deep thought anyway. Give my love to Godiva's remplaçant and lots of it to Alice whatever you cant use yourself that is but there is lots for all of you and more.

Toujours
Virgil

Mabel Dodge Luhan: Thomson met Stein's estranged friend at a party put on by Carl Van Vechten.
Capitals are in rehearsal: To be performed in the second Copland-Sessions concert in the Little Theatre, 24 February 1929. Thomson's pocket diary for 1929 notes rehearsals this week and next. (Thomson's diary commences 7 Feb. 1929.)
Muriel's book: In *Music at Midnight* (New York: Harper and Brothers, 1929), across from a photograph of Gertrude Stein "Being Monumental in a Field" (1928), Muriel Draper writes:

> Gertrude Stein was in London that year, and could be seen at most of the Drury Lane performances, stalking through crowds, adorned in a short corduroy skirt, a white silk shirt, sandals, and a tiny hat perched up on her monumental head. She was usually shadowed by a friend who was always draped in some semi-Oriental gauze of sorts with clinking bracelets, tinkling chains and earrings as big and oval as her gaunt eyes. A strange pair. They came to Edith Grove, where Gertrude would sit in Buddhistic calm until some topic of conversation arose which stimulated her interests. And then she would talk for hours, a steady flow of ideas in an almost boring logical sequence, some of them profound and others merely a form of brilliant dialectic. Her point once gained or, in any case, her opponent once retired, she would sink back into calm and absorb intuitively what no longer aroused her intellectually. . . . She was sensitive about attacks upon her own peculiar form of literary expression, at least sensitive to any expressed or felt doubt of her sincerity. The technical aspect of it she would debate for hours, but her motive for developing it she would protect to the last drop of her mind's blood. She would say abruptly: "I don't know anything about it. I take things in and they come out that way, independent of conscious process. I don't know anything about it." She said she could not "do" a portrait of me because I "swooped so" she could not keep me still long enough. . . . I like her. I like her very much and agree with Sherwood Anderson that she "may be, just *may* be the greatest word-slinger of our generation." (152–53)

Bernard's book: Faÿ's *Franklin, the Apostle of Modern Times* (Boston: Little, Brown, 1929).
remplaçant: replacement.

*****

140 E. 19
N.Y.C.
21 Feb. [1929]

Dear Gertrude

Nice letter today from Alice. May I [receive] many of them. Carl wrote you I suppose about the opera party at his house. Everybody wanted to come & was refused except useful ones. Grand impression. Mabel D.L. much impressed. Said if performed it would do to opera what Picasso did to Kenyon Cox, nobody could ever listen to opera again.* (* Later, we went to Harlem to a nigger drag and one of Carl's coon friends picked us up a millionaire dumb-bunny who gave us a ride in a Hispano-Suiza. Carl in Hispano repeated Mabel D.'s remark. "Mustnt do that," replies dumb-bunny, "What'll I do on Thursday nights?") Carl ravished. A Mrs. Harvey (née Dudley) sent you love & compliments & various things enthusiastic. Witter Bynner hated the words and asked me to write music for a play of his. A Mrs. Stettheimer having a party for me tomorrow and Theatre Guild people who are interested. Mrs. Wertheim will do something, maybe publish. I've been interviewed, caricatured, written about, talked about, and entertained. Sunday's concert (Capitals) will tell whether I'm to be really taken up or gently dropped. All agree my music makes you palatable to otherwise-not-having-anys.* (* That's the literary group. The musicians all find that my music is not much without your words.) I dont know whether you like that or not. Bernard Fay wrote an article about me. Very sweet. He leaves for France tomorrow. At Rochester I sang the Berceau & Susie & Preciosilla in my lecture. I am sending you some clippings and other Americana. I usually send same to Bérard, but thought these might amuse you. So please give them to him when you've done reading them. On second thought I am sending the comic Valentines to him direct because they go in some magazines & wont have to be folded. Ask to see them if such amuse you. Deems Taylor will please you I am sure with his momentous discovery. And the fact that artist's working-processes are now first-page news. We await Tonny's drawings. Nothing has shown up yet.

                Love
                 Virgil

---

opera party at his house: Stein's old friend Carl Van Vechten gave Thomson an evening party at his flat on West Fifty-fifth Street to play and sing *Four Saints* to twelve people influential in the arts and potentially instrumental in mounting a production. On 13 Feb., Van Vechten writes to Stein, "everybody loved it & I think your words are so right & inevitable in music" (*The Letters of Gertrude Stein and Carl Van Vechten* 191).
Kenyon Cox: (1856–1919), once much admired U.S. painter, now replaced in general esteem by Picasso.
nigger drag: The annual drag ball at the Rockland Casino, involving about 5,000 dancers and observers.
Witter Bynner: Forty-seven-year-old Harvard graduate and Santa Fé based poet and playwright.
A Mrs. Stettheimer: Ettie Stettheimer invites Thomson to her house at Fifty-eighth Street and Seventh Avenue to meet her two sisters, one being fifty-seven-year-old Florine Stettheimer, whose paintings he sees. Before seeing them, he was considering commissioning Picasso or Bérard to design the sets and costumes for *Four Saints*. After seeing them, he asks her to design them and sings her the opera. She agrees to be its designer, and starts "finding ideas right away for making it look like the Cathedral façade in Avila executed in crystal and ostrich feathers and red velvet and gold fringe" (*Virgil Thomson* 134–6). He later explains, "Florine's paintings are very high camp, and high camp is the only thing you can do with a religious subject. Anything else gets sentimental and unbelievable, whereas high camp touches religion sincerely and its being at the same time low pop" (quoted by Watson 74). She is the first American painter to participate in stage production (Watson 6).

Mrs. Wertheim: See note to Thomson, [7 Nov. 1928].
article about me: Two holograph copies of this brief essay, entitled "Modern Music in America," survive, the shorter in Faÿ's hand, the longer in Thomson's. In both, Faÿ writes that Thomson's present visit to America may diminish misunderstanding between composer and listener, which characterizes modern music owing to composers failing to understand "old things" and themselves. Thomson is a good ambassador because "his breadth of knowledge and his musical culture are astounding, his understanding of the modern spirit and modern technique is quite unique." "Everything he writes is endowed with this double quality, the boldness of the modern spirit and the enlightened irony of old art. In his most modernistic compositions there is a smile of wisdom. He never allows himself to be bluffed by himself. His music is daring but an atmosphere of kindness pervades it."
At Rochester: He lectured at the house of Hildegarde and Sibley Watson, on Sibley Place, at her request, to an audience mostly from the Eastman School of Music. In his lecture he "explained a little of what our group in Paris thought it was up to." In addition to his settings of Stein texts, he played and sang parts of *Four Saints* and played Satie's *Three Pieces in the Shape of a Pear*. He gave a similar lecture at the Art Museum. His solo performance of the opera was well received, as it had been in Whitinsville Mass., Kansas City, and Santa Fé. "And as so often happens in some regional center or university, everybody seemed to understand everything and to like it. . . . This can occur only before New York has told them what to think; afterwards they are more reserved" (*Virgil Thomson* 133).
Deems Taylor: Joseph Deems Taylor, popular U.S. opera composer and music critic. He serves as CBS radio commentator for broadcasts of the New York Philharmonic (1936–1943). He is remembered also as the master of ceremonies for Walt Disney's 1940 film *Fantasia*.

*****

To "M. Virgil Thomson / 140 East 19 Street / New York / N.Y. / U.S.A."

GERTRUDE STEIN
27 RUE DE FLEURUS
PARIS

[23 Feb. 1929]

My dear Virgil,

I was just going to write to you when your letter came because I had had a nice cable from Carl, he was so delighted with you and the opera at his house and so apparently were they all, I am awfully pleased and awfully pleased at all your good news, I do hope it all comes off well opera symphony sonata and Capitals and everything and then you will come back and tell us all about it, yes Mabel has a nice voice, she used also have uncommonly robust lashes to her eyes, and do give her my love, Muriel has done us all I think awfully well and I am delighted that she is a best seller, as to your portrait sure would be pleased to be paid at the regular rate only they need of course do it all, that is the only thing I would insist upon, I am glad you like it, I think the intensive study I am doing of the sentence is bearing fruit, I am working at it steadily, I am almost getting so I can xplain it simply I am in short quite on the verge of doing something, I do want to know if there is a sentence, I thought perhaps there wasn't but I am almost beginning to be able to xplain that there is, our news is various, Hugnet has fallen into the arms of a belle dame sans merci, and he is wan and palely loitering really wan poor chap, had not seen him for a while but had heard and yesterday saw him, he has lost well not kilos but certainly pounds, he is not sad but he is wan, Tonny's xhibition finished not ingloriously but he too was low in his mind but a bout of skating cheered his Hollandish soul and now he is quite active again, he too wanted to be wan but did not pull it off, I have one of his new pictures, called between them le repas solenelle [sic], pretty good, Bebé is thriving we are to see each other but haven't Hitchcock has disappeared, with the Spaniard so I understand, Hart Crane has joined the band, George Maratier who made the introduction which has led to Hugnet's joys and sorrows is busy being an editor, the Fabrication should be out fairly soon, otherwise finance weighs upon him, but we have almost certainly not completely certainly got our house for next summer, at Belley, but per contra we have domestic upheavals Helene hasn't been she is very ill then there has been a very funny literary intrigue going on when I have heard all about it there is only half just now, I will tell you it will amuse you, and the new Gody, I draw a deep breath there is a new Gody, and one is faithless

        Lots of love and the best always
            Gtrde.

---

intensive . . . fruit: Between the fall of 1928 and summer of 1929 Stein is engaged in a concerted investigation of the sentence, resulting in "Sentences" (*How To Write* 113–213).
belle dame sans merci: This affair will be short-lived, as Stein indicates in following letter. By summer he will begin his love affair with Marcelle Ferry.
le repas solenelle: the solemn [solennel] meal.
Hart Crane: The twenty-nine-year-old American poet arrived in Europe in December 1928 and is visiting Paris, a visit he considers "crucial to the curriculum of every American artist and writer" (Fisher 395). He hopes the excursion will propel his work on *The Bridge*, the long poem for which he will be best known. He introduced himself to Stein in a letter dated 31 Jan. He will leave Europe on 17 July after a brief incarceration for striking a police officer in a bar brawl.
Fabrication: *Morceaux choisis de La fabrication des Américains. Histoire du progrès d'une famille.* See note to Stein, [13? Dec. 1928].
house for next summer: After spotting the stone house on a Bilignin hillside, Stein and Toklas were determined to have it, though it was leased to a lieutenant in the French army. With help from influential friends, they instigated his transfer to Morocco, so that they can now assume the lease. They will rent the house until 1942 (Dydo 325–28). Bilignin is a mile from Belley.
per contra: by way of contrast.
Helene: Hélène, Stein's and Toklas's maid-and-cook until the end of 1913, when she stayed home with her husband and son. Now, her son dead and her husband in financial distress, she has returned for a year to work for Stein and Toklas. Stein writes, "We thought that really Hélène had come back to give the young generation the once over"— the older, prewar generation having included Picasso, Braque, and Rousseau. "She had in a way but she was not impressed in them. She said they made no impression on her which made them all very sad because the legend of her was well known to all Paris" (*Autobiography* 12).

*****

            140 E. 19
            26 fevrier [1929]

Dear Gertrude

    Capitals swell success. N.Y. talks of nothing else since three days. Audience roared with laughter during and bravos afterwards. Critics charmingly confused. Some thought it a good joke, some a bad joke and one or so got quite angry. It is being repeated next Sunday at the house of Walter Sacks (swell theatrical party with champagne and Winthrop Ames and such all got up by Gertrude Newell (the lady who had a brawl with a Sitwell in your house)) and the Chamber Music Society of Boston (toney private concerts they have) is asking for it next month & they intend to pay not only singers but composer as well. Which is swell. I shall do discreet opera selections also at the Sacks party. I enclose assorted clippings. Dont throw them away. Met your friend McBride. Liked him & him me & he heard some opera and liked it. Theatre Guild man not useful at present because he was mad he hadnt thought of it himself and he bit his finger nails in fury all during. I neglected to mention that at the Capitals show the poets were all disgusted with the words and the composers thought the music too low for anything. But the audience's way of taking it proved to me the possibility of having a regular boob success with the opera, at least it might run long enough to pay its expenses and it might just might (and without surprising me at all) make a little money. I return on Ile-de-France March 29. arriving April 3. I shall be glad.

                              Love
                              Virgil

I had after the concert a sweet and complimentary letter from a person named Lindley Hubbell whom I gather to be an acquaintance of yours. Terribly nice letter.

Ganna Walska gave a concert last week and sang an encore song entitled "If no one ever marries me".

Capitals swell success: performed 24 Feb. by Thomson and the Ionian Quartet. He recalls more fully:

    This came off as very lively indeed, with the audience hilarious, so much so in fact that at one point, to prevent the laughter from getting out of hand, from the piano I held up my right arm, palm out traffic-cop-wise, and stopped the fun from stopping the show. At the end there were bravos. There is no question that the performance constituted a success in terms of pleasure given, press space devoted to it, and intellectual excitement created. And a pattern in that excitement was established at this time which I have come since to expect whenever any work by Gertrude Stein and myself is given in America. The literary consensus is always that the music is lovely but the poetry absurd; whereas the music world, at least nine tenths of it, takes the view that Stein's words are great literature but that my music is infantile. The musical press on this occasion mostly took the latter view. (*Virgil Thomson* 136)

N.Y. talks of nothing else: E.g. W. J. Henderson in the *New York Sun*, 25 February:
    It is refreshing to discuss this piece first . . . a bit of burlesque, a travesty on inconsequential chatter such as one has to hear in many assemblies of entirely polite persons possessed of family pedigrees and college educations. The music is of the simplest, mostly chant and passages of patter with farcically solemn cadences. The text is often meaningless and of continuity wholly innocent. The Ionian Quartet sang the thing very seriously, as such matter should be sung, and the composer at the piano comported himself as if he were

publishing a message of pregnant worth to a waiting world. The audience rocked with laughter. And that was something novel at a concert of esoteric modernists.

Charles Isaacson in the *New York Morning Telegraph*, 25 February calls it a "masterpiece" and says, "nothing in seven years of investigations quite exceeded the completely lunatic presentation of 'Capital. Capitals'. . . . the audience roared. Some walked out."

Walter Sacks . . . and Winthrop Ames: The former a painter, the latter a writer, director, producer of Broadway plays.

Lindley Hubbell: Admirer of Stein's writing, author of two books of poetry published by Yale University Press and author of the poem "Promenade chez Nous," in which he recounts a visitor seeing on his wall a photograph of Jo Davidson's sculpture of Stein and exclaiming, "Gaea, the earth mother," and writes of watching the Mississippi moving "so slow and enormous and sure. There is no other river moves in the same way. / The Making of Americans moves in the same way. The Mississippi River comes out of the earth and the Making of Americans comes out of Gertrude Stein in the same way" (*larus* 1 nos. 5–7 [April, May, June, 1928], 40). He will publish a poem entitled "A Letter to Gertrude Stein," which neither addresses nor refers to Stein but implies that she laughs and inspires laughter (*Pagany* 1 no. 2 [Spring 1930], 37). In a letter to Stein, Hubbell writes of the concert, "It seems to me that Mr. Thomson has caught in his music all the charm, the humor and the loveliness of your lines" (24 Feb. 1929).

Ganna Walska: beautiful Polish-born opera singer, hugely rich through repeatedly marrying and divorcing wealthy men.

*****

To "M. Virgil Thomson / 140 East 19 Street / New York / N.Y. / U.S.A."

27 RUE DE FLEURUS
[11 March 1929]

My dear Virgil,

Delighted at the success perhaps we will get on the radio and the gramophone yet and have royalties and buy a prize Boddlington terrier and a telephone and pay for my new Ford car, perhaps, but anyway I am most awfully pleased. I also had a nice letter from the Hubbell man he is one of Larus's and wrote transition a nice letter in which he said that one should not be discouraged by the remarks of the articulate middle aged which I thought a nice phrase, and so we have been in correspondence a little since, I am awfully glad you and Henry McBride liked each other he is alright, we're seeing the band this afternoon, at Hugnet's, Hugnet now freed from thrall is himself again and wrote me a delightful letter of liberation, it will be nice telling them all about you, and it will be nice seeing you, Hitchcock René and Bernard all back, were separately here but we missed them but one would miss anybody with a new Ford car but I like your success even more, enough said and I am pleased with your interview and xplanations,

Alwys

Gtrde.

Boddlington terrier: Bedlington terrier, a breed often described as having the head of a lamb and heart of a lion. In two months' time, Stein and Toklas will adopt their lamb-like French poodle Basket. See [11 May 1929]. A year later Stein jokes to Thomson that Basket "has turned from a lamb into a lion" ([16 April 1930]).

Hubbell man . . . letter: Lindley Williams Hubbell (see note to previous letter). In his letter to *transition* XVIII (15 Nov. 1928), Hubbell thanks the magazine for reprinting Stein pamphlets difficult to obtain, explaining, "A knowledge of these works is indispensable to an understanding of the path that Miss Stein has taken from Three Lives to Useful Knowledge. And an understanding of that is indispensable to young American writers. I do not think that you realize how widely accepted Miss Stein is in America—not by the articulate middle aged, but by the young ones." Hubbell's letters to Stein typify the praise she enjoys from her devotees; in a letter of Oct. 31, 1930 he writes "Thank you for being what you are—a rock from which so many of us can quarry for our little structures."

letter of liberation: Referring to the "belle dame sans merci" of her earlier letter, Stein has received this news (translated here) from Hugnet:

It's "all" over, no more "Boo hoo."
I'm free.
I wrote a poem about it. At night sometimes it hurts, of course. But I'm free.
(March 1929)

pleased with your interview and xplanations: Thomson sent Stein clippings from various papers, all excerpting his typed "explanation" of "Capital, Capitals," copies of which he handed out to journalists. His explanation is most fully published in the *New York Herald Tribune* (24 February 1929):

The text of 'Capital, Capitals' represents a conversation among the four capitals of Provence—Aix, Arles, Avignon and Beaux and isn't about anything any more than any pleasant conversation is about anything although mention is made of various subjects which capitals might be likely to talk about if they talked, such as weather, climate, the seasons, visitors, beds, geography and mountains. It is about twenty minutes long, or fifteen, depending on how fast you sing it.

The music is of the greatest simplicity, mostly chanting; that is, it takes place in that border-land between chanting and singing where simple intonation gets tired of itself and breaks into melody every time it gets a chance. The accompaniment, when there is any, is a simple composition made out of four motifs, two of them short rhythmic figures on one note, and two of them short scale-figures. In the middle of the piece there are some plain chords and toward the end the descending scale-figure is amplified by being played in chords.

The vocal parts are written in what might be called normal or natural prosody; that is to say, there is very little distortion or false accenting of the words. And there is no polyphony. The piece retains its conversational character to the end and the singers refrain from interrupting one another or singing more than one at a time although there is a good deal of rapid back-talk. There are a high and low tenor, a baritone, and a bass.

*****

140 E. 19
21 March [1929]

Dear Gertrude

Boston was sweet and oh so sweet in gentle spring weather and she received me as one of her own and although lots of people didnt understand everybody took it very seriously and nobody there thinks anymore that I am a bad boy and the Harvard boys loved you and now I am home again and on April 4th (Ile-de-France) I shall be really home again. The Addises were sweet and nice to me and sent you love and I send you love. And clippings. And all. O dear wont it be nice to be home in quai Voltaire.

Love
Virgil

Letters with Notes   111

received me as one of her own: On St. Patrick's Day, Thomson conducted his *Sonata da Chiesa* at the Sunday concert of the Boston Flute Players' Club.

the Harvard boys: Thomson remembers, "The Harvard Musical Club evening was informal, companionable, and as to repertory comprehensive. My merrier works were received with jollity, selections from *Four Saints* with awe (no reserves), my *Symphony on a Hymn Tune*, played in four-hand piano version, with frankly expressed bewilderment."

His long American visit resulted in much publicity but, he writes, "No music publisher, . . . no opera house, no conductor was showing interest. Even the League of Composers had given me, through three different representatives, what I took for a planned brush-off" (*Virgil Thomson* 141).

Addises: Louise and Emmet, he a friend of Stein, who wrote a portrait of him, *Emmet Addis the Doughboy; a Pastoral* (*Useful Knowledge* 1928).

*****

To "M. Virgil Thomson / 17 Quai Voltaire / Paris."

   ROSE IS A ROSE IS A ROSE IS A ROSE [circular]
   27 RUE DE FLEURUS
             Tuesday [*9 April 1929*]

My dear Virgil,

 Are you nicely happy in your home will you come to supper to-morrow Wednesday, Hart Crane is coming in in the evening and it might amuse you and him to meet you and him, Let us know. Seven o'clock,

                  Gtrde.

to-morrow Wednesday: In his pocket diary, Thomson enters "7 Gertrude" on 10 April.

Hart Crane: See note to Stein [23 Feb. 1929]. Thomson will remember that Crane, whom he admired, "was too busy drinking and getting over it to make dates with" (*Virgil Thomson* 110). Crane will leave for the south of France on 19 April.

*****

             17 Quai Voltiare
             Wednesday [*10 April 1929*]

Dear Gertrude

 I have broken the emotional tension of return by my usual method of catching cold but that is some better and I shall be to supper tonight at seven hoping not to leave any of it at your house otherwise I am happy in my home though not really because the dirty carpet worries me and the curtains but my next door neighbor has died (not Lucy) and maybe I'll get his flat which is nicer.

                Love
                Virgil

tension of return: According to his pocket diary, Thomson left New York on 29 March. The diary is blank through 9 April.

Lucy: Lucie Delarue-Mardrus, fifty-four-year-old journalist, poet, novelist, painter, and amateur musician, "tall and dark-haired, with soft brown eyes." She and Thomson have become friends and frequent visitors in one another's apartments.

*****

To "M. Virgil Thomson / 17 Quai Voltaire / Paris."

27 RUE DE FLEURUS
[30 April 1929]

My dear Virgil,

We are off the end of the week and want you for supper before we go. Will you come in Thursday at 7.30, George Hugnet is coming too,

Lots of love
Gtrde.

*****

To "M. Virgil Thomson / 17 Quai Voltaire / Paris."

[11 May 1929]
Bilignin.
I did not get it spelled right ~~Billingen~~
par Belley
Ain

My dear Virgil

Here we are and very nice it is and even nicer and Basket and the car and the country and the house and everything has been so xciting that I have had no time to tell you that Carl is sailing on the 10 and he says you are a lamb and I guess you are from time to time,

Lots of love
Gtrde.

Basket: French poodle, Basket I (1929-1938). Stein and Toklas acquired Basket right before moving to Bilignin. In an embellished account, Toklas recalls, "For years after reading *The Princess Casamassima* I had wanted a white poodle. One day at the dog show in Paris Gertrude saw a pair of white poodles with a puppy and the puppy jumped into her arms" (*What is Remembered* 124). Stein says that "listening to the rhythm of his water drinking made her recognize the difference between sentences and paragraphs, that paragraphs are emotional and that sentences are not" (*Autobiography* 268).
Carl . . . lamb: In a letter dated 22 Apr. 1929, Van Vechten writes that he is sailing on the Majestic on May 10, hoping to arrive in Paris before Stein and Toklas depart for Belley. His letter ends, "Virgil is a *lamb!*" (*The Letters of Gertrude Stein and Carl Van Vechten* 194).

*****

17 Quai Voltaire
13 May [1929]

Dear Gertrude

I am glad you are proper and so in your new house. Mine is still in disorder but hope is eternal and I have also a visitor. Maurice Grosser, who is nice and I am glad Carl says I am a lamb and I guess I mostly was with him but then that wasnt much. Bébé did me again as portrait very good and I did him but very bad because it was premature and I shouldn't have really tried to make music just yet otherwise all fine and weather balmy. I was glad seeing Picasso at your house and in the flesh and I have remembered it a good deal so far also here is a clipping about literature.

Love
Virgil

I did him: *Christian Bérard: prisonniers,* 8 May 1929.

*****

To "M. Virgil Thomson / 17 Quai Voltaire / Paris"

[18 May 1929]
Bilignin
par Belley
Ain.

My dear Virgil,

transition is printing the opera, and there is to be a note saying there is music your music and also a statement of what and when the Harvard glee club are doing. It looks very nice in proof and send facts to me by return post as they want the proofs at once. Basket has been vaccinated and he is low in his mind otherwise we are happy and useful and next week I hope to be making sentences or liking sentences love to Bebé I am pleased he has made a good portrait,

Gtrde

---

transition is printing the opera: The libretto for *Four Saints* appears in *transition* 16/17 (June 1929): 39 72.

*****

17 Quai Voltaire
Monday of Pentecoste [*20 May* 1929]

Dear Gertrude

Please dont mention the Harvard Glee Club except to say if you like that there exists an excerpt from the Third Act known as *Saints' Procession* arranged by the composer for the Harvard Glee Club. I dont want to embarrass them in any way which is the surest way of making them change minds since no date is set although presumably the coming season sometime. I have a horrid feeling anyway that publishing the opera-words is premature and likely to cause trouble

    A. By satisfying one-half of the public curiosity about same.

    B. By removing from me all the honor your collaboration bestowed upon me. Because now it will look as if I just picked up a printed text and used it and no amount of explanation will do any good.

    C. In case of its performance, a previous publication of the libretto makes difficult its proper separate publication at that time.

I'm all agin it and state same for whatever right I may have therein which naturally is very small if any. But no no I am agin it really agin it and now I've got that bit off my chest where it has been weighing heavily since this morning. There is to be a concert on June 9th of American youth (Copland-Sessions auspices) at Salle Gaveau and they want your words so I thought we would give them Susie & Preciosilla prefixed by a little Hugnet and [Duchesse de] Rohan (provided a proper American singer can be found). It is to be the *bonne bouche* of an otherwise heavy and instrumental program, the only other vocal music being three short and uninteresting ditties by a kid named Robinowitch or something similar to three very dumb poems out of a book called Chamber Music by one J. Joyce. I find the juxtaposition amusing and entirely advantageous. (Not my suggestion at all, however.) But knowing the delicacy of your relations with said Joyce in public eye, I make possibility of your quick veto and if so please make it quick by which I mean telegraph. Otherwise all goes as is. Paris is nice and I went to Ermenonville for the day today

                    Momentary hiatus

Philip Lasell just came in it being midnight and now I suppose my troubles begin but that is spring and visitors and you are so wise to have only Basket on your hands.

                                    Love

                                      Virgil

[On the letter Toklas drafts the following in pencil:]
Written for an opera for Virgil Thomson An excerpt—from the third act known as Saints Procession has been arranged by the composer for the Harvard Glee Club

---

bonne bouche: best item (on the menu).
Robinowitch . . . Joyce: Israel Citkowitz (not Robinowitch) composed music for three Joyce poems. He was then a pupil of Boulanger, who arranged the program, which included Copland's *Vitebsk* trio and *Two Pieces for String Quartet*, Roy Harris's *Sextet*, Carlos Chávez's short piano sonata, and five of Thomson's works, including settings of Stein he mentions, sung by Marthe-Marthine.

                                      *****

To "M. Virgil Thomson / 17 Quai Voltaire / Paris."

[22 May 1929]
Bilignin
par Belley
Ain.

My dear Virgil,

There there you never can tell, I thought you would be pleased but you are not at all and yet I think you will be finally, you see they have as a foot note that the opera was written for you, then there will be a considerable notice in newspapers and that will reach the general public and make them curious and from past xperience I know that is a good thing particularly as it is the general public we are hoping to reach and they take a lot of preparation, I am quite sure I am right and when I am quite sure I am right I very often am, awfully pleased with your concert scheme and it will be nice and am sorry we won't be there. Had a [letter?] from Henry McBride he was pleased with you and most of all with your imperturbability combined with a perfect pitch.

Best to you alwys
Gtrde.

*****

[23 May 1929]

Dear Gertrude it's quite all right and I'm all used to the idea now and as you say you never can tell and I really got it all off my chest by writing it maybe I was just mad at not being asked. I went to Ermenonville for Pentecoste and it was lovely and the Rochefoucaulds live in the chateau now and they have made a hotel and a dancing and a bar next door to the park and called it Au Maxim's de la Rochefoucauld. And I have a new table and two blown-glass candlesticks with mirror inside and Philip isnt really bothering much and I have also four new linen pillow-cases and Tonny is looking fine and fat and Bébé is in Brittany with Max J. "on such a funny travel" and B. Faÿ gives a pendaison de crémaillère on Saturday and I tea today sous la coupole de l'Institut and the weather is of a grandeur. I dont like my new wall-paper and am having it changed tomorrow & my carpet is back and curtains coming tomorrow too. So by Saturday night I shall be really I hope & pray arranged and properly at home. Love Alice & greetings Basket &

Toujours à vous
Virgil

Pentecoste.... B. Faÿ gives a pendaison de crémaillère: Pentecost is 19 May. According to Thomson's pocket diary, he goes to the "Institut" on 23 May and Faÿ's party is on 25 May at 6 o'clock.
pendaison de crémaillère: housewarming party.
sous la coupole: under the dome.

new wall-paper . . . carpet . . . curtains: His former tenants, three young women, and their boyfriends made it necessary to redecorate his apartment.

*****

Sunday [26 May 1929]

Dear Gertrude

Here's a clipping and a greetings. Passed sweet soirée with Hugnet last night. We prepare a short opera. B. Faÿ gave party and Bravig & E. Paul played nice music. E. Paul made me sweet talk and I promised to write him a piece. Weather is hot and grand. I'm glad you are pleased about concert. Hugnet is off Gaby. Film is finished. I suppose he writes all this. Marthe sings you well. The Institute Tea was a frost. I arrived at five and every gateau was eat. I hope your country is as nice as my Paris. Life is nice but I remain quite sterile. No news of Carl except paper says he arrived.

Love.

Virgil

Hugnet last night: According to his pocket diary, Thomson met with Hugnet at 7:30, 25 May.
nice music: Elliot Paul plays accordion; Bravig Imbs, fiddle. See Thomson, 22 juillet [1929].
off Gaby: "Gabrielle" appears in the original text of Hugnet's "Enfances" (composed 1929, printed in *Pagany* 1931), but is revised as "Marie" in the book version (Paris: Editions Cahiers d'Art, 1933). Dydo notes that sometime later, Hugnet edited leftover copies by hand, crossing out "Marie" and restoring "Gabrielle." (An Yvonne similarly becomes "Irène," then Yvonne again). He also crossed out the dedication to Marcelle Ferry, suggesting the latter's role in the erasures of Gabrielle and Yvonne (Dydo 310).
Film is finished: Hugnet's *La Perle*.

*****

[Magazine article, "Gertrude Stein" by Patrice, *Paris Comet: Anglo-American Magazine* (May 1929) with photograph by Man Ray on facing page. Before her words to Thomson, Stein writes around the title:]
A Much Disputed Writer
Have you seen transition. It is timely if you like it say so sweetly if not say so sweetly, moralities unsuccessfully imposed upon Basket. There was a later thing in the Herald, did you see it, I sent it to Hugnet, supposing you had. have a good time and come to see us [in some?] way, have not seen Orbes, Best to Mrs L.

G.

Fabrication is rather splendid. Thanks. G.

Fabrication: The year before, Thomson was involved in the early stages of translating selections of *The Making of Americans* (published as *Morceaux choisis de La fabrication des Américains*). See note to Stein [*13?* Dec. 1928].
have not seen Orbes: See note to Stein [26 July 1929].

*****

To "M. Virgil Thomson / 17 Quai Voltaire / Paris."

[2 June 1929]
Bilignin
par Belley,
Ain.

My dear Virgil,

Carl is in London until June third at the Carlton then he comes to Paris and then to Berlin, and I guess then we will see him here, I am awfully sorry to be missing you all but we are awfully pleased with ourselves, Basket sometimes less so because he is being brought up and that never is an unmitigated joy it is such a natural feeling not to want to be coerced. There was a young fellow so like Tonny at the Bazar at Belley just now and he was most truculently buying a pair of suspenders. How do you wear them said the vendeuse, I wear them suspended says Tonny well the practic of these says the vendeuse is that you can wear them suspended or fastened. Now I ask you Virgil how do you wear suspenders suspended. The world is full of mystery, Elliot Pauls are here and they told us about Bernard's party it seems to have been quite hectic in efforts and in hours, I have not started to work yet but I am on my way, lots of love   Gtrde

---

Bazar: general store.
practic: pratique - n. practise, adj. handy.
vendeuse: saleswoman.
Elliot Pauls: Pauls' then wife was Camille Haynes; she was the second of what would be five.

*****

[from Toklas] Postcard of Goya's *La Pradera de San Isidro* to "M. Virgil Thomson / 17 Quai Voltaire / Paris / Seine"

[5 June 1929]

Dear V—Please please at once save poor Basket from starving or worse by sending me contre remboursement from a shop on the avenue Malakoff left hand side very shortly after the Place Victor Hugo—specializing in accessories for dogs
1 box Sprates biscuits pour jeunes chiens.
I'll love you if you do—A.B.T.

---

contre remboursement: I will pay you back.
jeunes chiens: young dogs.

*****

118   Letters with Notes

17 Quai Voltaire
7 juin [1929]

Dear Gertrude.

I sent off Basket's bisquits immediately and I hope they have arrived and that Basket is better. My house is now cleaned as I probably wrote you and I've had two nice parties and I've seen the Berman pictures and been properly knocked over and took him a customer. Also one for Tonny. Saw Pavelich's and wasnt. Remain faithfully to Baby's drawing. And certainly our little mystery story is not really over yet. Carl sends premonition of arrival from London. Aaron Copland publishes sweet tribute to me in a magazine called Modern Music. I saw a Russian ballet by Chirico. Awful low. You look well on a whole page of enclosed program. Please return the equally-enclosed clippings on the state of art and morals. Hugnet is sweet these days, when seen. Peter Smith's father died in Boston. Again across an ocean because wife & daughter are in chateau near Bath (England) and wife confined to bed of broken hip. So Russell [Hitchcock] went over to console, because he hadnt really left Paris at all as he was about to a month ago. Brewer arrives tomorrow. I have no idea how to suspend a suspender, though I may do it everyday without knowing. All the wachumacallits are triste about Barataud. The weather has gone rainish. I have a dark green wine bottle with round ridges all the way up. Strawberries are delicious, especially the cherries.

Love toujours
Virgil

---

sweet tribute: Copland writes:
Virgil Thomson can teach us all how to set English to music. If you insist on combining words and music you must be prepared to sacrifice one or the other. There is no such thing as equality of words and music, the few exceptions to this rule are special cases. To Thomson, words come first; so, in the manner of Satie's *Socrate*, he merely draws a frame of music around the words. In his setting of texts by Gertrude Stein—in the opera *Four Saints in Three Acts*, in *Capital Capitals*, in his numerous songs—he has caught the rhythms and inflections which make the English language different from any other. Without the complexities of the English madrigalists, he manages to superimpose over an elementary accompaniment an amazing variety of rhythms merely because he allows the words to have the naturalness of speech. It would be impossible to translate these compositions into any other language; what better test of their fineness could be asked. (*Modern Music* 4 no. 4 (May–June 1929): 17–18)
a Russian Ballet by Chirico: *Le Bal*, scenery and costumes by Giorgio de Chirico, music by Vittorio Rieti, directed by Diaghilev.
Brewer: In 1928 Joseph Brewer of the publisher Payson & Clarke arranged for Stein to collect her short pieces on America under the title *Useful Knowledge*.
wachumacallits are triste about Barataud: "Handsome Charlie" Barataud is a thirty-three-year-old war veteran who married money and become an amateur tennis player and a federal tennis referee. He has been convicted of murdering a taxi driver named Etienne Faure and, five days later, his own young lover, Bertrand Pegnet. He claims innocence of the first murder but refuses to name the killers, sons of upper-class families, his companions on the night of the crime. He claims that the second killing resulted from a mutual suicide pact. The sport of the elite, tennis had opened doors for him to Limoges high society, whose members are the "wachumacallits" sad about his conviction. Today, 7 June, at Limoges, the jury votes eleven to one for the death penalty, but he is sentenced to life at hard labour owing to an error, real or feigned, in writing down the jury's

response to questions about extenuating circumstances. This evening an outraged working-class mob of 3000 is rioting in protest that Barataud, one of "the idle depraved bourgeoisie" is not to be executed (*New York Times*, 8 June 1929; Brousseau, 9–78, 168).

*****

Postcard of "Sproat Lake, from Kleetza Lodge," to]"Miss Alice Toklas / Bilignin par Belley / Ain"

[8 June *1929*]

Dear Alice

The Goya was lovely and I do hope Basket is getting nourished and I am glad you asked me because there was a good Boissier cake shop in the same block and an adventure in the place itself.

Love
Virgil.

*****

To "M. Virgil Thomson / 17 Quai Voltaire / Paris."

[10 June 1929]

My dear Virgil,

Voici Basket looking for bisquits, and now he has them, also the clippings back and Eugene even to the toe, and otherwise very content with everything, the concert does look nice, have sent the tickets on to the deserving, Carl writes that he is hitting it up in London so I guess Paris will be less hectic, I delight in Russell's activities mostly when they are not which they are not active, The Elliot Pauls are leaving to-morrow, they have been in Belley, and liking it, so they may get to the concert, he was very sweet while he was here, I have just begun to work quite nicely, so many words to the line, and how many words to the line. It begins very well. Sentences for the moment are finished, also a nice little portrait of Basket, which might most *modernly* be put to music, lots of love and lets know all about how it went,

Gtrde.

Voici: Here is.
so many words to the line: From the work she is now writing, "Five Words In A Line" (1929), later printed in *Reflections On the Atomic Bomb, Volume I of the Previously Uncollected Writings of Gertrude Stein*, ed. Robert Bartlett Haas (Los Angeles: Black Sparrow, 1975), 142.
portrait of Basket: "Basket" (*Portraits and Prayers* 181). This spring Stein is also working on her film scenario, *Film. Deux Soeurs Qui Ne Sont Pas Soeurs*, which features a white poodle.

*****

To "M. Virgil Thomson / 17 Quai Voltaire / Paris."

[15 June 1929]

My dear Virgil,

Seventeenth your concert and Basket's fourth birthday, spanking monthly and the very best of good luck to us all, Remember me to Marthe Martine,

Alwys
Gtrde.

Seventeenth your concert: On 17 June 1929 at the Salle Chopin in Rue Daru, a "Concert of Works of Young Americans": Copland's *Vitebsk, Lento molto, Rondino*; Citkowitz's settings of the Joyce poems, Chávez's *Sonata for Piano*; Harris's *Sextette*; and Thomson's *La Valse Grégorienne, La Seine, Le Berceau de Gertrude Stein, Susie Asado,* and *Preciosilla*.

*****

[*Possible placement*] [1929]

Dear Gertrude

The duchess [de Clermont-Tonnerre] came across. Ordered a 20-minute play in French.

Love
Virgil

---

a 20-minute play: The Duchesse has commissioned Hugnet and Thomson to collaborate on a short opera, a project never finished. Hugnet wrote "L'Invention de la rose" and also "Pléthore et pénurie," but Thomson eventually pulled out of the collaboration "on grounds that Hugnet was a purely lyric poet without stage instinct" (*Virgil Thomson* 162).

*****

To "M. Virgil Thomson / 17 Quai Voltaire / Paris."

[26 June 1929]
Bilignin.
par Belley
Ain.

My dear Virgil,

It seems to have gone off [awfully?] well all of it, and everybody is happy about it including me and you, xpect to hear from you soon, but

Letters with Notes

anyway even Elliot Paul seems to be fallen. Have just sent care of you a letter to M. Marthine thanking her, I am most awfully pleased, and Carl is he there, am beginning to work and otherwise most awfully busy country busy which is busier than city busy but more not calm a little less calm but not xhausting, Love and best wishes   Gtrde.

It seems to have gone off . . . well: Reporting on the concert of 17 June, The Paris *Herald* of 20 June announces that "principal honours" went to Thomson. See note to Stein [15 June 1929].
M. Marthine thanking: Marthe-Marthine sang all the vocal works at the concert of 17 June.

*****

Sunday [*late June* 1929]

Dear Gertrude

Such a busy time and I didn't write you that the concert went off with much success to us you and me, and Joyce came & liked us and so did Adrienne [Monnier] who said sweet things next day to Mme. Langlois about "fine et spirituel et de l'ironie dedans" etc. which I suppose means that Antheil isnt "civilisation francaise" anymore since he has moved to Germany and written an opera in German and so with my duchess [de Clermont-Tonnerre] & Hugnet maybe I'm it anyway Tonny said it was like an arrived maitre who loaned his *concours* to a concert of aspiring young ones and the Gide faction it seems was also there and has passed around the word that I am the berries and the Fay's came and are passing around same and naturally my friends are doing same because they can say how lamentable American music is except me who live here and really it is surprising how much glory seems to accrue from a concert that cost nothing in fact was given with any intention but that of popularizing me who was supposed I guess to be just comic relief. I am sending you a poster and the E. Paul victory you have ready heard and it was lots of fun you triumphing in Belley with Joyce in person to receive the plaudits and Nadia Boulanger thinks my music is horrid and Marthe got a thousand francs for singing and Carl is here but drinking night & day and I still havent done a stroke of work since my reentry but am leaving Thursday for the midi and hope to be rewarded by saint pigeon with maybe a fragment of idea any way I'll make opera-score. Bravig laid poems on me and asked music for same and I said they didnt need any.
Maurice goes South with me and I come back 1st August to motor a minute with Mrs. Lasell and then in September I visit Madame Langlois at Flumet in Savoie so it doesnt look as if there were much tranquility for working but Maurice & Madame Langlois dont bother it is only motoring with Mrs. Lasell that is time out and that can be put down to profit and loss. G. Maratier is fat as anything. I sent Marthe her letter. Charles de Noailles gave a costume party (costumes de matières sans fil) and everybody was in

glass and aluminium and oil cloth & celluloid & such and Bernard said it was the prettiest party in years and now I sort of wish I had gone but I hadnt bothered to think up a costume and also I was extremely tired that night from having had a party myself the night before. Eugene's exposition is on and not selling well if Bernard is to be believed. The vernissage was hectic because he ran a kind of 1st and 2nd class compartments with chosen ones being invited back-stage for champagne, which offended all the others, and all his friends trying to encourage one another by saying how nice the pictures looked all together and how well they were hung. René [Crevel] says if this exposition doesnt réussit the only thing left for Eugene is to open a night-club. Russel did go to England but he came back in four days and he is still around and quite tiresome. So is Carl tiresome but he is sympathetic even with all his drinking and lechery. The *Americans*, making of, is beautiful as book, seldom seen better, and the translation is extraordinarily fine and the preface is darling. Havent seen portrait yet but presume it to be excellent, as the others I saw of yours were. The ensemble is in every way a knock-out and I should imagine it will be remarked same. My own *Saint in Seven* I have not seen. Hugnet writes me a one-act libretto called *L'Invention de la Rose* and some of it is good. Au revoir after this long letter and love thanks pretty photos and love to Alice and hoping you are same

Love
Virgil

Joyce came & liked us: Thomson will say, "I met James Joyce through Sylvia Beach and George Antheil. He never failed to tell me that he liked my work. He didn't come up after the concert and talk to me. He would go home, and I would see him later at Sylvia's bookstore" (to Dilworth, 3 Feb. 1981).
Adrienne Monnier, French writer and editor, runs her bookstore, *La Société des Amis des Livres*, opposite Sylvia Beach's bookstore, publishes the magazine *Le Navire d'argent* and will soon publish Larbaud's French translation of Joyce's *Ulysses*.
maitre: master.
concours: support.
the berries: 1920s slang for "great."
comic relief ... Boulanger thinks my music horrid: She helped arrange the program. When Thomson resumed studying with her in 1925, he found her direction stifling and quit, for which, he thinks, she has not forgiven him and regards his subsequent musical development with reserve (*Virgil Thomson* 146).
midi: noon.
saint pigeon: See note to Thomson, 31 July, 1927.
Charles de Noailles gave a costume party: 19 June (Thomson's pocket diary).
costume de matières sans fil: costumes of materials without thread, that is, the guests were not to wear cloth clothing.
réussit: succeed.
The *Americans*, making of ... and the translation: See note to Stein [13? Dec. 1928].

*****

Hotel des Bananiers
Villefranche-sur-mer
A.M.
4 July [1929]

Dear Gertrude

Thank you for *Comet* and for kind words therein. A gentleman from the Hessian State Theatre (Hessische Landestheater) in Darmstadt has written to know about maybe producing the *Saints* next season and I have answered where I can be seen and written S. Beach to send him a Transition. Also me one, because I havent seen it. And I shant be displeased, because that's all over now and one cant be sorry very long about what's already done and I must admit it comes in handy this time having it printed.

Weather is hot and pleasant and I have been laid up with an *insolation* but that is better although my back is still sore. And maybe I'll move in to Nice where the food is better but maybe not too. Anyway this is my address and I shall be around here likely all of July.

Sherry Mangan has sold *Larus* to a man with money to run it & same takes over unfinished subscriptions & editorial policy only hasnt any foolish ideas about poetry & prose. Sherry appears in Paris for a moment in August and commissioned to gather a few manuscripts for his successor among which you and so he will probably write you ahead of time and maybe he can choose from several pieces and return the superfluous before leaving France and I hope you wont hold his foolish ideas against the new administration.

I guess that's all just now except the usually appropriate sentiments and again thanks love Alice

            I embrace you
              Virgil

A.M.: *Alpes Maritimes*.
Comet: International culture magazine published simultaneously in Paris, London, and New York.
A gentleman . . . Darmstadt: Edwin Denby, poet, dancer, assistant stage manager, asking for the score of *Four Saints*, which now exists only in one pencil copy: "incomplete as to piano accompaniment and the choral passages. Of orchestral score . . . not one page." Thomson will send the complete piano score in September (*Virgil Thomson* 147). Hessisches Landestheater in Darmstadt has been interested in experimental works of late.
insolation: sunstroke.
Mangan has sold *Larus*: *larus* having ceased publication in 1928, earlier in 1929 Mangan transferred the unexpired subscriptions to Richard Johnson (called Johns) of Boston, who now edits *Pagany*, which will continue for three years, publishing Mary Butts, Ezra Pound, William Carlos Williams, Erskine Caldwell, Jean Cocteau, e. e. cummings, John Dos Passos, Paul Bowles, and Harold Rosenberg. It is in the opening issue that Georges Hugnet writes, in French, his two-page essay on Thomson's music (appendix A).

*****

To "M. Virgil Thomson / Hotel des Bananiers / Villefanche-sur-mer / ~~Haute-Marne~~ Alpes M^{imes}"

             [8 July 1929]
             Bilignin.
             par Belley,
             Ain.

My dear Virgil,

Darmstadt would be nice Hessen Darmstadt is so historical, and sure I forgive Sherry, I forgive any body who prints me and love anybody who prints and pays. It might be nice for them to do a little series of portraits of the rising generation, recent portraits of the rising generation, a nice little lot, yours and Bebé which are both very good Bernard Fay, Pavlik, a little one of Tonny, a little old one of Hemingway if they want to be timely and a very nice one of Basket. George Hugnet is appearing in a new American mag. the Blues and they seem very pleased with it. Otherwise we are growing vegetables are eating our own sweet peas and caging our own string beans, Basket is eating bread an art he is slowly mastering and I am making natural paragraphs which I hope will become a pleasant pastime, and that's all just now,

Alwys
Gtrde.

---

yours and Bebé . . . Basket: This idea would result in *Dix Portraits*. The portraits she refers to are "Virgil Thomson," "Christian Berard," "Bernard Fay," "Pavlick Tchelitchev or Adrian Arthur," "Kristians Tonny," "He And They, Hemingway," and "Basket."
Blues: A short-lived little magazine edited by Charles Henri Ford in Columbus, Mississippi, "perhaps the youngest and freshest" of the little magazines which, Stein liked to say, "have died to make verse free" (*Autobiography* 260). Her portrait "George Hugnet" appears in *Blues* 1, no. 6 (July 1929).

*****

Villefranche
Bananiers
22 juillet [1929]

Dear Gertrude

The Western Union sends me my money back for your birthday cable that never got there and same has been converted into a late but none the less birthday cake which will be arriving or has chez vous and may my love always seem as sweet to you and weigh as little. The sojourn has been lovely and some work done and much health restored and I am thin and brown and I can do portraits now for four clarinets. There are one of Maurice and three of Bébé (en prison, en soldat, en personne (chair et os)) and a waltz for Elliot P. & Bravig to play on accordion & fiddle. Frances Blood has a finished accompaniment and the opera has begun to develop some action and scenery ideas thanks to Maurice. I go back to Paris on Sunday to say au revoir Madame Langlois and meet Mrs. Lasell and in another week will start out in a motor with same and granddaughter for chaperon to see the Dôme and Le Puy and thence to Spain. I had thought of leaving Nice by auto-car for Grenoble and thence by train to Paris spending the day at Belley en route but it turns out to be dearer than I thought and very complicated as to hours and baggage and I have some more work to do here before leaving so that project gets sadly renounced and likely I shall be able to arrange same in September when I go to see Madame Langlois in Savoy. In the meantime many happy returns of everything and my thoughts to Alice. Je vous embrasse toutes deux.

Virgil

Birthday cable . . . , happy returns: Thomson's wishes and cake are mysterious, Stein's birthday being Feb. 3rd, Toklas's April 30th. The birthday in question could be Basket's, Thomson responding whimsically to last month's information that the 17th is the dog's "birthday, spanking monthly" (Stein [15 June 1929]). But Basket is not mentioned here. A clue may appear in "A Birthday Book": The line for July 14th begins "July the fourteenth July the fourteenth fifty," fifty being the age Stein turned in 1924, the year of its composition. Perhaps there is some private joke about a preferred birthdate recorded in "A Birthday Book" and shared with Thomson, 1929 marking Stein's fifty-fifth birthday so perhaps an occasion to act on it.
I can do portraits . . . fiddle: *Portraits of Ladies: Exercise in Composition: for 4 Clarinets; Christian Bérard, prisonnier; Christian Bérard, soldat; Christian Bérard en personne; Le Bains-Bar: waltzes for violin and accordion.*
chair et os: in the flesh.
Frances Blood: Stein's *A Portrait of F. B.* (published in *Geography and Plays*, 1922), which Thomson is setting to music.
Je vous . . . deux: I kiss you both.

*****

Postcard of "Sermon sur la Montagne par Loys Prat peint a freque dans le hall de la Chocolaterie d'Aiguebelle," to "M. Virgil Thomson / 17 Quai Voltaire / Paris."

[26 July 1929]

It was and is sweet and light and wonderfully brown sugar and we liked it. Sorry you did not make us we always can be made from Lyons, and better luck next time, say how do you do to Spain for us, and kind remembrance to Mrs. L. that is both the Mrs. L. I never did see Orbes, did you, and is the Dial dead, it said so in the Herald but is it and how did it die, and best to you always

Gtrde.

---

never did see Orbes: "Un Saint en Sept," Louise Langlois's translation of Stein's "A Saint In Seven," appeared in *Orbes* no. 2 (Spring 1929), 63–68. This piece is introduced by "La Vie de Gertrude Stein," 59–61. For an English translation of "La Vie," see appendix D.
the Dial: Little magazine publishing important Modernist writers, including T. S. Eliot, Marianne Moore, and e .e. cummings, ceased publication in July 1929. It had published Stein's "Composition as Explanation" and "A Long Gay Book" in 1926 and 1927, respectively.

*****

17 Quai Voltaire
3 August [1929]

Dear Gertrude the Dial a natural death because papa Watson that is Sibley's papa got tired of paying 50,000 dollars a year and I dont blame him. Mrs. Lasell is here. Greets you. We leave in motor the 10th. Pyrenees

& some Spain as per plan. Carl is here. Loved Madrid. Madame Langlois gone to Flumet. Writes its cold. Saw opera in Transition. It looks well. Godawful magazine. No news from Darmstadt. Nice cool weather. Wish August was over.

> Love
> Virgil

I suppose Henry McBride lacks a job now and several others.

---
papa Watson: James Sibley Watson, since 1919 co-owner and editor of *The Dial*.

*****

Postcard of "Le Puy - Le Château de l'Arbousset et le mont volcanique Denise," to "Miss Gertrude Stein / Bilignin / par Belay / Ain / Francia"

[Aug. 1929]

Dear Gertrude - I was where the picture says but now I am in San Sebastian and in three days I shall be in Madrid. Today I saw St. Ignatius's house at Loyola and it has a solid silver room & a lapis lazuli one and lots of nice relics. I hope you are well and right and writing and well and that Alice ditto & so also Basket but not writing

> Love, Virgil

St. Ignatius's house: His birthplace, the Renaissance granite palace of the Loyola family.

*****

Postcard of "Pont de La Balme (Savoie)" to "Mons. Virgil Thomson / Pension Freddy / à VILLEFRANCHES SUR MER/ ALPES MARITIMES"

[17 Aug. 1929]

My dear Virgil

Here we are but sadly without you, but better luck next time
> Love, Gtrde.

Ta lettre était belle et bonne. Je vais t'écrire en tâchant d'etre à ton niveau. Je t'embrasse.
> GEORGES [Hugnet]

Meilleur souvenir, et toutes mes amitiés
> Genia [Berman]

Ta letter . . . embrasse: Your letter was beautiful and good. I will write to you and try to be up to your level. I kiss you.
Meilleurs . . . amitiés: Yours ever, your good friend.

*****

Hotel du Mont Blanc
Flumet, Savoie
Wednesday [*4 Sept.* 1929]

Dear Gertrude

There has been a long and cordial correspondence with Darmstadt and they have read the libretto and like it and want to see the score and I very nearly went and showed it to them and then we couldnt come to any agreement about the language because I said no I didn't want it translated and they said they couldnt give it except in German and there the matter rests they protesting that they can make a good translation which no doubt they can and I hesitating to explain by letter that this opera isnt like any other opera because I presume every composer thinks that of his first child. Of course it is not at all impossible that even with all the linguistic sense cut out of it the musique might still have some intrinsic interest and of course the dramatic value of the libretto remains and whatever of the poetic texture they can translate. What do you think? And what do Alice and Georges think?
Lasell trip well over, nice trip, money continues. I'm glad it's all finished though. You know how exigent the rich are en voyage and how much attention they require. Flumet is a jewel. Went yesterday to Combloux which is grand. Shall be here till 15th about. Madame Langlois, Catherine Henri (friend of ditto), Maurice Grosser are here. Sherry Mangan will come for a moment. The 15th Madame L— goes to Burgundy. I South. I couldnt stop at Belley coming here because of luggage and Maurice. I could come and spend the day sometime from here if convenient, although I am not exactly certain of the communicatives. We have auto-car service to Aix-les-Bains (or to Grenoble), where I could spend the night, and I presume those towns have a short morning train to Belley or an auto-car by which I could return in afternoon. I fancy also you are having company a good deal this month so I count on your frankness to tell me if you would rather I didn't come. If there should be question of my spending the night in Belley I should stay at the hotel bien entendu. Give my love to Alice and there is always for yourself a perpetual fount of same.

                                          Toujours
                                          Virgil

---

money continues: In gratitude for his help during her illness in 1927—as he says, he saved her life—she has been giving him $125 a month. See note to Thomson, Sunday [*Sept.* 1927].
communicatives: An invented noun, "communications," in the sense of bus or train connections.
bien entendu: of course.

*****

To "M. Virgil Thomson / Hotel du Mont Blanc / Flumet / Savoie."

                                            [*6* Sept. 1929]

>Bilignin
>par Belley,
>Ain.

My dear Virgil,

Just as pleased as can be, sure have them translate after all it is important and when they will, always let them. It will be nice and we are looking forward to having you, George & Genia are here now and there is plenty of room for you too bed and board, Monday if you will telegraph me what time your auto car gets to Aix, and George and I will meet you there and bring you back here and then when you want to go back will take you back to Aix, come as soon as you can we all want to see you, lots of love, and I am awfully pleased about Darmstadt

>Gtrde

If Sherry Mangan is here at the same moment, he could go to the Hotel Pernollet, but for you there is lots of room so don't hesitate.

*****

>Flumet
>Hôtel du Mont Blanc
>Thursday [*12 Sept.* 1929]

Dear Gertrude

It was so sweet all of us together and I loved it so and Belley and your house and really I've seen you so little the last year what with my departure and yours and so we were really intimate again and it was sweet and also as guest I thank you for delicious visit. I'm afraid the lunch in Aix cant come off because Sherry cant be located yet, that is the bank doesnt know where he is and Madame Langlois has to go Monday to Burgundy to help somebody have a baby. Maurice leaves today for Villefranche. I stay with Madame Langlois till Monday. We will probably spend the week-end in Grenoble and leave from there for our respective destinations, because the weather isnt so good now and I think she is a little fed up with Flumet which is a little too high, over 900 metres. I'm sorry because it would have been so nice all together. I can arrange with Sherry however, all about what he can publish and George's letter whenever he turns up or even by letter from wherever I am. I am writing by same post to Darmstadt and I hope all that will turn out well. Love to Alice and best to George and Genia and

>toujours
>Virgil

Carl crossed with Bernard. B. told Carl I had brought Carl to B's house & Carl had met Bravig there. Carl writes to know, having no memory of any of it. It is all true, only Carl was boiled that day.

writing . . . to Darmstadt and I hope all that will turn out well: Visiting Stein and Toklas at Bilignin, Thomson proposed giving, as invited, a one-man performance of the opera at Darmstadt and asked Stein to share the cost since the benefit would be mutual. She refused on the ground that "the libretto has already been accepted." He did not argue but has decided not to go to Darmstadt (*Virgil Thomson* 148). Still the possibility remains open for a German premiere in German or English.

*****

[*12 Sept. 1929*]
Mont Blanc Flumet Thursday

Dear Alice

Here are nice clippings. Nougat by separate package.
Love
Virgil

Nougat: Candy made with nuts, usually almonds or pistachios.

*****

[From Toklas] Postcard of "HANSI—Prière de l'Alsace.—The Prayer of Alsatia . . . ," to "Monsieur Virgil Thomson / Pension Freddy / Villefranches s Mer / (Alpes M^{times})"

[*14 Sept. 1929*]

Dear Virgil. So many thanks for the delicious nougat—we are all enjoying it so much. Sorry we're not to be seeing you at Aix—but it was nice having you here. Madame Sylviac au telephone is superb and incredible—quite completely historical—indeed to such a degree that I cant picture myself in this period though Bach and the telephone equally filled '04 with joy for me—Have a good time at Villefranch—Ever yours A.B.T.

Madame Sylviac: When telephones were first used in Paris and each subscriber's line was connected to a designated switchboard operator, people trying to telephone were often frustrated by the ineptitude or laziness of their operators. One of the clippings Thomson sent 12 Sept. must refer to the story of the Parisian showgirl then known as "Mademoiselle Sylviac"—subsequently "Madame"—who was so abusive to her operator, apparently cursing and foully insulting her, that she (Sylviac) was dropped as a subscriber for "unspeakable behaviour," an action she fought in court (http://gepetel.fre.fr/dcmoi.html, 15 Feb. 2005, see *New York Times*, 8 May 1904, 4). Toklas is remembering dealing with switchboard operators in 1904, when she first acquired a telephone or began using one, a year in which she was also enamoured of Bach and playing a good deal of him on her piano.

*****

Pension Freddy
Villefranche-s-m. A.M.
22 September [*1929*]

Dear Gertrude

Thanks for card. I started for here over a week ago and got violently sick with diarrhoea and had to stay three days in Avignon and in bed and Sherry Mangan finally arrived and we came on here and I got all well and now he has left and will write you about his magazine. Also he wants to make arrangements for *Erasmus* in French and has no copy with him and would you mind lending him my copy long enough to show the publisher if so please mail it to him (Sherry Mangan, Hôtel d'Alsace, rue des Beaux-Arts, Paris) but if it isnt with you never mind because he is leaving quite shortly for home and he wouldnt get it unless it was pretty soon and even then you might ask on the envelope not to forward it if he has left but to return to you. I am glad to be back in Villefranche which is lovely and the hôtel is quite nice and the weather beautiful and now that Sherry has left the opera begins to make score and everything is nice and quiet once more. For which much thanks say I.   Love & thanks Alice nice card.

                              Love
                                Virgil

It wasnt brown sugar. It was what the Englishman calls *black treacle* a product which I identify as sorghum molasses.

Erasmus: John Mangan's *Life, Character and Influence of Desiderius Erasmus of Rotterdam Derived from a Study of his Works and Correspondence*. (see note to Stein, [7 Oct. 1928]). Sherry Mangan hopes that publication in French translation would elicit an honorary doctorate from Louvain for his father, who admires that university and has suffered a stroke that has precluded his going to collect honorary doctorates from Catholic University of America and Holy Cross at Worcester (Sherry Mangan to Thomson, June 1928).
It wasn't brown sugar: In her letter of 26 July, Stein remarked on the "sweet and light and wonderfully brown sugar" of the birthday cake Thomson sent from Villefranche. Perhaps he has enquired about it at the pâtisserie where he bought it, now that he is back there.

*****

To "M. Virgil Thomson / Pension Freddy / [Villefranche]-sur-Mer / Alpes Maritimes"

                              [27 Sept. 1929]
                              Bilignin
                              par Belley,
                              Ain.

My dear Virgil,

So sorry your tummy did misbehave in Avignon but tummys do Alice once scared me to death there by collapsing quite simply from too many muscat grapes eaten before a lunch of mackerel and pork in August in that beautiful place. So I know just how you did there in Avignon. Its a nice place good for popes and people not too fond of food but otherwise not all it should be well anyway I am glad you are alright again, did you get to Saint Remy for my sake and the Saints in seven and all the rest of that quite large family, some day I would like to see it again, I was awfully pleased by Mme Giraud a very intelligent french woman who said of the Saint en Sept she could make nothing of the sense but she was held by the music of the words, do tell Mme Langlois how pleased I am that the translation so well carried over and also it gives me good hope for the translation of the portraits since the *coadjuter* isn't that what you call it of hers will have the same job again. Genia B. has just done a very good portrait of himself to go into it. He has staid [sic] on a week after George left, we did love George he was so sweet and so gay and he is so devoted to all he loves and on the whole he chooses his loves well I am awfully fond of him, as for the Russian well the Russian any Russian makes it very difficult for me to like him, I suppose some day we must like some Russian, do you think it might be a writer, did you ever know a writer, I never did. I have read them but I have never seen one, I wonder well anyway I am fond of you and we were awfully pleased to have you here,   Alwys   Gtrde.

[Note on envelope:] I am not sure after all that Baby is not the best and the one of the three, tell him so for me.

---

good for popes: Avignon was the permanent residence of nine popes between 1305 and 1378.

Saints in seven and all the rest of that quite large family: A reference to her "A Saint in Seven" (1922), composed in Saint-Rémy-de-Provence along with other works, including *Saints and Singing* and "Talks to Saints Or Stories Of Saint Remy" (Dydo 61), this corpus perhaps comprising the "family."

Mme Giraud: Marthe Giraud. Dydo depicts her: "A cultivated woman who spent summers in Ceyzérieu near Belley and winters in Paris or Cannes, she was described by Toklas as 'one of those fabulous raconteuses' whose stories held Stein 'entranced'" (443).

Saint en Sept . . . Langlois: Louise Langlois translated Stein's "A Saint in Seven" for *Orbes*. See note to Stein, [26 July 1929].

coadjuter: assistant.

*****

To "M. Virgil Thomson / Pension Freddy / [Villefranche]-sur-Mer / Alpes Maritimes"

> [27 Sept. 1929]
> Bilignin
> par Belley,
> Ain

My dear Virgil,

Just as I sent off your letter that is my letter to you I got this inclosure from Jolas, he seems worried lest the gentleman be not serious and if he is should he be answered, no doubt the gentleman is serious, he wishes to say all he thinks but he also wishes to know something and what he wants to know nobody but you can tell him but you don't have to unless it would amuse you. I don't know anything about him of course evidently he was at Oxford, when you are through with the letter send it back to me but there is I imagine no hurry. As to the little remark outside my envelope, that is to say that I do really this time imagine that I know what I think, and that is that the piece of all that that is really alive is Bébé of that now I am quite sure there is a great deal to amplify but Bébé is alive and tell him so with my love, it is always pleasant to know one is alive,   Lots of love

Gtrde.

[Note on envelope:] Not Oxford, Cambridge.

---

inclosure . . . amuse you: Stein encloses a letter originally sent to the "Editor of transition" by twenty-four-year-old English composer Walter Leigh, who has read the *Four Saints* libretto in numbers 16 and 17:

> My difficulty is with the collection of works headed "Four Saints in Three Acts to be sung by Gertrude Stein." The reason I bother to try to understand her at all is that I know she does not subscribe to point eleven in your Proclamation—"The writer expresses. He does not communicate." because I heard her say so at some length when she read her paper "Composition as Explanation" to the Cam Literary Club at Cambridge.
>
> I am interested in this particular work of Miss Stein's as a composer. And my difficulty about it is that it does not seem to be a libretto of an opera at all, although she uses the words act and scene more than once. I admit that it could conceivably be turned into an opera of sorts if the title meant what it says, unpunctuated as it is, that it really is to be "sung by Gertrude Stein," but this can only be so taken in a spirit of facetiousness. So what I want to ask you is this.
>
> How many singers are employed, and how are the parts of the several singers indicated in the libretto? I have endeavoured to make this out for myself, but fail to see any other possibility than either a monologue, or a chorus, the composer being free to allot the words to the parts as he feels inclined. For such a setting the work is of course a little long and might be a trifle dull. I am also unable to separate the text from the stage directions, and indeed to understand Miss Stein's use of the word "scene." Miss Stein has not, I fancy, attempted an opera before? I imagine she is not widely experienced in music, and possibly not even very musical? There are many touches which indicate a lack of sympathy with stage singers.
>
> Virgil Thomson's setting of the work is presumably not published yet. But is the glee Saints Procession obtainable? I suppose Thomson is a leading expressionist composer in America. Does he successfully convey the continuous present? (to Elliot Paul 21 Sept. 1929, forwarded by Eugene Jolas to Stein, 25 Sept. 1929)

Leigh will go on to write operas, comic operas, and other music, much of it now published, before dying in combat in June 1942.

*****

Pension Freddy
Villefranche-sur-mer. AM
Sunday 29th [*Sept*. 1929]

Dear Gertrude

I am glad you have come to the same conclusions about Genia as I did. I looked him over (and the painting too) last spring after you left and arrived at ditto only I didn't say anything because I wanted to see if you wouldnt come to same on really seeing him some and of course the painting is good even very good only it isnt really what we're looking for and

Bébé comes out awfully well in the comparison especially for livingness and sweet humanity. Georges writes tenderly from St. Malo and enthusiastically of the floods and Tonny writes from Paris that he has no money and cant paint because he has no more canvases but that he promenades with Bébé in the Bois de Boulogne. Bravig sends card & I presume you have ditto. Cunning drawing. Score advances. Here is clipping in re B. Faÿ from this week's *Gringonè*. The one about Miss [Natalie] Barney is from same. The others I add for amusement. I presume you saw the further correspondence in Herald about *"words"*. We are having fête du pays today and the square is full of young wops in shiny shoes. One day we walked to Monte Carlo and Maurice goes swimming a good deal to keep out of *Saints* way. Weather fine, swimming fine. Score advances. Sun shines. Diarrhoea finished. Give my love always to Alice and

                                                toujours fidèle
                                                      Virgil

Georges sent my photo very good only why didnt those three paces he took work for everybody.

Gringonè: A scandal sheet, what today would be called a tabloid.
fête du pays: regional holiday.

*****

                                                   Freddy
                                               Villefranche
                                       Sunday [6? Oct. 1929]

Dear Gertrude

No I didnt get to St. Remy. We had a car hired to go to St. Remy and Les Baux but I wasnt moveable to that degree and that will have to be tried again. My score advances quite rapidly. Our weather stays good. Kirkpatrick is here for three days. Alice Branlière is at Cannes and we went there one day for lunch. I shall answer the English letter one day soon. Georges writes from the day before Paris. Tonny from sometime after but fancy I recounted that. All is quiet here till I get my score done. We think to come back in early November via *foire gastronomique* at Dijon.   Love toujours
                                                                             Virgil

---

Kirkpatrick: John Kirkpatrick, U.S. pianist who made a four-hand transcription of Thomson's *Symphony on a Hymn Tune*.
Alice Branlière: See note to Thomson, [26 March 1928].
foire gastronomique: food fair.

*****

To "M. Virgil Thomson / Pension Freddy / Villefranche / A.M."

                                                                        [21? Oct. 1929]

> Bilignin
> par Belley
> Ain.

My dear Virgil,

Yes alas we too are on our way well not on our way but about to be on our way to Paris and perhaps though not likely will be passing through the Gourmets, to be sure the cuisine of Dijon is just a little painting the lily for me, they just do do the cuisine a little beyond I prefer Chablis & Beaune but Alice has fallen for it again and again but I rather think we will be on our way the day before, anyway there is Paris, we are saying a tender farewell to our garden trimming our vines and gathering our quinces and all the rest, we were interrupted in these delightful activities by Laura Riding and Robert Graves but they have happily passed on to Geneva, and to Fribourg and further east, anyway a tres bientot, and lots of love

> Gtrde.

Laura Riding and Robert Graves: Graves, a thirty-four-year-old English poet who served as a junior officer with the Royal Welch Fusiliers in France and continues to suffer postwar neurasthenia. He married Nancy Nicholson in 1918, studied at Oxford, published his poetry regularly in Edward Marsh's *Georgian Poetry*. In 1926, twenty-five-year-old Laura Riding became emotionally and sexually involved with Graves and his wife, who, in 1927, left him, taking their four children. Riding is now publishing poetry in *transition*. She has discovered Stein and is greatly influenced by her writing, especially in work soon to appear in *Poems, a Joking Word* (1930). Recently she became entangled with the Irish poet Geoffrey Phibbs (a married man) and, distraught, leapt out a window on 27 April 1929, falling thirty feet, breaking her spine, an injury from which she will never fully recover. Suicide is against the law in Britain at this time, but Eddie Marsh, Chief Secretary of the Home Office, has persuaded the police to leave her alone and has assured Riding that she will not be prosecuted for attempting suicide (Riding to Stein, June 1929). She and Graves have left England not to escape the law but to put distance between themselves and Phibbs and Grave's wife, who, immediately after the suicide attempt, became a couple. Stein recommends the Spanish island of Mallorca (Majorca in English) where it is inexpensive to live, and they are about to go there, partly, also, because of its artists' community. They stayed with Stein and Toklas for three weeks and arrive in Mallorca on 23 Oct., cutting their intervening visit to Germany short because of rainy weather and annoying American tourists (Friedmann 162-63).
a tres beintot: à très beintôt, see you very soon.

*****

[*Possible placement*]   Thursday [*Oct.-Nov.* 1929]

Dear Gertrude

I've answered this. Nicely I think. I'm sick abed. Fever & bronchitis, as usual. Enjoying it but weak just now.

> Love
> Virgil

Catalog & clipping from Hitchcock.

---

answered this: Probably Walter Leigh's letter (see note to Stein [27 Sept. 1929]), returned to Stein with this note.

*****

17 Quai Voltaire
27 Octobre [1929]

Dear Gertrude

It started to rain so we just came home. Paris is nicer now than Nice. Carl sends illustrated edition of *Peter Whiffle* including you. Here is something you will like I think. Come home soon too I hope.

Love
Virgil

***Peter Whiffle* including you**: *Peter Whiffle, His Life and Works* (1922), Van Vechten's first novel, in which he twice mentions Stein (59, 121–22).

*****

To "M. Virgil Thomson / 17 Quai Voltaire / Paris."

27 RUE DE FLEURUS
[8 Nov. 1929]

My dear Virgil,

    Home sweet home, a nice home but we are all still a little lonesome for Bilignin, but will be a little less lonesome when we see you, otherwise everything cheerful,

love
Gtrde.

*****

[*Possible placement*]

Friday [Nov. 1929]

Dear Gertrude

    Welcome home and many of same. I am coming to see you tomorrow evening. Sherry Mangan writes *Pagany* publishes you.
Also includes nice clippings which herewith, saving your grace. And he has induced new owner-editor to pay flat page-rate. Mrs. Lasell writes my income stops 1st of May. But that's a long way off. I'm not down-hearted.

Love
Virgil

Program from Vermont arrives via Mrs. Lassell.

***Pagany* publishes you**: See note to Stein [31 Jan. 1930].

*****

Letters with Notes

[*Possible placement*]

To "M. Virgil Thomson / 17 Quai Voltaire / Paris"

27 RUE DE FLEURUS
[*Nov. 1929*]

My dear Virgil.

Robert wants back his farewell to all that because it is a proof and there is some discussion about cutting something out anyway I am to have another copy from Capes so you can read that so will you bring it back say to-morrow and come to supper 7 o'clock, that will be sweet, to-day being Friday, to-morrow is Saturday

Gtrde.

———

Robert wants back his farewell to all that: Graves's proof copy of his *Good-bye to All That: An Autobiography* (London: Jonathan Cape, 1929).

*****

To "M. Virgil Thomson / 17 Quai Voltaire / Paris."

27 RUE DE FLEURUS
[18 Nov. 1929]

My dear Virgil

We are to have here Tuesday evening Bob Brown and family probably and Ford etc certainly will you and Maurice come in, I imagine Maurice an xtremely useful young gentleman and you not so useful but also a pleasure,

Love

Gtrde.

———

Bob Brown: Author Robert Carleton Brown, whose portrait, "Absolutely As Bob Brown Or Bobbed Brown," Stein composes around this time. In his *1450–1950* (1929), Brown includes her in the distinguished list of dedicatees along with "ALL EARLY ORIENTAL ARTISTS," "SHAKESPEARE" and "PAGLIACCI."

*****

[*Nov. 1929*]

Dear Gertrude

Yes we'll come useful or ornamental or what has anybody.

Love

Virgil

*****

To "M. Virgil Thomson / 17 Quai Voltaire / Paris."

        ROSE IS A ROSE IS A ROSE IS A ROSE [circular]
        27 RUE DE FLEURUS

[26 Nov. 1929]

My dear Virgil,

Wednesday evening Bernard will be here and some others small and select and changeful may we have the pleasure of you too, everything seems moving gently

Gtrde.

*****

17 Quai Voltaire
[*12 Dec.* 1929]

Dear Gertrude

The Catesby Joneses are in town (for very short time) and want to come to tea tomorrow and be brought later to your house. I am in bed of a fever and bronchitis and cant possibly make a party. But can you get hold of Tonny for tomorrow and let Maurice bring them to your house. The time they suggested for here was 4 ½. Send me an answer so that I can let them know tomorrow morning.

Love
Virgil

*****

To "M. Virgil Thomson / 17 Quai Voltaire / Paris."

27 RUE DE FLEURUS
[12 Dec. 1929]
Thursday evening

My dear Virgil,

Did not get your Pneu in time to answer before but alas to-morrow Friday does not suit we are not free, some other time perhaps sorry you are not well

Gtrde.

*****

Calling card written by Toklas to "Monsieur Virgil Thomson / 17 quai Voltaire / Paris"

[1 Jan. *1930*]

MISS STEIN
MISS TOKLAS
    27, RUE DE FLEURUS

Happy New Year and fondest love

–Gertrude et Alice–

*****

To "M. Virgil Thomson / 17 Quai Voltaire / Paris."

GERTRUDE STEIN
27 RUE DE FLEURUS
PARIS

[7 Jan. 1930]

My dear Virgil,

Gorer is in town and will be here Thursday evening unless we hear to the contrary so will you come in then unless you hear to the contrary, Bon voyage to Maurice

                                    Gtrde.

hope tummy did not turn too much, am afraid it was the chill of the [drinking?] water.

Gorer: Geoffrey Gorer, who, as president of the Cam Literary Club, invited Stein to lecture at Cambridge in 1925. She lectured there the following year, and Gorer subsequently contacted Stein often when visiting Paris.
tummy: Maurice's. See postcard of [20 Jan. 1930].

*****

To "Miss Stein / 27 rue de Fleurus / Paris VI"

[*9 Jan. 1930*]

Dear Gertrude

I cant read the gentleman's name but I shall come with pleasure and may I bring Mary Reynolds because we are taking Maurice to the Gare at 9.30. You will maybe remember I think George Lynes brought her once. She is nice and no trouble but if I should not bring her send me a pneu.

                        Love
                        Virgil

Mary Reynolds: "The queen of American Montparnasse," "a war widow out of Minneapolis (by way of Vassar and Greenwich Village)" supported by a rich father, friend to artists and poets (*Virgil Thomson* 110, 204), beloved of Marcel Duchamp, introduced to Stein by George Platt Lynes. Thomson meets her at 6 today (pocket diary).
George Lynes: George Platt Lynes, twenty-three-year-old aspiring poet, recently turned photographer, from Englewood, New Jersey, one of the young men who visited Stein, who writes, "There were one or two under 20, for example George Lynes, but they did not count, as Gertrude carefully explained to them" (*Autobiography* 229).

*****

To "M. Virgil Thomson / 17 Quai Voltaire / Paris."

ROSE IS A ROSE IS A ROSE IS A ROSE [circular]
27 RUE DE FLEURUS

[17 Jan. 1930]

My dear Virgil

Clermont Tonnere this time signed C. [L.?] which is a pleasure to all concerned though we don't know which is her name proposes herself for tea Sunday at five will you do us the pleasure of meeting her I know you want to,

Alwys

Gtrde.

C. [L.?]: The second initial is unclear, but Stein's comments on the name confusion resonate with the various signatures to be found in the duchess's correspondence with her over the years (E. Gramont C. Tonnerre, Elizabeth C. T., Gramont Tonnerre, etc.). Born de Gramont, she was married for twenty-four years to the Duc de Clermont-Tonnerre, from whom she has been divorced since 1920. Her variable signatures may reflect uneasiness she feels with the title bestowed through this unfortunate union.

*****

Postcard of Stein and Toklas with nuns and soldiers in front of Hopital Simon Violet Père, to "M. Virgil Thomson / 17 Quai Voltaire / Paris."

[20 Jan. 1930]

I am awfully pleased I did think she was very favourable and I hoped something would happen, and everybody can be happy which is also nice I hope it happiness and the play will include Maurice's tummy,   love

Gtrde.

awfully pleased . . . happen: The Duchesse de Clermont-Tonnerre may have offered to contribute financial support; she did so previously, when she commissioned Thomson's setting of *Capital Capitals* in 1927. See note to Thomson [17 June 1927].

*****

To "M. Virgil Thomson / 17 Quai Voltaire / Paris."

GERTRUDE STEIN
27 RUE DE FLEURUS
PARIS

[31 Jan. 1930]

My dear Virgil,

Pagany is breaking out these may amuse you don't bother to keep them and I have found another announcement for Georges's 15 Boulevard Montmorency before March 31, somebody ought to see he gets there it is always all to the good moralement that somebody gets 20 000 francs,

Love
Gtrde.

Pagany . . . out: The first issue of *Pagany* appears in January 1930. It includes Hugnet's article on Thomson (see appendix A), followed by Stein's "Five Words in a Line," and William Carlos Williams' "The Work of Gertrude Stein."
George's 15 Boulevard Montmorency: Location of the reception at which Hugnet is to receive the award.
moralement: Stein's creative translation to indicate "for morale." "Moralement" in French means "morally."
Georges's . . . 20 000 francs: Hugnet has won this prize, worth $800 U.S., for a short story. Thomson later suggests that this and other successes contribute to Hugnet's "difficult" behaviour later this year (*Virgil Thomson* 192).

*****

To "M. Virgil Thomson / 17 Quai Voltaire / Paris."

ROSE IS A ROSE IS A ROSE IS A ROSE [circular]
27 RUE DE FLEURUS

[5 Feb. 1930]

My dear dear Virgil

It was nice coming home and finding the delicious and beautiful violets, Thanks ever so much and we will be seeing you soon if not before but perhaps before at the real pearl, symbol of all,

Alwys
Gtrde.

---

real pearl: Perhaps a screening of Hugnet's film, *La Perle*, the premiere having taken place in June of the previous year.

*****

To "M. Virgil Thomson / 17 Quai Voltaire / Paris."

ROSE IS A ROSE IS A ROSE IS A ROSE [circular]
27 RUE DE FLEURUS

[15 Feb. 1930]

My dear Virgil,

You are not too ill we are beginning to be worried, do you like Roselle Montgomery, I think she is rather nice, otherwise as we were, and you,

Alwys

Gtrde.

Roselle Montgomery: Fifty-six-year-old Georgia-born poet.

*****

To "M. Virgil Thomson / 17 Quai Voltaire / Paris."

GERTRUDE STEIN
27 RUE DE FLEURUS
PARIS

[26 Feb. 1930]

My dear Virgil

I hate to take Making of the Americans away from Maurice, but we have to abridge it for America and have to do it at once. could we have it. And best to you alwys

Gtrde

---

abridge it for America: A letter from Lee Furman of Macaulay Company dated 14 Feb. 1930 confirms his interest in publishing an abridgement of *The Making of Americans*, suggesting a reduction of the original 400, 000 words to 150, 000, so that they might sell the books for $2.50 each. Furman is enthusiastic, but publishing companies are sometimes nervous about Stein's marketability, and Stein later writes about Furman: "It's alright when he is over here, said Elliot Paul, but when he gets back the boys won't let him. Who the boys are I do not know but they certainly did not let him. Elliot Paul was right" (*Autobiography* 269). Later in the year, Macaulay will withdraw his offer to publish. The first abridgement of the novel will be published in Feb. 1934 by Harcourt, Brace and Co., with a preface by Bernard Faÿ.

*****

To "M. Virgil Thomson / 17 Quai Voltaire / Paris."

ROSE IS A ROSE IS A ROSE IS A ROSE [circular]
27 RUE DE FLEURUS

[6 March 1930]

My dear Virgil.

Alice and I are terribly pleased with the opera and I want to thank Maurice again for all he has done. As Alice says it not only sounds like an opera but it looks like an opera. May the saints have us all in their keeping and be as good to us as we have been to them

Love
Gtrde.

---

terribly pleased with the opera: Thomson visited with the score, and doubtless played and sang for Stein and Toklas, on 3 and perhaps 6 March (pocket diary).
I want to thank Maurice again: Maurice Grosser wrote a scenario for *Four Saints*, which will be used for its original production.

*****

To "Miss Stein / 27 rue de Fleurus / Paris VI"

[8 March 1930]

Dear Gertrude

It is arranged with the Cliquets for Wednesday evening. I will call for you about half-past eight. Or if it is not troublesome I might come for supper, but dont make any fuss and feathers for that. Glad opera pleases on reflection.

Love toujours
Virgil

Cliquets for Wednesday evening: Thomson notes this appointment for 12 March in his pocket diary.

*****

To "M. Virgil Thomson / 17 Quai Voltaire / Paris."

ROSE IS A ROSE IS A ROSE IS A ROSE [circular]
27 RUE DE FLEURUS

[10 March 1930]

My dear Virgil,

Yes with a lot of pleasure, you come to supper Wednesday and I'll have the car and we will go together, seven o'clock Wednesday tapestry, reduction of M. of Americans, portraits all looking like finishing.

Gtrde

---

tapestry: The petit point tapestry Alice did from Picasso's designs for two Louis XV-style children's chairs. In an article in *Nest* (Winter 2002–2003), Dydo identifies this as the period of their creation. They are now at the Beinecke Library, Yale University.

Letters with Notes

*****

To "M. Virgil Thomson / 17 Quai Voltaire / Paris."

Saturday [15 *March* 1930]

My dear Virgil,

We will come tomorrow evening about half past eight we cannot have you for supper for domestic reasons to-morrow but the good cook looks as if she will continue into next week and so we will arrange for later and Picasso was awfully pleased with [your mot?] about [Georges?] and [Sauguet?] c'est une autre ecole it is to be widely quoted, you can never tell what will make one famous, alors to-morrow at half after eight

Love
Gtrde

---

tomorrow evening: In his pocket diary, Thomson records the original plan to go to "Gertrude" at 7.
mot?: comment or note.
c'est un autre ecole: it's an other school (or faction).

*****

To "M. Virgil Thomson / 17 Quai Voltaire / Paris."

[19 March 1930]

My dear Virgil

On second thought I guess it is just as well to leave the book as it is it is less complicated and perhaps on the whole just as well well anyway as well so as we were,

Love alwys
Gtrde.

---

the book: *Dix Portraits*. This and the following letters suggest there is some discussion about including in the book of portraits a longer work, perhaps *Four Saints*, which Thomson offers to translate.

*****

[*19 March 1930*]

Dear Gertrude

I've gone and done it again and I am sorry. Out of an over-zealous and quite unnecessary loyalty to those absent I said an ugly thing to those present and that is worse because it hurt you whom I am ashamed to have hurt most of anybody and it was all so unnecessary on my part to hurt anybody especially my very dearest friend whom I love with all my heart

Yours very sorry
Virgil

Your pneu comes just now as I go to post and anything you say about the book is all right with me all that being your matter entirely except that please dont let the translation bother you if you want the longer book. It is really not much of a job and I can do it in two or three days and I dont really care at all whether I am paid (except something for the principle) and the little labor of love is really a pleasure both in the labor and in the love. So anything you prefer is right and "your slightest wish—etc."

Love,
V.G.G.T.

My opinion remains however that a longer book and a more choice selection of pieces is preferable to the original project. Especially since a piece of some length and variety shows the constructive aspect of your work and complements the incisive or precious quality of the portraits.

[*19 March 1930*]: This undated letter has been placed by other critics in the midst of the Hugnet-Thomson-Stein crisis of December 1930. While the emotional content resonates with that later struggle, the interrelated logic of Stein's two dated letters of 19 March and Thomson's letters (which we date 19 and 21 March) as well as reference to "the portraits," Stein's current project, compel us to place it here. Thomson's apology must relate to another of their not uncommon tiffs.

*****

To "M. Virgil Thomson / 17 Quai Voltaire / Paris."

ROSE IS A ROSE IS A ROSE IS A ROSE [circular]
27 RUE DE FLEURUS

[19 March 1930]

My dearest Virgil

No no I love you and we can tease each other always and always be all happy and trusting and about the book, I wobbled a good deal the way I do but I think really now its best to leave it as it is and hope that there will be more coming later, and lots of love and perfect friendship alwys

Gtrde.

*****

Friday [*21 March 1930*]

Dear Gertrude

Thank you for sweet forgiveness. Will you please bring the Etienne Marcel by Massot tonight to George's. I have need of it a little and will very thank you.

I have finished translations of portraits and will bring them. Maurice hunted for saints in Marseilles and didn't find exactly but says will next time.

Love
Virgil

---

translations: Thomson and Hugnet have translated ten of Stein's verbal portraits to be published in *Dix Portraits* by Hugnet's press in a limited edition by subscription. See note to Stein [*late* March 1930].
Etienne Marcel: By Pierre de Massot, *Etienne Marcel. Prévôt des Marchands* (1927), an account of the fourteenth-century provost of city merchants who defended Paris, instituted reforms, and was assassinated in 1358.
George's: In his pocket diary, Thomson records meeting with Hugnet tonight.

*****

To "M. Virgil Thomson / 17 Quai Voltaire / Paris."

ROSE IS A ROSE IS A ROSE IS A ROSE [circular]
27 RUE DE FLEURUS

[23 March 1930]

My dearest Virgil

Yesterday I forgot or I forgot yesterday to say that the Massons are coming in Thursday evening and I am asking the stray Englishmen and anything else that comes along and will you come and meet them, one does not know what the stray Englishman may be, Lots of love

Gtrde.

Massons: Andre Masson and his wife Odette (née Cabale), he a French painter most often associated with Surrealism. Stein owns some of his work.

*****

[*Possible placement*]

To "M. Virgil Thomson / 17 Quai Voltaire / Paris."

27 RUE DE FLEURUS
[*Spring 1930*]

My dear Virgil.

Will you come in Saturday evening and have your fortune read, the Countess is bringing her cards and she will tell you all about the next 6 months, she really has done it well for Alice, it is all coming to come true, funny little things happen more anon

Gtrde.

Countess: Margherita Pecorini. See note to Stein, [*21 Nov. 1927*].

*****

Postcard of G.S. and A.B.T. with nuns and soldiers in front of Hopital Simon Violet Père, to "M. Virgil Thomson / Hotel Freddy / Villefranche-s-mer / A.M."

[*late* March 1930]

The candle will be lit V.G.G.T. Alice's middle one is a B. I have no middle one you see, so there for me. The contemporaries are just finished. They end with you and they are awfully cute. And the family, best to the family and love to you and alwys

Gtrde.

late **March**: The initial postmark of 7 March must be in error, as the arrival postmark indicates April, the card is addressed to Villefranche, and Thomson's replies of early April respond to "the candle" and the topic of middle initials.
V.G.G.T.: Virgil Garnett Gaines (his mother's maiden name) Thomson.
B.: Alice's middle initial, for Babette.
The contemporaries: Later to become *Dix Portraits* (Paris: Editions de la Montagne, 1930): ten portraits by Stein followed by Thomson's and Hugnet's translations. When published they do not end with Thomson, but appear in the following order: Pablo Picasso (second portrait), Guillaume Apollinaire, Erik Satie, Pavel Tchelitchev, Virgil Thomson, Christian Bérard, Bernard Faÿ, Kristians Tonny, Georges Hugnet, Genia Berman.

*****

Hôtel Freddy
Villefranche-s-mer
5 April [*1930*]

Dear Alice

Mightn't one more candle do the work. À l'intention dun Herrn Musikdirektor.

Love
Virgil

All well and fine here. Sun and battleships. Swimming. I've found some nice La Fontaine fables. (Contes are too dirty.) And a swell cutting from Bossuet's funeral oration for the Queen of England Henriette wife of Charles I.

Love and tenderest to Gertrude and I am writing her shortly. V.G.G.T.

Herrn: Lord.
Contes: Tales, *Les Contes* of Jean de La Fontaine (1621-1695). In 1906 Fernande Olivier read aloud to Stein La Fontaine's stories to keep her amused while she sat for Picasso's portrait of her (*Autobiography* 46).

Bossuet's funeral oration: The text by Jacques-Benigne Bossuet (bishop, theologian, court-preacher) Thomson will set it to music and entitle it *"Oraison funèbre de Henriette-Marie de France reine de la Grande-Bretagne / Bossuet,"* referred to in subsequent letters as "Bossuet."

*****

Freddy
Villefranche
11 avril [*1930*]

Dear Gertrude

Darmstadt is silent. Bossuet is pushing enormous cries. The sun is shining. The family is well. And quiet. Carl writes he cant swallow Eugene. Hitchcock is arriving. La Fontaine has already come. Come out nicely. The British navy is impressive and serious and drinks only beer or even lemonade and every morning they sing hymns and do physical culture to musique. You are quite welcome to one of my G's. Either one you like or both. Marthe & Cliquet retire from the concert. I presume Sauguet remains. I dont care. I shall do it anyway. Please write any news. I hope to see *Contemporaries* when I return.
No arrival announced from Squire.
Madame Langlois sent you saints.
Alice shall have a cake from Vogades.
A big one if Genevieve crashes through.
Twice I've been to movies.
All the British sailors are trying to talk American in imitation of the talkies. "Anybody come from Richmond?" seems to be the practise-phrase. In Southern dialect. They're learning too. And Ghandi gathering salt on the other hand. It's really too bad, because I've taken quite a fancy to them. Maybe that's why they're all so nice though.

Love and embraces
Virgil

Eugene: Eugene MacCown, friend of Thomson since Kansas City days and roommate in Paris in the early months of 1922, graduate of the University of Missouri, painter, and jazz pianist. His relationship with Thomson became strained with the 1923 death in New York of Bernard Faÿ's brother Emmanuel. MacCown suspected that neglect by Thomson was a contributing factor (Tommasini 58, 133). Thomson asked Carl Van Vechten to meet with MacCown, and on 22 March 1930, Van Vechten writes from New York that he has taken an immediate and hearty dislike to "E. MacC."
Hitchcock is arriving: Thomson's portrait of Henry-Russell Hitchcock, *Russell Hitchcock, reading*. See note to Thomson, [*4 June 1930*]. Hitchcock is renting a room in Paris near Thomson's apartment and writing his first works on architectural history. He will accompany Thomson on long walks through Paris, reading its buildings to him. Thomson writes, "He interested very little Gertrude Stein, more Georges Hugnet, . . . a great deal Madame Langlois, who could spot a proper scholar when she saw one" (*Virgil Thomson* 108).
La Fontaine: Thomson's composition for voice and piano to "Le Singe et la Lèopard" based on a tale in *Les Fables de Jean de La Fontaine*.

Squire: W. H. Haddon Squire, London-based music critic for the *Christian Science Monitor*.
Genevieve: St. Genevieve, before whose statue Toklas is lighting candles in hope that the opera will be produced.
Ghandi gathering salt: From 12 March to 6 April 1930, Mahatma Ghandi walked 250 miles from Ahmedâbâd to the Arabian Sea, delivering speeches along the way protesting the British monopoly on making salt and promoting Indian independence.

*****

Freddy's
Villefranche
13 Avril [*1930*]

Dear Gertrude

"Es kann sein kein Fried' auf Erd' mit Ruh' mit Ruh'". Haddon Squire announces self for Apr. 22. I shall reenter for Sat. 26th unless he wants me earlier. I invited him for 2.30 Saturday and will you come at 4.30 for tea? Sauf contraire. Georges writes of Yves de Longevialle. It's horrid. What of Bernard's job? I cant write him till I know whether to congratulate. Silence from Darmstad. Hope same gives consent

Love
Virgil

Es kann . . . Ruh': Probably apropos of current events in India, referred to by Thomson near the end of his previous letter, and translating the English words of Stein's libretto: "There can be no peace on earth with calm with calm" (*Four Saints*, 21).
Yves de Longevialle: Twenty-three-year-old poet, reviewer, translator, Grace-Ives de Longevialle reviewed Thomson's concert of 30 May 1928. He was a gifted student and friend of Bernard Faÿ, who introduced him to Stein. He and Faÿ translated Stein's "Melanctha" into French. Stein included brief portraits of him in "Absolutely As Bob Brown or Bobbed Brown" (1929) and her play *At Present* (1930), and wrote a full portrait of him, "Grace Or Ives de Longevialle," in January or February 1930 (published by Wendy Steiner in *Yale University Library Gazette* 50 no. 1 [July 1975], 41–45). On 24 March he died in a car accident. Faÿ will commemorate him as a true poet but one of the spiritual casualties of the war. (Dydo 222, 388, 389, 390).

*****

To "M. Virgil Thomson / Freddy / Villefranche / Alpes Maritimes"

[15 April 1930]

My dear Virgil,

Helas, one of the few French words I loved in the books when I was little, we are leaving for the country the 25, Villemorin says flowers have to be planted before the first of May and anyway we are ready to go or will be, and Helas Bernard did not get his job, the senate voted down the chair, but that does not make any difference since the College had voted it so it will now depend upon other means, but anyway no one talks about it and he is as sweet as can be. Yes it was horrid about poor Yves and poor Bravig has pretty well gone to pieces under it, Yves was good to them when all the rest of us were not and poor Bravig feels it deeply, I was with them at the church, a very xtraordinary thing and the father, well anyway, don't bring any fruit Alice says because we are leaving and anyway we love you very much

Gtrde.

Helas: Unfortunately.
Villemorin: Vilmorin-Andrieux and Co., long-standing French horticultural firm and publisher of planting guides.
Yves: Yves de Longevialle. See Thomson, 13 Avril [*1930*]. With the help of Bravig Imbs, he translated Virginia Woolf's story "The Mark on the Wall." He was godfather (Toklas godmother) to Imbs's daughter Jane Maria Louise (b. 17 Sept. 1929).

*****

To "M. Virgil Thomson / Freddy / Villefranche / Alpes Maritimes."

[16 April *1930*]

My dearest Virgil

Whats the news well first Basket has been turned from a lamb into a lion a sweet little lion but a lion nonetheless, and now Alice is combing out the Lion's tangles in the salon but we all like it, second we have a marvellous Alsatian domestic who makes most wonderful cake cookies and pies so do not send cake but if you want to send something make it sugared fruits that she can put into cakes (a very very little because otherwise she would do nothing but cake) and as she loves us she is going to the country with us so either here or there you can eat them. Third Sherry Magnan's [sic] thing about ~~Elliot~~ T.S. is wonderfully funny it is catholic bright and awfully well done and I had a charming time with it and read lots of it aloud with joy, his descriptions of anglicanism by the way the steel Gothic is just developing gothic as if it was the measles as we come down the quays, we are leaving the 25 and we are frightfully busy, *George & I* have translated Composition as xplanation, he has shown me the translations of the portraits they are darn good, his which was very difficult has spots that are awfully satisfactory, Pierre is still working I have not seen him but George has and all of it is to be ready Thursday, the little things came do thank Mme Langlois and I will too very shortly and I did kind of not think it was Maurice, and Lucy Church Amiably is being printed and [Havoth?] is taking it all over and is to do some more in fact a whole edition of my unedited anyway we begin, and I just bought myself to-day a romantic landscape of Francis Rose, a charming villa picture, and its raining, and George Maratier is to arrange a show for Eugene in Chicago and they are coming back in June, so Georges Maratier says if on the proceeds this I do not know. And in between I work a little pas mal and I am pleased about La Fontaine et Bossuet, and let me see what else, there have been lots of Poles some of them nice, Bernard is very sweet, Tonny has done his drawing of him Bernard is pleased George H. is giving a party, and why are Cliquet & Marthe not going,

Love
Gtrde.

Sherry's thing about T.S.: Sherry Mangan, "'A Note': on the Somewhat Premature Apotheosis of Thomas Stearns Eliot," *Pagany* 1 no. 2 (Spring 1930), 23–36. In this witty and cogent essay, Mangan ridicules Eliot's neglect of art (poetry) for the mere craft of criticism—worse, it is oracular, not scholarly, criticism—and for his declaraton of allegiance to royalism and Anglicanism, all of which represents a spiritual collapse and retreat into "snobbism," a form of "insecurity" inimical to "artistic courage" and tending to preclude the "abundance and enthusiasm" requisite to art. Mangan's essay appears immediately before Lindley Williams Hubbell's "A Letter to Gertrude Stein," 37.

Pierre is still working: Pierre de Massot is a thirty-year-old French poet, prose writer, critic, pamphleteer, a former Dadaist, struggling with poverty, illness, and opium addiction, formerly a close friend of Satie, long a friend of Thomson, who may, as he claims, have introduced him to Stein (she could have known him earlier through other friends), and who is attempting to revive his career. De Massot is writing the preface to *Dix Portraits*, in which he speaks of Stein's attempts to free words from constrictions of grammar and idiom and reliance on memory.

[Havoth?]: This is what the word looks like, but she most likely means Harry Horwood, an American editor and literary agent whom she considers a worthy manager for the Plain Edition. By the end of the year he will be deemed unsatisfactory, and Stein and Toklas will run the publishing venture on their own.

Francis Rose: Francis Cyril Rose, twenty-year-old painter, his work recently "discovered" by Stein, who will buy nearly one hundred of his pictures and insist for the rest of her life that he is a great painter (*Virgil Thomson* 172). He keeps a flat in Paris, designs for Diaghilev, exhibits this year with Dali, associates with Cocteau, Bérard, Picasso, Christopher Wood. Stein and Toklas will meet him within a year and become fast friends.

*****

Villefranche
19 avril [*1930*]

Dear Gertrude

Happy times to you and a prosperous planting. Bossuet is finished. The cake was already sent. I'm sorry. I dont even know whether it was good or not, because it was a kind I hadnt tasted. Darmstadt still quiet. Your letters were full of news and mostly swell news except about Bernard's job. But the publishings! And the cook! Pagany arrived here and I had a hilarious breakfast with the "lotuses of prose style and Anglican theology". No news but Bossuet and some rain and today a magnificent double rainbow and tender sweet letters from George. Cliquets not asked to his party because Madame H— wont have Marthe in the house any more. Something Marthe did or said once, I dont remember what. Georges's Pagany article quite good. I'm won over. (Incidentally, it isnt hardly at all the same article.) You'll like Bossuet. It is quite grandiose and style-funèbre-Italian-opera. I'm sorry not to kiss you goodby. But sweet so-longs to you and nice weather and I'll do my best about the Xian Science Monitor.

Love
Virgil

lotuses of prose style and Anglican theology: A quotation from Mangan's "A Note: on the Somewhat Premature Apotheosis of Thomas Stearns Eliot": "If Mr Eliot has sailed grandly into a haven with a gesture which only the exact brilliance of his mind keeps from looking pitiably resignatory, that is not a cause for us of other instincts and tastes to blindly direct our lesser barks in after him, and (of all things) to live on the lotuses of prose style and Anglican Theology" (29). See note to Stein [16 April *1930*].

George's Pagany article: Hugnet's "Peinture Poesie," concerning modern painters and focusing on Christian Bérard, Kristians Tonny, Eugène Berman and Léonide Berman in *Pagany* 1 no. 2 (Spring 1930), 105–12, which Thomson is currently reading. Thomson may have been displeased with an earlier version of the article.

funèbre: funeral.

the Xian Science Monitor: Thomson is trying to get its music reviewer to preview *Four Saints*. See note to Thomson, 26 april [*1930*].

*****

To "M. Virgil Thomson / Freddy, / Villefranche / A.M."

> ROSE IS A ROSE IS A ROSE IS A ROSE [circular]
> 27 RUE DE FLEURUS
>
> [23 April 1930]

My dear Virgil,

Regret nothing, the cake was xcellent, we had to tell Jacqueline that it was not as good as hers but that was to save face, anyway it was neck and neck, Hitchcock at least from the concierges description I imagine it was Hitchcock passed by yesterday but we were out, otherwise xcept that Basket had worms we are as we were, inclosed is a page to be put in cardboard proof of Lucy's clothes, rather pretty I think, George is in Brittany, Bernard at [Saleux?], Bravig at Chartres, Janet [Scudder] in town and [renting?], and [inventing?] and Margherita [Pecorini] telling pleasant fortunes, otherwise absolutely nothing new,

> Alwys
> Gtrde.

[Note on envelope]: Come come it was entirely the same article, M. [Kristians?] here said he writes with real facility, after reading.

Jacqueline: Stein's Alsatian domestic. See Stein [16 April *1930*].
Lucy's clothes: Cover for *Lucy Church Amiably* (Paris: Plain Edition, 1930), rich blue with black lettering.

*****

> Villefranche
> Saturday 26 april [*1930*]

Dear Gertrude

Squire wired sorry must postpone visit so I ditto reentry and I go back to arrive the 29th and I thought all my work was done but I have suddenly given birth to a violin sonata and I am glad the cake was edible. Lucy

Church is beautiful so beautiful she could hardly be more so. Francis Rose is here and covering us with amiabilities and the British Fleet left singing Goodby Broadway and Senabre is in Mallorca, Puerto Soller, maybe I'll go a while in summer and Maurice is well and behaving handsomely. Georges' article may be same but my opinion remains changed. Changed that is enough to admit the article is respectable reading. I thought *L'archipel* also much improved by print. Lady Rose told my fortune with tarots and went into a trance and told me marvellous things many of them same as Pecorini and she described my music to me and finally gave me advice and then it wasnt she any more at all but the guardian angel who spoke directly in the first person and gave me hell for being stupid and not running my own affairs. I hope you had a nice trip and you will have a nice garden and I am awfully glad about Lucy and the edition.

Love and to Alice too
Virgil

Squire wired: The music reviewer of the *Christian Science Monitor*, W. H. Haddon Squire, repeatedly postpones coming to Paris to hear the opera, though he says he has "seldom looked forward to any critical task with greater interest" (to Stein, 25 February 1930). On 4 December 1931 he writes to Thomson, delaying again, adding that if Thomson wants a notice of *Capital Capitals* in the *Monitor* he should send seats and he will send someone if he cannot do it himself.
a violin sonata: *Violin Sonata No 1*, 1930.
Senabre, Ramón: Catalonian painter, friend of Thomson, who composed his portrait for piano.
L'archipel: a poem by Hugnet read aloud by Marcel Herrand in the concert with music by Thomson and Cliquet-Pleyel on 14 November 1928.
Lady Rose: Francis's mother, who lives in Villefranche.
Pecorini: See Stein, [23 April 1930].

*****

Postcard of "La Maison de Jeanne d'Arc à DOMREMY," to "M. Virgil Thomson / 17 Quai Voltaire / Paris."

[28 April 1930]

My dear Virgil,

If one has to have the way of Saints one can accept Jeanne d'Arc and here we are and best to you and Bossuet and all good things
Love
Gtrde.

*****

Postcard of "Birth Place of Marechal Joffre at Rivesaltes april 1917," photograph of Stein and Toklas in ambulance, to "M. Virgil Thomson / 17 Quai Voltaire / Paris"

[3 May 1930]

But Hell if affairs won't get to be affairs how can one run them, do they know or do you know, you nor I nor nobody knows how everything else and barley grows, roses have little things we have spent the day spraying and now all is well,   Love

                                                          Gtrde

*****

                                    17 Quai Voltaire
                                    11 May [1930]

Dear Gertrude.

    Please excuse silence very busy with Bossuet now finished and very beautiful indeed with a great ampleur and I had a party last night and Cingria loved it and nobody can find fault with French prosody (thanks to slight aid of Mme. Langlois who knows more than all of them about it) and everyone is terribly impressed. Mrs. Lasell has sent sweet letters & a check for May & no mention of stopping. Darmstadt is at a stand-still with everyone sold on us but the musical director who is standing pat. Who would have thought it? The score has been carried off to Vienna by representative of Universal Editions for examination in view of publication. If St Genevieve isnt tired of us by this time, I suggest a candle for that, but perhaps best not to insist. She knows our story by now. George Kates old college friend later Oxford Doctor now Hollywood mogul has fine stories about it all. Marion Davies who when in England was asked what she thought of British pictures replied "I have a Reynolds in my own home." Hitchcock is here and departing daily for Germany but still here and god knows when and Maurice had a tiresome visitor from Duluth so we put them together and it has become a tender idyll for them & a great relief for us. Antheil writes tender letter (dictated) encouraging my attendance at Frankfort premiére of his opera. Nothing further from Squire. I am very well. I have some red lilies. Sénabré remaining at Puerto Soller I shall probably join him in June or July. Carl predicts June arrival. I hope your garden is doing as gardens should and that you are having nice time. Corrected proof on *Dix Portraits* with Georges. Baby's is a scream. Génia is mécontent at being spoken of in the feminine. Massot still promises preface. I've no confidence. I suppose you saw this clipping.

                                                     Love toujours
                                                          Virgil

    I'm a bit chagrined that Darmstadt finds my music not *à la hauteur*.

---

ampleur: fullness.
Cingria: Charles-Albert, forty-seven-year-old eccentric, impoverished, scruffy, alcoholic Swiss poet, close friend of Max Jacob; according to Thomson, "his mind ingenious, his talk both learned and funny"; living in an unheated sixth-floor garret room near St. Sulpice

with a bicycle, five hundred books, and a fifteenth-century spinet on which he plays Bach, Byrd, Pasquini, Stravinsky, and jazz (*Virgil Thomson* 110, Imbs 262).

the musical director: At Darmstadt, the *Generalmusikdirector* is Dr. Karl Boehm. In retrospect, Thomson will be glad the premiere of his opera is not in Germany but in the United States:

> Its text would have acquired for twin a German version, and the whole work would have taken on the mood of the German art-theatre. I would have scored it, moreover, for a much larger number of musicians; and its future life, in consequence, would have been led in middle-to-large-size repertory houses. Its American production, had there come to be one, would not therefore have been a possibility for the museum director in Hartford who allowed me eventually to give it a Negro cast, an English choreographer, and cellophane scenery designed by an American painter, and where exiguous theatre-pit led me to score it for a very small and special-sounding group. The repertory houses might or might not have taken it on, but its whole Hartford and Broadway adventure and its production as choreographic theater in the Diaghilev tradition would most likely never have taken place. (*Virgil Thomson* 149)

George Kates: Thirty-five-year-old supervisor of Hollywood set designs, specializing in their historical accuracy, educated at Columbia and Harvard with a doctorate in fine arts from Oxford, lost most of his money in the 1929 stock market crash, is about to leave Hollywood to live in Beijing.

Marion Davies: Former dancer in the Ziegfeld Follies, for twelve years now the mistress of William Randolph Hearst, who relentlessly promotes her film career. By the end of this year, she will have acted in thirty five films including, recently, four talkies.

Antheil . . . his opera: *Transatlantic*, his first opera and a popular success.

Dix Portraits: See note to Stein, [*late* March 1930].

tiresome visitor: Cary Ross, young American poet (with poems in *transition*, March 1928), friend of Grosser, soon of Thomson. While in Paris in the spring of 1928, bearing a letter of introduction by Claribel Cone, he had met Stein, who mentions him at the end of "Finally George A Vocabulary of Thinking," finished in the spring of 1928 (Dydo 214). In New York, Ross is interested in visual art and has been a junior participant in informal discussions about the future of the newly-founded Museum of Modern Art. His friends include Henry-Russell Hitchcock, Philip Johnson, and the museum's director, Alfred Barr Jr. and his wife—Ross officially witnessed their New York wedding (they had a second marriage ceremony in Paris).

his opera: Antheil's *Transatlantic*.

Massot: See note to Stein [16 April *1930*].

à la hauteur: noble, lofty

*****

Postcard of "HANSI—Prière de l'Alsace. –The Prayer of Alsatia . . . ," to "M. Virgil Thomson / 17 Quai Voltaire / Paris."

Bilignin   [15 May 1930]
par Belley
Ain.

My dear Virgil.

As Elliot Paul has so charmingly said the pleasures of frustration are that it is the common lot anyway Bossuet and Mrs. Lasalle standing by is satisfaction and I am very pleased. That whole story about Picasso is xceptionally nasty and as he has been and I by accident know it in detail an xceptionally good son. C'est come c'a que c'a se fait. and lucy church is turning out as pretty as she looks and the same to Bossuet and lots of love   Gtrde.

story about Picasso . . . xceptionally good son: Picasso's mother sold more than 400 of his boyhood drawings and paintings to the dealer Miguel Calvet Martí for 1,500 pesetas, which he then sold in Paris for 200,000 francs. Picasso launched a suit against Calvet, who misled María Picasso into thinking the payment was a deposit for loan of the art, and forbade his mother and sister to sell any more of his youthful works. Stein is likely responding to the sensationalized treatment of the affair in the newspapers, which included suggestions of María Picasso's poverty (and thus Picasso's neglect of her). Picasso's mother had said to him, in Stein's presence, "you are very sweet and as a son very perfect" (*Autobiography* 239).
C'est come c'a que c'a se fait [*C'est comme ça que ça se fait*]: That's the sort of thing people do.

*****

> Beavaisq-Hotel
> Tréport, S. Inf.
> 21 mai [1930]

Dear Gertrude

    I'm come to northern sea-shore to repose from visitors and certainly it is nice with a Catalan proprietor who cooks like angels and the scenery is pleasant and weather very and excellent pears from Canada are to [be] bought for a dime in Eu. I've read proof twice on your book and I guess it's in press now. Bébés exposition is large and fancy and there are a couple of real good pictures and a great deal of pretty painting. Hitchcock has not left yet but the Berlin-bound (3 of them) are departed. Maurice has finished and received good money for two portraits and sold another picture to New York by mail. Saw Bernard chez lui with fancy countesses but the proprietress didnt come.

The Duchess [de Clermont-Tonnerre] is silent in re Bossuet. Unless she peeps shortly I shall go away in early June.

In any case now I plan a high-class concert (alone) in December with a carefully chosen program. Carl announces June arrival. Massot's preface actually got written. Koussevitzky has pronounced the word masterpiece sans reserves from two hearings of Bossuet. I have a nervy idea. I think I'll do the Phèdre of Racine. Entire. René [Crevel] is in town. Not seen by me. But weakish, says Bernard. I return Saturday. How does your garden grow?

> Love
>
> Virgil

exposition: exhibition.
chez lui: at his house.
the Phèdre of Racine: Thomson's *Aire de Phèdre*.

*****

Postcard of "Environs de BELLEY—Château de Musin," to "M. V. Thomson / 17 Quai Voltaire / Paris"

[30 May 1930]

My dear Virgil

Good luck to Phedre, I heard [Sarah] Bernhardt do it in San Francisco when I was sixteen, it moved me. George Antheil seems to have had a large party who went and didn't go, good luck to us all   Gtrde

*****

Wednesday [*4 June 1930*]

Dear Gertrude

Complicated times and many visitors all wanting something and usually getting it but not offering much. Eugene is back. Not seen yet. All sides agree a failure. Toutes les gaffes possibles et de suite. Muriel got him away by holding an auction of his pictures & realized a couple of hundred dollars. George A. is here in glory at the Georges V. I believe Miss Barney, [Ford Madox] Ford, and the Monnier-Beaches went to Frankfort. Plus [Ezra] Pound. I had another party. Lots of people & Bernard & Gaultier-Vignal and Les Lasell and Madame Langlois & Alfred Barr & wife & Cary Ross who is in tenderest relations with Hitchcock. I did a portrait of Hitchcock which is good like Ramon [Senabre]'s and terribly funny.

The atelier show with Marthe & Cliquet not much of a success but it continues. Mrs. Lasell does not seem to be continuing to continue at least no letter for a month & it's the 4th already of this. The Duchesse [de Clermont-Tonnerre] has disappeared and doesnt answer my letters. In short life is very triste but otherwise all is excellent. The morale is good (mostly) and the work of the highest quality. Hugnet says book sells swell. All love and embraces.
                    Virgil

Daisy Barr, née Scolari identified Koussevitzky as a person known in Rome & in Brussels as what you divined.

Toutes les gaffes possible et de suite: all the mistakes possible and one after another.
Muriel: Possibly Muriel Draper, unconventional, flamboyant, dictatorial salon hostess in New York, friend of Stein (see Thomson 12 fevrier [1929]), in Europe to see the premier of Antheil's opera, Antheil being one of her protégés.
Georges V: Landmark Paris hotel, famous for luxury and architectural distinction, built in 1928.
party: According to his pocket diary, Thomson's party was on 29 May.
Monnier-Beaches: Booksellers and publishers Adrienne Monnier and Sylvia Beach, the hyphen marking them as inseparable both personally and professionally. They went to Frankfort for the premier of Antheil's opera. See Thomson 11 May [1930].
Gaultier-Vignal: Louis Gualtier-Vignal, author, formerly a friend of Proust.
Alfred Barr: Alfred Barr Jr. is the first director of the Museum of Modern Art in New York, the world's first museum devoted to modern art.
portrait of Hitchcock: *Russell Hitchcock, reading,* Paris, 29 May 1930.
triste: gloomy.
Daisy Barr: Born Margaret Scolari, wife of Alfred.

*****

[*Possible placement*]

[Note on small torn page, to Gertrude Stein, n.d.]:
Our friend C[ary]. Ross presented translations of poems by our equally friend G. Hugnet to our more or less friend E. Jolas latter remarking in re same (but not reading poems) that publication was impossible because Hugnet belonged to the wrong French group. Does this mean transition gets money from surrealists? (who in turn ditto from Russia says Bernard).
V.G.G.T.

[Possible placement]: The note is undated, but American Cary Ross is in town, and this Spring is the only period during which Thomson signs his name "V.G.G.T."

*****

Monday [June 1930]

Dear Gertrude

I'm going Wednesday to join Sénabre in Mallorca (Puerto Soller). Maurice avec.
The sheets have arrived and I shall sign them today.
I've let my flat to a banker from N.Y. for 3 months.
Duchesse not having a party. Finishing a book–instead. She writes me sweetly–also Miss [Natalie] Barney. Hitchcock left finally. Yesterday. Cary Ross remains. He has improved. Hitchcock has not. Tonny has been here twice, unknown to Anita. Gave me a picture. Georges has a new love-affair, a lesbienne, a "triste & belle histoire." Carl arrives in London tomorrow. Eugene is back. Nothing changed. I shall stay in Mallorca till the Sirocco arrives if any. With luck till September.
Love
Virgil

Here are some good skits from *Judge*. Mangan sent them.

Maurice avec: with Maurice.
Anita: Anita Thompson Dickenson, introduced to Tonny by Van Vechten (Van Vechten to Thomson, 2 Aug. 1930). She is twenty-nine years old, black, a psychologist, teacher, artist, actress, dancer, and model.
triste & belle histoire: sad and beautiful story.
Judge: Periodical of American wit and humour, published in New York.

*****

To "M. Virgil Thomson / ~~17 Quai Voltaire / Paris~~. Casa Francisco Vicens / Puerto Soller / Mallorca / Iles Baleares/ Espagne"

[17 June 1930]

My dear Virgil.

Love to Mallorca from us, eat enzaimadas, and the honey of the orange blossoms and oranges the Soller ones are good, also the sardines and above all the melons confit, red inside green outside wonderful, and there is no sirocco but a hell of a lot of mosquitoes [pursued?] both English and American, we are very cheerful even with the rain, abridging Making of Americans, Macaulay has signed for this fall, it turns out rather good, but has been a task, some amusing people turning up, I guess it is going to be good weather as Henry McBride comes to-day and he always has luck lots of love to yourself Maurice and Mallorca

Gtrde.

Love to Mallorca: Stein and Toklas spent a year (1915–1916) on Mallorca after fleeing air raids on Paris.
enzaimadas: Mallorca is famous for these spiral-shaped pastries, with sweet or savory fillings, dusted with sugar.
confit: candied.
abridging . . . Macaulay: See note to Stein, [26 Feb. 1930].

*****

Two postcards not addressed or stamped, sent in envelope: the first of "Vista Gral de Palma", the second of "'Truyol' Mallorca, España"

> Casa Francisco Vicens
> Puerto de Soller
> Mallorca
> Islas Baleares
> 29 june [1930]

Dear Gertrude - It is all very nice & we have a house with Senabre & a good cook and it all costs practically less than nothing and it is very hot but with a breeze and mosquitoes dont come under my net and the pastry is excellent and do you know the whistles if you like I will bring or send you some it seems we are staying till September and then making some visits in Valencia & Madrid & a French aviator has invited us to fly Madrid-Paris and it all sounds well and I am astonished at how cheap all around even Barcelona is less than France and our maid cooks with butter. Tonny came to see me in Paris several times and was angelic and awfully nice and I enjoyed it again & he gave me a picture and said I mustnt let Anita [Thompson Dickinson] know he had been there. And Bernard seems to have got off handsomely with Mme. Langlois because he has been grand & tender ever since with me ever since. Hitchcock finally left for Germany in an auto with three lovers. Cary Ross gave me a present! And G. Hugnet took me to the train. Your card arrived as I left.   Love & all
         Virgil

we have a house: Thomson, Grosser, and Senabre are renting "a roomy flat in the fishing village of Puerto de Soller" from where they do "a great deal of walking and mountain climbing" (*Virgil Thomson* 165).
the whistles: *siurells*, inexpensive clay children's whistles, usually in the shape of a man on horseback, white with red and green ornamentation, made on Mallorca since Arab times.

*****

Postcard of "BELLEY (Ain)—Monument de Brillat-Savarin et le Promenoir," to "M. Virgil Thomson / ~~17 Quai Voltaire / Paris~~. à Casa Francisco Vicens / Puerto Soller / Mallorca / Iles Baleares/ Espagne"

[30 June 1930]

My dear Virgil,

The book has come and I am really awfully pleased and the translations are good and thanks so much, and the island is it still funny and nice and edible, it used to be so xtremely edible and the melons and the orange honey, and the cakes and the oranges, and the sardines and lots of love to you alwys

Gtrde

The book: *Dix Portraits*. See note to Stein, [*late* March 1930].

*****

Postcard of bull fighting "Juan Belmonte dando media veronica," to "Miss Alice Toklas / Bilignin / par Belley / Ain / Francia"

7 July [1930]

Dear Alice

We have come to live in Palma rather just outside on the sea at Hotel Calamayor and it is good here. Yesterday was fine comida. Weather hot and pleasant. Palma is flirtatious. Food excellent. Best pastry in Soller.   Love.   Virgil

We: After a month of walking and mountain climbing near Puerto de Soller, no longer able to bear "Senabre's daily distress when the postman failed to bring the check owed to him by his Paris dealer," Thomson and Grosser moved to a seaside hotel near Palma. "From there," Thomson can "go by tramcar to the bullfights, or shopping to order shirts and shoes, beautifully made and absurdly inexpensive." He also stays in his room, writing music in bed under a mosquito net (*Virgil Thomson* 165–66).
comida: eating

*****

To "M. Virgil Thomson / ~~17 Quai Voltaire / Paris~~. Hotel Calamayor / Palma de Mallorca / Iles Baleares / Espagne"

[*12* July 1930]
Bilignin
par Belley
Ain

My dear Virgil

Its nice to know you are in Palma I always liked Palma better than Soller and the people are more amusing. I like the decayed pirate quality of Palma and do go out to Terreno and drop a tear for us in calle dos de Mayo I forget the number but it was about the third house to the left after you climbed the stairs and it belonged to a major in the army I forget his name but anyway it had two nice mandarin trees in the back and the most beautiful heliotrope in the little front garden and Polybe I guess Polybe is no more, he used to dance along with the other dogs in the moonlight, dear Terreno, perhaps Mark Gilbert is still in the land it was to him the sharp English lady said you are either old enough to fight for your country or young enough to eat cake so he had to eat cake although he didn't want to. Anyway everybody is delighted with the ten portraits and the translation thereof which is very nice and pleases me a lot thanks so much. I have done George's Enfance, I dunno I think its interesting its a mirroring of it rather than anything else a reflection of each little poem, well you'll see anyway here we are, string beans are abundant so is rain and cold but we all seem to be happy and we hope you are the same

        Alwys
          Gtrde.

---

calle dos de Mayo I forget the number: In 1915–1916 Stein and Toklas stayed at Calle Dos de Mayo 45, the number subsequently changed to 17A, which is half a house divided into smaller units. They rented one of these units. Locally called a "little village," El Terreno is a residential area a half-hour walk from the centre of Palma (Moad 420–22).
Polybe: Stein and Toklas's first dog, purchased during their stay on the island. He was unruly and loud, aggravating the neighbours to the extent that he had to be given away.
Mark Gilbert . . . didn't want to: Stein remembers him in *The Autobiography of Alice B. Toklas* as "an English boy of sixteen with pacifist tendencies" and the English lady scolding him as "a descendant of one of Nelson's captains, a Mrs. Penfold" who objected to his refusal of cake at her house (177). "Mark" appears in "Turkey and Bones and Eating and We Liked It" (1916), both "Mark" and "Gilbert" in "Letters and Parcels and Wool" (1916).
George's Enfance: Hugnet's *Enfances*, a suite of thirty poems, which Stein has not so much translated as responded to in her own styles of English.

*****

Hotel Calamayor
Palma de Mallorca
27 July [1930]

Letters with Notes

Dear Gertrude

Yes Palma is nice and the weather has been superb and the water delicious and Ramon [Senabre] is still at Soller and Maurice has been in Barcelona and Madrid and I have enjoyed my splendid isolation and I have written a sonata for you to play on white keys and also but not for you a violin sonata and the isolation now is less splendid so on the first I shall leave and join Maurice in Barcelona for a few days and then probably go back to France for a little. In September I am due for a visit to Madrid and to Madame Langlois near Biarritz but during August I shall probably rove a bit as is my habit.

Would it be convenient if I paid you a short visit at Bilignin sometime before the end of the month? I have a little money. Mrs. L— having sent another stray check my way. So that my proposal is moved entirely by a desire to see you and Alice and to hold a slight intercourse with a piano in the privacy of its home. Please consider only your own convenience about it. Carl wrote from Carcassonne that he was coming to Barcelona if his cheauffeur could get a passport & hence here. I've been expecting news for 2 days now but none so I dont know maybe he got delayed by the Santiago celebrations. I have read The Bible in Spain with much pleasure. The *Dix Portraits* has never arrived to me though Georges sent it three weeks ago. I have shed appropriate tears at Terreno for you also sweat because I go through it always to get to Calamayor which is further on just beyond Porto Pi and before C'as Catalá. It is beautiful and tranquil and Palma has lots of movement especially from six to eight. Mosquitoes havent bothered here but there are lots of ants. It's best to write me always in Paris because on principle I leave here the first.

            Love and always same
            Virgil

---

a sonata for you to play on white keys: Thomson's Piano Sonata No. 3, "for Gertrude Stein to improvise at the pianoforte," a work composed for the white keys, which are the only keys she plays (*Virgil Thomson* 190).
a violin sonata: Violin Sonata No. 1.
I shall leave and join Maurice in Barcelona: He does go to Barcelona, where he finds Grosser in "a dismal room near a noisy beach and beside the railway tracks" and rescues him "from this self-punishment," going with him by train to Villefranche on the Côte d'Azur, where he writes more music and Grosser paints. In his autobiography Thomson opposes "cheerful France" to Spain, which he experiences as "intense . . . always, even when the intensity is that of a deep dissatisfaction not unlike the irretrievable boredom that seems to be endemic among male Spaniards over thirty" (166).

*****

To "M. Virgil Thomson / ~~17 Quai Voltaire / Paris~~. Hotel Quintana / à Collioure / Pyrènées Orientales"

            [1 Aug. 1930]
            Bilignin

par Belley
Ain.

My dear Virgil,

Sure it will be a pleasure arrange to suit yourself because just at present August is free, we had a delightful visit from Bernard and we all thoroughly enjoyed it, the Picassos are due to-morrow and Carl the end of the week although the last four days he has disappeared, Bravig and family are about six kilometers away, Bravig was a bit seedy but is now looking very fit so let us know when in August you want to come, the piano would like to be played on, what with gardening proofs poetry and visitors I have had no time to improvise, you have not seen my thing of Enfances, it is interesting but more of that when we meet, did you see Laura & Robert on the island or is censoring a letter merely a coincidence. Emily C. has opened communications again, via Ellen I said back that I was pleased and thought she had been millionarish the message will probably not be transmitted so there we are, and I am happy that supplies have recommenced, I was that sad about it, that it was disturbing, I was about to suffer as much as you although as the small boy remarked to an admonishing father not in the same place, but now may she bloom and give, I am now deep in history, what is history history and audiences, but more of that anon, Mary Butts poem in Pagany is good, but they seem to have not done Pierre's poor Pierre. well anyway lots of love

Gtrde.

Enfances: See note to Stein, [*12 July 1930*].
Laura & Robert on the island: Riding and Graves, living, writing, and publishing in Mallorca.
Ellen: LaMotte, long-time companion to Emily Chadbourne.
Mary Butts poem: "Heartbreak House" in *Pagany* 1 no. 3 (Summer 1930): 1–4.
poor Pierre: In this issue (*Pagany* 1 no. 3) appears an advertisement for Pierre de Massot's *Prolégomènes à une éthique sans métaphysique ou Billy, Bull-Dog et Philosophe* (Editions de la Montagne) but he is never published in *Pagany*.

*****

Hôtel Freddy
Villefranche-s-mer. A.M.
9 August [1930]

Dear Gertrude

I stopped 2 days at Callioure where I had your letter & I saw the Darmstadt man & we got on fine and I'll tell you the opera-story later. Anyway he wants a ballet for Berlin and it's already begun. It is very pleasant to be here again & the weather is fine and I shall be coming to Belley in about two weeks. Is Carl there? I've lost track of him.   Love and best

Virgil

the Darmstadt man: Edwin Denby. Thomson later remembers that Denby
> told me the explosion my opera had caused. Darmstadt's bright history in producing left-wing or far-out operas and ballets had been the work of a house-team with progressive ideas, encouraged by and protected by the *Generalintendant* Carl Ebert. . . . but these productions had also been costly, losses being only partly recuperated through works of standard repertory needing little rehearsal and no new scenery. Someone in authority, presumably the *Generalmusikdirecktor* Dr. Karl Boehm, had decided to begin tapering off on modernism by taking a firm stand against *Four Saints*. (*Virgil Thomson* 148)

*****

Postcard of "Environs de Belley—Vieux Pont de Bognens," to "M. Virgil Thomson / Hotel Freddy / Villefranche-sur-mer / A. M."

[11 Aug. 1930]

Hurrah for Berlin, its a sure case of veni vidi vici. Carl and Fania were here and very sweet we had a good time, and have you seen my film in Revue Europeenne, and has Georges sent you my version of Enfances, its nice weather even when it rains and lately it has not been raining   Love
                                                                                       Gtrde.

my film: *Deux Soeurs Qui Ne Sont Pas Soeurs*. Published in *Revue Européenne* 5–7, 1930.

*****

                                                            Freddy
                                                            Villefranche
                                                            14 August [1930]

Dear Gertrude

    The book has just come at last and I see now it is very pretty. Pavlick's drawing is pretty swell. And the Tonnys. Cant say much for Bébé and less for Genia. Preface is nice very nice. And the translations read off all right. I am glad you were pleased & I see now there was some cause because it's a distinguished book. I'll look for the film. Enfances I havent seen. Nor heard from Georges for some time. Carl's new book arrived. It is usual. And we are mentioned. You will like the ballet about Mallorca & priests feeding ensaimadas to the olive-trees.

                                                                                      Love
                                                                                      Virgil

The book: One of the 110 copies of the illustrated version. In addition to Stein's ten verbal portraits, this version of *Dix Portraits* contains visual portraits: that of Pavlik Tchelitchev by himself, those of Bernard Faÿ and Kristians Tonny by Tonny, that of Virgil

Thomson by Bérard, and those of George Hugnet and Genia Berman by Berman. 400 copies were printed without illustrations.
Carl's new book: Van Vechten's 1930 novel, *Parties: Scenes from Contemporary New York Life*, contains the following paragraph:
> I went to Isabel Pollanger's the other night, Claire Madrilena was explaining to David, to hear Virgil Thomson's new opera with words by Gertrude Stein. It is called Four Saints in Three Acts and I was so thrilled by it that on the way home I said to the banker who had taken me that a performance of this work would end all opera, just as Picasso with his imagination had put a stop to repetition in painting. My rich escort looked at me in consternation and exclaimed, End all opera! What would I do Thursday nights? (68-69)

For Thomson's account of the actual exchange on which this is based, see his letter of 21 Feb. [1929].
ensaimadas: Mallorcan pastries. See note to Stein [17 June 1930].

*****

Postcard of "BELLEY—Le Promenoir," to "M. V. Thomson / Hotel Freddy / Villefranche / A. M."

[16 Aug. 1930]

Let us know a couple of days ahead when you are coming and where you want to be met Virieux le Grand or Amberieu, or Culoz, it will be very nice having you, nice and quiet, if you are ready to risk weather,   Love
                                                                    Gtrde

*****

Postcard from "Cote D'Azur—Villefranche-sur-Mer" of "Les Casernes et la Darse," not addressed or stamped.

Monday 19th [*18 Aug. 1930*]
Freddy. Villefranche

Dear Gertrude. I will come to Culoz next Monday afternoon at 3.32. I could also arrive at 8.17 in the morning if you preferred. I imagine that's a bit matinale. Phèdre has been pushing melodious cries. She's a preposterous old thing. We've been having Jacques Viot. Also Marcel Duchamp & Brancusi as neighbors. And the perennial Francis Rose. I'll do my best about weather without water
                         Love,   Virgil
No word from Georges in a month. What's he up to?

Monday 19th: Thomson is mistaken about the date—Monday in August is the 18th.
matinale: morningish
Jacques Viot: Probably the art dealer by that name.
Marcel Duchamp: Forty-three-year-old painter—famous for *Nude Descending a Staircase* (1912)—and sculptor, former Dadaist, associated with the Surrealists, famous as a pioneer conceptual artist for his "readymade" urinal wall-mounted and entitled *Fountain*, later, in an art world dominated by conceptual art, regarded as the most influential artwork of the century. Stein considered him and René Crevel "the most complete examples of french charm" (*Autobiography* 256). Thomson later said about Duchamp, who will become a lifelong friend:

He was like Pierre Boulez. Both of them were the type of super-intellectualized Frenchman who dislikes other people's art so thoroughly that he has to make something his own way that would outdo theirs in some way. They outdid what they were rivalling in complexity. With this kind of work, by the age of thirty the artist has made five absolutely unforgettable works of an extremely elaborate and complex composition. And then he can never relax. He can't be easy-going enough so that by forty he can create easily and be a great master, with freedom. (to Dilworth, 3 Feb. 1981)

Brancusi, Constantin: The Romanian sculptor, fifty-four years old, resident in Paris since 1904.

*****

HOTEL JACOB & D'ANGLETERRE
44, RUE JACOB - PARIS   4 Sept [*1930*] Thursday

Dear Gertrude

I had a pleasant night and I met Carl and gave him the offerings and he was pleased and he will do whatever we say about Mary only she is busy getting ready La Dame aux Camélias and always with the composer and he recommends waiting till after the première (Dec.) to approach her and then he will see her in Chicago and I can see her next spring. In case of emergency he will give me now a letter to her I can present any time an opportunity might arise and that's that. Otherwise I find him immersed in own affairs and not very interested in mine. Nor in Paris now that Berlin has given him the illusion of his lost youth. Paris is sweet and lovely. My tenants are behaving. All seems quite right and I am remembering happy times at Bilignin and the terrace and Basket and Aix and the romantic storm and I thank you for the happy times and I embrace you both and I remember the Enfances whole sentences sometimes and dozing on the train I was playing with Basket who was pale yellow pink and instead of fur had almonds stuck in him like the stewed peaches had. I left a pants-hanger (steel) in my cabinet de toilette. It isnt large. You might put it among your things and bring it when you come back if not too much trouble. I shall go Sunday to Ascain.
                                         Again thanks and always my love
                                                                    Virgil

Carl doesnt really understand anything.
I think God is a better bet.
He is nice though & we have a good time.

Mary: Mary Garden. Stein and Thomson want her to sing the female lead in *Four Saints*. She is a fifty-six year old Scottish-born American soprano, star of the Chicago Opera Company since 1910, an exponent of "the bravoura style," "the French singing style as Jean de Reszke invented it," characteristic of the period preceding the First World War. She used "her lovely voice . . . as an instrument of dramatic projection, not, for all its extraordinary qualities, as the subject of the evening's entertainment." He first heard her sing in 1911. (*The Art of Judging Music* 224–45, 89)
La Dame aux Camélias: title of opera by Verdi based on Dumas's novel of the same title but the reference is to *Camille*, likewise based on the novel, libretto and music by Hamilton Forrest.

happy times: In the late summer of 1930, Stein writes to her friend Ellen du Poy: Virgil Thomson spent about two weeks with us and we had a nice time and he put my film to music [*Deux seours qui ne sont pas soeurs*] . . . we played our whole opera together and were more pleased with ourselves than before. And then Virgil has done some awfully good piano things lately. And then we had an idea he caught a glimpse of Mary Garden in the south, and he says she looks exactly like St. Teresa, and would she be ours. She might, only we don't know quite how to bell the cat, have you any Chicago connections that track her seems to me I had a vague recollection that you at one time knew he[r] very well. . . .
See note to Stein [3 Oct. 1930].

*****

Postcard of "SAULE PLEUREUR . . . Weeping millow [sic]. - Published in 1795 . . . Expiatory Chapel, Square Louis XVI, Paris," to "Miss Alice Toklas / Bilignin par Belley / Ain"

Paris
7 Sept. [1930]

Dear Alice. I am leaving tonight. Paris has been fun. C[arl] has been nice & nasty as usual but mostly nice very. Your chocolates have been a pleasure. The memory of Bilignin is a constant delight.
  Best & always
    Virgil
Hôtel Etchola, Ascain, B.P.

*****

To "M. Virgil Thomson / ~~17 Quai Voltaire / Paris~~. Hotel Etchola / Ascain / B^{sses} Pyrénées"

[8 Sept. 1930]
The pants hanger was found and will be preserved and brought

My dear Virgil,

  Well that is alright, and I will keep Carl going later and he will do all he can and now my idea to start the ball a rolling is for me to write a letter to Mary just so that later it will be in her mind, find out for me her xact address and I will write to her, I think that's the way to begin if she answers me it will be a start, and if she doesn't then it will have been a start anyway, Basket has had fleas but no almonds growing yet and besides he says it is a hell of a hot day and it is, no news otherwise, I have begun well I don't quite know what I have begun [mais?] we will see, and we did enjoy having you and it was very very nice and lots of love and best to Maurice and Mme Langlois   Gtrde

[Note on envelope:] I have played my piece and A. says it sounds quite like it only I had to skip the left accompaniment but that was short and the time changed on me 4 to 5 without warning otherwise O.K.

I have begun . . .we will see: Probably referring to *Madame Recamier: an Opera*. See note to Stein [3 Oct. *1930*].
mais: but
my piece: See note to Thomson, 27 July [1930].

*****

Etchola
Ascain. B.P.
10 Sept [1930]

Dear Gertrude

I suppose it wont hurt to write Mary but she is all wrapped up Mr. de Forrest who is constantly with her and his Dame aux Camélias which has première in December and you know those one-track prima donna minds also Scotch but it wont hurt anything and all the address we know is Beaulieu, A. M. which ought to reach her and dont forget as Carl says that she has probably never heard of either of us but maybe she has at that and you might give her a chance to reply and hear the opera in Paris or I could I guess maybe manage to go to Beaulieu if necessary though Paris is better and in any case I prefer showing to sending because I know what happens to wandering scores. The score I have. It came back from Vienna in answer to my letter but with no word about it. Ascain is very lovely and the garden is nice and the food delicious (though hardly Bilignin) and the country is of an extraordinary beauty you must see it one day with mountains near by and not high and both gentle and grandiose and pretty fields and photogenic oxen and noble Basques and pretty femmes de chambres who speak Spanish in black with white aprons and espadrilles and Madame Langlois is pleasant to see again and she sends you sweet greetings. She was ill in Paris and bored in Cauterets and is thin but I hope the good air and food will pick her up. I am interested in what you have begun and shall be eager to see and if there should ever be an extra copy of Enfances I could use same to good advantage. Georges writes a little depressed at the great beauty of the translation which he fears quite crushes his little poem and says "vraiment j'ai des amis trop forts pour mois".
The weather is good, a little rainy evenings. St. Jean is horrid but sea is sea and I swam today. Bébé, as we supposed, is in Venice. Sauguet writes a number for London Chauve-Souris. Other friendly activities are accounted for by enclosures.

Love to both of you
and many of them.
Virgil

Mr. de Forrest: See note to Stein, 4 Sept [*1930*] Thursday.
vraiment . . . mois: truly I have friends too strong for me. In a letter dated 11 July, Hugnet responds to the Steinian version, "This isn't a translation, it is something else, *it is*

better. I more than like this reflection, I dream of it and I admire it. And you return to me hundred-fold the pleasure that I was able to offer you" (translated, Hugnet to Stein, 11 July 1930, Beinecke Rare Book and Manuscript Library).
Sauguet writes something: *La Nuit* (1930), set design by Bérard.

*****

Ascain
13 Sept [1930]

Dear Gertrude

It's floody and cold. We leave Monday for Paris. I've copied Basket and he is charming. Write me at Quai Voltaire.
Love
Virgil

---

copied Basket: *Deux soeurs qui ne sont pas soeurs* now proceeding as a film project, Thomson set it as a vocal score, suggesting the accompaniment was a musical portrait of Basket at Bilignin.

*****

To "M. Virgil Thomson / 17 Quai Voltaire / Paris."

[17 Sept. 1930]
Bilignin
par Belley
Ain.

My dear Virgil,

Pagany has just written that they are wholly delighted with the two Enfances and are going to print them face to face in the winter number that pleases me very much and you too I know, and beside nothing much, the thing is going on quickly but what it is this I do not know, but it is something, the sun is shining but the nights are cold and Christiane Jouffray was here that is all the combined families and she played my piece on the piano and she did something with it and I dunnow it kind of had a future and it was nice. Otherwise nothing more, I liked all of George Antheil's eight premieres but might he not once in a while pretty soon have a segonde, la segonde empire, well anyway best to us alwys

Gtrde.

Christiane Jouffray: Married daughter of Stein's friend Marthe Giraud.
my piece: See note to Thomson [27 July 1930].
segonde empire: Reference to Napoleon III's second empire after the mid-nineteenth century, Stein suggesting that Antheil's many-times-premiered *Ballet mécanique* (1924) has been his empire, and that it's time he writes something new. See note to Stein [6 May 1927].

*****

Letters with Notes

29 Sunday [*28 Sept. 1930*]

Dear Gertrude

Looking always for flats none yet. Maurice is home busy copying which he does assiduously and prettily also Georges back with lady (Alsatian) and she is divorcing her husband & has a small child & it all looks black for Georges but he is happy & I guess that's enough for us just now. Cliquets also back & quarreling & I guess Marthe is getting restless again for change. Mme. Langlois ill with anthrax on temple dangerous but [Hartman?] operated & she is better but will remain at hospital a week or two. It is Neuilly & I go every evening at 7 and that is a long way at dinner time. If you wanted to write her a card it is 26, Bd. Victor Hugo, Neuilly. Otherwise nothing. Mrs. Lasell writes occasionally, always without check. Paris has never been more beautiful than now. Today walked from Versailles to St. Germain & it was lovely. My stairway remains a mess. Elevator being installed. Elliot Paul is back. For good he says this time. Wife said to be following. Rumors that Tonny & Anita [Thompson Dickenson] have gone & got married. And that's that.
I read Lucy Church every night. I am overjoyed about *Enfances'* publishing. I've boasted of salmon carp to everybody & practically none have ever even heard of it. I had a good dinner last night with liver & raspberries. At my corner bistro. Coq de bruyère remains a memory.

Love & Love to each
& all
Virgil

---

lady (Alsatian): Marcelle Ferry. She and Hugnet met in 1929, Ferry leaving her husband and child to be with Hugnet for a relationship that will last a few years.
29 Sunday: Thomson is mistaken about the date—Sunday in September is the 28th.
Coq de bruyère: capercaillie or wood grouse. Thomson must have eaten this during his recent visit to Bilignin. There is a recipe for Braised Grouse in the *The Alice B. Toklas Cook Book*.

*****

To "M. Virgil Thomson / 17 Quai Voltaire / Paris."

[*3 Oct. 1930*]
Bilignin
par Belley
Ain.

My dear Virgil.

The Herald says Mary Garden is in Paris visiting friends. I wrote to her and she got it alright I guess because it did not come back so that is that for a beginning, now I think it should be followed up gently do you know anybody in Paris who knows her in any case I think it would be worth while to have Maurice go for us and gently xplain to her all about us and our work, I think he would be better than you or me or Carl, anyway

170   *Letters with Notes*

Carl will begin again later, you see your insuces facile and my firm conviction might say profound conviction that nothing will happen does not make us a very good team of go getters. Now I think Maurice can do for us what we cannot do for ourselves and I think that it ought to be done now as Ellen du Poise who is in Chicago and thinks Mary Garden will make and has made and can make an xcellent nun will be talking about it out there, well of course nothing will happen but it is awfully important that it should for your sake, really and truly for your sake, so send Maurice and quickly, don't go yourself send Maurice, don't think this is foolish it isn't. Say they are doing funny things matrimonially all our little friends, and George whom we xpect Monday he does not want to marry the Alsatian does he gare the only thing more single track than Wilson an opera singer or a Breton or a Scotchman is an Alsatian, well there is nothing to do about that, I play my piece almost every day and Alice says it is begin[ning] to sound quite like it, since I have finished my play opera I have been taking it easy I got kind of xcited over it, I don't yet know whether it is anything but that we will have to see too   Lots of love
                                                                                        Gtrde.
I am writing to Mme Langlois. I was awfully sorry about her being so ill, you know I like her and think awfully well of her but when I see her she bothers me, G.

---

insuces [*insuccès*] **facile**: easy failure, a tendency to give up.
Ellen du Poise . . . nun: Also spelt Du Poy, friend of Stein, novelist and journalist, will publish several articles on Stein in the *Chicago Daily Tribune*. In response to Stein's request about Mary Garden (see note to Thomson, 4 Sept [*1930*]), Du Poy writes, "No, I don't know Mary Garden but she does look like a nun and I suspect she *has been, or is,* or *will be* some day."
funny things matrimonially all our little friends: By now the younger friends of Stein and Thomson included the composer and writer Paul Bowles, a poet named John Latouche, and a photographer named Paul Durham, all in their early twenties, all gay. Bowles and Latouche married lesbians. Durham is engaged to a heterosexual woman he will marry in 1940.
gare: French interjection, meaning "Watch out!"
single track . . . Wilson: Woodrow Wilson (1856–1924), Democratic president of the United States from 1913–1921. Stein's interest in Wilson is evidenced by her early work "Fernhurst," where she incorporates aspects of his personality into her portrait of the professor Philip Redfern (Katz xxvi), and by her portrait of him in *Useful Knowledge*. Wilson's "single track" nature was most famously apparent in his refusal to compromise with the Republicans on the Treaty of Versailles, resulting in the failure of the United States to join the League of Nations.
I play my piece: See note to Thomson [27 July 1930].
my play opera: Probably *Madame Recamier: An Opera*. Published in *Operas & Plays* (Paris: Plain Edition, 1932).

*****

Postcard titled "Souvenir de BELLEY (AIN.)" with 8 vignettes, to "M. Virgil Thomson / 17 Quai Voltaire / Paris"

[6 Oct. 1930]

Mary seems to have gotten away before even Maurice could get there helas well anyway she says she aint going to sing anymore, so now it will have to be another, Georges is here and we are all happy

love

Gtrde.

[in Georges' hand:]   Affection sous
                       cutanée GEORGES

---

ain't going to sing anymore: Mary Garden will retire from the opera stage in 1931.
Affection sous cutanée: Deep affection, punning on *injection sous-cutanée*, subcutaneous hypodermic injection.

*****

Tuesday [7 Oct. 1930]

Dear Gertrude

Mary left Paris the day I had your letter. Maurice is sorry. I think he was rather pleased at the idea of calling on her. I've told Carl to write her. Georges & lady spent Sunday here. I like her. As you have likely learned from Georges, practically all the informations in my last letter were false. Mme. Langlois is getting better. Still at hospital. It was nice of you to write her. I am staying in my flat for the present (at Maurice's expense) and we both live here and work here and it's a little close but better & cheaper than a hotel and doesnt really go badly. And we both eat. And I am pleased with my summer's work. And I am copying. And hunting flats. There is one near Pantheon, new, ready in April, we may take. Carl writes. Cingria much in view. We share ideas on Gregorian music. His book on Saint-Gall very good. Bravig calls. Church visible at café. Departs tomorrow to be a don at Oxford. Mrs. [Elliot] Paul still said to be arriving. On water I believe. Mrs. Lasell writes of poverty & Mr. Lasell has sold 60 horses. All but his best ones. I kidded her sweetly about it. Georges brings you the rest of news

There remains love & kisses.

Virgil

Church: Ralph Withington Church, American doctoral student in philosophy at Oriel College, Oxford (writing his dissertation on Malebranch), friend of Sherwood Anderson, who wrote him a letter of introduction to Stein. He and his wife, Georgia, became friendly with Stein in 1927 when he began trying to place her writings with publishers. He gave a talk on Stein to the Johnson Society of Pembroke College on 17 June 1928 and published "A Note on the Writing of Gertrude Stein" in *transition* no. 14 (Fall, 1928): 164–68. He subsequently became a professor of philosophy at Cornell and then Berkeley (Dydo 108).
very good: Thomson considered Charles-Albert Cingria's *La Civilisation de St. Gall* a masterpiece, "the most erudite and yet most readable hypothesis of the origin of the Gregorian chant I ever read" (quoted by Imbs, 258) and written "in the most beautiful French prose" (*Virgil Thomson* 110).

*****

Postcard entitled "Environs de BELLEY—Pont d'Aignoz sur le Seran," to "Monsieur Virgil Thomson / 17 Quai Voltaire / PARIS / 6"

[8 Oct. 1930]

My dear Virgil.

Lets be strong, lets send Maurice to interview O. Kahn and tell him to put us in sans blague Hotel Ritz and as he is a friend of Carl and Jo why not, so let us be strong and send Maurice, George and I have come to a nice conclusion for a book of you, that is your music and I am most happy that it is arranged but he will tell you all about it, Love and kisses

Gtrde.

[in Hugnet's hand:]
Oui, je crois, je suis sûr que
notre projet est très bien. Donne
moi rendez-vous vite. Ton GEORGES

Kahn: Otto Kahn, founder of the Metropolitan Opera Company in New York. Stein suggests that Grosser propose to him that he hear Thomson play and sing *Four Saints*.
sans blague: no kidding.
conclusion for a book: Stein and Hugnet have agreed to publish a special edition of Thomson's music in Hugnet's Editions de la Montagne, for which Hugnet's father agreed to put up $200, Stein pledging to supply the remainder, which, they estimate, could go as high as $800 (Tommasini 212).
Oui ... GEORGES: Yes, I believe, I am certain that our project is very good. Let's meet soon. Yours GEORGES.

*****

Friday [*10* Oct 1930]

Dear Gertrude

I was strong and showed your card to Maurice and he said no and I said nothing at all because I couldnt think of any and as a matter of fact if Otto Kahn must be seen it is plainly my duty to do it myself or even you who could give him the high-hatting that he loves and bestow the honor of an acquaintance for the service demanded. Mary is different because she is professional and a woman and personally sympathetic. However, I will write to Otto today and I think it would be more impressive if you wrote also saying you hope he will see me. I shant mention Jo or Carl.
I copy music & I *may* have a flat in April. Maurice copies music & feeds me. Madame Langlois leaves her hospital next week. On Monday. Paris remains beautiful. My chauffe-bains has gone away to get a new insides. I have read Bravig's Cat book & find it extremely dull. Cingria is much about & very nice.

Love toujours
Virgil

Letters with Notes

[on separate sheet, likely written later in the day and mailed with above:]

I have written Otto & said Carl urged me show him the opera & will he do me the honor of inspecting the score or of allowing me to sing him same. I mentioned you in the last sentence as author of the text.

I think it would be nice if you wrote (just as one greatman to another) and said you hope he will see me. The idea being that it is my opera & you as author of text have a paternal interest in my career and can allow yourself to write him about me without seeming to be really asking a favor for yourself too much.

Otto Kahn . . . Mary: he influential at the Metropolitan Opera in New York, she at the Chicago Opera. Owing largely to the recent stock market crash, nothing will come of attempts to interest these U.S. operatic centers in *Four Saints*.
chauffe-bains: water-heater.
Bravig's Cat book: *The Cats*, published in 1935 in Dutch translation (Dydo 417).

*****

Sunday [*12 October* 1930]

D.G.

Here's Otto [Kahn]'s answer. And a card from Cingria he asked me to send you. Paris is colder but lovely. Bernard writes from Ohio of fausse naiveté. I have become very fond of my violin sonata. I am eager to see the historical tragedy.

L. & K.
Virgil

---

fausse naiveté: false naiveté.
historical tragedy: Stein's recently completed *Madame Recamier* (see note to Stein [3 Oct. *1930*]), which may particularly interest Thomson because it is subtitled *An Opera*.

*****

To "Monsieur Virgil Thomson / 17 Quai Voltaire / Paris 6" [in Hugnet's hand], postmarked Paris, rue Danton, so probably written by Stein at Bilignin and mailed by Hugnet in Paris

[13 Oct. 1930]

My dear Virgil.

Voilà I write and tell him as if I had the habit of telling him what he should do that he should listen to you, sure he will have left before our letters get there but then you can't do everything, you can't think of it and get there in time, however it is an effort, and we will save Maurice for another time, I am glad things are going nicely, we have had a nice time with

Georges although the weather has been bad, but projects are many and I hope they come off, and lots of love

Gtrde.

Cher et grand Virgil, je pars, ce soir. –

Entendu pour mardi 6^H, chez toi. Je trouverai ta letter chez moi demain avec mon petit déjeuner.

Je pense que nos projets, à Gertrude et à moi, te conviendront et même te feront grand plaisir. Alors à mardi. Je te raconterai cela.

Ton GEORGES

Cher et grand Virgil . . . GEORGES: Dear great Virgil, I'm leaving this evening. Tuesday 6 o'clock at your place is fine. I'll find your letter at home tomorrow with my breakfast. I think Gertrude's and my plans will suit you and in fact will give you great pleasure. I'll see you Tuesday then. I'll tell you all about it. Yours, Georges.

*****

Sunday [19 Oct 1930]

Dear Gertrude

Otto [Kahn] as you know. Miss [name?] has been written to but not yet replied from. Duchesse is having me this week to lunch and sing. I am delighted with plans for edition & much obliged to you for aid. The plans however seem to be some different after reflection and discussion. Namely.

It seems hardly gentil to advertise an *amitié à trois* with 3 painters looking on from the 2nd class compartment. So I presume the amicable nature of the collaboration had better be left to the préface.

I dont approve (commercially) of mixing vocal with instrumental music or French texts with English. So I guess it must be all vocal and (to include Georges) all French.

I had consequently imagined 3 Tableaux de Paris. *The Seine, The Berceau, the Film.* But Georges objects to appearing between two ladies and really feels very deeply anyway on subject of D^{chesse} de Rohan. And he prefers Racine but that makes a funny mixture and so we settled for the present on 4 pieces. *Fable of La Fontaine, Phedre of Racine, Valse Gregorienne* of Georges, & *Film*. I think it is a nicely varied program myself.

Also my copyist says phototypie is ruinous in expense. I personally think it not *trés serieux* comme édition. Especially since there is Viennese fac-simile edition of scores by the great masters done as nothing in Paris could touch. I prefer zinc engraving* (* Or an imitation of same. It costs half. We are going Tuesday to the engraver & look at everything to see what is best.), in-quarto, each piece in a cover† (†The title of the piece might be written in upper corner in pencil so as not to interfere with the picture & still be recognizable without opening.) of real eau-forte by a different artist, the whole in a plain printed cover all pages simply folded loose, no sewing. This is a high-class musical format & the quarto size makes it feasible for both the piano and the book-case. I have an early Satie edition something like this with cover by Puvis de Chavannes which Georges thought an excellent model & we can change it where we like but it is a thing to start from. We suggest Leonide [Berman] as the fourth artist.

> Leonide for La Fontaine
> Pavelich for Phèdre
> Marcoussis for Georges
> Tonny for you.

Or any way you like, for that matter, or any body.

I propose a preface by Carl Van Vechten in English. I should like a small avant-propos also myself in French.

I imagine one might do 150 or 175 copies at 150 francs & 25 at 750 with signatures & mss. of something not in the book, perhaps the Marquis de Sade piece, or Susie Asado, or a portrait or a part of your Sonata. That might be varied for each subscriber, anyway something trick. I suggest these figures because they seem feasible in dollars, 6 & 30, however I am open to any kind of reason. We can figure accurately as soon as we have full prices on everything. I do think all copies should contain the illustrations.

I have no really swell title yet. *Four French Texts* might do.

Let me know any changes you would propose and what you think of this plan.

Paris is still grand & lovely. Tonny is visible. Anita is reconciled because there is money in the offing from some old Dutch pictures Tonny discovered somewhere. Jo & Nora Lasell are back. My summer's work is all corrected and copied & recorrected and learned & ready for customers. Madame Langlois has gone to recuperate in Burgundy. *Lucy Church* has been loaned to Janet Flanner for New Yorker mention. A violinist is coming to tea. The week is opening hopefully. Will you be back soon?

Love & happiness
Virgil

---

delighted with plans for edition & much obliged to you for aid: See note to Stein [8 Oct. 1930].
an *amitié à trois*: friendship of three, Stein, Thomson, and Hugnet.
The Seine, The Berceau, the Film: By Duchesse de Rohan, Hugnet, and Stein respectively.
Puvis de Chavannes: French symbolist painter, 1824–1898.
Leonide [Berman]: see note to Stein [19 June 1928].
Marcoussis, Louis: Forty-six-year-old Polish-born leading Cubist painter, engraver, cartoonist, book-illustrator, an associate of Picasso, Braque, Apollinaire, close friend to Gris and Max Jacob, who introduced him to Stein.
Jo & Nora Lasell: Josiah Lasell, brother to Philip, and his wife. In 1926, Thomson wrote *Ten Easy Pieces and a Coda: For Josiah Lasell to Play on the Pianoforte*.

*****

To "M. Virgil Thomson / 17 Quai Voltaire / Paris."

[21 Oct. 1930]

> Bilignin
> par Belley
> Ain.

My dear my dear,

Yes of course you have a weakness for french texts thats alright but we want to sell the darn thing and we got to have the reclame of English texts in other words mine to help sell it believe me it is not for anything xcept selling and also I definitely want some thing that has no words, this is a sample we are offering of one Virgil Thomson in whom we believe as well as a pretty book and we want it to reach as many people as possible and we want the samples as various as possible, no rather a few pages of the opera than any more french and cut down the artist illustration as much as possible, I don't think they will help sell this particular book a lot, and what I want is to have something that will reflect credit on the three of us as a book and will show you to the best advantage, it was really a concession to Georges to have any painters at all I would much rather do more of you than that, think about it from that end, I personally think the three friends and practically confined to that with the intention of your being shown in as much music as possible is my firm idea.

I don't think using Carl as a little forward is a bad idea but go slow on that until we talk it over and your forward must be in English as well as in french, your little xplanation of your aims and fancies, now be good control the french passion, I like the french alright but English ain't so worse, et la musique avant tout, give my very very warm regards to the Duchesse of whom I am really awfully fond and I am awfully pleased that we are going to do you, you have done an awful lot for all of us and I want to do a little for you but remember, this is to show your music and it has to sell and be seen because that is important for you just now, my dear Virgil

lots of love

> Gtrde.

And now this pour my idea more or less, Have the Gregorian Waltzes of Georges, Preciosilla & a piece of the opera. mine. A sonata mine or others for piano or violin, (I like the one for [C.?]P. a lot) And a movement of the church sonata which Alice likes a lot,

I don't say just this but something like that and enough of each so it is something, then do the whole thing in a loose cover based on the one Tonny did for the Berceuse and this could be done by Marcoussis & Tonny together, and cut out the introductions entirely, this is just a general scheme but the kind of thing I have in mind,

> Our real love and kisses
> Gtrde.

---

reclame: *réclame*, publicity.
et la musique avant tout: and mainly the music.
pour: for.

the one for [C.?]P.: C. P. is probably Thomson's close friend and colleague Cliquet-Pleyel, for whom Piano Sonata no. 1 or Piano Sonata no. 2 could have been written, Thomson considering him an expectional pianist. In 1928 Thomson composed his portrait, *Cliquet-Pleyel in F*.
church sonata: See Thomson [9 January 1929].
Berceuse: *Le berceau de Gertrude Stein*, a poem by Georges Hugnet.

*****

To "M. Virgil Thomson / 17 Quai Voltaire / Paris."

[22 Oct. 1930]
Bilignin
par Belley
Ain.

My dear Virgil,

I am being quite thoughtful you see I want this book to do for you something like Geography and Plays did for me, make something definite and representative that can occupy, and now this is a possible idea which will if it is not too costly if you can perhaps be [feasible?] and sufficiently meaty, Capitals, Bossuet and Gregorian Waltzes of Georges, that is all on the same more or less idea, and represents three distinct periods and would be saleable, and would show you at your heights, think this over, very carefully you see I want you shown at your best and want you saleable to those who are your natural audience, and so far this is the only combination that seems to me to have raison d'etre, I don't mind being with two gentlemen, it may of course be too long, that is another matter anyway think about it, inclosed two tickets that may amuse Maurice, I am finishing my tragedy of Maurice etc, the first Mme Recamier, faded too gently for a real tragedy but its pretty good, lots of love my dear, Yours Gtrde.

tragedy of Maurice: See note to Thomson [*late* Nov. 1930].

*****

Wed. [*22 and 23* Oct. 1930]

Dear Gertrude

Yes of course I see now what you are wanting from me I didn't from Georges explanation and I am entirely amenable. I had the idea that a mixed collection wouldnt sell at all. I remember a collection of piano & vocal music by Ethelbert Nevin called *Sketch Book* that nobody bought although there were some wows in it that sold like anything when they were brought out separately. You see there is one public which buys vocal music, another piano, another fiddle & so on, also a different public for French and for English. This of course is the public of professionals and of private persons who sing or play something, the important public in fact, and I hesitated to exclude them by addressing myself only to book-collectors & complaisant friends. A collection such as you propose would be very imposing, like Antheil's musical supplement to This Quarter, and if you think we can sell it, all right.

As for including more pieces & less pictures I am all for it. Georges thinks books dont sell without pictures. We might have one portrait of me perhaps. If you want to do a big book, we might even publish the opera no less. That will be seen about when we know costs. In any case we'll do whatever you want to do and I am just stating objections. I remain with a leaning toward a professional book which might have some possibility of a legitimé sale. If we make expenses I can always publish others. It isn't as if this was the only music I was ever going to get printed at least I don't like to think so. And I imagine a book with some unity should sell better than just morceaux choisis. Also that my newer pieces will appeal more to my friends than ones they know.

Now it's tomorrow & I have your other letter and now you see what I mean and I like what you suggest. Capitals Bosseut & George's Waltz, plus maybe Preciosilla makes an excellent book. Or prelude to opera instead of Capitals if you prefer. It's shorter and extremely good. Anyhow we are getting close to something.

Duchesse hasnt written yet as she promised but I presume she will. Ch. de Noailles invited me to his film. I think I shall ask him over one day for music.

I want to see the tragedies.

Love & soon
Virgil

Thanks tickets. Embrace Alice.

---

legitimé: legitimate.
morceaux choisis: selected pieces.
his film: The Vicomte Charles de Noailles has produced and financed Cocteau's first film, *Le Sang d'un Poète*, which was completed in September 1930.

*****

To "M. Virgil Thomson / 17 Quai Voltaire / Paris."

[25 Oct. 1930]
Bilignin
par Belley
Ain.

My dear Virgil,

Yes we will get something that will combine all distinction professionalism and saleability, all three good things, meditate encore, the Capitals have one advantage they would be dedicated to the Duchess but is that an advantage does she really help to sell about that I don't know, I would naturally prefer the prelude but is it better to have a whole thing than a part, also about Carl would his introduction help sell and to the public you want [to] meditate upon that of course he would be pleased, also investigate cheap printing of music because if done on good paper it looks swell as voila the Ten Portraits, and about pictures you see what I mean is that if you put in pictures then the public kind of don't want it without pictures they think they are being done that I think has been a mistake about the other editions de la Montagne, the difference should be paper but all the edition should have the same content xcept signatures and ms. pages and such personal knickknacks think about that also, well thanks a lot and we will be home soon now the snow is in the hills opposite and the fires in the chimney are nice and it is very nice but all the same we will be in Paris soon and that will be nice

Gtrde.

A title just pops into my head quite simply

The Music of Virgil Thomson

(and then below as if we were illustrators) texts of Gtrde Stein, Bossuet and Gge Hugnet.

---

encore: again.

*****

Mardi [*28 Oct. 1930*]

Dear Gertrude

Yes d'accord in re illustrations.
How's this?

Capitals,	
Valse	Preceded by a Preface of Carl Van Vechten & an essay by me on musical prosody.
Song of Solomon	
Bossuet	

This will bring out my largest clientele, the one that respects me on musical matters & especially this matter. And Carl is excellent. Highly respected on music. He is the only man in America whom all sides read. (He did a good preface to launch Rimsky[-Korsakov]'s autobiography, I remember.) The book makes sense and raison d'etre. The four pieces illustrate the problems of recitative or conversation, lyric poetry, coloratura singing, and ceremonial prose.

It might be called *Words with Music* or *Music for Words*.
I'm afraid it makes a pretty big book. About 100 pages.
I've been grippy and havent been able to go to the
engraver-places. I will eventually.

A book like that neednt be too well printed if paper is good. But it must be sewed to cloth, like opera scores. Here's a good proposition anyway. We can always cut it down.

L. & K.

Virgil

Thanks pretty photo & 4-leaf clover. I dine tonight with the duchess. I've read a Jules Vernes book with pleasure.

Rimsky[-Korsakov]'s autobiography: *My Musical Life* (New York: Knopf, 1923).

*****

[*Possible placement*]
To "M. Virgil Thomson / 17 Quai Voltaire /Paris."

[15 Nov. 1930]

My dear Virgil,

We were stupid, Carl gives us the best answer in his letter, he says that it is possible perhaps to find a publisher over there for the opera, in which case of course he introduces it and all is well and over here unfortunately the xigencies of the editor of the Press of the Montagne forces the use of the mixed languages, so there you have the thing ready made and actually I think Carl would prefer if he is to be connected with the opera to have the New York glory, so I imagine that is the thing to do and if he could introduce and get the opera published over there we would not ask anything better, as soon as I know from you I will write to him too

Love

Gtrde.

[Possible placement]: We propose that this and the following note belong in November, rather than December, the month an earlier editor identified in the smeared postmark. Carl Van Vechten writes on 14 December, "Dear Gertrude: So glad to hear from you & Virgil and to hear that Santa Theresa may be published, introduced by me!" (*The Letters of Gertrude Stein and Carl Van Vechten*, 231). Such a response would logically follow, rather than precede, these notes from Stein and Thomson. Furthermore, Van Vechten's note from New York would not arrive in Paris by 15 Dec.
Carl . . . introduces: After its appearance in *transition* (June 1929), the opera libretto is next published in *Operas & Plays* (1932). In 1934 it is published separately by Random House, with the Van Vechten preface.

*****

[*Possible placement*]

[*Nov. 1930*]

D.G.

Yes its swell idea I've wrote Carl. Sent him some music avec.
I have some other good ideas about things too.
See you soon.

                                    Love
                                         Virgil
I said fine find us an editor. Mine exiges I write preface. So we save you for opera.
---

music avec: with music
exiges: demands.

*****

To "M. Virgil Thomson / 17 Quai Voltaire / Paris."

GERTRUDE STEIN
27 RUE DE FLEURUS
PARIS

                                         [22 Nov. 1930]

My dear Virgil,

   We don't seem to be getting chez vous this afternoon with the vegetables but we will Monday afternoon and will you leave chez your concierge Mme Recamier, on Monday because I have to have it for Tuesday and best of good luck to the tea-party,

                         Alwys
                             Gtrde

Mme Recamier: Stein wrote *Madame Recamier: An Opera* in September and loaned it to Thomson, possibly to consider setting to music.

*****

                                         [*late* Nov. 1930]

Dear Gertrude

   Thanks many for the fine tiny carrots and for the squash which I cooked last night & mashed with butter and it was delicious. I reread the plays and I am a little bothered with the Maurice & Eugene one. It is on its way somewhere quite new from Enfances & Mme. Récamier & maybe it will get tragic. It's one of those stark ugly little stories, you know, all drab & realistic, but it starts to take flight every now & then & I suppose that's what tragedy is, something ugly that takes flight. Anyway it's very different from Mme. Récamier which is really Lucy Church & Enfances & not much new except the shape. She is very beautiful of course but she doesnt bother me like the other.
                         Love   Virgil
It's the pastorale texture of Mme. R— that keeps her safe & sound. It's the harsh texture of the other that pushes the cataclysm away. If you make the texture impersonal like Mme R— but nobler, I think the catastrophe will

happen. (And of course, one may find on reflexion that it has happened already.)

Krembourg came & was all sold on me & opera, wife too. Everything O.K. Mrs. Wertheim excused herself at the last moment. Probably I got off better with Krembourg for being alone.

Maurice & Eugene one: *They Weighed Weighed-Layed*, which features eight Maurices and four Eugenes. Like *Madame Recamier*, it was written in the fall of 1930 and published in *Operas and Plays* (Paris: Plain Edition, 1932).
Krembourg: Alfred Kreymborg, poet, playwright, novelist and editor of the little magazines *The Glebe*, *Others*, and *Broom*. The famous first Imagist anthology, *Des Imagistes*, was published as an issue of *The Glebe*. He visited Thomson at 2 on 18 November (pocket diary).
Mrs. Wertheim: See note to Stein, [7 Nov. 1928].

*****

To "M. V. Thomson / 17 Quai Voltaire / Paris."

[26 Nov. 1930]

My dear Virgil,

The trouble with tragedy is that it is if it could be something else but that really is not for us, it could not be something else and if it could it still would not be tragedy but it used to be, I'll bring them back to you Saturday to see about Maurice, and he has indeed forced me to my favorite problem of narrative, I think if I could once really understand narrative I would know what to use and what not to use in plays, so I am at it again, it has commenced not surprisingly, I am pleased about Kreymborg, and something may happen, anyway I am pleased,

Alwys
Gtrde.

*****

Saturday [6 Dec. 1930]

Dear Gertrude

I'm afraid I have a coeur sensible after all. I thought I had won the little incident with Georges about Pierre's book and I was proud of myself but I came home and went to bed of a grippe and so I guess I didn't after all. However, it seems to be leaving sooner than last year.

Love
Virgil

It seems (via Mary Reynolds) that Pierre & Robie are being thrown out of their flat (yesterday or tomorrow) unless they raise 2000 francs & that the reason for selling the bed was to have money & prevent same but they cant get any money out of Mme. Ferry nor sell bed elsewhere.

coeur sensible: soft heart.
the little incident with Georges about Pierre's book: Thomson has greatly helped Pierre de Massot with his book *Prolégomènes à une Ethique sans Métaphysique, ou Billy Bull-dog et philosophe* and, expecting a complimentary copy from the publisher, Georges Hugnet, did not subscribe to purchase a copy. He subsequently demanded one from Hugnet and got it. According to his pocket diary, Thomson saw Hugnet on 1 and 2 Dec.
Robie: Robbie, Scottish wife of Pierre de Massot, for whom see note to Stein [16 April 1930]. They were impoverished partly owing to his opium addiction.
Mme. Ferry: See note to Thomson 29 Sunday [*28 Sept, 1930*]

*****

To "M. Virgil Thomson / 17 Quai Voltaire / Paris."

[*9 Dec. 1930*]

My dear Virgil

Sorry about the grippe but look here I am not awfully anxious to mix in but you must not be too school girlish about Georges and also after all he is putting down his 5000 francs of his fathers credit for your book and hell it is a gamble and he could do things with it that would be surer and after all he is doing it and after all nobody else is, its alright but nobody else is so remember the Maine and even if there is a minority report you must not overlook this thing, and beside why the hell should not Pierre give you the book as well as George but anyway that is another matter, this is only to cure the grippe, anyway I love you all very much but I always do a little fail to see that anyone is such a lot nobler than anyone else we are all reasonably noble and very sweet   Love to you and to Maurice
Gtrde.

---

remember the Maine: American patriotic slogan during the Spanish-American war. The *Maine* was a battleship whose sinking, in 1898, was blamed on Spain and precipitated the war. Stein is advising against making a pretext for hostilities.

*****

Tuesday [*9 Dec. 1930*]

Dear Gertrude

Do you know Krembourg's address. If you do would you mind sending it to Mary Reynolds, 14, rue de Monttessuy, VIIeme? She wants to give him her house in Villefranche which would really be a nice little gift. My flat didnt come thru. The woman decided against taking in young men. I've put an advertisement in Figaro. Thanks for therapeutic letter. I'm silly enough but not really school-girl because I havent used my sorrows for black-mail & the incident is closed. It was that I got angry which I dont do often & not being in a position to fight back on account of music-publishing & the girl being present & we being at your house & several other services Georges was doing me I just caught cold before I knew what had happened. Whatever feeling is left is turned against the girl who is after all none of my business. And we are all being decent & patient with her for the moment. Anyway that's all that & I've payed my nobility with a sore throat.

Love
Virgil

---

the girl: Probably Marcelle Ferry. See note to Thomson 29 Sunday [*28 Sept, 1930*]

*****

To "M. Virgil Thomson / 17 Quai Voltaire / Paris."

[10 Dec. 1930]

My dear Virgil,

We have Rosenfeld's book and he gives you a pretty good send off, all the more reason for the book to get out in time, and your little piece to be written but you'll see it, Robbie is an ass, about Mary Reynold's je n'en sais rien, but all of this will be xplained, about your house in the rue St Louis really and truly we are glad that it isn't yours we did not say anything because you were pleased but the Bradley's who live there go from one slight fever complaint to another and so does anybody on the island and neither of you are just made for that kind of thing, I hope something turns up on land, have done another play not a play every day but a play every other day,

Love
Alwys
Gtrde.

Rosenfeld's book . . . pretty good send off: Paul Rosenfeld, *An Hour with American Music* (Philadelphia : J. B. Lippincott, 1929), 96-98. He writes:

> The flippancy so specially Satie's and his progeny's, the Parisian Six, plays a large role in Thomson's art. His Valse Grégorienne and his half absurd, half grandiose settings of . . . the Duchesse de Rohan, charming as they remain, are bits of Gallic clowning. . . . The one American poet he has distinguished is Gertrude Stein; but his musical arrangements of her opera of St. Teresa and St. Ignatius, and her cantata Capital Capitals, are ultimately *jeux d'esprit*. To be sure, both works are musically effective; and the fourth act of the opera, with its processional and its chorus Dead as Dead, has a real worth; the words being changed very rapidly to an original kind of monody. . . . Still, the music in these works is to be found chiefly in Gertrude Stein's wonderfully melodious prose; Thomson having contented himself particularly in the opera, with the purveyance of a mere accompaniment of wilfully banal chords and arpeggios, and simple figures comically emphasized. . . . Thomson began by writing some tangos in the style of Satie's best disciple, Milhaud. (Thomson's were much better than Milhaud's, too.) And one of the most respectable of his pieces, the Sonata da Chiesa for clarinet, trumpet, viola, horn, and trombone, is still suggestive of Satie's influence. Thomson not only places a tango between the chorale and a fugue; but strives for and attains the simplicity of line and purity of expression of Satie's serious works. Some more recent compositions . . . are more radical and original. All of them have a primitive naiveté. . . .

je n'en sais rien: Who knows.
rue St. Louis . . . island: Running east-west, the Rue St. Louis-en-L'Ile bisects the Ile St-Louis. This is the island in the Seine west of the Ile de la Cité, the heart of ancient Paris. Bradley's office is at 5 rue St. Louis-en-L'Ile, and he and his wife, Jenny, live next door.
a play every other day: This phrase appears in "Politeness," a piece written a couple of months earlier, later published in *Painted Lace*. Stein is now a prolific playwright, composing eleven plays in 1930 alone.

*****

Postcard of: "S.A.R. Monseigneur le Comte de Paris" to "M. Virgil Thomson / 17 Quai Voltaire / Paris."

[1x? Dec. 1930]

My dear Virgil.

We did have a good time last evening and I think our plans good ones, and we better see right away if Prahl could be heated up about the opera, it would be nice to give a private show of it and if it worked we could have a semipublic one with Bernard introducing us that would be chic, anyway we will [have?] something about something and have a lively winter, go to it, I am awfully pleased with Basket and Alice is awfully pleased with the violin sonata, next time I will listen to that first, I have started a new one at least I think I have,   Love
                                                                Gtrde.

Prahl: Victor Prahl, American baritone.
violin sonata: No. 1

*****

To "M. Virgil Thomson / 17 Quai Voltaire /Paris."
27 RUE DE FLEURUS
PARIS

[16 Dec. 1930]

My dear Virgil,

I forgot to add that I would rather you did not do the Berceuse at your concert, there was every reason for doing it the first time but there is no reason for doing a thing as intimate as that a second time now. Just had a Christmas card from Mrs. Laselle [sic],
                    Love to you both
                         Alwys
                         Gtrde.

I would rather you did not do the Berceuse: Stein thought Hugnet's "*Le Berceau de Gertrude Stein*" not amusing, as it tries to be, and too intimate (Tommasini 212-13).

*****

To "M. Virgil Thomson"

[*Dec. 1930*]

My dear Virgil

I must send a cable to Pagany to-morrow morning and I have not their New York address as I left all the letters in Bilignin. Will you bring me their New York address early for to-morrow, the last act of the drama was played this aft. you have been very sweet about not saying I told you don't imgne I don't appreciate it

Gtrde.

---

last act of the drama: Stein and Hugnet were planning to publish their *Enfances*, accompanied by illustrations by Picasso, Tchelitchev, Marcoussis, and Tonny. The book was to be issued by Jeanne Bucher. Stein received a copy of the subscription for the book, in which Hugnet's name appears first in large type, then, after the title, in small type, "suivi par la Traduction de Gertrude Stein." She was furious since they had already agreed that her version was no mere translation (*"traduction"*) but part of a collaboration in which his poetry inspired her poetry. She objected, but he insisted on the title page design, lest readers think he translated her. So she withheld permission to publish her text, and when she and Hugnet met "this afternoon" at the Bucher art gallery, she refused to shake hands with him. Stein is too late to stop the publication of her version of *Enfances* (on facing pages with his) in *Pagany* but at her insistence in a telegram received by the magazine 22 Dec., the poem will appear as "Poem Pritten on Pfances of Georges Hugnet." Thomson's recent tension with Hugnet over the complimentary copy of de Massot's book intensifies her feeling of camaraderie with Thomson. Hugnet will ask Thomson to heal the breach and save the book. She will agree that the difficulties can be resolved and asks Thomson to act as her "agent."

*****

[from Toklas] [*22 Dec. 1930*]

-Monday-

Dear Virgil.

Gertrude has just told me of her conversation with you apropos of Madame Ferry's advances (?)—She—G- of course—now sees more in detail than when she was talking and I've a point or two to add—this latter is the reason I'm writing instead of Gertrude.

First for G-'s points. This is her definite—only—and first and last title for all uses—for the title of the book—for the announcements and for anything that may crop up in the future in connection with the book.

```
┌─────────────────────────────┐
│        Georges Hugnet       │
│            1929             │
│                             │
│          Enfances           │
│                             │
│       Gertrude Stein        │
│            1930             │
└─────────────────────────────┘
```

Secondly—that he does not presume to represent her concerns [to] Madame Bucher—She will attend to her interests herself or appoint some one to do so.

All this net and clair without further discussion or hair splitting from Georges—

As for my additions—that these propositions are not offered to George but are offered by him to Gertrude—without any ifs or ands or further conditions—now or for the future. No conditions at all for the future use by Gertrude of her poem with George's until she knows her further rights legally outside of France.

You really are taking on too sweetly the difficulties only Georges can create. Dont please get worn out with it. Perhaps where it's a friend's vexations one is struggling to dissipate the good actions of being a boy scoutie sootheth and turneth away wrath.

Ah yes—Tonny was here yesterday obviously to ask if his eau forte would be needed immediately—to which G- replied that there was no need to make it at all as one had changed one's mind –

   Love to Maurice   Ever Yours
                 Alice

[Note on envelope:]
Will you or M- telephone results tomorrow morning before ten—please—

Madame Ferry: See note to Thomson 29 Sunday [*28 Sept, 1930*]
Madame Bucher: See note to previous letter.
net and clair: clean and clear.
eau forte: Term for nitric acid solution used in engraving. Tonny's engraving is no longer wanted to illustrate the book of Thomson's music, which was to have been published by Hugnet.

*****

On the telephone, Toklas repeats to Thomson that the proposal arrived at must be "distinctly understood" as coming from Hugnet. When Thomson presents the proposed title-page layout, Hugnet scribbles on it, "I accept." Thomson delivers this sheet of paper to Stein after dinner in her flat on Christmas Eve. She says, "This seems to be all right," but Toklas remarks, "It isn't what was asked for." The evening continues and concludes amicably, but Alice decides to break off relations with Hugnet.

*****

To "M. Virgil Thomson / 17 Quai Voltaire / Paris."

[26 Dec. 1930]

My dear Virgil.

When you come to-morrow will you bring with you my Mme Recamier, and Maurice plays and the Enfances. Thanks so much

Alwys

Gtrde

When you come: Staying home nursing a cold and practicing for his concert, Thomson will return the manuscripts by messenger (Watson 124).

*****

Preoccupied by an illness of Madame Langlois, Thomson remains out of touch with Stein for two weeks, an unusually long and silent absence, causing Stein to suspect that he has sided all along with Hugnet against her. Considering her willingness to put up most of the money for a book of Thomson's music, this presumed disloyalty is especially galling—even though she is now determined that there will be no such book (see Toklas, [*22 Dec. 1930*]). When Thomson does return, she meets him at the door with a curt, "Did you want something?" He says, "Merely to report on my absence." She says, "We're very busy now." He leaves. He sends her an announcement of a concert including his setting of her texts. She replies with the following calling card.

*****

[21 Jan. 1931, Calling card engraved with her name and continuing in her hand writing:]

MISS GERTRUDE STEIN
declines further acquaintance with Mr. Thomson.

*****

Described by Thomson (*Virgil Thomson* 196) and Tommasini (216) but not, or no longer, in the Yale archives, this card inaugurates two years of non-communication between Stein and Thomson. He recalls: "If she expected flowers, as after my former moments of offensiveness, she did not receive them, for I was aware of no wrongdoing, unless my failure to discipline Georges for her advantage might be so viewed. In any case I took her at her word" (*Virgil Thomson* 196). He later speculates that she may have been "terrified by George's rapid mobilization of the French intellectuals" and, feeling outnumbered, was disappointed at his (Thomson's) disinclination to fight for her. Toklas engineered the rupture between Stein and Hugnet, whom she felt Stein loved too much, and she probably encouraged the break with Thomson. She was usually the breaker of relations. She was responsible for Stein's break with her brother Leo, with Mabel Dodge, with Pavel Tchelitchev, and with Ernest Hemingway. About her effecting such separations, Thomson writes, "she did them so skilfully and so carefully that Gertrude hardly knew what happened, and maybe even thought that she herself was the responsible one" (*Reader*, 207). In his autobiography, Bravig Imbs claims that Toklas never liked Thomson: "She realized that Virgil could be one too many for her in any battle of wits, that he could whip out as nasty a sarcasm as she any day, and she was even disconcerted at the sinuous way his mind worked" (160). In 1963, when Thomson asks why she interfered when Hugnet and Stein were finally in agreement, Toklas will reply, "I was only trying to protect Gertrude," adding that Stein's friendship with Hugnet "was never a permanent attachment—a youthful thing" (197).

Here are excerpts from Stein's fictionalized version of events, entitled "Left to Right," published in *Story* (November 1933) 17–20, with real identities disclosed in square brackets:

> Arthur William [Georges Hugnet] came to see me while I was in the country. He proposed to me that we should have a book together. This was not really true; he had done his and I had done mine. We both had seen the others.
>
> I accepted all that he proposed. The book was to be illustrated by drawings by people we both knew. . . .
>
> One evening we were all going to a circus to see a man do some marvellous giant swinging. Arthur brought with him the announcements for our book and I did not notice anything. The next morning I looked and it said it was his book and it did not say it was my book and I did not say anything.
>
> I wrote to him and said not at all it must be half mine or something. He said nothing. Then he wrote and said that the way he had decided was the right way and therefore it was too late to change something. Then I went to the editor and said it was necessary to change something. She said why yes of course that is what I think. Just then she was called by someone to come to the telephone. She came back and said that he had said to her he would not let them change anything. I said all right there is nothing to do I am not allowing them to have anything. And that was the way the thing was then.
>
> Generale Erving [Virgil Thomson] was a writer, that is to say he had written not writing but something. That is to say we were writing we were writers who were writing. We were both very fond of him. He was never interfering but he knew everything and he always said something. I knew what he said and I noticed everything. I never noticed that he said a thing. And so it went on. He had been for some time not liking Arthur William. That is to say he had not for some time said anything about liking me or anything. . . .

Generale Erving called me one afternoon on the telephone to tell me something. I said I knew all about Frederick Harvard [Bravig Imbs]. Fredrick Harvard is a writer who has written... and for Arthur William it was very interesting. He was seeing Frederick Harvard and Frederick Harvard called him Arthur but that was nothing everybody called Arthur Arthur but Arthur was calling Frederick Harvard Frederick and that was because Frederick Harvard was going to be writing something that Arthur would be coming to find interesting. I told Generale Erving I knew all about that anybody could have seen that coming.

Generale Erving told me over the telephone that he wanted to fix up everything. It was all right but it would be all right and Arthur was not at all there but he General Erving would see him was I willing. Yes I was willing but not so willing that I was willing to be refusing anything before I said it. I was not giving and refusing anything. I was willing. Yes. Yes said Generale I understand.

Of course you do I said but let us repeat it. Are you coming or are you going. I am not doing anything. I will see you to-morrow evening. Well you do not want to forget that I am not here only to be accommodating. I do not need anything and it has to be said just like that or nothing. I understand said Generale Erving. I am seeing you tomorrow evening.

Everybody was quiet in between.

Generale Erving came and we spent a pleasant evening. We talked about everything.

He told me some things that Arthur had said that I did not know he said but he did say them. He told about how long Arthur had been saying he had been thinking that he had better do what he was doing. I said I had heard that Arthur was like that from someone who long ago had had enough of him and I said that I was through with him and this was after Generale said that Arthur was ready to say that he was ready to ask me to have him give in. Generale had had a piece of paper on which Arthur had written this thing. When Generale was leaving I gave the paper back to him.

The next day I did nothing. And then there was another week and then I had a letter from Arthur asking me to arrange everything. I did not do anything.

All this time I thought that it was all Arthur William. Perhaps it was and then perhaps I had better not have anything further to do with Generale Erving. Perhaps not. Perhaps I might think over everything. Perhaps I might remember everything. Perhaps Generale would come again and I would see him and I would not say anything. Perhaps he was worried about everything. Perhaps Generale would come again and I would tell him I was busy and could not see him....

When I had waited a little longer I said to the editor that I was not giving her anything and so Arthur did not have anything and that was all over. . . . I sent a card to Generale Erving and I said I did not want to have any further acquaintance with him.

And now before I go out I always look up and down to see that none of them are coming. We were after that never friends or anything. This is all this true story and it was exciting.

Stein includes Bravig Imbs (Frederick Harvard) in her story because she suspected him of collusion with Hugnet. Shortly after dismissing Thomson, she severed relations with Imbs through a telephone call made by Toklas. Toklas announced, "Miss Gertrude Stein has asked me to inform you that she thinks your plan of sending Valeska to Belley, considering Valeska's condition"—Imbs's wife was pregnant and Stein and Toklas were the only people she would know in Belley—"a colossal impertinence, and that neither she nor I ever wish to see either you or Valeska again" (Imbs 296). This completed Toklas's purge of Stein's young friends. In her published story, Stein does not implicate Toklas in her decision to sever relations with Thomson, but then Toklas was decisive in breaking relations with Hugnet and Stein deliberately obscures that.

In 1963 Toklas will tell Thomson of Stein's separation from him that "Gertrude had been 'very disturbed by the separation' and 'deeply relieved by the reconciliation'" (*Virgil Thomson* 197). Stein never again communicates with Hugnet, who goes on to associate himself with the Surrealists until excommunicated by Breton in 1938. In May 1931, Stein publishes 120 copies of her "reflections" of Hugnet's *Enfances* under the title "Before the Flowers of Friendship Faded Friendship Faded." After Stein's death, Hugnet will attempt in vain to renew acquaintance with Toklas.

*****

15 January 1931–22 January 1933

*****

If Toklas ended the relationship between Stein and Thomson, after a two-year hiatus William Aspenwall Bradley renews it. What had been a three-party relationship, with Toklas as the third party becomes, at least initially, fourfold. Bradley's objectivity now balances Toklas's antipathy to Thomson. Bradley's firm equanimity in the service of Stein's career neutralizes Toklas's proprietary attitude.

Stein became acquainted with Bradley in 1928—see the note to Thomson, 17 juin [1928]. Increasingly dissatisfied with small-press publication and the diminishing of the inheritance she lives on, in 1930 she engaged him as her agent in hopes of making money (see Bradley to Stein, 7.6.34). He began working assiduously to get her published with major houses, a difficult enterprise during the Great Depression, which had begun in the United States with the stock-market crash of October 1929 and subsequently spread to Europe. In 1930 he negotiated with the Macaulay Company for an English equivalent of *Morceaux Choisis* but was unsuccessful. In 1931 he negotiates with Librairie Stock in Paris for the publication of *Américains d'Amérique* and is successful, owing to the active intersession of Bernard Faÿ. In 1932 he unsuccessfully negotiates with Harcourt for publication of *Three Lives* and *The Making of Americans*. In December 1932, Stein shows him her newly finished *Autobiography of Alice B. Toklas*. Reading it, he realizes at once its potential, and sends it to Harcourt, stating that "with a little clever handling this book could be made into a best-seller." Harcourt accepts it. Bradley manages the contract for publication and arranges serial publication in *The Atlantic Monthly*. Owing partly to his agency, Stein enjoys greater fame in the United States than she has previously known and is making money as never before.

In 1933, Bradley learns of plans to mount a production of *Four Saints* and undertakes to act as "peacemaker" between Stein and Thomson (see Dydo 416, 543–48). And so the correspondence resumes, but it is changed in style and substance. It begins as a three-way exchange, with Bradley as mediator. Initially, Bradley's contributions are cool, rational, politely impersonal business letters, their formality a means of disallowing Stein's aggressive, sometimes unrealistic ambitions. Emphasis is on business, money, contracts. Aesthetic matters are limited to interpretation and performance. He stamps her undated letters to him with "received" and the date, information potentially important legally.

*****

WILLIAM ASPENWALL BRADLEY
5, RUE SAINT-LOUIS-EN-L'ILE
PARIS 4

23 January, 1933

Dear Mr. Thomson,

Miss Gertrude Stein, for whom, for some time past, I have been acting as literary representative, has learned indirectly of the project to inaugurate the new model theatre in Hartford, Connecticut, in January 1934, with a production of the opera FOUR SAINTS. Naturally this interests her very much and she would be very happy to have further particulars concerning the production itself, your arrangements with the director, Mr. Austin, etc. Perhaps you will be kind enough to write me supplying them.

May I add that I had the pleasure of meeting you in Paris on various occasions as well as of attending one of your concerts some years ago? I was glad to learn from Miss Stein that you contemplated returning to France in June and shall hope to see you here then.

With kind regards, I am,

Very sincerely yours,
W.A. Bradley

VIRGIL THOMSON
17, Quai Voltaire
Paris, 6e
c/o Philip Johnson, Esq.
230 E. 49th St. NYC

---

a production of the opera: By late 1932, Thomson has interested a group of Harvard art-history alumni in producing *Four Saints in Three Acts* at the Wadsworth Atheneum in Hartford, Connecticut. The group is largely homosexual, devoted to visual art, and associated with Alfred Barr Jr. and the Museum of Modern Art.

Mr. Austin: A. Everett ("Chick") Austin. The magnetic centre of the group of Harvard alumni mentioned above, which includes Russell Hitchcock. Austin is daring, playful, enthusiastic, receptive to the new, a connoisseur of aesthetic value, with an extraordinary eye for visual art. He teaches art history at Trinity College, Hartford; directs the Wadsworth Atheneum, the oldest American art museum; and works for a firm of Bond Street art dealers in London and New York, his enthusiasm being chiefly the Baroque. He is President of The Friends and Enemies of Modern Music, which "brought to Hartford since 1929 programs of modern music and musicians about whose work contemporary critical opinion has been far from unanimous" (Program for *Four Saints*, Hartford, 1934). He is building a new museum-wing to be opened with exhibitions of Picasso and ballet-sketches by Diaghilev and with the world premiere of *Four Saints in Three Acts* in sets and costumes designed by Florine Stettheimer. He and his friends want to produce the opera as a way of expanding their modernist displays beyond the visual arts.

Philip Johnson: Millionaire graduate from Harvard in classics, now enamoured of modern architecture and a friend of Hitchcock, who introduced him to Thomson in 1930. Johnson paid Thomson's fare to New York in November 1932, and has lent him his east-side apartment.

*****

WILLIAM ASPENWALL BRADLEY
5, RUE SAINT-LOUIS-EN-L'ILE
PARIS 4

4 May, 1933.

Dear Miss Stein,

... I had a letter from Virgil Thomson and a first preliminary talk with him yesterday. He is now coming to lunch with me today and I will then write you fully about the FOUR SAINTS affair at Hartford. ... W.A. Bradley

*****

WILLIAM ASPENWALL BRADLEY
5, RUE SAINT-LOUIS-EN-L'ILE
PARIS 4

6 May, 1933.

Dear Miss Stein,

Virgil Thomson lunched with me on Friday [5 May] and we passed the whole afternoon together in my office going over the matter of the proposed production of FOUR SAINTS IN THREE ACTS in the new Model Theater, Hartford—which, incidentally, is being built *expressly* for that production—and sketching out tentative forms of agreement both between you and Thomson and between you both and Austin, curator of the Wadsworth Athenaeum and the Morgan Memorial of which the theatre will form a new department. It is, of course, on a small scale, with a seating capacity of 300 only, but Thomson says that the stage will have ample wings providing all the space necessary for a completely satisfactory theatrical or operatic production. He gave me a great deal of detailed information about his plans, the composition of his personnel, etc., but I thought it better, to avoid errors or omissions on my part, to ask him to write all this out in a letter which he has promised to send me and which I will transmit to you. All I will say here [is] that, as musical director, he has secured the services of Stokowski's assistant at Philadelphia and some one of the first class, whose name I do not recall, to do the costumes and the settings which are already designed and which will, from what he told me, be extremely original and striking.

The date for the opening is at present [set] for 24 January and it is planned to give at least six consecutive performances, after which the production will be moved to New York for at least three performances at a high price—possibly as high as $25. the place. Thomson has very high hopes that once production is thus actually made of your joint work, the commercial managers will begin to take an interest or, rather, to throw off the fear which they usually have of everything that is radically new and which has held them back thus far. It is not at all impossible, therefore, that this beginning may turn into something very important for both of you, hence the drafting of the contracts, on the model of that provided by the Dramatists' Guild of The Authors' League of America, thoroughly protecting your rights in all circumstances, becomes a matter of prime necessity.

Something, however, even more pressing just now, is the question of protecting your joint work by securing, as far as possible, a valid American copyright. You have, of course, lost the possibility of acquiring such copyright protection for your text by itself, through having first printed this, in English, in a foreign country, that is France, so all that is left now is for Thomson to apply for a copyright of the work as a whole, your words with his music, which, of course, has never been published anywhere as yet. I am doubtful, myself, whether this device will assure you *absolute* literary protection, but it seems to me an excellent practical expedient and, indeed, the only one now left. In any event, it will completely prevent the unauthorized use of the words with the music, which is, after all, the important point in the case of an opera.

To secure such copyright for the joint work, Thomson will have to have made a complete manuscript of the words and music together, as for actual performance. This will cost, he informs me, between $25 and $50, and he wants me to ask you whether you will be willing to share with him that expense, half and half. This is the *only* expense he would suggest thus sharing with him. All the rest he will stand himself, including the trip back to America especially for the supervision of the details of the production, the direction of the rehearsals, etc. Please let me know about this as early as possible, so that the copying work can be put in hand without delay, also in order that a stipulation covering same may be inserted in your personal agreement as collaborators.

I may say that Thomson seemed to manifest the friendliest feeling for you and an entirely unabated admiration for your work, as well as, I thought, a most sympathetic and penetrating appreciation for it. Indeed, he would be, apparently, only too happy to see you and talk over with you the project for a new opera which he now has in mind and which he thinks might interest you too. Since the *"froid"* between you seems to count for little or nothing in his attitude towards you, perhaps it would be possible for you, as well, to bury whatever little hatchet may be involved and to resume relations as in the past. Of course I make this suggestion—which is hardly even a suggestion—with the greatest diffidence, not knowing anything of the character or seriousness of your past differences. Were there, however, the slightest possibility of my patching things up between you, or were there any place for me whatsoever in such a role, I should be only too delighted to serve as a "peacemaker."

I will write you again as soon as I have the promised letter form Thomson to forward, and I shall no doubt be able to let you have the agreement drafts at the same time.

With our very best to you both,
Ever sincerely, W.A. Bradley

Miss Gertrude Stein,
Bilignin, par Belley,
AIN.

*****

17 Quai Voltaire
6 May [1933]

Dear Mr. Bradley,

Here are details of opera plans. New Theatre in new wing of Morgan Memorial Art Gallery of Wadsworth Atheneum, Hartford. Seats 300 people with plenty of room. Stage 30 by 30 feet, plus large wing-space. Orchestra-pit seats easily 16 musicians.
Four Saints to open the new wing of the art-gallery on January 24, 1934. Decorations and costumes by Florine Stettheimer with aid of A. Everitt Austin Jr. and Maurice Grosser.
Musical direction, Alexander Smallens.
Stage direction, Herbert Osborne.
These people are high-class professional men who are giving their services free out of admiration for the work and friendship for me. The cast and orchestra will be hired.
I am making a special score for the following instruments. String quartet, double-bass, guitar, accordion, trombone, 2 saxophones, trumpet, small clarinet, bass clarinet (interchangeable), flute, piccolo (interchangeable) and a battery to consist of harmonium, celesta, glockenspiel, kettle-drums, cymbals, sicle-drums, tambourines, etc.

The choral parts to be sung by Hall Johnson's Negro choir.

The solo parts to be sung also by negroes, excepting maybe the compère and commère.

The negroes will, however, be painted white, at least their faces. The first act (living pictures) takes place on the steps of the Avila cathedral. Backdrop represents clouds, made of white cellophane gauze draped in puffs, with gold fringe. Cathedral made of contiguous strings of clear crystal beads with curtains of starched white Nottingham lace in the Gothic arch. The lions on the steps are gilded and chained by chains made of gilded paper links to a tulle Gothic rainbow. Rose carpet on the steps. St. Teresa in cardinal red velvet with red cardinal's hat and Nottingham lace veil.

The second act décor is not yet precisely imagined, except for the maypole dance. For this, the minor saints will be in bright colored robes, something like in Fra Angelico's pictures, with hats like gold halos on the sides of their heads and scarves wired to float in fixed folds (reading *Gloria in Excelsis* and similar mottos), the robes also wired and transparent, revealing the negro bodies underneath.

In the third act, the various visions will be built in low relief out of divers cloths and materials and raised from under the stage on a platform. Mr. Austin, who is a professional magician, will perform the miracles of sudden appearance and disappearance of pigeons and the flowering of a small three into large bouquets of red feathers.

With the exception of the storm-scene and one night-scene in the second act, the entire opera is played in white light.

There will be at least three and maybe six performances in Hartford.

Mrs. Murray Crane has offered to organize 3 subscription performances in New York.

No other performances are as yet definitely planned.

Any comment Miss Stein may make on these projects will of course be very valuable, as will any other ideas she may have about the opera. We are all very desirous of her counsel and collaboration.

> Very sincerely yours,
> Virgil Thomson

Maurice Grosser: Thomson's long-time lover is creating the scenario, a series of scenes that loosely suggest dramatic progression, so that the opera can be staged.
Alexander Smallens: Assistant musical director and conductor to Leopold Stokowski of the Philadelphia Orchestra, has accepted Thomson's invitation to conduct the *Four Saints*.
Herbert Osborne: Subsequently replaced by John Houseman.
negroes: African-American singers are cheaper to employ than white professionals and, able to rehearse in their church, don't need to rent rehearsal space. But there are more compelling reasons for Thomson's choice. He decided on a black cast in the Ha-Cha Bar and Grill on Seventh Avenue in Harlem while listening to Jimmy Daniels singing "I've Got the World on a String" (Watson 199). "Realizing the impeccable enunciation of Jimmy's speech-in-song," he turned to Russell Hitchcock and said, "I think I'll have my opera sung by Negroes." He recalls, "The idea seemed to me a brilliant one; Russell, less impressed, suggested I sleep on it. But next morning I was sure, remembering how proudly the Negroes enunciate and how the whites just hate to move their lips." "I was not to be stuck with . . . the poor enunciation of professional opera singers" (*Virgil Thomson* 217, 219). In the racist culture of the time, his decision is revolutionary.

painted white ... faces: An idea later dropped, probably Stettheimer's, since she advocates, till the last week of rehearsals, that all exposed black skin be covered with white makeup (Tommasini 255) and white gloves. She worries that varied brown skin-tones will diminish the brilliance of her brightly colored costumes (Watson 263).
Mrs. Murray Crane: Josephine Boardman Crane, patron of the arts, wife of Winthrop Murray Crane, former governor of Massachusetts.

*****

[*May 1933*]

My dear Bradley,

... About Virgil and the Opera. Virgil knows perfectly well that he and I had no cause for quarrel, the quarrel was with George Hugnet and was a perfectly legitimate authors quarrel, and with Virgil it was a failure of personal loyalty on his part which hurt me shrewdly at that time because he knew that I with what I thought good reason had counted on his loyalty to me as he had always been able to count on my loyalty to him, in the same way that we had always counted on each others understanding of each others work. So there is nothing further to be said about that but that does in no way change the fact that our work does naturally go together.

About your proposition of my sharing the xpenses of copying that seems to me very fair. About a new opera of course I am interested we had already talked about that before we parted so now you know all my feeling in the matter, and I leave everything in your hands. I would be enormously pleased if the opera turned out a success both for my sake and his ...

Alwys
Gtrde Stein

*****

WILLIAM ASPENWALL BRADLEY
5, RUE SAINT-LOUIS-EN-L'ILE
PARIS 4

10 May, 1933

Dear Miss Stein,

... To Virgil Thomson I communicated, discreetly, the substance of what concerned him, and I believe he will now write to you himself directly.

Herewith I enclose a draft of your joint agreement which I helped him to draw up and which has carefully been gone over by him. If there are any modifications you would like to make, please let me know. If not, when you return the paper, I will have it redrafted *en double exemplaire*, on *papier timbré*, returning both copies to you for your signature.

The production contracts—those, that is, with Austin—are still being worked over, and a draft will go to you in a day or two. I did not imagine a contract could be so complicated! Thomson has an excellent head, and although he tells me he has never had anything to do with contracts before, and has never even had anything published, he thinks of everything. It is true we have had the standard form of the Dramatists' Guild of the Authors' League of America to help us.... W. A. Bradley

---

en double exemplaire: in two copies.
papier timbré: stamped paper, special paper for legally binding agreements.

*****

WILLIAM ASPENWALL BRADLEY
5, RUE SAINT-LOUIS-EN-L'ILE
PARIS 4

12.5.33

Dear Mr Thomson,

Thank you for yours of the 10th enclosing draft of your agreement with Miss Stein. This went off to her at once & I ought to have it back today or tomorrow. Unfortunately there is no second copy of the agreement so I shall have to wait till you return it to me to make the further modifications. You can either send it to me or can bring it yourself, so that we can go over it again together. In that case you had better call me up & make an appointment.

I wrote to Calvocoressi (O.U.P.) as agreed & hope to hear from him also in a day or two.

Francis Rose & Ruth called here at the office yesterday. Today they are leaving for the South, as you no doubt know. I am wondering whether I shall see you this afternoon at Miss Barney's ....

Sincerely yours,
W.A. Bradley

Calvocoressi: M. D. Calvocoressi, musicologist, author of books on many composers, translator of books by composers for Oxford University Press.

*****

WILLIAM ASPENWALL BRADLEY
5, RUE SAINT-LOUIS-EN-L'ILE
PARIS 4

15 May 1933

Dear Mr. Thomson,

Here is what Miss Stein says in comment on your letter which I sent her:

"Of course, I can tell very little by description of what they are going to do, you can only tell when you see the maquettes, and I suppose they have good reasons for using negro singers instead of white, there are certain obvious ones, but I do not care for the idea of showing the negro bodies, it is too much what the English in what they call 'modernistic' novels call futuristic and do not accord with the words and music to my mind. I liked Virgil's original Sunday school ideas on the whole better, but still as it is up to them to make a success of the performance, I do not wish to be critical, the great thing is to get it done and successfully done both for his sake and mine"

I have not heard from her yet about the Agreement, but then there has hardly been time. I will let you know as soon as it arrives.

Sincerely yours,
W.A.Bradley

I suppose they have good reasons for using negro singers . . . I do not care for this idea of showing negro bodies: Giving tight-lipped expression to her own racial prejudice, Stein writes in her *Autobiography of Alice B. Toklas* "that negroes were not suffering from persecution, they were suffering from nothingness. . . . the african is not primitive, he has a very ancient but a very narrow culture and there it remains. Consequently nothing does or can happen" (257).

maquettes: mock-ups, models.

*****

[received 16 May 1933]

My dear Bradley,

... There are several points to take up about the Virgil Thomson contract. In the first place there are other things of mine that he has set to music Capital Capitals and a number of songs, while we are at it should we not include these other things in our arrangements or should that be done separately, we are hoping for all three of us that they may become valuable property.

In clause 2 I also wish to add a clause that all the profits of this production or publication should be received by a third party at the present time W. A. Bradley and that he should receive the sums due and divide the profits or the royalties of any kind between the author and the publisher; if for any reason W. A. Bradley ceases to act they should then jointly appoint another third party to act for them.

I want this introduced whenever there is any question of receiving money.

Following clause b. I want taken out (such acceptance not to be unreasonably withheld) that does not mean anything, for of course neither of us are going to withhold acceptance unless we see what we consider a good reason.

I always wish added after clause b. Neither composer nor author are privileged to use their part of the opera with anyone else's work, that is the author may not use the libretto with any other composer's music nor the composer the music for the opera with any other libretto.

In clause 6 I do not like that form, said contract to be duly accepted and signed by both parties, it should be replaced by the usual formula used in paragraph 3 and there should be mention of the royalties to be collected by the third party W. A. Bradley

Otherwise it seems alright. . . .

     Alwys   Gtrde Stein

*****

WILLIAM ASPENWALL BRADLEY
5, RUE SAINT-LOUIS-EN-L'ILE
PARIS 4

16 May 1933

Dear Mr. Thomson,

I have just heard from Miss Stein about the agreement and as there are a few suggestions she has to make, perhaps another séance would be in order. I am leaving town in the middle of the morning but will return by noon or after three-thirty. Will you telephone which would be most convenient for you?

  In haste,
   Sincerely yrs.
    W.A. Bradley

*****

WILLIAM ASPENWALL BRADLEY
5, RUE SAINT-LOUIS-EN-L'ILE
PARIS 4

20 May, 1933

Dear Miss Stein,

I had another long session with Virgil Thomson yesterday and we went over together the various points concerning your personal agreement with him which you brought up in your last letter. I now enclose a revised version of this agreement, the result of our joint labours, and, though Thomson proposed slight modifications of some of your suggestions, I think that, on the whole, you will find it satisfactory. If not, we are ready to try again! I will take up the several clauses in their orders.

1. *Clause I c.* The phrasing here is slightly different from yours, but only in the effort to make it even tighter and clearer. The suggestion was a good one, and Thomson accepted it at once, without discussion.

2. In *Clause 3*, Thomson is perfectly ready to leave out, as you propose, the words "such acceptance not to be unreasonably withheld," but neither he

nor I can quite see why this should be necessary, especially as you accept the principle of arbitration between you for the settlement of any differences or disputes between you, in Clause 9. The word "reasonably" leaves the door open to such arbitration and gives the ground on which the arbitrators would work. Hence I have left the clause as it stood originally, though you have only to amend it again as before, if you still feel so disposed.

3. *Clause 6* has been rewritten more in accordance with Clause 3 and I think will meet your objection to the original wording.

4. The most difficult to manage was the agency clause which you wished to have inserted and which was intentionally omitted in the first draft for the reason that it was hard to find a formula which would fit your two cases. You see, I am your general agent, and hence it would be normal for me to have a continuing interest in your share of the opera under as many different contracts as might be made for it during its entire life. But I am not Thomson's general agent, but merely an "agent of record" in this particular instance—that is, he comes to me as to a lawyer to have certain papers drawn up for him for a particular purpose—and my interest in *his* share of the opera is limited to a *single* contract, namely the one which we are now engaged upon with Austin for the Hartford production and any other productions which may be made by him, either directly or indirectly, during the life of that contract. It is quite conceivable that Thomson, who has been very nice in all this so far as I am concerned, might still, for one reason or another, wish to avail himself of the services of another agent at some future time for a second, or a third, contract. I cannot, therefore, very well impose myself upon him in perpetuity, as would be the case were your instructions as to a third party, who should receive and divide between you the returns from both of you [be] carried out to the letter. Hence we have drafted a kind of compromise clause which, while it accepts the principle established by you and, it seems to me, quite fully protects your interests, leaves him free, under certain definite restrictions, to receive his share of the earnings through any production directly from the producer.* (* Remember, too, that while both you and I are likely to remain in Paris till the end of our lives, Thomson will certainly spend a good deal of his working life in America, so it would be rather a hardship for him if his share of the earnings had always to cross the ocean twice before reaching his pocket!)

As you will see, no mention has been made of publication, as opposed to production, for the reason that it has been specifically stated in Clause 6 that your agreement shall remain in force only so long as the musical part of the opera exists in manuscript only, after which it shall be replaced by a contract with the publisher. It will be time enough then to draft and insert an agency, or "third party" clause, which will exactly fit the new circumstances.

I hope that all this is quite clear and will be found satisfactory. There is, of course, a complete agency clause drawn up in conformity with the standard agency clause of the Dramatists' Guild of The Authors League of

America, in the contract with Austin which is now being typed and which will follow in the next two or three days—a very elaborate document!

The only point which I have not covered in the foregoing is your initial point as to the extension of the present agreement to cover not only the opera but all the work which you and Virgil Thomson have done together. Frankly, I think that this would make of it a rather clumsy and cumbersome instrument and might lead to all sorts of confusion. Remember, too, that production hardly counts in the case of a piece like "Capitals, Capitals," which still remains in manuscript. The appropriate moment to make an agreement for it, as well as for the other things he has set to music would seem to be when they have found a publisher. At least this is Thomson's suggestion, and it appears to me perfectly reasonable. What do *you* think?

With our very best greetings to you both,

Ever sincerely,

W.A. Bradley

*****

[rec. 23 May 1933]

My dear Bradley,

The agreement seems now alright with one xception, I do not wish the words unnecessarily withheld, because, the only reason, would be one connected with making it a revue feature or other thing to which I might object or might not but if I did or if he did a third party might not find it unreasonable, I think we had better take for granted each others reasonableness. Did you tell him what I wrote you about the scheme of decoration, I sent the letter at the same time as the article for Wings and some clippings and as you did not mention any of these things, I am asking about the part of the letter that concerned the opera....

Alwys

Gtrde Stein

*****

WILLIAM ASPENWALL BRADLEY
5, RUE SAINT-LOUIS-EN-L'ILE
PARIS 4

24. 5. 1933

Dear Mr. Thomson,

Miss Stein still clings to her objection to the word "unreasonably". So, as I know you do not insist, I am striking it out. Although she finds the revised agreement entirely acceptable, and I am having it drawn up at once in *papier timbré*. . . . If you will drop in Friday morning, I think you will find it ready for your signature. Or I could see you that afternoon at three o'clock. Will you ring me up?

The production contract has already been copied up & sent to Miss Stein. Perhaps I shall have had some word from her as to that when I see you on Friday.

In her last letter, Miss Stein asks if I told you what she wrote me concerning the scheme of decoration etc, and, since she is intensely curious to have your reaction, it occurs to me you might send her a word repeating what you said to me as to the merits of the present scheme over that of the inspired "Sunday school" project. I think she would appreciate it, and such artistic indication can, I believe, be better treated with her directly than through the "third party" of your [word?].

Don't forget your promise to let me have a little outline of a possible musical book. The moment is a propitious one, with Knopf at present in London and in a buying mood

Very sincerely
W. A. B.

---

papier timbré: stamped paper.

*****

WILLIAM ASPENWALL BRADLEY
5, RUE SAINT-LOUIS-EN-L'ILE
PARIS 4

25 May, 1933

Dear Miss Stein,

. . . all the essentials have, I believe, been taken care of—the contracts etc. That between you and Virgil Thomson has now been established on *papier timbré*, and I am expecting him to call and sign them tomorrow. I will also take up with him then the changes suggested by you in the production contract, which came back to me from you this morning. . . .

Yes, I communicated to Thomson that part of your letter relating to the costuming and the *mise en scène* of the opera. As usual, he did not show himself in the least dead-set or dogmatic. All that he is thinking of, he says, is the most effective presentation, and, inasmuch as he will be there himself to take general supervision, he thinks he may be depended upon to arrange all such details as the exposure of the negro bodies etc with a view to the maximum of artistic effect. In other words, he is not in any way committed to such details in advance, and his own ideas are all perfectly fluid at the moment. As to his original idea for the Sunday-school setting, he has a feeling now that this setting has been rather overdone recently and tends to give a somewhat sad and subdued effect. If he is now rather in favor of an outofdoors setting, it is, in large measure, because this seems to promise the utmost brilliancy in lighting and general atmosphere. However, as all this is rather delicate ground for me to tread on, I have suggested to Thomson that he write you himself in fuller and more accurate explanation of his own ideas, and I have no doubt he will do so. . . .

With best greetings,
Ever sincerely,
W.A. Bradley

*****

[rec. 27 May 1933]

My dear Bradley,

There are three points in the contract that I want to speak of.

Clause 2 Since we have paid together for the making of the score should not the instrumental and vocal parts be made over to the author and composer and become *their* xclusive property etc.

In clause 7 I would wish the last clause to be taken out, unreasonably withheld. It allows too much latitude to others beside it is taken for granted that we would consider our best interests.

Clause 10, I think this should be completely taken out, we should never give another person a right to sell your property. If it is a valuable property then you can sell it better, and if it isn't it is of no importance.

I am inclosing this that came this morning, in the Paris Weekly information, I thought it might please Stock,

Alwys
Gtrde Stein.

*****

WILLIAM ASPENWALL BRADLEY
5, RUE SAINT-LOUIS-EN-L'ILE
PARIS 4

29 May, 1933

Dear Miss Stein,

I was going to write you yesterday in response to your last letter, dealing with production contracts, but a day in bed prevented that, and now, this morning, I receive a letter from Virgil Thomson, enclosing a copy of his to you. As he told you in this, I did not feel that I could transmit to you his proposal for a revision of the basis on which you are to share the profits from the opera, but naturally I could not withhold from him my permission to write to you himself on this business matter, which concerns a basic arrangement between you both. Personally I have no knowledge as to what is the customary division between composers and librettists and was interested to listen and learn.

I wish he had also written to you in answer to your first point, affecting clause 2, as I thought he was going to. This matter too seems to me rather a technical one, and all I can do is to pass on to you his contention that the orchestral material and choral parts are more normally his property than yours jointly, because they represent—at least insofar as the instrumental parts are concerned—his work only, while they are *all* at least half his own labor, since he will have corrected them all by hand—a job which, he claims, is nearly as great as the original copyrighting. He adds, in his letter to me:

"The choral parts will be mimeographed and Miss Stein might easily have a few if she desired, but the orchestral parts would seem to me to be naturally my property. Any small sum I might make on renting them out for a future performance (they are very fragile and don't last long) would be an extremely modest recompense for my labor in connection with their making. If spoken parts existed for the opera, their script would naturally return to Miss Stein. Maquettes for décors and costumes will similarly remain the property of the artist who makes them. I should have no objection to depositing said parts with you, as agent for the opera, but I don't see that Miss Stein has any property rights in the orchestral."

The point, as I see it, is that what *you* are getting, for your half share of the cost of copying, is the relative protection of your text by the general copyright covering words and music. In view of that very definite advantage, I believe you could afford to yield on this point, whatever you might think of Thomson's main contention.

With regard to your third point, affecting clause 10, I think that, perhaps, you misunderstand a little the real meaning of this clause, which is to protect the producer against the loss of his capital investment, as would be the case did he not have the right to sell to another producer ready to reimburse him for his original outlay. In other words, it is not merely a matter of copyright which is here involved, but of property rights as well. Such a clause is absolutely a standard one (as you will have seen by The Dramatists' Guild form of agreement) and is universally included in book contracts as well. As a matter of fact, you are both fully protected, both financially and artistically, but the stipulation contained in the clause that the assignee, whoever he may be, shall be "bound by all the terms and covenants" of the agreement. I am sure that, without such a clause, no producer would ever be found to put on an expensive production, any more than any builder would put up a house on a piece of land for which he had not a perfectly clear title and a long term lease.

Mr. Thomson says he will take up with me later the question of the words "unreasonably withheld," which he regards as of no great importance in any case.

I am returning your marked copy of the production contract for your further consideration of the above points. Sincerely yours. W.A. Bradley.

*****

17 Quai Voltaire
30 May [1933]

Dear Gertrude

    Mr. Bradley has communicated to me a passage from one of your letters to him in which you express some reserves about the opera-mounting as I described it, and he has suggested that I might correspond directly with you on that subject, which is after all a part of our artistic collaboration and outside his domain. I am eager that the production should represent your text as closely as possible and so is Miss Stettheimer. Hence my eager acceptance of Mr. Bradley's suggestion to establish, if that is agreeable to you, a direct correspondence on the subject.

    Before I go on about the mounting, however, I am taking the liberty of mentioning a business matter which I have already spoken of to Mr. Bradley and which I have his permission to write to you about, he being slightly embarrassed, as both your personal agent and our joint agent, about reopening the question.

    At the beginning of my conversations with him I mentioned that although the usual practice was otherwise, I preferred, in view of the closeness of our collaboration and of the importance given to the text in my score, to offer you a 50-50 division of all profits. It has since been called to my attention by the Société des Droits d'Auteurs that such an arrangement defeats its own end and that the contract commonly made in France allowing two-thirds to the composer and one to the author is designed to establish that very equality:

    1.) because the manual labor involved in musical composition is so much greater than that of writing words that half the proceeds is an insufficient return for the composer, considering him as a joint worker,

    2.) because a literary work is perfectly saleable separate from the music and thus brings further profit to its author, whereas the music is rarely saleable in any way separated from the text it was designed to accompany. The 2-1 division of profits is already, it would seem, to the advantage of the author in that an inferior text is assured of paying profits as long as the music lives, and a poem of merit is in no way injured in its independent literary career by the performance of an inferior musical setting. In cases where the musical setting is noteworthy, the sale of the book has often surpassed the normal sale of that author's work, thus bringing a very considerable independent profit to the author in which of course the composer has no share at all. I am told that this has been true recently of Claudel's *Christophe Colombe* (music by Milhaud) and of Edna Millay's *The King's Henchman*, which was written for Deems Taylor. *Four Saints* has already, if I mistake not, been published twice, and I hope Mr. Bradley will arrange to have it printed in America (with perhaps a few minor changes to permit American copyright) so that it can be sold as a libretto at the operatic performances.

In view of these considerations would you consider it just on my part to ask that our projected contracts (and any eventual publication of the score) be based on the 2-1 rather than the 1-1 division of profits, a proportion which, as I said above, is the one used in France to secure an equable division of benefits? The same proportion would naturally apply in sharing the expense of copyright.

About the mounting, we are all in accord that the idea of a parochial entertainment must remain. Miss Stettheimer suggested, however, that since any interior is less joyful than an outdoor scene, and since Sunday-school rooms and chapels have been done in so many religious plays (black and white), perhaps the same entertainment might take place on the steps of a church, in this case the cathedral of Avila itself, although represented in a far from literal imitation. Spring at Avila could thus be expressed doubly. Also the general atmosphere somewhat lightened. The colors and materials she suggests are merely an amplification of the dazzling fairy-tale effect ordinarily aimed at in the construction of religious images out of tin and tinsel and painted plaster and gilding and artificial flowers. Her idea seems to me to be more efficacious than our original one in expressing the same thing, especially in view of the enormous heightening of every effect that is necessary in order to get a dramatic idea across the barrier of foot-lights and music. I must admit I am rather taken by the whole proposal, having seen the extraordinary grandeur and elegance which Miss Stettheimer has produced in her own rooms with exactly those colors and materials. We are all, however, open to persuasion and to suggestions, and no maquettes have been made.

The idea for the May-pole dance in Act II is even less definite than the other. That also is Miss Stettheimer's. The negro bodies, if seen at all, would only be divined vaguely through long dresses. The movements would be sedate and prim, and the transparence is aimed primarily not at titillating the audience with the sight of a leg but at keeping the texture of the stage as light as possible. This end is important to keep in view when there are as many things and people on a stage as this opera requires and all frequently in movement. Naturally, if the transparent clothes turned out in rehearsal to be a stronger effect than we intended, petticoats would be ordered immediately for everybody. I think the idea is worth trying, however. If it can be realized inoffensively, the bodies would merely add to our spectacle the same magnificence they give to classic religious painting and sculpture. One could not easily use this effect with white bodies, but I think one might with brown.

My negro singers, after all, are a purely musical desideratum, because of their rhythm, their style and especially their diction. Any further use of their racial qualities must be incidental and not of a nature to distract attention from the subject-matter. Hence, the idea of painting their faces white. Nobody wants to put on just a nigger-show. The project remains doubtful, anyway, till I find the proper soloists.

Very faithfully yours
Virgil

I am eager that the production should represent your text as closely as possible and so is Miss Stettheimer: Here Thomson is stretching the truth. Interviewed in the *New York Sun*, 24 March 1934, Florine Stettheimer will say about Stein, "I've hardly read her. I've started to a number of times." She has not read the Stein libretto "except in part. I got tired." The set is, instead, an expansion of her portrait of Thomson, painted in 1930. "I worked for a long time on that... I tried to put into it everything I knew of Mr. Thomson, so that in the end it was Mr. Thomson. Then I translated what I felt to be all the qualities that appeared in Mr. Thomson's portrait into the opera set."

the bodies ... purely musical desideratum: Thomson later said, "Their skins, light or dark, take light beautifully." In contrast "we look like oysters on stage. They were not in any way put out by religious subject matter, which embarrasses white people so deeply" (quoted in Watson, *Prepare* videotape).

*****

May 30 [1933]

My dear Bradley,

... No I have not had the letter from Virgil yet. However for clause 2, I am quite definite, any score of the opera must be owned by us in common, however made, he will perfectly understand that I have had enough xperience with young men to know that if we are to act together we must act together throughout, otherwise difficulties will ensue. The question of the small sums he may make in renting out said scores he need not worry about, there will be no dispute about that, but the ownership must be composer and author. if you show him this he will I think perfectly understand.

In reference to clause 10 I think there should be included, with the consent of the owners of the opera, but if you think not I am willing to abide by your decision...

Alwys

Gtrde Stein

*****

[*1 June? 1933*]

My dear Bradley,

I am sending you the letter you left here the other day and the Minimum Basic Agreement of the Dramatist guild in case you have not it, so that we can talk it over over the telephone Monday morning, and by that time you will perhaps have found out what is the custom about the song writers. As stated by him it seems manifestly unfair, but of course we will have to do what is customary. On the other hand I know you will make him understand in your firm but pleasant way that while I am so very manifestly important in the opera equally important as important the words as the music, the music as the words that he should not think or say that 50–50 is not a just arrangement, that it is a very perfect union, and both parties should realize that graciously and gratefully, but I know you will do all this xactly as it should be done. If you have not yet heard from Austin, we will talk that over the telephone Monday morning,

  Alwys
  Gtrde Stein.

*****

WILLIAM ASPENWALL BRADLEY
5, RUE SAINT-LOUIS-EN-L'ILE
PARIS 4

1 June 1933

Dear Mr. Thomson

Forgive my delay in returning enclosed letter. Frankly I still feel it's a bit late to propose a reduction of Miss Stein's part but that of course is your business. Have now written to Miss Stein myself saying she will hear from you shortly on certain points. . . .

  (we are in plein déménagement.)
  Sincerely yrs
  W.A. Bradley

---

in plein déménagement: in the middle of moving house. Bradley is moving his office from 5 to 3 rue St-Louis-en-l'Ile, immediately next door to where he lives.

*****

To "M. Virgil Thomson / 17 Quai Voltaire / Paris."

[6 June 1933]

My dear Virgil,

Have just received your letter. I think, in fact, I wish to keep to the original terms of our agreement, half share of profits. It is quite true that upon you falls all the burden of seeing the production through but on the other hand, the commercial value of my name is very considerable and therefore we will half it 50-50. the only other point in the agreement between [us] is the one referencing to the phrase, unreasonably withheld. Bradley will have told you that I think that we should take for granted one another's reasonableness.

They are three points to be mentioned in the contract with Austin.

The first one is clause 2. I have xplained to Bradley that in everything that concerns the opera we must be joint owners. You need not worry that

210 *Letters with Notes*

I will not treat you generously what any small sum which could accrue to you from renting but the ownership must be a joint one. the said instrumental and vocal parts shall be made over to the composer and author and shall become their property. As I xplained to Bradley long xperience has taught us that if we are to be together in this thing we are to be together all the way through.

The second thing is clause seven, the use of unreasonably withheld.

Clause 10. This is a matter for you to carefully consider with Bradley. It seems to me that the way this is worded allows the producer and other producers to speculate in an opera without our consent, and I think it is not very well stated. I think we should be consenting parties to such a sale. Think this over. Otherwise everything seems alright and I hope that we and the opera will have all the success we can have which will be very nice for all of us.

I am entirely agreed that the stage setting of out of doors scenery would be the best, and I hope there will be the [o]xcarts, (with the [nuns?]), and the river and the landscape. Would it not be possible to have something in the nature of their out of door processions, with daylight and candle light and overhead canvas stretched between the houses. It altogether makes a beautiful light. I suppose one of the reasons for using Negroes was the diction, it all sounds very hopeful and about all these things I am quite ready to accept what seems best to those who are doing it. The best of luck to us all

      Alwys   Gtrde.

I forgot to say that a ms. copy of Capital Capitals was brought to the rue de Fleurus by a taxi driver do you know anything about it.

*****

17 Quai Voltaire
9 June [1933]

Dear Gertrude

Thank you for your kind and frank letter. If the only reason, however, for holding to a 50-50 division, aside from the natural enough desire to obtain as favorable an arrangement as possible, is the commercial value of your name, I should like to protest that although your name has a very great publicity value as representing the highest quality of artistic achievement, its purely commercial value, especially in connection with a work as hermetic in style as the Four Saints, is somewhat less, as I have found in seeking a publisher for our various joint works, although I have (with some difficulty) found a publisher for other works of mine. Moreover, it is not the value of your name or the devotion of your admirers (I except Mrs. Chadbourne, who began very practically indeed but didnt continue very long) that is getting this opera produced, but my friends and admirers,

Mr. Austin and Mr. Osborne and Mr. Smallens and Florine and Maurice, who are all giving their services at considerable expense to themselves, and a dozen other friends who are contributing $100 or more each to Mr. Austin's costly & absolutely disinterested enterprise. The value of your name has never produced any gesture from these people, whereas every one of them has on other occasions manifested his interest in my work by creating commercial engagements for me and by offering me further collaborations with himself. And dear Gertrude, if you knew the resistance I have encountered in connection with that text and overcome, the amount of reading it and singing it and praising it and commenting [on] it I have done, the articles, the lectures, the private propaganda that has been necessary in Hartford and in New York to silence the opposition that thought it wasnt having any Gertrude Stein, you wouldnt talk to me about the commercial advantages of your name. Well, they *are* having it and they are going to *like* it and it isnt your name or your lieutenants that are giving it to them. If you hadnt put your finger on a sensitive spot by mentioning this to me, I should never have done so to you. However, I've got it off my chest now and the fact remains that even were the situation reversed, a 50-50 contract would be, so far as I know, absolutely without precedent.

About joint ownership of the musical material, I accede to your reasoning and thank you for your generous gesture about the hiring it out, although I think, in view of the fact that we are making a business agreement that may involve heirs or something, everything had better be divided properly.

The other matters can, I think be easily arranged with Mr. Bradley, and I shall take his advice about the statement of Clause 10. The "unreasonably withheld" phrase can be eliminated from our personal agreement if we are convinced of each other's reasonableness, and it can be kept out of the other if Mr. Austin doesnt mind. It is usual, however, in such contracts to offer some protection to the producer, who may have spent real money on a show only to find himself completely at the mercy of an author who might use his right of forbidding the performance as a weapon in some minor dispute which could normally and fairly be settled by arbitration.

I am glad you approve of the scenic plans. The second act includes just such a night scene as you have described. I dont know whether a river can be got on the stage too, but I hope so.

The Capitals was in a folder with the opera text which I took to the copyist. Bringing it home, it dropped out of my pocket in a taxi. I am glad it has been found and if you will instruct your concierge to give it to me, I shall call and get it. I'm terribly glad it isnt lost.

         Best of greeting
           Always faithfully
             Virgil

---

resistance . . . overcome: Thomson will recall:
> their final adoption of it had been brought about by my singing it and playing it on everybody's piano till all could recognize it as something possible for them to admire without intellectual shame. And they could admire it all the more as a property about to be launched by their world rather than by some group mainly

musical or literary. Moreover it was through their support that Chick knew he could find the money for producing it. Certain friends of mine would gladly contribute (though not one of Gertrude's did); and his art dealers, from the smallest up to Lord Duveen, would feel obliged to. (*Virgil Thomson* 217–18)

*****

To "M. Virgil Thomson / 17 Quai Voltaire / Paris."

BILIGNIN
PAR BELLEY
AIN

[11 June 1933]

My dear Virgil.

Yes yes yes, but nous avons changer tout cela, because the important thing is this, the opera was a collaboration, and the proposition made to me in the agreement was in the spirit of that collaboration, 50-50 and the proposition that I accepted was in the spirit of that collaboration 50-50 and the proposition that I continue to accept is the same. When in the future you write operas and have texts from various writers it will be as you and the precedents arrange, but our opera was a collaboration, we own it together and we divide the proceeds 50-50. and we hope that the proceeds will be abundant and we wish each other every possible good luck.

My brother Mike has the ms. of Capital Capitals. I will write to him to send it to you or you can communicate with him yourself if you like, Chemin de la Plaine, Vaucresson S. et O. I am awfully pleased that some things of yours have been published, anything that we know or the later things

Alwys

Gtrde Stein.

---

nous avons changer tout cela: we have changed all that.

*****

WILLIAM ASPENWALL BRADLEY
5, RUE SAINT-LOUIS-EN-L'ILE
PARIS 4

17 June, 1933

Dear Miss Stein,

. . . Virgil Thomson has written me a letter from which I quote the following:
"Miss Stein is being nice but quite firm about the money proposition and giving no reason at all. Which justifies my former hunch that an arbitration clause is absolutely necessary in our agreement and that the phrase

"unreasonably withheld" should not itself be unreasonably withheld. Unless we put arbitration in, there is no way of settling the simplest minor difference that might arise between us, and unless we have the other, the withholding of consent becomes just a way of getting what one of us might want by the unreasonable exercise of that privilege."

It seems to me that, in the circumstances, some sort of compromise is absolutely necessary or we shall never get on with the making of the contracts. Thomson writes me that he does not expect anybody to take his reasonableness for granted, so he does not quite see why he should be expected to take yours. It is evident that, in all such agreements, unless precautions are taken in advance, a dead-lock may arise, which is the reason why the Guild itself in its standard form of agreement includes the disputed phrase "not to be unreasonably withheld." It is, so far as I can see, the only possible safeguard against one or the other of the two parties imposing absolutely upon the other his own will or point of view about any matter under discussion. . . . W.A. Bradley

*****

WILLIAM ASPENWALL BRADLEY
5, RUE SAINT-LOUIS-EN-L'ILE
PARIS 4

19 June 1933

Dear Mr. Thomson,

I have just had a conversation with Miss Stein on the telephone and think the way of compromise has now been found. Will you come to my office again for a final conversation. . . . How about turning up three o'clock? . . . If not we can make another appointment.

Sincerely yrs,
W.A. Bradley

---

compromise: Not much of a compromise, Stein gets her 50–50 profit split, Thomson the inclusion of the disputed "unreasonably withheld" phrase in their contract.

*****

17 Quai Voltaire
22 june [1933]

Dear Gertrude

Everything is arranged now, at least for the duration of our present contract and I have signed it and Mr. Bradley is sending it to you. The copy of score is ready (or will be tomorrow). It is in the original form plus Maurice's stage-directions. I suggest (since they are neither your nor my invention & though they will be used in the production are not the only ones that are possible) that I cross them out of the copyrighted work. Also that you make in your text a few minor changes, sufficient to permit it to be copyrighted should it be printed in America. I will make the corresponding musical changes and we will thus have an authoritative version for all purposes. If you care to do this, please send me the corrected text as soon as you can, because I should like to finish off that copy and leave town by the 1st of July.

I find on working over the opera and orchestrating it that I should very much like to make a few simple cuts. You offered me that privilege at the beginning of our collaboration & I didnt care to avail myself of it, preferring to set everything and wait for a later time to make any such cuts in view of an actual performance. I find now that there is a little too much singing & not enough instrumental relief. I should like to eliminate for example a few of the stage-directions as sung, especially where they are repeated frequently. I dont mean systematically remove them, just a few repetitions now & then, in every case (or nearly) to replace them with an instrumental passage of the same length & tune. This makes a rather amusing effect & is as if an instrument were saying the words that somebody has just sung. There are also a few passages that I should like to eliminate for the purposes of this performance, substituting in one or two cases a short instrumental passage, in others nothing at all. This in view of tightening the structure musically and making a more simple & effective musical continuity. The aria in Act III about roses smell very well, for instance, comes right after another aria for tenor & rather impedes the advance of the spectacle toward the ballet. I should like to cut it out.

The cuts I propose are only for the purposes of my score for this performance. The copyright score would include everything. I mention the cuts because I dont want to avail myself of a permission offered so long ago without its being renewed. I hope you will allow me to do this. I assure you the theatrical effectiveness of the work will be enhanced.

Many thanks for your gracious acceptance of the consent clause in our agreement. We now have, I think, a simple way of settling any differences that may arise without bitterness. As a matter of fact, we understand each other so well and our interests lie for the most part so close together that I am sure we shall always be mostly reasonable with each other anyway.

Best of greetings

Always devotedly yours
Virgil

*****

WILLIAM ASPENWALL BRADLEY
5, RUE SAINT-LOUIS-EN-L'ILE
PARIS 4

23 June 1933

Dear Mr. Thomson

We are sending you herewith enclosed the contract (in three copies) for the production of FOUR SAINTS IN THREE ACTS, re-typed with the corrections made yesterday by yourself and Mr. Bradley. Kindly let us have them back, duly signed, so that we can send them to Miss Stein for her signature.

Very faithfully yours
W.A. Bradley
[Madelaine] Dhermy
Secretary

P.S.—Mr. Bradley's lawyer now assures him absolutely that a single copy of the manuscript score with words of the Opera will be sufficient for purposes of copyright protection in America. If therefore, you will send us the manuscript, we will forward it to Washington ourselves at once.

---

the contract: Appendix E.

*****

To "M. Virgil Thomson / 17 Quai Voltaire / Paris."

BILIGNIN
PAR BELLEY
AIN

[23 June 1933]

My dear Virgil,

Yes of course you are to make the cuts, the burden of making it a successful performance lies upon you. It would perhaps be a good idea that the changes in the text necessary for the copyright, should be made in the parts you cut, in that way it would not be necessary to make any changes in the words and music to be used. If you think this a good idea mark in the copy of Operas and Plays I am sending you the passages that you want to cut and also what proportion of those cuts should be changed for the copyright, I will then send you back the book and the changes and you can go ahead. I am very pleased that everything is arranged, Bradley will be sending me the agreement and I will sign it, and I hope it will all be as successful as possible, we certainly deserve it, do we not. I am sending you the book to-day and I will make the changes necessary at once so it can all be finished as promptly as possible. You are quite right about not using Maurice's suggestions in the copy for copyrighting, I am glad he is to be in the show, he certainly helped a lot

Alwys
Gtrde.

*****

WILLIAM ASPENWALL BRADLEY
5, RUE SAINT-LOUIS-EN-L'ILE
PARIS 4

24 June, 1933.

Dear Miss Stein,

I send you herewith the agreements between you and Virgil Thomson, which have now been put in order and signed by him. Please return one to me, invested with your own signature and witnessed by Miss Toklas, for him to keep. Three copies of the production contract, revised in accordance with our latest understanding, went to him yesterday, and I will send them to you as soon as they come back. As you will see then, we have, as you wished, put into the assignment clause 10 the words: "with the consent of the Authors" and "such consent not to be unreasonably withheld," so all is well in that quarter, unless Austin himself raises any objection. . . .

Virgil Thomson has now received the complete manuscript, with words, of the score of FOUR SAINTS IN THREE ACTS and will let me have this for copyright purposes as soon as he has heard from you with regard to the slight changes in the text which would make the protection for you more sure. In consulting my lawyer here in Paris with regard to the copyright, I also discovered that it will probably be possible to secure copyright for *your text*, for *play production*, independently of its publication as a literary work. For this, however, you will be obliged to give me a typewritten manuscript. Will it be too much trouble for Miss Toklas to prepare this, or would you prefer to have me get it done for you from my own copy here in Paris? I will then forward it also to the Copyright Bureau of the Congressional Library, in Washington. . . .

Ever sincerely,
W.A. Bradley

*****

June 25 [sic] / 33

My dear Bradley,

Have just had a nice letter from Virgil saying that everything is arranged. He suggests that I should make the necessary changes to insure the American copyright, will you find out for me and let me know as soon as possible just what changes are necessary in a work to make it eligible for copyright, what proportion of the work and what the character of the changes, will you let me know this as soon as possible as he wishes the changes to be made as soon as possible. I have suggested that the changes should be made in the parts of the opera that he intends to cut for this performance. I have given him permission to make such cuts as he considers necessary. I am glad that this has all been arranged so happily, and thanks to you . . .

Alwys
Gtrde Stein.

June 25 [sic]: Since Bradley receives and answers this letter on the 24th, and the 25th is a Sunday, Stein must be mistaken about the date.

*****

WILLIAM ASPENWALL BRADLEY
5, RUE SAINT-LOUIS-EN-L'ILE
PARIS 4

24 June, 1933

Dear Miss Stein,

Your letter of the 25th arrived just as I had signed the enclosed letter. I am glad that you have already heard from Thomson and everything is understood between you. As for the question of the changes, *any* changes whatsoever—slight verbal changes or the recasting of a line or sentence here and there—are all that is necessary. Thomson will then modify his *music* as required, to harmonize it with the words. Your suggestion is ingenious that the changes should be made in the part he intends to cut for the Hartford performance. . . . W.A. Bradley

---

Your letter of the 25th: see note to Stein, June 25 [sic].
enclosed letter: i.e., his of 24 June, 1933.

*****

June 26 / 33

My dear Bradley,

Here are the documents signed and witnessed, we will shortly be sad when we haven't a contract to sign at least once a month will we not. As soon as I get back from Virgil the marked copy of Operas and Plays which tells me the parts he is to cut for the Hartford performance, I will send you a typewritten copy of it as arranged for Play Production. . . . You do not tell me how many lines would have to be changed, ten, twenty, thirty, I have no idea at all, will you xplain it to me a little more, is it any proportion of the work, is it whole lines or only words. Will you let me know as soon as possible so I can do it as soon as I get the corrected copy from Virgil. It

would be very nice if it could be printed and sold as a libretto for the performances at the performances, as he suggests ...
      Alwys
       Gtrde Stein.

*****

       17 Quai Voltaire
       3 July [1933]

Dear Gertrude

 I have made the changes in the printed text, indicating everywhere who sings what & restoring the original reading whenever there was a difference. That ought to be enough changes for your own copyright. I did not make the cuts in the score for copyrighting because it was too long a job & there is no reason, I think, for not copyrighting the whole thing. Another copyright, in case of publication, will cover those and also any changes & restorations I might make in rehearsal. I have delivered the score to Bradley & received payment for half of the cost, which was altogether 660 francs, donc 330 francs. You can copyright the version I am sending you for non-musical performance. Also for publication whenever it is printed in U.S.A. Our mutual version will be copyright for performance & publication, there being a difference, if I am correctly informed, between musical & literary copyright in that the latter requires no printing, though neither requires it for performing rights.

 I am going away now for a little bit but I can always be reached here. Best wishes for a good summer and affectionate greetings to you both.
      Always faithfully
       Virgil

I have seen a good [deal] lately of the Comte and Comtesse d'Aiguy who admire you no end and make me sing your works for all their guests.

———

donc: therefore.

*****

       July 4 / 33

My dear Bradley,

 I am sending you the marked copy of the Four Saints with the cuts and changes that Virgil Thomson has made for the performance. I suppose there is no question of copyright until you have made some arrangement for printing it for libretto purposes. Anyway so much is done ...
    Alwys   Gtrde Stein.

*****

5 July, 1933

Dear Miss Stein,

I believe I have not yet acknowledged receipt of the signed production contracts for FOUR SAINTS IN THREE ACTS, which I immediately turned over to Thomson, for him to forward to America. He has, incidentally, just brought in the nicely bound copy of the manuscript *partition* (words and music) of the opera for copyright purposes. The total cost of this is Frs 660, and, since he was anxious to have the money at once, I gave him a cheque for one-half that amount, being your share. . . . Ever sincerely, W.A. Bradley

---

partition: score.

*****

July 26 . 33

My dear Bradley,

I am so sorry that I did not answer about 4 Saints, surely have it copied right away and copyrighted, and then you can be free to try and get someone to print it to be sold as a libretto, if the opera is to be given this winter, all that should be attended to as soon as possible . . .

Gtrde Stein

*****

Hôtel Ste. Anne
Ile de Porquerolles (Var)
9 August [1933]

Dear Gertrude

Many thanks for the lovely book which reached me some time ago at Honfleur and then I went to London & later to Besançon and here and so busily en voyage I was that I didnt thank you before although I read it at Honfleur and so did Maurice and we had a lovely time. It is so much about all of us and an epoch and I now see that Madame Récamier is very beautiful which you told me all the time but I never made head nor tail of it before. Not that I do a lot even now because it is all about Belley & environs I presume but I see that is very grand.

Ford (the small young one) wrote me and then I was only in Paris a minute in passing and didnt see him but another time I will.

Again many thanks. And good wishes to you both

toujours
Virgil

Opera scoring advances rapidly.

---

the lovely book: *Operas & Plays* (Paris: Plain Edition, 1932).
Ford: Charles Henri Ford, editor of *Blues*. Stein has recommended him to W. A. Bradley, on whom as agent, he relies for a book contract that results in publication of his and Parker Tyler's homoerotic stream-of-consciousness novel, *The Young and Evil* (Paris: Obelisk, 1933), which is heavily influenced by James Joyce, Djuna Barnes, and Gertrude Stein. She thinks him "fresh . . . and also honest" with "an individual sense of words" (*Autobiography* 260).

*****

HOTEL LEONORI
Madison Avenue at 63rd Street
NEW YORK

6th Dec. [1933]

Dear Gertrude - Here is a newspaper article that will amuse you from the Hartford Times. The cast of the opera is hired and rehearsals begun. I have a chorus of 32 & six soloists, very, very fine ones indeed. Miss Stettheimer's sets are of a beauty incredible, with trees made out of feathers and a sea-wall at Barcelona made out of shells and for the procession a baldachins of black chiffon & bunches of black ostrich plumes just like a Spanish funeral. St.Teresa comes to the picnic in the 2nd Act in a cart drawn by a real white donkey & brings her tent with her and sets it up & sits in the door-way of it. It is made of white gauze with gold fringe and has a most elegant shape. My singers, as I have wanted, are negroes, & you cant imagine how beautifully they sing. Frederick Ashton is arriving from London this week to make choreography for us. Not only for the dance-numbers, but for the whole show, so that all the movements will be regulated to the music, measure by measure, and all our complicated stage-action made into a controlable spectacle. The Houseman man mentioned in the clipping is a play-wright, friend & collaborator of Lewis Galantière. He "understands" the opera too, if you know what I mean by that word. Everything about the opera is shaping up so beautifully, even the raising of money (It's going to cost $10,000), that the press is champing at the bit and the New York ladies already ordering dresses & engaging hotel rooms. Carl's niece has taken a Hartford house for the opera-week. Rumors of your arrival are floating about and everybody asks me is she really coming and I always answer that it wouldnt surprise me. Certainly, if everything goes off as fancy as it looks now, you would be very happy to be here and to see your opera on the stage and I would be very happy to see it with you and your presence would be all we need to make the opera perfect in every way. (February 7th is opening date, I believe.)

Many people seeing my copy have asked me where *Operas and Plays* can be bought here and those who have tried tell me it isnt to be had. Couldn't you send a consignment to several of the good book-stores? Big stores are best now. Nobody goes to little ones anymore & they've mostly gone out of business, anyway.

Always affectionately
Virgil

c/o Avery Claflin, Esq.
65 Broadway
N.Y.C

Could you send me also some photos for publicity use? Glossy prints are best, of course.

V.—

---

how beautifully they sing: Thomson is glad he chose black singers:
> Not only could they enunciate and sing: they seemed to understand because they sang. They resisted not at all Stein's obscure language, adopted it for theirs, conversed in quotations from it. They moved, sang, spoke with grace and with alacrity, took on roles without self-consciousness, as if they were the saints they said they were. I often marveled at the miracle whereby slavery (and some crossbreeding) had turned them into Christians of an earlier stamp than ours, not analytical and self-pitying or romantic in the nineteenth-century sense, but robust, outgoing, and even in disaster sustained by inner joy. (*Virgil Thomson* 239)

Van Vechten will write to Stein, "The Negroes are divine, like El Grecos, more Spanish, more Saints, more opera singers in their dignity and *simplicity* and extraordinary plastic line than *any* white singers could ever be" (8 Feb. 1934; *The Letters of Gertrude Stein and Carl Van Vechten* 295).

Frederick Ashton: Twenty-nine-year-old dancer, choreographer, whom Thomson met in London. He has agreed to choreograph the opera, is on his way from England, will arrive with Maurice Grosser on 12 December. He will create for the opera a new kind of choreography from his background in classical ballet, his experience of the Catholic rituals of his childhood in Peru, and black popular dance. Thomson will remember, "He spent his childhood living next door to a nunnery. He knew how nuns moved. He had that awareness of the ritual nature of their lives" (Watson, *Prepare* video). Like Thomson, Smallens, and Stettheimer (everyone except the orchestra and cast), he agrees to work temporarily without pay.

The Houseman man: Thirty-one-year-old John Houseman. Freed by the recent failures of his grain business and marriage, he is shifting his energies to the theater. With no apparent prospects other than as a conventional playwright, he has agreed to direct the opera and acts virtually as its producer while supporting himself by translating from French and German. Near the end of a fifty-year career on stage, in film, and in television, he will call *Four Saints* "the womb of my career" (Watson 6).

Lewis Galantière: French-American friend of Thomson, translator, playwright, and journalist best known for his translations of Antoine de Saint-Exupéry.

the press . . . is she really coming: The surge in interest is due in great part to the popularity of *The Autobiography of Alice B. Toklas*, published by Harcourt, Brace and Co. on 1 Sept. 1933. Having been serialized in *The Atlantic Monthly*, featured on the cover of *Time Magazine*, quickly selling out its first four printings, the book makes Stein for the first time a best-selling author. Its success will make *Four Saints* economically performable and contribute to its publicity. In the book, using the persona of Toklas, Stein writes of herself:
> Virgil Thomson she found very interesting although I did not like him. . . . Virgil Thomson and Gertrude Stein became friends and saw each other a great deal. . . . Gertrude Stein was very much interested in Virgil Thomson's music. He had understood Satie undoubtedly and he had a comprehension quite his own of prosody. He understood a great deal of Gertrude Stein's work, he used to dream at night that there was something there that he did not understand, but on the whole he was very well content with that which he did understand.

She delighted in listening to her words framed by his music. They saw a great deal of each other. Virgil Thomson had asked Gertrude Stein to write an opera for him. . . . She . . . worked very hard at it all that spring and finally finished Four Saints and gave it to Virgil Thomson to put to music. He did. And it is a completely interesting opera both as to words and music. (244, 246–47)

Avery Claflin: Thirty-five year old Brooklyn-born businessman, lawyer, financier, and composer who had studied music at Harvard and in Paris with Erik Satie.

*****

To "M. Virgil Thomson / ~~c/o Avery Claflin / 65 Broadway~~ c/o Hotel Leonori / 63rd St. & Madison Ave / New York / U.S.A.

27 rue-de-Fleurus
Paris
[31 Dec. 1933]

My dear Virgil,

I am very pleased that it looks like beginning so well, happy new year to you, it sounds very very amusing, my brother Mike says will they make records of it but really perhaps they will make a film and that would be even more xciting as well as everything else. At any rate I am glad it is being done and glad it is being done in February I like February. I will send you some photos, Marcoussis is just doing an etching of me, if he gets it done and he says it will either be done in a week or in a year I will send it to you. In any case I will send you something. Alice is writing to the book-shops. I do indeed hope that everything goes off as well as it promises and again all best wishes for the new year. We saw the D'Aiguys a great deal this summer and had some amusing conversations,

Alwys
Gtrde.

*****

HOTEL LEONORI
Madison Avenue at 63rd Street
NEW YORK

8 january [1934]

Dear Gertrude

Happy New Year. All goes very fancy. Tickets mostly sold already. Doing 4 extra shows in Hartford. Then Philadelphia. Then opening New York.

Just thought this little folder might please you

toujours
Virgil

*****

3. Photograph of the original production of *Four Saints in Three Acts* (1934): Act One, second tableau, "Saint Teresa could be photographed"

27 rue de Fleurus
Feb. 4 [1934]

My dear Bradley,

    This is to authorize you to have Virgil Thomson's share of our royalties paid to him in America the share coming from the Hartford and New York performances of Four Saints.

                  Alwys
                          Gtrde Stein.

*****

To "M. Virgil Thomson / ~~c/o Avery Claflin / 65 Broadway~~ c/o Hotel Leonori / 63rd St. & Madison Ave / New York city / N.Y. / U.S.A.

[12 Feb. 1934]

My dear Virgil.

    Thanks so much for your message. I am awfully pleased that it has all started off so well, I had a number of cables and they all seemed to feel that it had really been done, which will be most awfully nice. I had a charming cable from Bryher do you know her address because I want to write and tell her how much I liked her doing it. I am now waiting for the letters and they will be coming along soon. May it go on and prosper. It has been an xciting winter in every kind of a way, and the opera way is a very nice way, and I am very happy about it,

Alwys
Gtrde.

---

all started off so well: Both the preview (7 Feb.) and opening (8 Feb.) of *Four Saints* were sold-out, elegant, grand occasions. The first performance received twelve curtain calls after Act I, the curtain calls at the end lasting half an hour (Watson 276, 280).
cable from Bryher: Winifred Bryher's cable of 10 Feb. from New York reads, "SAINTS TRULY HEAVENLY."

*****

HOTEL LEONORI
Madison Avenue at 63rd Street
NEW YORK

16 February [1934]
c/o Avery Claflin Esq
French-Amer. Bank
65 B'way

Dear Mr. Bradley,

Thank you for letter and enclosures. Mr. Houseman of whom I spoke is my stage director and business consultant for the opera. I wrote Miss Stein about him. He is a play-wright and director of considerable experience and has been invaluable in directing the production. He is the dramatic collaborator of Lewis Galantière and a devoted and indefatigable director for us. We are not going to Philadelphia just now. We are expecting something of a run here, leaving the road till later. I will send clippings in the future. I am sorry I haven't saved them so far. The papers have been full of nothing else. We are opening Feb. 20 at 44th St. Theatre.

Please thank Miss Stein for her willingness to readjust the proportion of profits on movie and other extra rights. For the moment everybody seems satisfied and pleased, but I will quote your letter whenever the question rises again. It looks as if we are all going to make some money.
About *Susie Asado*.

The usual American practise is to pay $5 outright to the poet ($10, if the poem is long or the author insistent). In this case the composer receives the full amount for himself of the royalties. If Miss Stein prefers that arrangement I shall be more than pleased. I offered her a share of my royalties because of my esteem for her work and my belief in its ultimate commercial value. I offered the proportion that I am assured by the Société des Auteurs is the maximum currently demanded in France by poets of high artistic or commercial value in the *theatre*. The French practise about songs is the same as here, Max Jacob, Jean Cocteau, & Paul Eluard (the poets most in demand by composers there) usually receiving 100 francs from the publisher for their work. They can share in addition 1/3 of the royalties paid for performances if they join the Société. This is separate from publication, can in fact be collected on unpublished works, and does not regard the publisher at all. I believe, however, although I don't know how much, that he gets a small royalty too on published works.

Anyhow, please believe that I was far from wishing to keep from Miss Stein her just rewards in proposing what I did. I allowed the 50–50 proportion to go then about the opera because I injudiciously proposed it myself and when I asked to have the error corrected she refused. My ultimate capitulation was due to the necessity of her accepting an "unreasonably withheld" phrase, the phrase itself quite unreasonably withheld, as you will remember, until I sacrificed some of my rightful royalties for it.

The Cos Cob percentage, by the way is 10, not 1, as your letter mentions. I presume my writing was not clear.

In case my information about French royalty practise is incorrect (your letter indicates at any rate that you have been informed otherwise), I shall be glad to change my demands to conform to what is really done. My informants have been Sauguet, Cliquet-Pleyel, Milhaud and Max Jacob. Supposing you ask the two Sociétés about it.

I learned from your first letter that you are expecting to be here April 1st. I hope the opera will be on still. The gala first-night has been changed for a much more profitable one at $6.60 a head and which is already sold out. I haven't time to write Gertrude just now. It would be very good of you to share all this news with her.

Very cordially yours,
Virgil Thomson

Cos Cob: Music press. Thomson had met the publisher, Alma Morgenthau Wertheim, at Carl Van Vechten's party for him in New York in 1929.
I hope the opera will be on still: *Four Saints* played at Forty-fourth Street Theatre, one of the largest on Broadway, from 20 February to 17 March, doubling the planned two-week run, and reopened at the Empire and played from 2 to 14 April.

*****

Telegram to "Thomson 65 Broadway New York 21 Feb 1934"
Happy as can be newyork news

Gertrude

*****

Telegram to "Virgil Thomson care of Claflin French American Bank 65 Broadway New York 27 Feb 1934"

Have received cable from Moses and Houseman proposing reduction royalty NewYork production and road run to six percent stop Before considering Gertrude demands payment Hartford royalties also expression your opinion please wire
Bradley

Moses: Harry Moses, retired Chicago women's underwear manufacturer, now a Broadway producer financing the production of *Four Saints*—his office is at the Empire Theater, Broadway and 40th St. Thomson later remembers, "Moses scented prestige in *Four Saints*, also a bargain, since our production was being made at off-Broadway prices. He realized that the work was not a commercial venture but an art piece, and that if it could be made to pay its way, or nearly, both he and Broadway would gain intellectual credit" (*Virgil Thomson* 240).
Hartford royalties: Neither Stein nor Thomson would ever be paid them (Watson 289).

*****

HOTEL LEONORI
Madison Avenue at 63rd Street
NEW YORK

2 March 1934

Dear Gertrude

You will have had by now most of the big critical fire-works. Here are a few rarer tid-bits. Also see, if you can, perhaps at Amer. Library, Catholic weekly *America* for February 17. Fancy high Jesuit Father La Farge, did us proud. He, incidentally, was the author of the phrase "baroque fantasia. Usefully."

Everything grows and grows. Seeing two publishers today.

Always devotedly yours
Virgil

La Farge . . . "baroque fantasia. Usefully": Son of the American painter of the same name, John La Farge, SJ, is editor of the Jesuit weekly *America*. On pp. 475–76, in his column "With Scrip and Staff," over the signature "The Pilgrim," he reviews *Four Saints in Three Acts*, writing of its "impressive and poignant music, conducted by the dynamic Alexander Smallens, and interpreted by splendid choruses in solemn ballet; the tempo ranging from the sedateness of a minuet to the comparative speed of a Victorian garden party." He praises the "superb soloists. Actors all Negroes. Not as Negroes, not written for Negroes, but chosen by the composer, Virgil Thomson, for their skill and voices." He thinks they seemed "worried, at least at first, by the unintelligibility of the Steinian words. . . . But they were the words to be sung: and that ended it. Usefully." He expects that many will be "annoyed by the curious incongruity between passionate, heartrending chords and words that sound like reminiscences of an Ollendorff exercise book." He says that Stein's "idea seems to be a baroque fantasia. She wishes to convey to the spectator and hearer the vague general impression of how baroque appears to her; of what she particularly loves in baroque: its contained grandeur; its dignity of high noon and blue skies." He continues:

> But this is not done too seriously. It is ironical; seriously ironical or ironically serious. The passionate chorus set to walk-in-the-park words may be a mild satire on most operas, where after all you rarely hear the words; and when you do, find you have not gained much.

She conveys too, in a strange way, the impression that a spiritually illiterate person receives from the accidentals of the Catholic liturgy. To such a person, the chanted lessons of the Church, the intonations and movements, appear solemn yet inconsequential grave announcements of the inexplicable. Not that she resents this; she enjoys it, as the most precious element in the baroque. Her attitude toward it is of interest; of pleasure; possibly of something deeper, a sense that there *is* something profound and meaningful beneath these forms. So with an immense number of moderns; a nostalgia for something they have lost. Yet she remains slightly ironical.

St. Teresa and St. Ignatius are but symbols of this something in the baroque which lifts it above a gorgeous garden party. They are the foci of baroque dignity, restraint, expansiveness. They are vaguely reminiscent of a vaguely apprehended period: agreeable figures. St. Teresa is two figures, one who sings, one who postures. They have many conversations: pleasant conversations. These symbols are chosen because for some reason or other Gertrude Stein does like the historical Teresa and Ignatius, or what she knows about them. But in the opera they remain mere symbols.

And above all not to be taken too seriously. Cherry blossoms surrounded by space. Usefully? I do not know.

Reflected in his praise of the cast is La Farge's dedicated opposition to racism, evident in his writings. In the mid 1950s, the Pope will commission him to draft an encyclical entitled *Humani Generis Unitas* opposing Nazi racial policies. La Farge will submit it but Pius XII will die before being able to issue it, and the encyclical will disappear into the Vatican archives.

*****

Telegram to "Virgil Thomson care of Claflin French American Bank 65 Broadway New York 3 March 1934"

Sorry cannot discuss reduction till Hartford New York royalties now due are paid in full according contract with all broadcasting to date suggest cable remittance
Bradley

*****

HOTEL LEONORI
Madison Avenue at 63rd Street
NEW YORK

6 March [1934]

Dear Mr. Bradley,

Moses is not obliged to pay Austin's debts. Austin will pay our royalties when the FOUR SAINTS shall have made a profit. At present Austin is in extremely difficult circumstances and the opera deficit is very large. We and everybody else will be paid in due time, but we mustn't bother him about it. Moses, on the other hand, is entirely solvent and pays everything regularly. He is objecting firmly to paying 10% royalties, because nobody ever does pay that on a run. If we refuse to accept six %, he will be very difficult and probably close the show. I wash my hands from now on of the whole matter. It is up to Gertrude to decide. I think that if you and she were here we could all sit down together and decide things properly. Across an ocean all is different and nobody ever really understands what anybody else is talking about. I do hope she will come with you. If the show is going to be the eventual money-maker that we all believe here, it is worth while setting these matters equitably and to everybody's satisfaction right now.

Two more matters:

Maurice Grosser's scenario, which rendered possible the putting of the opera on the stage, must be paid for, and it must be paid for out of the librettist's share of royalties, because it is literary work. My musical directions are sufficient for a musical execution of my score. Gertrude's stage directions (beautiful and suggestive as they are) are in no way sufficient to the staging of her libretto. If she will consent to pay him 1/2 of 1% out of her share, that will be in fact, a minimum payment as such matters are figured in the theatre. 1% would be more just.

The other matter is your commission, which I [am] going to ask to reduce, along with the general reductions taking place. I offered it to you and now I see that I was foolish. It isn't as if you had sold the production. On that basis you and Gertrude would owe me a commission. Your services to me consist in handling money and 10% is too large for that. Also there is a slight feeling in my mind that in all matters of contention between Gertrude and me, you are acting for her interest (as is natural and right) rather than for mine.

I have instructed Moses to withhold your commission, it being kept to my credit at his office, until you get here and we can rearrange all that amicably together.

O. Yes, I have publishers too. Marks of N.Y., Birchard of Boston and a private individual in N.Y., are all dickering for it. I have made no offers to anyone, but I have informed myself of the local practise and the normal and maximum figures and I expect to have some definite proposals to submit to Gertrude shortly. (Please prepare her mind to accept an adequate and generous division of profits, but which cannot on a musical publication be 50-50). Random House is selling FOUR SAINTS hand over fist. VARIETY states that FOUR SAINTS has had a bigger line press (you know what that means, I presume) than any show in 10 years. It costs $10,000 a week to run. Business is only fair, but growing. The prognostic on Broadway is that we will continue doing business (here, on the road, in London, etc.) for at least two years. Moses has put money into it and is continuing to do so. He deserves to be handled carefully, he is not a bad man; his good will is of value to us. Austin has ruined himself for us and deserves only the greatest thanks and consideration on our part. Miss Stein, incidentally has never taken the troubles to thank him, or anybody else connected with the production, nor did she even wish us well by cable at either of our openings. I beseech you to impress upon her that Austin will pay us (as he will pay his other creditors) and that he deserves even at present only gratitude from us. The cables you have been having, signed Houseman for

Austin, are not of course from him at all but from Moses, that signature formula merely representing the fact that our contract is with Austin. Houseman, of course, like Ashton and Miss Stettheimer and myself, gave his services free and still does to the production, because he believed in it and signs those telegrams and letters because Austin isn't in New York and Houseman is sort of general manager of the Friends and Enemies production. This to explain that it is not Austin who is complaining about the royalties figures (which is all right for a few performances) but Moses, who is sinking money into us to make a run on a profitable and normal commercial basis.

(My private advice to Gertrude, if she wants it, is to accept Moses's royalty-checks of 3% as "on account of royalties" and to get the matter settled definitely when you or she comes. There is, I think, no urgent need for doing anything at all about it for a week or two, except to answer telegrams sweetly and diplomatically.)

(You *are* coming soon, however, are you not?)

Best greetings
Virgil Thomson.

Grosser's scenario . . . must be paid for: Moses will end up paying Grosser half a percent out of his own (the producer's) share of the profit.
Marks . . . Birchard: Edward B. Marks Music Company, New York; C.C. Birchard & Co., Boston.
we will continue doing business (here, on the road, in London, etc.) for at least two years: Owing to arguments between Stein and Thomson over royalties and a share for Grosser, Moses will cancel plans to take the opera on tour after performances on Broadway.

*****

Bradley arrived on 1 April in New York (Thomson 16 Feb. [1934]) and will stay till 3 July, principally to negotiate on Stein's behalf with publishers, at the end of this, her most financially rewarding year as a published writer. He ceases acting as agent for Thomson and represents her in negotiations concerning the production of *Four Saints*.

*****

New Canaan, Conn.

6 April 1934

Dear Miss Stein,

I received your welcome letter yesterday, forwarded from New York, where I shall be again on Monday. Mrs. Bradley will already have told you what I wrote from here the other day of my meetings with Thomson and John Houseman, so there is no need in repeating it here. I now enclose the latter's letter which I agreed to forward if he would care to write. The only new point advanced, so far as I can see, is the danger that Grosser might possibly withdraw his consent to the further performance of the opera, but there does not seem to be any too much conviction behind this veiled threat. The other arguments you know, and was myself prepared for in the long discussion I had with both Thomson and Houseman separately. Thomson, of course, claims that whereas Grosser's scenario was already made at the time of signing the contract, it was not then definitely decided to use it, which explains why it was not mentioned—which seems to me decidedly specious! to say the least! However, I had to give them this space to state their case over again and put it before you. Houseman, personally, is a nice boy, with greater integrity, I should say, than Thomson, whom he judges rather accurately. He said to me, "Thomson is like any man who, never before having made any money, is boggled by the prospect suddenly opened to him and determined not to lose any part of it." As for my own feelings towards Thomson, it is enough to say I felt compelled, at once, to withdraw as his agent and representative. He asked me definitely to espouse his point of view in the present instance and act as his champion—"though I know it will be very difficult for you in the circumstances." Well, that is all settled anyway. You might let me have a word in reply, at your leisure. There is no hurry and this exchange of letters at least enables us to gain time. Incidentally, in his cover letter to me, Houseman says: "In my own opinion the best solution would be ¼ % from Mr. Thomson and ¼ % from Miss Stein. I know that Thomson would agree to this but he does not want this suggestion." Thomson hinted to me as much, and also said he would do nothing about the publication of the opera till this point was satisfactorily settled—in which case, he also makes it sufficiently clear that he would accept the 50/50 division. I shall be seeing Houseman again, Monday or Tuesday, to collect the money from the fifth week. I hope it has been a success. I will probably see Thomson also, and will then take up with him the question of the London broadcasting of "Capitals, Capitals" etc. . . . I had no conversation with Cerf other than about the contracts etc. for *Four Saints*. . . .

 My best to you both,
  Sincerely,
   W.A. Bradley

Cerf: Bennett Cerf, thirty-five-year-old New York publisher, journalist and, in 1927, cofounder of Random House. Currently its president, Cerf undertook to publish *Four Saints* for distribution during the production of the opera after Harcourt decided not to (Dydo 598).

*****

           April 14/34

My dear Bradley,

 I was very glad to have your letter and I had already had all Mrs. Bradley's news, and now she has all mine. . . .

And now about the Grosser business.

The facts are these. Grosser living with Thomson and as a friend worked with him quite naturally, as one always does with a housemate. As I remember in those conversations the intention was to represent the whole thing as taking place in a sort of American Sunday school. As I understand, the opera is not at all that, is not at all the thing they talked of then, but naturally it is what everybody has made of it, Miss Stettheimer, the stage director the lighter expert everybody, as always it [is] in that sort of thing. That Thomson had no idea at all of considering Grosser as anything but a friend and house mate who helped with the opera as he helped with the copying of the music is perfectly evident by the fact that he never mentioned him at any time during the very prolonged discussions of the contract. Indeed I imagine that I was the first to mention him in this connection as when I was first interviewed about the 4 Saints before it went on at Hartford, in speaking of everybody in connection with it I said Maurice Grosser had been most helpful as he had a very good sense of the theatre. So little did Thomson think of him in this connection that his Grosser's going over was rather an after thought, however all that is naturally their own affair. My position is perfectly clear, I consider that no one has any property rights in this opera except Thomson and myself, and just how much and just how little Grosser helped Thomson, I do not know, but once again that is not our business. So I think the matter is perfectly simple. In the case where the author pays the scenario writer it is where the author has called in or hired the scenario writer. I most certainly did nothing of the sort and as I say as I understand the opera is not at all staged as we all talked it over but as it naturally found itself under everybody's impetus and Grosser was important in it all as a friend and housemate of Thomson whose intent was naturally vivid and his suggestions very frequently very good. There that is my point of view in the matter. And of course I am not writing to any of them myself. This makes my point of view perfectly clear that no one has any property rights in this opera xcept Thomson and myself....

     Alwys
      Gtrde Stein

*****

HOTEL LEONORI
MADISON AVENUE AT 63rd STREET
NEW YORK

21 April [1934]

Dear Gertrude

I am enclosing check and statement from B.B.C. for 4 guineas minus income tax for broadcasting of Capitals, Capitals. The entire fee was ten guineas, two of which was reimbursement for cablegrams sent by me in arranging the matter and postage on the music. I had intended to include a small fee for the hire of score and parts in this two guineas but by the time I had paid the cables and postage the remainder turned out to be nominal. The actual broadcasting fee of 8 guineas was divided equally between us at my request in separate checks and that is what I am enclosing here.

The opera is closed now for the summer and everybody has had a lovely time about it and I must say that in every way it was very very beautiful and of course there were some who didnt like the music and some who didnt like the words and even some who didnt like the décors or the choreography but there wasnt anybody who didnt see that the ensemble was a new kind of collaboration and that it was unique and powerful and I wish you could have seen the faces of people as they watched and listened. In the fall a tour is being planned and in the meanwhile I am treating with various publishers. I have given Susie Asado to the Cos Cob Press and you will have a contract about it shortly. The usual 50-50 is all right and I will do the proof-reading and mss work free because I happen to have an extra copy and the proof-reading on it will be easy because the piece is very short. I dont think I can do that on the opera. Any fair arrangement that you think of will probably be all right with me. You see I sold the *Four Saints* to a producer and I didnt ask for any commission and I gave my services to the preparing of the production just as everybody else did and I made two trips to America to do these things at my own expense and all that was all right because I wanted the opera produced and it couldnt have been produced if I hadnt done those things. But I cant go on doing them free, of course. If you prefer to keep our profits on a 50-50 basis, that is all right, provided I can be reimbursed for one-half of the expenses I will get into in preparing the mss. for publication (the old one being temporarily the property of the production and pretty well scratched up at that) and for one-half of the time & trouble involved in correcting the proofs. I will undertake all these expenses if you care to make a 65-35 split. Otherwise, I leave it to you to make some fair proposal about them so that the real division of profits may continue to be equal, and as I said before, any means you suggest of accomplishing that end will probably be all right with me.

I have explained all this to Mr. Bradley and I am writing it to you at his suggestion. I am meeting him next week again to arrange a similar status for Capital, Capitals and once such an arrangement has been agreed upon it can serve I hope for all the work we have done together and for any possible future collaboration.

I should like to add that I have always considered that our not seeing each other in the last few years was a completely personal and sentimental matter and that I have never had any reason to question your fairness about anything or your good-will and I dont think you have ever had occasion for disbelieving in mine.

Always devotedly and loyally yours
Virgil

c/o French-American Bank
  65 Broadway. New York City

P.S. I undertook the B.B.C. thing without asking you, because they cabled hurriedly, & I couldnt imagine you would object to its being done. I had the checks made separately in order that your money should not pass through my bank account. I hope I have acted correctly.

*****

Paris April 21/34

My dear Bradley,

I am sorry that the opera is not going on, I was cheered by a newspaper clipping that Hubbel sent me that it was playing to sold out houses, but these things never mean anything. However there is one thing we must remember and that this is the ticklish moment for us. Now when they are making new arrangements they will once more try to get us reduced. Moses and Houseman may be alright but one has to remember that they were chosen by Virgil and they may be very easily playing his game. However our position is simple, wherever and whenever it is played we get our 3 percent, and we stand absolutely pat on that. Cerf turned up to-day. He seems very pleasant. We had considerable talk about the Plain Edition he seems not unlikely to be willing to dispose of the remainder of the edition that we have and if he does so successfully to go on he said when he got back to America he would go into the matter. He says that they have sold 2500 already of the Saints and that pleased him very much. Oh and does Austin get payed at all by Moses. If he does of course he should at once pay us what he owes us. Have you found out about this. It is very important. . . .

Alwys
Gtrde Stein.

---

if he does so successfully to go on: Cerf is inclined to publish a book by Stein every year. On 29 May, he will offer to publish *Three Lives* in a Modern Library edition. On 23 October, he will offer to publish *The Making of Americans* complete as a Modern Library Giant, but he will be too late, to Stein's great regret, since, one day earlier, Harcourt will have contracted to publish the abridged version. Stein will propose instead that he publish a collection of her portraits, which he publishes in November 1934 as *Portraits and Prayers*. On 26 July 1934, he will express his wish to publish all her works. In him, she will have found what she has always wanted, a New York publisher (Dydo 549–50).

*****

4 West 43rd Street
New York

26.4.34

Dear Mr. Thomson,

In accordance with my promise to you last night and as holder of Miss Stein's representation, I herewith authorize you to take out in your own name the copyright of her SUSIE ASADO, in its musical setting.

It is understood that she will receive one half of the joint royalties paid to you both by the Cos Cob Press (1% on the retail price of the book) but that she shall be accountable to you for one half of the expense incurred by you in securing said copyright, namely, the making of a copy of the words and music to send to the Library of Congress for that purpose, postage on same, and Government fee of $1.00 for registration. A check for the amount then due will be sent you immediately by me on receipt of the first royalty cheque from the Cos Cob Press.

Sincerely yours, W.A. Bradley

*****

April 28/34

My dear Bradley,

Mrs. Bradley is sending you a copy of Thomson's letter and also of the accounting for the broadcasting of Capital Capitals. Of course he had no business to do his own accounting but it opens the whole question. I am writing him a personal friendly note but referring him to you for all business xplanations. I think we should absolutely stand pat on a 50-50 basis. Proof correcting I am always willing to do, that need not be done for me, if he considers that a service and as for his trips of course that is not my affair, I do what I can for our mutual benefit in my way as he does what he can for our mutual benefit in his way and we each attend our affairs beside and that is all very simple. The fact that we received 8 guineas for part of a programme is interesting and makes it very necessary that we should come to a definite statement about all our performances in whatever country they take place. But I am certain that you are attending to this matter in xactly this way, and of course if Thomson cables he should be paid for his cables but he must let you do the subtracting.

It is very important that all this is clear and that he recognises it, because undoubtedly our future together is sufficiently important. But in this case undoubtedly for us eternal vigilance is the price of peace.

You have never said whether Austin has been eliminated or is still receiving his share in the proceeds. If he is he must either pay us immediately or be out of the contract, that seems only reasonable. It is a pity Moses could not have held out longer as the middle classes do seem to be coming round to it. Griggs has just telephoned me and said his people and friends are all going and say that for the last performances there were a great many people almost a block long standing in line. However I imagine it will begin again and perhaps with better organization. Griggs is using the Carl Van Vechten photographs of the singers in the Figaro Illustré, and in a Catholic weekly called St Sept. The Catholic weekly is very interested, so he says.

In this letter Thomson does not of course mention Grosser. I am asking Mrs. Bradley to send along to you a copy of Operas and Plays. As I told you Grosser had some very definite ideas how some of the plays in Geography and Plays could be played. It might be possible that something could be done about that, and in that way he of course would come into the affair. . . .

Alwys,
Gtrde Stein.

Griggs: Arthur Kingsland Griggs, editor, translator, author of the popular guidebook *Paris for Everyman* (1926).

*****

To "M. Virgil Thomson / ~~Hotel Leonori / Madison Avenue at 63 Street~~ / 166 east 61 St. / New York / N.Y. / U.S.A.

27 rue de Fleurus
[29 April 1934]

My dear Virgil

It was a glorious victory and very pleasant and very moving to all concerned. Undoubtedly we must graciously and gratefully accept that we do go very well together. All the business part of your letter I have answered to Bradley, and otherwise well really there is no otherwise. Carl sent beautiful photographs of the St Theresas and St Ignatius, they too were quite moving, and a great many personal decriptions beginning with Whittemore.

It has been a beautiful winter for us. And I hope we will enjoy many returns of the same
      Alwys
       Gtrde.

Whittemore, Thomas (1871–1950): Old friend of Stein from Cambridge-Boston days, charismatic art historian and archaeologist who studied with Matisse and taught at Columbia. He raised funds for Russian émigrés after World War I, and founded, and now directs, the Byzantine Institute of America in 1930.

*****

WILLIAM ASPENWALL BRADLEY
5, RUE SAINT-LOUIS-EN-L'ILE
PARIS 4

11.5.34

Dear Miss Stein,

'... I have waited for a long time for the enclosed letter from Moses, who told me he was going to take up with his lawyer the possibility of Grosser getting an injunction which might interfere with his projected road-tour of 26 perf[ormance]s in the autumn—I had a long talk with him in April about the situation created by your refusal to yield to Houseman's letter. He himself has had some difficult passages with Thomson, and he said he understood perfectly your point of view in the matter, and sympathized with it. He has lost $15,000 in the production, however, and is unwilling to risk the $25,000 extra which he is planning to put up for the tour if there are going to be any legal complexities. Apparently, however, his lawyer does not take very seriously Grosser's threat, which is really Thomson's, since the latter told me he was going to *urge* Grosser to get an injunction, even if he stood to lose by this measure! There is no doubt that T. hates you, and I couldn't help smiling when I read his letter to you, which my wife sees soon, with *fausse douceresse* and its insincere protestation of good faith and of loyalty. He *talked* in a very different vein, and it is no doubt he who has poisoned the minds of everybody against you—you will readily understand that, in the circumstances, it has been impossible to enter into relation with Grosser himself. Since Houseman did not respond to my last letter suggesting a further interview, you will also see in the foregoing that there have been *no* profits as yet from the production of *Four Saints*, with a deficit of $15,000. The arrangement between Moses & Austin is that, in the doubt of eventual profit, they will take 4% each, the remaining 20% to be distributed among the various producers: Miss Stettheimer, Houseman, F. Ashton etc—

As to the opera being played to "sold out" houses, you will have seen in their statements that this is not so. Of course, when Moses announced the end of the run, the box-office receipts rose sharply, as they did before at the 44th-St. Theater, and as always happens in such circumstances.

Further negotiations with Thomson are going to be difficult, as I believe he has already left for France, so you may have news of him over there before this reaches you. His letter to you was not written at my suggestion, and he knew perfectly well that I was acting for you, as your agent. I had already asked him about the prospect of the London Broadcast, so he knew I was expecting it. But he was glad, I think to take this little "dig" at me, if only because I had rather forced his hand over here. He is at once sly & malicious and actively untrustworthy. When I see you, I will tell you a number of things. Of course we take the attitude now that if you don't accept the division he offers you, he will not have the opera published at all. But I don't think this is any more serious than the threat of an injunction. Of course it was not possible to do anything about the other musical matter (your *Susie Asado*) because he wanted to hear you first on the matter of principle, and then make a general arrangement . . . W.A. Bradley

---

the possibility of Grosser getting an injunction: Stein refuses to pay Grosser from her percentage of royalties for writing the scenario for the opera. See Thomson 6 March [1934], Bradley 6 April 1934, Stein April 14/34.

road-tour of 26 performances: This will not occur.
his lawyer does not take very seriously Grosser's threat: In his letter to Bradley (of 7 May), however, Harry Moses does mention that his lawyer is looking into the matter further.
fausse douceresse: The word "douceresse" does not exist, but an Anglophone might confuse it with "doucereux" (honeyed), so Bradley means something like "false sweetness."

*****

Bilignin
par Belley
Ain
May 25/34

My dear Bradley,

  I was glad to get all your letters with all their mixed news. I am including a letter from Bureau Voorhies about the opera. He seems to be doing a vigorous propoganda judging from all the fan letters which are steadily increasing in number, whatever that may mean.

  But first about the Four in America in respect to Harcourt. Of course my feeling and I am not sure that even practically it is not the right course is that Harcourt should publish books of mine that are not what he calls open and public, if he does not it would eventually be bad business, spoil the market. He should recognize that my reputation is and was made by the kind of book that the Grant is and that a certain proportion of them should be printed by him before he does another of the kind he likes which will be the volume of essays or lectures which I am doing for the lecture series. Do try to make him see that what he calls open and public books are really illustrations for the other books, and that illustrations should be accompanied by what they illustrate. You see he was wrong about Four Saints. Cerf told me that he was sorry that he had not made it a dollar and a half book because it would have sold as well as that and it is apparently doing very well, and Harcourt was afraid of it. Now I cannot be sure but I am not altogether doubtful but what the Four in America would have the same xperience. One thing is entirely clear and about that I have always felt strongly, that Harcourt ought to be willing to risk some of my real kind of books if he wishes to go on with the volume of essays and later the Confessions. The body of my real work should be edited by the same man who does these other books, you know I even suggested that this should be incorporated in the contract but you wisely said no and Harcourt justified that by printing the Making of Americans. He says in his letter that that book has only done a quarter as well as the Autobiography, but that of course to me is very well indeed and in the long run it will win out. Look at Three Lives. No I do think that if Harcourt wants to do and does as beautifully and sympathetically the what he calls open books, he should do the others in between and I am sure for the durability of the sale of my works it is the right thing to do. . . .

About the Thomson I think you have done admirably and indeed he is as he always was. As Sidney Smith says, The most delicate and sensitive turpitude is always to be met with in Scotland and he is a beautiful xample, there is no doubt about that. Of course his vanity is terribly hurt as is natural because he feels that way, but the only thing to do is what you have done, just go on and hold out and always keep a watchful eye, because after all he is in the wrong. I really don't think of what I know of Grosser that he has anything much to do with it. I have heard nothing of his return to Paris.

Mrs Bradley will have sent you the scheme of lectures. I have begun work on them, and I want them to be very simple and very direct. I have about finished the one about pictures. And I will slowly go on with them until all six are done. I do hope you will like them. I keep quite definitely not thinking about anything concerning it xcept the writing of the lectures so that I will not get nervous. Of course some one will have to act for me over there but that you will find satisfactorily I am sure. . . . Best wishes and so many thanks,

Gtrde Stein.

Voorhies: Rousseau Voorhies, a southerner working for the Chicago office of Macmillan Company introduced to Stein by Faÿ. Voorhies acted as advance man publicizing her in Chicago in order to increase the audience for her lectures there. He wrote, lectured, and, without her permission, published a letter from her to him in the *Chicago Daily News* (14 March). This and his aggressive publicity nearly caused her to cancel the Chicago lectures (Dydo 604–605).
Four in America in respect to Harcourt: Alfred Harcourt, fifty-three-year-old co-founder of Harcourt, Brace & Company, has refused to publish *Four in America*.
the Grant: i.e. *Four in America*, which features Ulysses S. Grant, Wilbur Wright, Henry James, and George Washington.
the Confessions: Conceived as a follow-up to the successful *Autobiography*, this book project would be abandoned, material from it appearing in a brief work entitled "And Now" (*How Writing Is Written*, pp. 63-66) (Dydo 572-73).
Sidney Smith (1771–1845): English clergyman, cofounding editor of the *Edinburgh Review*, who became a canon of St Paul's Cathedral in 1831. He told Francis Jeffrey that "the most delicate and sensitive turpitude is always to be met with in Scotland" ("A Memoir of the Reverend Sidney Smith by his Daughter Lady Holand," *Dublin Review* [Sept. 1855], 252). A famous wit, Smith was a writer, a popular preacher and lecturer, an abolitionist, a promoter of education for women, Catholic emancipation, and parliamentary reform. Queen Victoria collected his works. His enduring fame in the United States rested on his rhyming recipe for salad dressing.
he is a beautiful xample: While many of Thomson's ancestors who arrived in North America in the seventeenth century were Welsh, the rest, who came a century later, were Scottish (including the Thomsons) and Scotch-Irish (*Virgil Thomson* 5).
the scheme of lectures:
    1. The gradual making of Making of Americans and its gradual change into something else.
        The American W[omen's] Club lecture with the development into the Long Gay Book.
    2. The conception of personality and its expression in portraits, poetry, and Tender Buttons.
    3. The question of tenses grammar, and its relation to telling a story. The later period.
    4. Pictures that is paintings and what they mean to me.
    5. The History of English literature as I understand it.
    6. Plays and what they are.
All illustrated by readings. (Stein to Mrs. Bradley, n.d.)

*****

Columbia University Club
4 West 49th Street
New York

7.6.34

Dear Miss Stein,

I have your long letter of 26 [sic] May, which rather fills me with dismay, since the views expressed therein are so utterly at variance with my own. . . .

You are wrong if you think that Harcourt for a moment regrets that he did not do *Four Saints*. He rejoices, for your sake, that it had a good sale but feels, as before, it was not a book [for] this list. As for my attempting to persuade him that he did wrong in declining *Four in America* and that he does not know his own business, I should merely make myself ridiculous if I took that line and destroy my standing. Moreover, he *did* publish *one* of your more usual books, and the results were such as to dissuade him. . . . For not only did the *Making of Americans* not sell itself, but it actually retarded the sale of the *Autobiography*. Thus you can see what would happen if he undertook to publish, as you suggest, a series of books of the same character . . .

You say that *Three Lives* and *Four Saints* have sold well, but remember that they were published in the wake of the *Autobiography*, that they were *short* books, that the former was already a classic and that the latter was stimulated by the *succès d'estime* of the opera. As for *Geography & Plays*—well, I won't say any more on that score!

I repeat, you came to me in the first place because you wanted to make money, and you *have* made money. If you are not interested in making money any longer, you ought to tell me so. You have been good enough to say, in the past, that I have acted "wisely", even admirably in the conduct of your affairs. It would seem, therefore, that I should by this time [have] acquired a certain increased credit in the present. I am sorry to note that the reverse seems rather to be true, and that you are more and more inclined to argue with me on the question of "practicality." Now, this is *my* domain, just as it is your domain to write books, and if you do not recognize it as such . . . my usefulness to you, as I see it, is finished. That is for you to decide. But, just now you have also got to decide whether you will accept the specific arrangements I have tentatively made for you and my general campaigns for the publishing of your books in this country. Otherwise we will get nothing done at all, and you will not have profited from my long sojourn in this country, where I have worked almost exclusively for you.

As my time is getting short, please cable.

Regards to you both.

Sincerely, W.A. Bradley

P.S. Leigh is now going ahead hard on your lecture arrangements. As Mrs. Bradley will have told, I was obliged to go ahead on my own responsibility if we were to get ahead at all, so made the best arrangement possible with the best man in this country. . . . I did not see Thomson again, though I talked with him just before he sailed a fortnight ago on the "Ile de France". I told him what you had said in your last letter and asked him what he, or Grosser, was going to do about the injunction. He was a little embarrassed and said they had decided it was not necessary since he was informing Maurice that if you would not yield, he would have nothing further to do with the production. W.A.B.

Leigh . . . your lecture arrangements: Stein's American lecture tour was originally the idea of William Rogers, an editor for *The Union* of Springfield, Massachusetts (Stein to Bradley, 14 May 1934). In January 1933, Bradley inquired about arranging a speaking tour for Stein with the W. Colston Leigh Bureau of Lectures and Entertainment in New York, but Leigh replied that Stein was insufficiently well known to justify a speaking tour. Then the *Autobiography* was published, and Leigh became interested. Bradley and Leigh negotiated through most of 1933, until Stein declined to "bind" herself "to anything in the future" or put herself "in other people's hands" (to Bradley 13 Oct 1933). With the Broadway success of *Four Saints*, her fame increased, and Harcourt suggested a lecture tour. She begins to rely on Bernard Faÿ for advice about such a tour. He proposes his friend Marvin Ross, a young historian, to organize her lectures and warns her of engaging a lecture bureau. Faÿ gets his friend Voorhies involved (see Stein, May 25/34). Bradley has engaged Leigh to organize the lectures. On his own, Leigh approaches Alfred Barr of the Museum of Modern Art and Bobsie (Mrs. Charles) Goodspeed, with whom Faÿ has already put Stein in contact about her lecture tour, indicating that he (Leigh) is arranging Stein's tour. Stein hears and furiously protests to Bradley, who ceases contact with Leigh. Marvin Ross will organize Stein's tour, which will bring her to Chicago, where she will see and hear *Four Saints*. (See Dydo 595–616).

*****

WILLIAM ASPENWALL BRADLEY
5, RUE SAINT-LOUIS-EN-L'ILE
PARIS 4

19 July 1934

My dear Miss Stein,

My secretary has, I believe, answered all the questions contained in your letter of the 13th to Mrs. Bradley, excepting that about arrangements made by me concerning the performances of the opera and the publication of musical scores.

With regard to the former, as I think I have written you already, Harry Moses, undeterred by Thomson's threats of an injunction, is preparing a road tour this autumn, which will begin in Boston, in October, and which he hopes to continue west, through to the Coast—this in spite of the fact that, when I last saw him, just before leaving New York, he had received a letter from the Austin-Houseman group saying they *thought* they had found someone else to finance future performances.

Thomson also told me, on the eve of his sailing for France, that he had dropped the matter of the injunction for the present but was notifying Moses that he would have nothing further to do with the production, which he believed would have the same effect. Moses some time after informed me that he had never received any such notification and that, so far as he was concerned, Thomson's absence would not embarrass him in any way—quite the contrary!

With regard to the publication of musical scores, etc., nothing has been, or can be, done while both you and Thomson maintain your present attitudes, since he has declared his unwillingness to take any further steps in the matter until you yield on both points, namely the percentage to Grosser for the use of his scenario and the division of profits between you both. The one trifling exception he was willing to make was for the publication of SUSIE ASADO, so I wrote him a letter of authorization covering this (April 26), of which I send you herewith a copy.

I am,
Very faithfully yours,
W.A. Bradley

Miss Gertrude STEIN
Bilignin par Belley
(Ain).

*****

In late July 1934, Bradley ceases acting as Stein's agent. The decline of their relationship is not fully recorded above, since we reproduce only correspondence related to the Stein-Thomson ventures. Letters from Stein to Mrs. Bradley written in May, while Bradley is in New York, exhibit early sparks of the trouble to come. In these letters Stein grows increasingly frustrated at not hearing from Bradley regarding various projects, *The Birthday Book* in particular. Bradley expresses his own growing exasperation in a note, on Stein's letter of 2 June, which includes her detailed responses to Richard Jones' proposed drawings for *The Birthday Book*; Bradley writes, presumably to his wife, "You see busying herself with carved cherrystones, while I am occupied with the big things for her!"

In his letter of 19 July (above), along with a note sent by his secretary on 16 July, Bradley responds in a business-like manner to an accusatory letter from Stein dated 13 July. There her principal complaint is that Bradley did not cancel arrangements made with Colston Leigh regarding her lecture tour. She declares that "serious injury [is] done my affairs by this flagrant violation of my direct and positive cabled orders," and demands the return of the power of attorney she granted him when he left for New York. Toklas's editorial hand is clear in the drafts of both this letter and one dated the 19th, which is more vitriolic. Stein's complaint about

Leigh stands, and again she accuses Bradley of acting "in direct opposition to my verbal and written instructions" and of acting in ways "harmful to my interests" and which "seriously injured my prestige." The latter charge arises from her contention that Bradley has failed to adhere to her wishes that a chosen publisher should accept both her popular and her more difficult manuscripts; Stein believes that the more accessible books "illustrate" the challenging works (see May 25/34) and that publishing only the accessible books would amount to offering "Hamlet with Hamlet left out" (Stein to Mrs. Bradley 26 May 1934). She concludes her letter by stating that she will be informing a list of publishers that Bradley no longer serves as her agent. Advising and supporting Stein all this time is Bernard Faÿ, who tells her that Bradley has been serving her badly. Faÿ is urging her not to entrust herself with a professional organizer of lecture tours but to let him arrange her tour through a friend or friends.

In a second letter of 19 July, Bradley responds without reserve, writing "In answer to your abusive letters recently addressed both to my wife and to myself." He says that (1) Stein never objected to Colston Leigh being asked to arrange her lecture tour in America, and that now he sees that she "had been merely using me as a pioneer to clear the way for some vague project" of her own; (2) that Stein never insisted, as she claims, that Harcourt can only publish her lectures and *Confessions* if he also published *Four in America*. Bradley concludes:

> I shall not dwell upon your statement that, in your opinion, I have done your publishing programme "incalculable harm." As a matter of fact, you have never had such a programme—except that which I have sought to establish for you—only the publication of individual books here and there, according to circumstances.... Your friends will agree with me, I am sure, that no necessary relation exists between the two categories of your work and that to seek to create a purely artificial one for your publisher would be fantastic, if not fatal. It would be hardly worth while to point out and to correct the numerous misstatements with which your letters abound. I will mention one only. It is your statement to my wife that I have never sold a book of "the other kind," i.e., not "open and public." You forget it was I who, for better or for worse, placed with Harcourt THE MAKING OF AMERICANS. That was not one of the days when I was "influenced" by Harcourt—rather the reverse!

Writing the following day, Mrs. Bradley lists some further facts to disprove Stein's various grievances, and betrays serious frustration with Stein. In response to Stein's comment about injury to her prestige, she writes: "The only injury to your prestige is that done by yourself in writing the letters which you send somewhat imprudently in order to quiet your nerves. They have, as a matter of fact, definitely destroyed it for me, but may in time prove priceless documents for your biographer." She notes that all papers belonging to Stein will be returned, that if she proceeds as promised in her last paragraph, "we will at once take legal action against you," that "if my husband, when writing to you yesterday, did not already tender you his resignation, so thoroughly justified by your evident bad faith, it was to leave you the entire responsibility for a situation which you, and you alone, have created."

After this heated exchange there exist a few short notes exchanged between Toklas and Bradley concerning the return of all paperwork related to Stein. On 27 July, Bradley states that he is sending said material and that they should refer to his lawyer if they are not satisfied. The last note from Bradley is sent in response to a demand from Toklas that he send her cable texts, presumably so that she can confirm fair charges have been claimed against the Stein account. Bradley admits that "In looking over these attentively, I note the use of a word, in two places, which it was not my intention to make you pay for. Therefore I send you stamps for frs. 4.65, in reimbursement of same." He encloses the cable texts and twice underlines the word in question. The word is "LOVE."

Although Bradley reported "There is no doubt that T. hates you" (11.5.34) and the friendship between Stein and Thomson never recovers its former intimacy and warmth, it does survive. Thomson remains loyal to her and not just for the sake of his future career prospects. Proof of this will occur in 1936, when James Joyce approaches him with the suggestion that he make a ballet of chapter nine of *Finnegans Wake*, which incorporates children's rhymes and games. Thomson would remember:

> Joyce offered assured production at the Paris opera under the direction of Leonide Massine. Massine was riding high at the Paris opera and putting on ballets, and he sort of proposed this to Joyce, I think. News of the Gertrude Stein success in America had reached everywhere. And he knew me. We were on the best of terms, and he thought I might be interested to do a dramatic work. I knew that that would have been a wounding blow to Gertrude, and Gertrude was my good friend. I didn't see why I should do that to her. When Adrienne Monnier published the French translation of *Ulysses,* she asked Picasso to make some illustrations. He often made illustrations for books. He turned her down. He wasn't going to do that to his old friend Gertrude either. You don't move around that way. It didn't matter that I was friends with Joyce, but to have done a public thing, to have moved over from her to what you might call the enemy, at least the store across the street, I thought would have been ungraceful. So I took the chapter home to read and I wrote him afterwards, "This is not a scenario for a ballet; it is a chapter in a book that is a piece of literature. If I simply take the subject of children's games in Dublin and use it for a ballet, I'm not using any of the Joyce in it, because the Joyce is in the words." I didn't mention, of course, that I could have made a musical setting of a sort of cantata nature, involving chorus, soloists, and words. Actually, I never liked singing with dance. Instrumental music loves dance, and dance loves it. But the old song-and-dance, while it is a routine in Vaudeville, has never worked terribly well in the serious

ballet business. Anyway, I felt justified in refusing it on legitimate grounds (to Dilworth, 3 Feb. 1981).

*****

New York
2 October [1934]

Dear Gertrude

A young Jewish boy named Sawyer asked me to his house to see the version he does of Four Saints & I went & it is entirely pleasing & quite original & when I told him so he said would I write you that & I said yes with pleasure & so I am only I am not going to tell you what it is like because you should make him do it for you and that way it will be all surprise and very pleasant I assure you.

Pleasant remembrances & good wishes.
Virgil

French-Amer Bank
65 Broadway.
N.Y.C.

*****

Telegram to "Stein 27 Rue de Fleurus Paris"   [9 Oct. 1934]

OPERA CHEERED VERY HAPPY

VIRGIL

OPERA CHEERED: Presumably, Thomson has just learned that Stein and Toklas will sail on the S.S. *Champlain* on 17 Oct. and will attend the Chicago premiere of a five-performance run on 7 November in the Auditorium Theater.

*****

HOTEL LEONORI
MADISON AVENUE AT 63rd STREET
NEW YORK

31 October [1934]

Dear Gertrude

Alexander Smallens who conducted our opera last year (and like all our collaborators, quite gratuitously out of admiration for the work) asks me to please if possible induce you to give him a signed photograph of yourself, he presumably passing on to me the buck of asking you because he didnt care to risk being refused directly. So in case you care to honor him, you may as well communicate directly with him at 45 Prospect Place New York City.

A slighter favor I should like for myself, if you care to do it, is your autograph for the *Four Saints* program belonging to Miss Nora Shea, who is Secretary to Arthur Judson of the Columbia Broadcasting & Concerts Corporation and who has been of very considerable service to Mr. Smallens and me about the musical side of the opera. If you would be so good as to sign her program, simply mention it to me in Chicago and I will see that it is deposited at your hotel & called for.

Always devotedly yours
Virgil

Again my compliments on the beautiful lecture. I am very happy that everything about your visit is going so handsomely. Last night's audience will not soon forget what they heard.

---

the beautiful lecture: The first lecture on Stein's American tour, "Plays," delivered the previous evening at the home of Mrs. John W. Alexander, 170 East 78th Street. Although Thomson visited Paris the previous May, his meeting with Stein last night is their first since the break in their friendship three years and ten months ago.

*****

To "M. Virgil Thomson / Hotel Leonori / Madison Avenue and 63 Street / New York."

Algonquin Hotel
1 Nov. 1934

My dear Virgil,

It was nice seeing you the other evening and I am glad you liked it, and we are very very xcited about Chicago next Thursday, of course tell Mr. Smallens that I will send him a photo autographed as soon as I can get hold of one, you know very well I never refuse anybody and certainly not Mr Smallens who did so beautifully for us, so please tell him that as soon as I have a photograph I will send it to him with so much pleasure and that I will be having some very soon. And of course about the four Saints program for Miss Nora Shea.

Thursday then and the best of luck to us all now and
  Alwys
    Gtrde.

Chicago next Thursday: Stein and Toklas are flying to Chicago for the first of five performances of *Four Saints* being financed by Grace Denton and conducted by Thomson (Smallens being unavailable) in Chicago's Sullivan Auditorium.

*****

HOTEL LEONORI
MADISON AVENUE AT 63rd STREET
NEW YORK

28 January [1935]

Dear Alice

Please remind Gertrude of the signed photo she promised to send Alexander Smallens. He lives at 45 Prospect Place, New York City. Felicitations on continued and colossal successes

Toujours à vous
Virgil

*****

HOTEL LEONORI
MADISON AVENUE AT 63rd STREET
NEW YORK

25 February [1935]

Dear Gertrude

The boys of the Berkshire School have been so desirous of obtaining Pigeons on the Grass for the use of one of their own numbers that they have taken up a collection among themselves and raised about $60, which will underwrite the publication of the piece. J. Fischer & Brother[s] of New York, an excellent firm of music publishers, have agreed to do the publishing and to put the piece in their catalogue. They are thus enabled to experiment with the sale of the opera material and find out whether eventual publication of the whole is a good risk for them, all of which is to our advantage and to theirs. Hence the following arrangement has been made, subject to your approval, and a contract will be sent you as soon as I hear from you whether it is acceptable or what corrections you wish to add to it.

1.) The copyright remains our possession.

2.) We receive 10% royalties on sales; that is, 5% each, or 2 1/2 cents each, as the piece will sell retail for 50 cents.

3.) The Berkshire School Musicale Association will receive 100 copies in special covers which they are free to sell privately at any price they like. The publisher pays no royalties on these copies. We can ask the Association for royalties on sales if you insist. I have not mentioned the matter. I have in addition offered to autograph ten copies and I hope you will be willing to do the same. The boys are not interested in making money, but I thought it preferable, in view of their trouble and generosity, to make possible the retrieving of their investment at least. In this way, they are pleased with their venture, the publisher with having his edition underwritten, and we with having our work made available to the public on

Letters with Notes

good publishing terms. Please let me know as soon as possible your wishes about the matter, so that the engraving can be started, providing everything is all right.

Congratulations on your continued and complete successes.

Affectionate & devoted greetings
                              Virgil
When you come to N.Y. again, I should like to visit Mr Fischer with you & make an arrangement whereby his firm becomes the depository of score & parts for future hirings & distributions of same.

---

the Berkshire School: Sheffield, Massachusetts. One hundred copies of *Pigeons on the Grass Alas* will be published 8 May 1935 by J. Fischer & Bros. for the Berkshire School Musicale Association. There will be a signed edition of ten copies.

*****

To "M. Virgil Thomson / Hotel Leonori / Madison Avenue 63 street / New York / N.Y."

THE
MIDWAY DREXEL
APARTMENT HOTEL
6020 DREXEL AVENUE
CHICAGO

[27 Feb. 1935]

My dear Virgil,

That sounds alright, send me the contract here care of Thornton Wilder, I will be here for some time that is to say two weeks. and I will sign the Berkshire Boys copies of course. I am glad everything is going nicely with you, we are enjoying every minute of it all and hope this finds you the same
                         Alwys
                    Gtrde.

Thornton Wilder: Thirty-seven-year-old graduate of Yale (BA) and Princeton (MA), author of Pulitzer Prize-winning *The Bridge over San Luis Rey* (1927), and part-time lecturer in comparative literature at the University of Chicago. He began corresponding with Stein in 1934. See *The Letters of Gertrude Stein and Thornton Wilder*, ed. Edward Burns, Ulla Dydo, and William Rice (New Haven: Yale, 1996).

*****

166 E. 61
New York
9 April [1935]

Dear Gertrude

I am sending you contracts with Fischer for *Pigeons*. Yours for signing, if satisfactory, mine for inspection.

Concert performance & radio broadcast are permitted by Moses. Concerts pay no royalties. Radio pays a yearly lump to members of Amer. Assoc. of Comp. & Publishers. I am not a member; Fischer is. There is no way of calculating what he may get for this being sung; hence Moses & I were disposed, not being able to collect ourselves, to let Fischer have whatever there might be, considering radio performance just like concert performance as an advertisement for the opera and for the sale of printed copies. Whenever I shall have six pieces of music published, I shall join the A.S.C.A.P. myself & have the copyright returned to my name.

The American Arbitration Association, a quite interesting and very important organization for settling out of court industrial & commercial disputes, has asked me [to] provide appropriate music at the end of your lecture on April 29th. I am honored and will be only too delighted and we will probably have the two nice saints also.

It will be lovely seeing you again before you leave and give my love to Alice

always affectionately
and devotedly
Virgil

The Pigeons should be out by the end of the month. I will sign the bon à tirer whenever you return the contracts.

Fischer: Of J. Fischer and Brothers. See Thomson 25 February [1935].
bon à tirer: final corrected proofs. He will give final authorization to print.

*****

HOTEL MARK HOPKINS
NOB HILL
SAN FRANCISCO

[*April 1935*]

My dear Virgil,

The contracts are alright xcept the clause IX of the return copyright, and the ownership of the copyright. That clause should be put into my contract with both our names and my name should be put into your clause IX as common owner of the copyright and perhaps by that time, that is by the time you have six pieces printed I too will join up and we will proceed together in any case the clause IX must be in my contract too, it is better so, I am sending it back to you by air mail, attend to it at once send it back to me by air mail we are here until the 19 so that you can easily get it back in time, it will be nice seeing you in New York we will talk things over, we have been having a wonderful time. I have met Florine Stettheimer out here several times and like her a lot,

Lots of love
Gtrde.

*****

166 E. 61
New York
12 April [1935]

Dear Gertrude

As long as the musical copyright of Four Saints is in my name, it would seem irregular to make a contract with a third party as if it were in both names. Consequently, Clause IX, as corrected by you, has been eliminated from my contract. There will be no transfer of copyright to Fischer; the copyright in my name will appear on the song, as it does on the manuscript score of the entire work, and the formula for revoking publication-rights to this piece becomes a mere notification on my part whenever there may be a proper offer of publication for the whole score, even from another publisher.

Any action I might take in this matter is of course covered in the contract between you and me, which requires concerted action in all matters regarding our mutual interest. This is an arrangement between us and does not interest Mr. Fischer.

If you desire a change in the copyright registration, we can arrange that between ourselves when you come to N.Y., although your own literary copyright is, I gather, completely taken care of by Random House, and your equity in my copyright of the musical work is taken care of by the contract between us which Mr. Bradley wrote.

I enclose again your contracts and mine as corrected. If anything about them is still unsatisfactory, fire them right back at me and they will be changed.

Always devotedly yours
Virgil

*****

To "Mr. Virgil Thomson / 166 East 61 Street / New York."

HOTEL ALGONQUIN
59 TO 65 WEST FORTY-FOURTH STREET
NEW YORK
FRANK CASE

[22 April 1935]

My dear Virgil,

We are back and will you come to-morrow morning at eleven and bring with you a copy of the printed Susie Asado, I want to see how that was done, will you telephone here if you cannot come, and we will arrange some other time,

                             Alwys
                                Gtrde.

*****

To M. Virgil Thomson / ~~French American Bank / 65 Broadway~~ / 2 Beckman Place / New York / N.Y. / U.S.A"

[23 April 1936]

My dear Virgil

There is a possibility quite a real possibility that they will do Four Saints in Paris in June, this year. there is a great deal of enthusiasm a fair amount of hope a very very slight amount of certainty, at any rate there is enough so that you might find it worth while to get in touch with all the singers and the décor so that if they do cable you to come over with it no time will be lost. They want the production in English just like it was in New York. Of course and that is of course you never can tell, it can be nothing and it can be it. We leave for Bilignin next week, but if it comes off we will be back for it, If it is to be at all it is to be in Paris this June. Carl writes that you have done the Voodoo music for Macbeth I hope it comes off well, best to you

                                Gtrde.

Voodoo music for Macbeth: Now co-director of The Negro Theatre Project, Houseman produces an all-black version of *Macbeth* in Harlem, directed by twenty-year-old Orson Wells with music and sound effects arranged by Thomson. The witches are voodoo priestesses, backed by the music of an African drum troupe led by Asadata Dafora Horton (later minister of culture for the Republic of Sierra Leone). Thomson will say of Welles, "Oh Orson knew everything" (to Dilworth, 3 Feb. 1981).

*****

To "M. Virgil Thomson / ~~French American Bank / 65 Broadway~~ / 2 Beckman Place / New York / N.Y. / U.S.A."

                                Bilignin
                                par Belley, Ain
                                [23 May 1936]

My dear Virgil

The idea was to do the 4 Saints in the Theatre Champs Elysee but unfortunately they got the idea too late and there just really is not time for this spring, but the idea is not dead and they are going to try to fix it up for next spring, and perhaps it will come off and if it does it will be nice, I am glad you are having a successful winter, I am very interested in the Macbeth music, remember me to all the saints and I do hope it will come off yet,   Love

Gtrde.

*****

To "M. Virgil Thomson / Palace Hotel / 131 bis Bould. St. Germain / 11 rue du Four. / Paris."

[14 Dec. 1936]

My dear Virgil

Thanks, we will be pleased, I am asking the Countess d'Aiguy and her brother and father the M. Merinos to come too as they are acting as intermediaries with the possible producers

Alwys
Gtrde.

Countess ... producers: La Comtesse Diane d'Aiguy and her family were involved in plans to stage *Four Saints* in Paris. The production never materialized.

*****

To "M. Virgil Thomson / ~~French American Bank / 65 Broadway~~ / New York / N.Y. / U.S.A Chelsea Hotel / 222 West 23rd Street / New York City"

BILIGNIN
PAR BELLEY
AIN

[24 June 1937]

My dear Virgil.

They write me from San Francisco that there is a possibility of them doing the 4 Saints there, what is that, the ballet went off very very well and I met Cochran and he was interested he said that he had thought about doing 4 Saints at the time that it was done in America and he did Porgy the play instead which did not succeed, I saw him several times and he kept coming back to it, if he said it would be a success, he said he was surprised at the popularity of this ballet and did I think the 4 Saints would be as popular, well anyway if you want to begin with him I think you were in communication at that time there is a chance, we had a good time in England it was rather fun being at a premiere of one of my things and it is pleasant doing that in London, I hope everything is alright with you alwys

            Gtrde.

Daniel Webster is done.

Chelsea Hotel: This will be Thomson's New York address for the rest of his life.
the ballet: Stein attended the premiere of her *A Wedding Bouquet* 27 April 1937 in London. Gerald Tyrwhitt-Wilson (Lord Berners) composed the music and Frederick Ashton choreographed.
Cochran: Charles B. Cochran, "the British Ziegfield," producer and promoter of musical comedies, including those by Noel Coward and Cole Porter. In the winter and spring of 1932, Thomson wrote to him to interest him in producing *Four Saints* in London. Cochran replied (25 Feb. and 22 March) saying he was too busy to meet him. In an undated letter draft, Thomson writes to him, "It is hardly advisable to submit you the bare script of *Four Saints in Three Acts* as Gertrude Stein wrote it for me, as you know her style being highly obscure and in need of some interpretation. One of the particular excellences of my score is the ingenuity with which I have interpreted the text and made it clear."
Daniel Webster: Stein's *Daniel Webster. Eighteen in America: A Play*, which anachronistically brings together both historical figures and acquaintances of Stein's.

*****

            French-American Bank
            65 Broadway
            1 Feb. [*1938*]

Dear Gertrude

  A negro troupe belonging to the Federal Theater wants to produce Four Saints in Philadelphia for two weeks, starting rehearsal as quickly as possible. Since the admission charges are low, the authors' fees are low too, but we are offered the maximum figure, which is $150.00 a week ($75 each). This is all right by Dramatists' Guild. I consulted various persons, including Carl V.V., as to the advisability of allowing it to be done, and the advice is to go ahead. I also am in favour of allowing it.

  Since, however, your consent must be delayed by the mails, I have told the Federal Theater to go ahead with their plans, under all reserves of course regarding your wishes. No contract will be signed until I know them. Please inform me immediately. If you care to cable,

  Virgil Thomson Frenambank New York
  yes Stein

will be enough to assure permission and keep everybody happy till the mails get here.

  As to the contract itself, the Federal Theater doesnt seem to be quite equal to the novelty of signing a contract with two persons, and since I should prefer not to do the signing & handling of money, I have prevailed upon Bennett Cerf to act as both your and my agent. He was willing enough to act as yours but not too eager to act as mine, since it means nothing to him except as service to you. So if you are willing to let the opera be done, please write him authorizing him to sign the contract for you and handle the fees and requesting him to be so kind as to render a similar service to me (since that seems to be the only solution that doesnt present elaborate red-tape difficulties). He doesnt really mind doing it.

I've no idea what sort of show is planned, but it must be mostly a new one, since none of the old directors is available. It is the idea of new & different production that mostly tempts me about the whole idea. Because sooner or later that must be done. Otherwise the work is frozen. Like Satie's *Mercure*, which had such a fancy production by Massine and Picasso in 1923 that nobody has dared try it since. I didnt see Cochran, as you suggested last summer, but I sicked Henry Moses on him (Cochran being in N.Y.). I never knew the result & then Harry died and anyway my conviction is that the work is known and anybody that wants to do it will ask for it and that selling-talks from me would more likely interfere than help.

I am very busy just now with a ballet. I did another movie too (*The River*, all about the Mississippi) and some plays and I shall be in Paris before very long. I read your
Autobiography with pleasure.
I enclose my devoted affection

          Virgil

---

your Autobiography: Gertrude Stein, *Everybody's Autobiography* (New York: Random House, 1937); (London and Toronto: Heinemann, 1938)

*****

To "M. Virgil Thomson / 222 West 23 Street / New York / N.Y. / U.S.A."

<del>27 RUE DE FLEURUS</del>
5 rue Christine

[11 Feb. 1938]

My dear Virgil,

 I cabled Yes and with great pleasure, yes the great thing is to get it done to get it sung after all the opera is the thing and neither you nor I have ever had any passion to be rare, we want to be as popular as Gilbert and Sullivan if we can, and perhaps we can, we are almost dead with fatigue but we are completely happy in our new home, it is a delight full of sun and lovely wood-work, and charm, and we cannot understand how we ever stayed where we did, and I saw Maurice the other day, after we are really settled in we will see him again, he was as sweet as ever, a little thinner a little older but just as sweet and I always did think he was sweet, did Jay Laughlin send you the new Directions with Daniel Webster in it. if not I will give it to you when you come over, and I am writing to Bennett Cerf at once alwys

          Gtrde.

---

5 rue Christine: Stein relates the circumstances of the move to Carl Van Vechten:

254 *Letters with Notes*

We are leaving rue de Fleurus for rue Christine, we are so xcited we can't see, the landlord said he wanted to put his son in and at one o'clock he told us and at 3 we had found a lovely apartment seventeenth century panelling, in the rue Christine ancient home of the Queen Christine daughter of Gustavus Adolphus, and it costs the same as this and it has a terrace roof in front of it, oh well we will be in it the 15 January, and its address is 5 rue Christine, and we are so xcited. (25 November 1937, *The Letters of Gertrude Stein and Carl Van Vechten*, 578)

Jay Laughlin: James Laughlin (signs letters to Stein "Jay"), writer, editor, publisher. Published *Daniel Webster. Eighteen in America: A Play* in his *New Directions Prose and Poetry* anthology series in 1937.

*****

To "M. Virgil Thomson / ~~French American Bank / 65 Broadway / New York / N.Y. / U.S.A. C/o Hottinger & Cie / 38 Rue de Berne / Paris / France~~ Hotel de Tours / 15 Rue Jacob / Paris (6ième)"

GERTRUDE STEIN
~~27 RUE DE FLEURUS~~
~~PARIS~~
5 rue Christine,

Bilignin
par Belley
Ain.

[1 June 1938]

My dear Virgil,

It is always just on the eve of departure that they spring propositions on you, we are leaving to-morrow morning and to-day somebody acting for Mrs. Dolores Harding, 19 Park Place Villas London W. 2, who is a producer, and wants to produce Four Saints called me up, she is a Mrs. Harry Kaufman, and they have already written to Smallens about it, but he said he could not and so they came to me, they think of using Robeson for St. Ignatius and finding somebody in London to do St. Therese so as to avoid trades union troubles, so you see they are serious, they want to know about scenery I said it would not be difficult nor costly to do it in London newly and it would probably interest Miss Stettheimer to do it, I could not give them Miss Stettheimer's address so I referred them to you and Carl, their idea is to do it this fall, it sounded more like something than any proposition yet, and so I am writing to you about it, to do whatever you want to do about it, it would be nice if they did it, it has been a very lively winter, what with moving and a great deal happening it has been pleasant and xciting, and now for a little calm we are off to Bilignin

lots of love
Gtrde.

Hotel de Tours: Thomson is returning to Paris and will stay in France through the early, Phony-War period of World War II.

Robeson: Paul, famous black actor, political activist, *basso profundo* concert singer.

*****

To "M. Virgil Thomson / ~~French American Bank / 65 Broadway / New York / N.Y. / U.S.A. C/o Hottinger & Cie / 38 Rue de Berne / Paris / France~~ Hotel de Tours / 15 Rue Jacob / Paris (6ième)"

BILIGNIN
PAR BELLEY
AIN

[4 June 1938]

My dear Virgil

They seem xcited enough to ask what royalties we wanted so they could figure on the matter, I told them that you could tell them what percent we had in New York which would probably be what we wanted in London but that I did not know xactly, so will you let them know, we are pleased to be here just got here a few hours ago after a hectic winter in Paris ending up with Francis Rose,

Alwys

Gtrde.

*****

38 rue de Provence
Paris IX
25 June [1938]

D.G.

I sent you a check from N.Y. on June 7th. Did you get it? I've had two letters from you here. I've seen Mrs Kaufman. She seems a trifle vague. I enclose a letter from her. Can you send her a copy of Four Saints? I havent one available. I am leaving here next week for Evian but please write me always to the above which is a bank address. I shall be in France (and environs) all winter.

Cordially and always
Virgil

*****

To "M. Virgil Thomson / 38 rue de Provence / Paris"

[27 June 1938]

My dear Virgil.

No the cheque didn't come and I would like to have it, will you send me a duplicate and notify your bank that I never had it, that is the first one I am asking Maratier to take a copy of Four Saints to Mrs. Harry Kaufman, he has one, I have not met either of the two who are interested but if they did do it it would be nice we might make some money and have a good time both pleasant things, if they really do want to do something since you are to be here all winter it will be very pleasant, I have just finished my Faustus, it makes a very honest opera, well its hot

Gtrde.

my Faustus: Her libretto *Doctor Faustus Lights the Lights*. Lord Berners was involved in its development and began composing the music. But he will abandon the project after a personal breakdown brought on by the war, and will suggest passing the work on to Thomson, who will also decide against it. American composer Richard Banks will compose incidental music for its 1951 performance in New York.

*****

Nantua - 8 july [1938]

Dear Gertrude

I am writing to my bank to refuse the first check. Here is another. The sum paid was $25 and I included the C.B.S. voucher in my other letter to you, so now it is lost I suppose you will take my word for the sum. As a matter of fact you are getting more than you really should, as I made a special arrangement of the orchestra for the boadcast and should have charged a fee (say $5.00) against the total sum for hire of score & parts, but I forgot to do it and the amount is small anyway, a difference of $2.50 and so no matter. If the letter ever turns up, please send me back the check *and* the voucher. It was the *Pigeons* aria sung on Columbia Broadcasting "Workshop" hour in a program of "Surrealiste" music. As you know, anything at all fantastic is now in the U.S. called "Surrealist". It all came up two days before I sailed and I had the rearrangement to make and no time to be difficult about anything. So I dont know what the rest of the program was, but I think (as I am sure you do) the work is entitled to be performed by practically anybody who is interested enough to ask for it and we wont quarrel over there about surrealism.

Best & faithfully
Virgil

Write always to
38, rue de Provence Paris ix

*****

To "M. Virgil Thomson / 38 rue de Provence / IX / Paris Hotel des Bains / Thonon (H^te Savoie)"

[9 July 1938]

My dear Virgil

I have had sent to Mrs Kaufman 4 Saints, and she has received it, and that seems to be that, did you notify the bank and did you send a duplicate

to me, because it has not come, do let me know, Francis Rose does seem to be having a very lively success, I liked his portrait of Hitchcock, yours not quite so good, but perhaps you do look like that now, well anyway,
     alwys,
Gtrde.

*****

To "M. Virgil Thomson / 38 rue de Provence. Hotel des Bains / Thonon / H^{te} Savoie"

BILIGNIN
PAR BELLEY
AIN

[11 July 1938]

My dear Virgil,

Thanks for the check but of course I had thought it was the one for the Philadelphia performance of Four Saints, did anything happen there, I never heard anything more, Bobsy Goodspeed telephoned me that she was giving Maurice a show in Chicago, I was very pleased
     Alwys
          Gtrde.

*****

Hotel des Bains
Thonon - H^{te} Savoie
16 July [1938]

D.G.

We know eagerness of old friends to believe the worst but your first guess was right I dont look like the portrait. Not yet anyway. I am back in Thonon my old love and doing a cure d'eau et de solitude and writing things and having a lovely time. I was with Maurice in Nantua (delicious site) and in the high Jura, where he remains because he liked the altitude and the landscape all of which was fine by me because it gave me pretext for coming here which I've had on my mind for 12 years. So all is happy and I quite forgot to write you about Philadelphia after being very firm indeed with Bennett Cerf that he must act as financial agent for us both because the Federal Theater couldnt think up a way of signing a contact with two authors of the same work and I didnt see any reason to do all the signing myself when you had a perfectly good publisher around and so he said he would and divide the proceeds and then there were long delays and it finally turned out that the man who was to direct everything had administrative troubles because having got himself temporarily assigned to some radio work the radio unit found him valuable and wouldnt let him be assigned back or even loaned to a theater so that's what happened to Four Saints in Philadelphia and it's really kind of a shame because it was Tommy Anderson who was to run it and he was in the original company and knows everything by heart and he had a brand-new idea of making it all modern and about the Spanish war which I think might be quite fine. Regularly once or twice a year somebody has a plan to revive the Saints and I always say yes naturally but I dont really believe in any of them just yet. The epoch isnt right. The original production isnt forgotten enough. All of a sudden one day it will be forgotten and then *Four Saints* will be very easy to perform and it will start its natural life as a classic repertory piece which I know will be a long life. But dont forget we had 60 performances in 1934 and 60 in a year is a lot of performances for an opera and we had them because of Freddy & Florine & Mrs. Wayne, etc., so we cant regret our elegant production or its 60 performances but at the same time said elegant production weighs heavily on the mind of anybody who thinks of reviving the work now. All this to explain why I dont do anything myself about putting it on again. Nor will Mrs. Kaufman & her English friend, if I read them correctly. It is really all all right and the score is all ready for any time anybody is serious about it. It's like Satie's ballet *Mercure*, which Massine & Picasso both outdid themselves in production of, and nobody has dared try it since. That was in 1923.

Love toujours
Virgil

Tommy Anderson: He sang the role of St. Giuseppe in the original version of *Four Saints*, has kept a prompt-book, and knows every movement.
Mrs. Wayne: Beatrice Robinson Wayne, the female lead, St. Teresa, in *Four Saints*.

*****

To "M. Virgil Thomson / ~~38 rue de Provence / IX / Paris~~ 116 Rue de Vaugirard / Paris"

[6 Aug. 1938]

My dear Virgil,

This looks as if it were not dead, it would be nice if it really happened, I have not heard anything from Mrs. Harding, I do not know whether she is writing to you or to me, I would want whatever is to be done to be first seen by my agent in London, I have a very good one there, he really does do things, and I would like him to represent me, I have told him about the whole matter, about our meeting in September, that could be done here if agreeable to everybody, well anyway we will keep each other au courent of anything that happens, I hope you are having a nice hot summer, it is lovely here alwys

Gtrde.

Mrs. Harding: See Stein, [1 June 1938]
au courent: *au courant*, up to date.

*****

38 rue de Provence
[1938]

D.G. Yes I continue to have correspondence with Mrs. Harding and I've heard from English friends in Paris signs of interest which lead me to think maybe London has to have a big negro show of some kind next season so maybe we are it you never know. I'm glad you have a good London agent. So have I if I should need one. And certainly we wouldnt think of signing anything without somebody of that kind to advise us. All I've done so far is informal preliminary negociations to see if the lady meant business. When she asked for a royalties-figure, I proposed 8% as a figure which would be satisfactory to me and probably to you. Nothing formal nor any firm offers, just a figure to satisfy her temporarily. When she wrote me last week asking for an option I replied that the Dramatists Guild did not allow the giving of options without an advance-payment & that the usual price was $500 for six months. She also asked for your address in order to write asking you for an option. I gave her the address but discouraged her from making separate negotiations, since any action taken by you & me must be taken jointly anyway. If after being told that options cost money she still wants to do business, then I think we should all meet without further ado and sign some real contracts.

You understand, I am sure, that I am not wishing to do your business for you. But it seems always to facilitate everything when I tell people I am empowered by you to speak informally for both of us, even (in small matters like radio or concert) signing the release which allows the performance to take place. In a matter involving serious money we must both of course have lots of skilled counsel and I wouldnt attempt to do real business without you or your agent to help me. The first days of September would be a good time for me, as I expect to be in Paris round the 10th. And Belley a very convenient place. I wrote Mrs. Harding this morning all this and asked her to write you and agree with you on a date convenient to you both.

Always affectionately
V—

I am in Paris just now, but going back tomorrow to Savoy and the Jura.

*****

To "M. Virgil Thomson / ~~38 rue de Provence / IX / Paris~~ Hotel Bavoux / Lamoura (Jura)"

[12 Aug. 1938]

My dear Virgil,

You were quite right about the option, if she comes through with the money then it will be likely that the rest will follow, let me have your address in Savoie, if she takes up the option we will go over to see you and make arrangements about future meetings, so keep me informed as to it all, it would be fine if it did happen,

Alwys
Gtrde.

*****

Postcard of "Abbaye d'HAUTECOMBE / La Grange vue de l'abside de l'église" to "M. Virgil Thomson / 38 rue de Provence / IX / Paris Hotel Bavoux / Lamoura / (Jura)"

[16 Aug. 1938]

My dear Virgil just had another letter from Mrs. Kaufman in which she says that Mrs. Harding has already written, will you let me know if you have received anything so I can let her know alwys

Gtrde.

*****

Hôtel Bavoux
Lamoura-Jura
17 August [1938]

D.G.

I enclose letter from Mrs. Harding. Also mine to her which please read and if O.K. mail. If not send it back with suggestions.

The one she wrote before to you she sent to me to be forwarded but since she said (it was sealed) it was to ask you for an option and since I had her sized up as a muddle-head anyway, I reflected about further complications and then I sent the letter back to her, giving at same time your address so she could write or send it on if she still wanted to but explaining that the preliminary arrangements etc. (as I wrote you before) had better be conducted thru me since they had started that way and that options were being granted a. jointly and b. for money.

I had thought if she meant business I would stick around here till September. Now I am not counting on it and I am leaving the end of this week for Villefranche (probably Friday afternoon). So keep on sending mail to 38 rue de Provence. If you want to communicate for any reason before I leave here, telephone (avec *avis d'appel*, because the hotel has no phone, but the post is right across the street) and we can converse about whatever has come up or whatever ideas you have re La Harding.

    Sorry to miss your visit. It would be nice having you to lunch or something. Perhaps later. Anyway in Paris.

And always affectionately
Virgil

---

avec *avis d'appel*: with a message to call me.

*****

To "M. Virgil Thomson / ~~38 rue de Provence / IX / Paris~~ Hotel de la Colline / Villefranches s. Mer / (A.M.)"

[18 Aug. 1938]

My dear Virgil,

    You are holding our end up well, it looks as if she would come through if she could get the money, and in England as our dear old friend Ford said, they do or they do not. heres hoping she does, its lovely weather and I am working a lot and I hope you have a good time, and I hope we will have to meet re Harding, if not Paris this winter

    Alwys   Love
                 Gtrde

---

if she would come through: On 9 September, Mrs. Harding returns the score to Thomson, saying she cannot interest a manager in it and, since Stein wants her to pay for an option, she cannot continue with the project, over which, she adds, she has already wasted a great deal of time.

*****

[On a Letter from the BBC dated 30 Nov. 1938 regarding possible broadcast of "Three Saints in Four Acts" (sic)]:
My dear Virgil Once more and yet again dear friends so will you answer them

lots of love alwys,
Gtrde

*****

17, QUAI VOLTAIRE
PARIS VII
March 11 [1939]

Dear Gertrude

BBC writes it is still making up its little mind about 4 Saints. The score is there since Christmas. Capital, Capitals is however being given by same shortly and I will let you know the date when *I* know it. I have asked for the same fee as before (ten guineas minus income tax). This sum includes two fees, one for hire of scores and the rest for performing-rights. The usual practise of musical publishers is equal division between rental-fees and performing-rights fees. That means that I will send you one-fourth of the amount received, as soon as I receive it. All expenses of shipping and insurance and the like are charged against the rental fee.

That is why the rental fee is placed as high as the other. When one adds up the cost of musical copy and the frequent replacements necessary (it wears out very quickly because musicians are very careless with music) plus postage (often merely for inspection of the piece) plus insurance plus customs duties (which I frequently have to pay when music is returned to France), there is no profit in it anyway. In the case of orchestral music there is usually a loss.

Sorry not to have seen you more this winter. I seem to be constantly at that damn book. It gets on. When do you go away?

Always devotedly
Virgil

---

damn book: *The State of Music* (New York: William Morrow and Company, 1939), which will be published to rave reviews, including one by Copland saying: "Virgil Thomson has written the most original book on music that America has produced. . . . the wittiest, the most provocative, the best written, the least conventional book on matters musical that I have ever seen (always excepting Berlioz). If you want to have fun, watch how people react to this book. . . . It will make many readers hopping mad. It will simply delight others" ("Thomson's Musical State," *Modern Music* 17, 1 [November 1939]: 63–65). The following year this book will get Thomson appointed as chief music critic for *The New York Herald Tribune*.

*****

To "M. Virgil Thomson / 17 Quai Voltaire / Paris."

[15 March 1939]

My dear Virgil,

I will be pleased with my portion of the ten guineas and let us know when and we will try and hear it, it will be fun if the opera comes off or on
Alwys
Gtrde.

*****

17, QUAI VOLTAIRE
PARIS VII
Monday 28 March [*1939*]

Dear Gertrude

The BBC decided not to try Four Saints. I've had no date yet for the *Capitals*.

Affection
Virgil

*****

To "M. Virgil Thomson / 17 Quai Voltaire / Paris."

[28 May 1939]

My dear Virgil,

Agnes Capri is very much interested in the film Dix Soeurs que sont pas soeurs and wants to sing it, I said you had already put it to music, I also told her about the Hugnet poems, I don't suppose they pay but it might be nice if they did it, we are leaving for the country so I can't arrange it myself but will you see her, she leave[s] for Cannes to-morrow and will be back next Tuesday, a pleasant summer to you

Alwys
Gtrde.

Agnes Capri: Esteemed singer planning to open a night club, solicits Stein for a text to be set to music. Stein ultimately writes a new work for her, "Les Superstitions," but the proposed setting is never completed.
film Dix Soeurs . . . soeurs: *Deux Soeurs Qui Ne Sont Pas Soeurs*. See notes to Stein, 11 Aug. 1930 and 10 June 1929.
the Hugnet poems: Thomson's collaborations with Hugnet, *"Berceau de Gertrude Stein"* and *"Valse Grégorienne."*

*****

Postcard of "Golfo di La Speria - Porto Venere," to "Miss Gertrude Stein / Bilignin par Belley (Ain) / Francia"

[3 Aug. 1939]

D.G. I wrote a nice note to Capri but she didnt answer and I went away. I will try to arrange something in the fall. Are you having a nice summer? I am.

affection
Virgil

*****

17, QUAI VOLTAIRE
PARIS VII
6 September [1939]

Dear Gertrude

I am rather wondering about you and wishing for your news. Is there anything I can do for you here? I am staying on for a while, at least.

love
Virgil

---

anything I can do for you: An expression of concern owing to recent events. On 1 Sept., the Germans invaded Poland. On 3 Sept., Britain and France declared war on Germany.

*****

To "M. Virgil Thomson / 17 Quai Voltaire / Paris"

[17 Sept. 1939]

My dear Virgil

It was nice of you to write, yours was almost the first letter we had, we are staying on a bit and then we go to Paris I'll let you know when we get there, For the first time in my life I have had a radio in the house and it does discourage me about music, why should there be so much of it, it going on all the time in the air certainly has something to do with the world's troubles, well anyway it will be nice seeing you again and I hope the book is going on well, we saw Hitchcock, he came, that now seems very long ago,

Alwys
Gtrde.

---

the world's troubles: See note to previous letter. On 17 Sept., the Soviets invade Poland, which they will divide between themselves and the Nazis on 29 Sept.

*****

On 10 May 1940, the Germans invade France. Stein and Thomson are in Bilignin. Most of Stein's and Thomson's young French friends are mobilized. On 26 May, Allied troops are evacuated from Dunkirk. On 3 June, the Germans bomb Paris. Afraid of being caught behind German lines with insufficient money, Thomson travels by train on 8 June 1940 to Moumour in the Pyrenees to stay with Gertrude Newell. Six days later the Germans occupy Paris. On 22 June, the new Prime Minister of France, Marshal Pétain, signs an armistice with Germany. Thomson embarks from Lisbon to New York on 12 August. Among people he knew aboard ship with him were Salvador and Gala Dali, Man Ray, the movie-maker René Clair, and Arthur Sherril, a former Harvard boy working for *Time* magazine in Rome (to Dilworth, Feb. 1981). Shortly after arrival in New York, on the basis of the success of *The State of Music,* Thomson becomes principal music critic for the *New York Herald Tribune*. Stein and Toklas have been advised by the American Consul at Lyon to flee France but they stay. Bernard Faÿ has been made head of the Bibliothèque Nationale and is an advisor to Pétain, whom he gets to order the subprefect at Belley to ensure safety and adequate rations of food and coal for Stein and Toklas.

*****

To "M. Virgil Thomson / Care of M. Carl Van Vechten / 101 Central Park West / New York / N.Y. / U.S.A."

BILIGNIN par BELLEY (Ain)

[15 May 1941]

My dear Virgil

It is nice to be going on together again, Chaucer says something like that, and it is just that kind of weather. I am very anxious to know how it sounded as an oratorio. And I am awfully pleased that success has come to you at last, you were always a believer in longevity, and I must say it is a pleasure, and I know you are liking it.

When and if we make more money will you send my share to the Mercantile Trust Company of Baltimore for my account.

You probably have a secretary now, so do lets hear from you and all about everything, lots of love

    Alwys Gtrde

It is nice . . . weather: Reference to the General Prologue in Chaucer's *Canterbury Tales*:
  Whan that Aprill with his shoures soote
  The droghte of March hath perced to the roote
  . . . Thanne longen folk to goon on pilgrimages . . . (lines 1–2, 12)

an oratorio: *Four Saints* is being performed this spring in New York with the original cast but without staging, one performance conducted from the piano by Thomson in the auditorium of the Museum of Modern Art, the other conducted by Alexander Smallens at Town Hall.

*****

To "M. Virgil Thomson / Care of M. Carl Van Vechten / 101 Central Park West / New York / N.Y. / U.S.A."

[2 Sept. 1941]

BILIGNIN
PAR BELLEY
  AIN

My dear Virgil,

I have not heard from you yet, did you send the money to the Mercantile Trust Company of Baltimore to my account and how much was it.

Here we are in the best French manner living on luxuries but not on necessities, truit écrevisses lemons and pigeons, but anything simpler not to be had and as no hotels are open and no means of transport, luxuries have to be consumed sur place. well anyway, write and tell me if the money has been sent and how much it was, when will we meet again, it looks not so far away as it once seemed that we will be back in Paris, and that would be nice, lots of love

Gtrde.

---

truit [*truite*]: trout.
écrevisses: crawfish. The chapter, "Food in the Bugey during the Occupation," in *The Alice B. Toklas Cook Book* details culinary challenges and peculiarities during this period, featuring two recipes for crawfish, both calling for wine and cognac but no butter.
sur place: on the spot.

*****

222 W. 23
New York City
December 5, 1941

Miss Gertrude Stein
Bilignin par Belley
Ain, France

Dear Gertrude:

I have been putting you off for months because I had so many things to tell you I imagined I would need a full free day to write them. Here goes a little of it, anyway.

The *Four Saints* performances came off very brilliantly last May. I am sending you by slow mail programs and a handbill. The audience was brilliant; the press was fine; the sound of it all was ravishing. It is now obvious to everybody that we don't really have to have scenery every time. Words and music held the attention for two hours without any trouble at all. I sent to your bank in Baltimore two checks, one from the Museum of Modern Art for $15.86, and one from the Town Hall for $30.78. This represents one half of five percent of the box-office gross. I did not ask for a larger percentage, because the performances were certain to lose money anyway and I did not wish to seem greedy about small amounts in view of Miss Crane's willingness to lose $1,000 or more on a concert of sheer musical prestige. (The work has been recently referred to in the press as a "classic".) Its paying public, however, remains, though intensely devoted, moderate in size. School children and college people love it also, and I am constantly refusing inquiries about it from schools. In order to take advantage of these, the work will have to be published. And since no commercial publisher wants to take it on just yet, I am thinking of publishing it myself. I have a little cooperative publishing firm called the Arrow Music Press, which I started with Aaron Copland and two other composers several years ago. Each composer published pays what the publication costs. Then, instead of receiving only ten percent royalty on sales, he receives all of the returns, minus distribution expenses, which makes a royalty figure of 65 percent. If I publish the work in this way, I shall pay the cost and reserve all of the royalties excepting the five percent of sales price that you would normally receive from a commercial publisher. You would also receive 25 percent of all performing rights fees, which is the same proportion that you would receive from the commercial publishers, who reserve half of such fees for themselves.

If this proposition seems reasonable to you, and if the printing does not turn out to be more expensive than I can afford, I shall have a contract drawn up and submit it to you. If you prefer to share the expense of publication with me, we will share equally in all the receipts. I think the whole cost will amount to something around $700, maybe a bit less. I intend to print 25 copies on special paper with both our signatures and to sell these by subscription for $25 a piece. I do not think it will be difficult to sell most of these. This will enable me to price the ordinary edition of 1,000 copies at $4, which is cheap for an opera score but which will bring it within the means of choral societies and school organizations. Please write me by airmail what you think of the idea and which way you would like the contract drawn up.

It was nice having letters from you. I wish I had them oftener. I miss you a great deal but do hope that you are right that we shall be seeing each other soon in Paris. I wouldn't know; I have no prophetic sense about wars. I am glad for your own sake that you have stayed in France, because I think you will not regret it. I should have done so myself if I had not been obliged to earn my living. I stayed until August of last year and I saw both parts of France after the war was over, the part with Germans and the part without. If there is anything on earth that I can do for you or send to you, please let me know.

I am having a pleasant and busy (but very busy) life. My music gets played and published and quite a lot of new gets written. When the war is over we must write another opera. Only we must wait till then, because I don't think we could choose the subject very well by mail. I hope you are both well and enjoying your diet of luxuries and I embrace you both affectionately.

Always faithful,

Virgil

The *Four Saints* performances: See note to Stein, 15 May 1941. At the Town Hall performance, Thomas Beecham first heard the opera, afterwards telling Thomson that it is "a child of the Elizabethan masque" (*Reader*, 260).

Miss Crane: Louise Crane, lesbian, philanthropist, and patron of the arts, daughter of Josephine Boardman Murray (see note to Thomson, 6 May [1933]). She has financed this revival of *Four Saints*.

after the war was over: In 1941 this can only refer to the fall of France, 22 June 1940, concluded by the armistice in which Pétain surrendered to the Germans and began heading the Vichy government.

*****

To "M. Virgil Thomson / 222 W. 23 Street / New York / N.Y."

March 27, 1942

BILIGNIN par BELLEY (Ain)

My dear Virgil,

Glad to hear from you, I have known that all your news is good news, everybody has told me so but it is nice to hear it from yourself, your arrangements about publishing 4 Saints seems to me very fair so go ahead, in the paris you mention, in these days naturally I cannot share the xpenses of publications with you, contracts came through alright, I have just had one sent me for my book for children called To Do, I think you will like it, you are in at least your name is in it's a book of alphabets and birthdays, it is being printed by Smith and [Dewell?]. and you will be pleased that Paris-France in french is having a real success, for the first time I have written a book that everybody can read, as one of the farmers said to me, it is very curious, my domestique de ferme can read it my wife can read it, I can read it, and it would appear that it is much admired by the elite. You know Virgil I always did want to be a popular author, that is one that anybody could read, I am one that am personally quoted by everybody but as not yet my books and I want that to[o], which brings me to the opera, I wish that we could write an opera that would be as popular as Carmen, it would be nice for the money but it also would be nice for satisfaction, an opera anybody would like including the farm hands and the elite let us some time go to it, I wonder what has happened to all our young friends in this present unpleasantness but then most who were young then are not young enough to be young now and so I suppose nothing happens, well anyway

lots of love

Gtrde.

To Do: *To Do: A Book of Alphabets and Birthdays*. Despite the contract, first publication was posthumous, in *Alphabets and Birthdays*, vol. 7 of the *Yale Edition of the Unpublished Works of Gertrude Stein*.

you are in at least your name is: In *To Do: A Book of Alphabets and Birthdays*, Stein writes:

V is Van Virgil Valeska and Very. . . . And then there was a hill and its name was Virgil . . . Virgil is a hill and a hill would not make such a mistake not until he did make such a mistake. It would be lighter to make such a mistake than heavier.

Van then, he is a man.

Virgil till, he is a hill.

No mistake at all about that.

Now what happened

What did happen.

Certainly something did.

By mistake.

And a mistake is mistaken.

Oh yes.

What happened.

It is all very confused but more confused than confusing.

Papa Woojums took a picture of a hill which he will, Virgil.

And on the hill grew forget-me-nots. . . . I am Papa Woojums and I'll climb a hill.

Virgil Virgil Virgil.

And he went on writing a poem.

I have a hill, Virgil, I have forget-me-nots when I will, and I was born not on a hill, no Vigil not a hill

. . . . Do they have hills Vigils,

Do they have forget-me-nots,

Plots forget-me-nots,

. . . . measles and mumps would go up the hill to Virgil

(*Alphabets and Birthdays*, 61–64)

Earlier she had included his name in her libretto, though in a context likely to recall his Classical namesake: "They can remain latin latin there and Virgil Virgil Virgil virgin virgin latin there" (*Four Saints* 21).

Paris-France in french: In 1941, *Paris France* was published in Algeria by Éditions E. Charlot, translated by May d'Aiguy.

domestique de ferme: farmhand.

*****

As 1942 closes, the Germans occupy Vichy France. In February 1943, the subprefect at Belley warns Stein, through her lawyer, that they are about to be arrested by the Gestapo. She telephones Faÿ. He saves them. They are obliged by landlords (who wish to live there) to leave their house in Bilignin, and they move in February to a house at Le Colombier in the mountains outside Culoz fifteen kilometres up the Rhône. In August 1944, the Gestapo breaks into their Paris apartment, Picasso notifies Stein, she notifies Faÿ, and he ensures that the apartment is sealed and the pictures unconfiscated. On 31 August, American GIs arrive in Belley, and Stein greets them. In mid-December, she and Toklas return to Paris, where Stein is now a celebrity for GIs, her fame soon being renewed by *Wars I have Seen* (New York: Random House, 1945), which appears to rave reviews and sells over 10,000 copies.

*****

Radiogram 22 March 1945
LC VIRGIL Thomson NEWYORK HERALD TRIBUNE NEWYORK
TOUCHED BY YOUR REVIEW MANY THANKS AFFECTIONATELY
GERTRUDE STEIN

> **YOUR REVIEW**: In the *Herald Tribune*, 11 March 1945, Thomson writes:
>> Gertrude Stein's story of her life in France between the armistice of 1940 and the liberation of 1944, "Wars I Have Seen," reads as clearly as her three previously published books of memoirs, "The Autobiography of Alice B.

Toklas," "Everybody's Autobiography" and "Paris, France." Its style is that of her conversation, easy, colloquial, direct. Its subject matter is that of all her most hermetic poetry, namely, the domestic life. It begins with some memories of earlier wars, and it returns to these constantly, just as anybody's account of what happened today uses events that happened before as a point of reference and comparison. But mostly it is a day by day, week by week, month by month account of Miss Stein's life among friends and neighbors, food, animals, ideas, and current events—which has always, rather than the narration of things past, been the subject of her best writing.

The book has, therefore, all the vividness and immediacy of her most recondite compositions without any of their obstinate, if fascinating, obscurity. It has, too, the warmth and the friendly humanity of her previous memoirs without any of the slightly fatuous quality that autobiographies of the great (Miss Stein's included) do have, that never quite convincing theme of "look what a good (or bad) boy am I!" It is really the most charming and the most realistic picture imaginable of a life that has been closed to our knowledge for more than four years. Stories from France are beginning to come through now, but none is so convincing as Miss Stein's. It must have been like that there; it would not have been any other way. It is a true picture.

Miss Stein has always liked to walk every day and to write every day. She also likes to eat every day and to talk with people. So every day she walked places on errands about food and talked with people she met on the way. And every night, or nearly so, she wrote about where she had been, whom she had talked to, what had happened to her neighbors and to their relatives, stories they told her, rumors, jokes, adventures and many reflections regarding it all. The daily life is all there, the daily fear, the daily unusual, the daily contempt for the Germans (she found the Italian troops rather agreeable on the whole, and Miss Toklas bought cigarettes from them) and the daily faith that the Americans would eventually arrive.

The suspense of waiting for the Americans and the joy of finally having them there is the real drama of the book, just as the details of daily living are its poetry and theme. Not that there is not also much good talk about history and tactics and politics and death. That is a part of any one's daily life, too, especially in the presence of disaster. Miss Stein's theory about the war, the conviction that sustained her through it, is that it had to be in order that the nineteenth century should be killed off finally. Her faith in the future is that France will arise like the phoenix from its ashes and that the twentieth century everywhere will be able now to start living its own life. It all came about because Germany (and a little bit England) insisted on thinking and acting as if the nineteenth were still going on. It accomplishes, therefore, what the other world war failed to accomplish. And she suspects that it will be followed by a longish peace, a "peace without progress," without any of the outmoded nineteenth-century notions, in fact, in it.

And she finds to her great delight that American soldiers are not like the ones she knew in the other war. They don't ask questions or criticize foreign customs, and they converse. "In the last war they had their language (as different from British English) but they were not yet in possession of it. . . . It was beginning to possess its language but it was struggling but now the job is done, the G.I. Joes have this language that is theirs, they do not have to worry about it, they dominate it, they dominate their language and in dominating their language which is now all theirs they have ceased to be adolescents and become men."

If the twentieth century is really finally to stop being a cause and become a going concern, as indeed we all hope it is, Miss Stein can be proud of her role in the heroic early days of it. Living through the war takes nothing, as courage, compared to being for forty years a one-man literary movement. And to have become a Founding Father of her century is her own reward for having long ago, and completely, dominated her language.

*****

To "M. Virgil Thomson / Hotel Ritz / Place Vendome / Paris"

[12 Sept. 1945]
5 rue Christine
Wednesday

My dear Virgil,

Alice tried to get you in the morning but you seem to be out even in the morning, it is understandable, I have achieved quantities of literature about the period and am now reading Clemenceau about the impeachment, he might be the hero, you know he was over then, might make a nice hero, also the copy of the play is here here, for you, so ring us up, lots of love, and lovely weather
   Alwys
    Gtrde.

I told Pierre Balmain to invite you to his opening next Tuesday,

---

Virgil Thomson .... Paris: Thomson returned to Paris to discuss collaboration with Stein on a second opera. Douglas Moore, the chairman of the Music Department at Columbia University had seen and loved *Four Saints* on Broadway, and, in 1945, wrote to offer Thomson a commission from the Alice Ditson Fund to write a second opera with Stein. From the Palace Hotel in San Francisco, Thomson wired to Stein proposing renewed collaboration, saying he had an idea for an opera. She sent back "her delight," in a wire or letter now lost. Soon after, Thomson's friend the attorney Suzanne Blum got the Cultural Secretary at the Foreign Office to award Thomson a "mission" to go to France for two weeks, partly for having helped to organize concerts benefiting a Free French group called France Forever. In August he flew to Paris and is discussing the subject with Stein (Thomson, *Reader* 210, 252*)*.

I have achieved quantities of literature: In preparation for writing the libretto for *The Mother of Us All*, she is reading nineteenth-century history, exhausting the American Library in Paris and sending to the New York Public Library.

Clemenceau ... might be the hero: At this time, she is considering for a subject the impeachment of President Andrew Johnson in 1868 from the point of view of George Clemenceau, then a young journalist visiting the US.

Pierre Balmain: Thirty-one-year-old fashion designer, opening his Haute Couture on the Rue Francois to present the elegant new French style that will dominate postwar French fashions. A close friend of Stein, in 1943 he created the costumes for two of her plays for children, *In A Garden A Tragedy In Act One* and *Look and Long, A Play in Three Acts*.

*****

To "M. Virgil Thomson / Ritz Hotel / Place Vendome / Paris."

[24 Sept. 1945]
5 rue Christine
Monday,

My dear Virgil,

Will you bring with you to-morrow evening the copy of the play, some young actors wanted to give it a reading and they need the two copies, till to-morrow, and I will show you a wonderful passage, they seem to be sending me from the New York public library all the literature of the period, if it comes off it will be a most erudite opera,
   Toujours
    Gtrde.

the play: *Yes Is For a Very Young Man*, Stein's play about the French resistance. The Biarritz American University Theater is interested in putting on the play, but negotiations will ultimately fail and the production will be cancelled. For details see *Staying on Alone*, 80–81.

*****

To "M. Virgil Thomson / Hotel Ritz / Place Vendome / Paris."

[8 Oct. 1945]
5 rue Christine.

My dear Virgil,

I just have been looking over my sonata, alas without a piano because there is none, but you got just what I wanted, it does make a design, and the design changes, which is so much better than a picture, perhaps we can find a piano before you go, I would like to hear and play it, also I made out a list of characters for the mother of us all, they came out kind of funny and there is a kind of a prelude, well one meeting more Virgil is almost necessary, bless us all,
Alwys Gertrde and again so many thanks,

my sonata: Thomson's Sonata No. 3, "for Gertrude Stein to improvise at the pianoforte." See note to Thomson [27 July 1930].

*****

To "M. Virgil Thomson / Care of Herald Tribune / New York."

5 Dec. [1945]
5 rue Christine

My dear Virgil,

This is to introduce Lamont Johnson who has just bought the option of Yes is for a very young man. I am sending him to you because perhaps you will help him in a way, as I know you can, we have had the cast here and I think they will do it well. I think you will like him, it has all been very xciting and now I will quiet down and think about the opera, I know a lot now about Susan B. and I am beginning on Webster, lots of love
Alwys   Gtrde.

Lamont Johnson . . . Yes is for a very young man: Having met Stein during the war while on a USO tour, twenty-three-year-old actor Lamont Johnson has acquired the rights of *Yes Is for a Very Young Man*, which he will direct in Pasadena, California, and, in 1948, in New York, off Broadway, at the Cherry Street Theatre. It is the first play he directs in what will be a long and renowned career as director and producer in theater, cinema, and television.

Susan B.: Susan B. Anthony (1820–1906). In the autumn of 1945, Stein chose her as the heroine of her opera. Anthony was a pioneer of the women's movement, an organizer of a women's temperance association, an advocate in obtaining legal rights for women over their children and property, and president for eight years of the Woman Suffrage Association. Her fifty-year relationship with co-suffragette Elizabeth Cady Stanton caused scandal and, for both, scorn. Clearly Stein saw her as a fictional counterpart to herself.

*****

VIRGIL THOMSON   222 WEST 23ᴿᴰ STREET
                              NEW YORK CITY
                              15 March [1946]

Dear Gertrude

Carl says the opera is nearly finished. I hope so. I want to see it. I pine for it. I shall be leaving here sometime between the 15th of April and the 1st of May. It would be nice if I had it before I left. A theatrical producer has offered $1000 for an option on the completed work, sight unseen. I am looking into the matter; and if it seems proper to accept, I shall write or wire for your approval. My lawyer can make the contract, since you have no agent here; and we can split his fee, which will be reasonable. I spoke to Carl about this today, who approves my procedure. I think I have an engraver for *4 Saints*.

I have a can-opener for Alice and a book for you. Write for what else I can bring you. And do send me *The Mother of Us All* if it is done. Or a couple of acts. I like to look at things a while before I start writing music to them.

affection
Virgil

*****

To "M. Virgil Thomson / 222 West 23rd Street / New York / N.Y. / U.S.A."

19 March [1946]
5 rue Christine

My dear Virgil,

It will be nice seeing you again, the opera finished (registered) is on the way to Carl, put at the post four days ago, I hope it gets there before you leave, I think I did make her quite magnificent, well we'll see, and when you get here I have a very good agent, Mrs. Bradley is doing all my theatricals in America, Alice is most xcitedly looking forward to her can opener, pleasant days
Alwys

Gtrde.

Letters with Notes

4. First page of the manuscript score of *The Mother of Us All*

Mrs. Bradley: Stein became reconciled with William Bradley and his wife, Jenny, early in the war, when he resumed his role as Stein's agent. At Bradley's death in 1939, Jenny took over the agency and now acts on Stein's behalf in contract negotiations.

*****

April 15 [1946]

Dear Gertrude

The libretto is sensationally handsome and Susan B. is a fine rôle. I am sailing on May 1. Shall be at 17 Quai Voltaire on the 8th or 9th. I am having more copies made of libretto. Sending one to Columbia University. Douglas Moore, their music head, is writing you to ask where you want your money sent. Arnold Weissberger is writing you about the offer of Courtney Burr to pay us $2500 (the price has gone up) for first option on producing the opera after Columbia Univ., this money not to be charged against royalties. He is a high class producer, will give us free hand in the production. The offer is most advantageous, and I hope you will agree with me that we should accept. The kiddies from California are expected next week. If they arrive before I leave, I shall use what little influence I have to mate them up with a producer for the Resistance play. The Pasadena performances, though they aroused naturally much interest, do not seem to have been decisive with regard to Broadway. All the serious theater world seems to admire the play but to resist something about it at the same time. My suspicion is that a little more rewriting on your part would clear up the difficulty, probably the American woman needs making into a bigger rôle, a more ample character, something for a good actress to get her teeth into. At present she *is* a little flat. She seems smaller than the French people, just as Americans in France often do. But an American audience is not going to understand easily how an American, especially a woman, can not be a more interesting character than any foreigner. Anyway, if local producers continue to resist, the kiddies can do it again out of town, probably in Cleveland; and if you are here you can see whether it still needs more script.

Maurice wrote a review of *Brucie* [sic] *and Willie* for an Atlanta paper which he writes me from Chattanooga he will send you when it appears. I read the galley proofs when he did and we both loved it dearly and it all comes out clear now what you meant last summer by "pioneering" which is just what we all, that is the little friends, have always been doing and maybe it isnt so easy for all of them though certainly it wasnt always so easy for us but anyway it is the only thing any American can admit doing and respect himself because a pioneer is the only thing we can imagine ourselves being noble as or understand. And certainly Susan B. comes out as a noble one. She is practically St. Paul when she says "let them marry". And the whole thing will be easier to dramatize than *4 Saints* was, much easier, though the number of characters who talk to the audience about themselves, instead of addressing the other characters, is a little terrifying. Mostly it is very dramatic and very beautiful and very clear and constantly quotable and I think we shall have very little scenery but very fine clothes and they do all the time strike 19th century attitudes. Agnes de Mille will be useful for that; she is after all a granddaughter of Henry George.   à bientot and full of affection,

Virgil

Douglas Moore: See note to Stein [12 Sept. 1945].
Arnold Weissberger: Thomson's attorney.
the kiddies from California . . . the Resistance play: The cast for *Yes Is for a Very Young Man* includes Anthony Franciosa, Gene Saks, Michael Gazzo, Bea Arthur, and Kim Stanley.
Brucie **[sic]** *and Willie*: Stein's Brewsie and Willie (New York: Random House, 1946).
Agnes de Mille: Forty-one-year-old, Harlem-born, UCLA-trained dancer, choreographer, writer, original member of the Ballet Theater (later renamed the Morkin Ballet), for

which she wrote and choreographed *Black Ritual* (1940) for an all-black cast. Her Broadway choreography credits include *Rodeo* (1942), *Oklahoma!* (1943), and *Carousel* (1945).

Henry George: (1839–1897), author of *Progress and Poverty*, which made him one of the most famous living Americans at the end of the nineteenth century.

*****

To "M. Virgil Thomson / 17 Quai Voltaire / Paris."

5 rue Christine
1 July [1946]

My dear Virgil.

We will be going away for a month or so at the end of next week, do you want any consultation before we go,
Alwys
Gtrde.

---

do you want any consultation before we go: Stein and Toklas are leaving to spend the summer at Bernard Faÿ's country house at St. Martin, southwest of Paris. Thomson has returned for his second postwar visit to Paris, meeting Stein and Toklas several times in May and June. On Stein's part, the friendship is fragile, and when, at a party, he begins teasing her, Toklas warns him that Stein might cry. On 14 June, Stein wrote to Van Vechten that she is cutting the character "Virgil T" out of the opera. Van Vechten persuaded her to restore him (Watson 320). During the last of her conversations with Thomson, which may be the "consultation" she here proposes, he will urge against a fifty-fifty split of profits for their new opera, since, as composer, he will be involved in many post-compositional expenses. He will urge agreement to a one-third, two-thirds split, the latter going to him to compensate for these expenses, or else that they retain the fifty-fifty split but share expenses equally. Stein will agree in principle in Toklas's hearing (Thomson to Van Vechten, 15 Oct. 1946). Specifically, for the publication of his musical setting of her *Preciosilla*, Stein will agree to the one-third, two-thirds split in profits in favour of Thomson. This will be their last conversation.

*****

Letters that Cannot Be Dated or Placed Precisely in Sequence

Sunday

Dear Gertrude

Thanks for the list. Hugnet thinks I should include your card with invitations. If you are of same accord you might bring along a dozen or two on Monday. I'll write *de la part de* above your name.
Love
Virgil

---

de la part de: on behalf of.

*****

[n.d]

Dear Gertrude

    I found this which I had lost. It may gently divert you. Anyway. Thanks nice party.

                          And many loves.
                            And Alice too.
                            And
                                  Virgil

*****

[Postcard, photograph of Stein and Basket on chaise longue, probably taken Fall of 1930]

Love and kisses
                Gtrde.
Had to have it enlarged
for a New Zealand young gentleman
so had on[e] for you
                G.

New Zealand young gentleman: Len Lye, modernist filmmaker and kinetic sculptor, born in Christchurch, New Zealand in 1901, moved to London in the late 1920s, then to New York in 1944.

Epilogue
Thomson and Toklas

At 6:30 p.m. on Saturday 27 July, Gertrude Stein died of cancer in the American hospital in Neuilly. The next day, Thomson read of her death in the paper on the train from Trieste to Paris. Upon arrival, he went immediately to Toklas, who was grieving and alone. Stein had made a will naming her and Allan Stein, her nephew, as her executors and Carl Van Vechten as her literary executor. In the will, she left Picasso's portrait of her to the Metropolitan Museum of Art in New York, her papers to Yale, and the rest of her estate to Toklas, making provision for payments to her from the estate, including the sale of pictures. What follows is an account of Thomson's relationship with Toklas after Stein's death insofar as it concerns his relationship with Stein, their collaboration, and their mutual friends.

Living now largely on his salary as chief music critic for the *New York Herald Tribune*, Thomson began composing the music for *The Mother of Us All* in the fall of 1946. He had his attorney, Arnold Weissberger, draw up the contract for the opera, which he sent first to Van Vechten for approval and then to Toklas. The terms of this contract are identical to those in that for *Four Saints in Three Acts* with two exceptions. Reflecting Thomson's final conversation with Stein, the first exception stipulates that "the Author and Composer shall share equally all profits there from and all expenses or obligations in connection therewith." The other exception states that "Because of the death of Gertrude Stein, it is understood and agreed that the right to sanction, negotiate for, and contract for performance, translation, publication, arrangement, adaptation, etc. of the joint work shall be solely the right, and within the discretion, of the Composer."

Toklas had never been comfortable with Thomson's easy familiarity with Stein and their collaborative, creative intimacy, which had bypassed her. For a time, Toklas remained leery of Thomson and relied for advice on Van Vechten. But Thomson won her over with gifts, letters, and, when in

Paris, visits and excursions with her to good restaurants, she as his guest. His motives undoubtedly included self-interest, since, as Stein's heir, she would be signing contracts involving his settings to music of Stein's texts. A reading of all the letters between them suggests, however, that affection for her outweighed self-interest and that her affection for him increased with her gratitude and with evidence of his continuing dedication to work done in collaboration with her beloved Gertrude.

Initially they almost fell out over Bernard Faÿ, who had become a close friend of Stein and Toklas, affording Stein entry to the stratosphere of French intellectual life. In 1932, Stein had helped him strategize to acquire the Chair of American Civilization at the College de France, defeating Andre Siegfried. Faÿ had increased Stein's literary recognition in France by helping to translate her writings. He ensured the publication of *Américains d'Amérique* in 1933. Under the Vichy regime in 1940, he accepted the directorship of the Bibliothèque Nationale, replacing a Jew. Pétain having outlawed secret societies, Faÿ's duties included accumulating and organizing 170,000 files on Freemasons seized by the French police from Masonic lodges. Personally opposing Freemasons for being anti-Catholic and for meddling in French political life, Faÿ oversaw the integration of these files into a single coherent Masonic file and the development of lists of names and addresses of Freemasons—his secretary, Gueydan de Roussel, doing most of the work. Initially the purpose for all this was to exclude Masons from government administration. Eventually, however, the Gestapo used these lists to imprison, deport, and murder large numbers of Freemasons—six thousand were imprisoned, 990 deported, 540 murdered (Malcolm 80). Faÿ may not have known that any or all of this would happen, but once it began happening he probably knew, since his secretary, Roussel, acted as liaison with the Gestapo, some of whom worked in the library, and Roussel was, for most of the war, his lover. Faÿ also edited the anti-Jewish journal *La Gerbe*, which the Nazis funded (Burns, Dydo, Rice 405).

As Director of the Library, he was an advisor to Pétain, spending one week each month with him at Vichy. In this capacity, he arranged for Stein to translate Pétain's speeches, which she began while the United States still maintained diplomatic relations with Vichy France and continued after the full German occupation of France in November 1942, stopping only when advised that continuing would draw the attention of the Germans.[1] As we have seen, at Faÿ's urging, Pétain personally ordered the subprefect at Belley to look after her and Toklas, and Faÿ saved Stein's collection of paintings from confiscation (see after Stein [17 Sept. 1939] and after Stein March 27, 1942). In February 1943, Stein's lawyer informed her that she and Toklas were to be arrested for deportation to a concentration camp and advised her to flee to Switzerland. They stayed in France, unmolested, doubtless

---

1. She translated about three-fifths of the printed text of Marshal Pétain, *Paroles aux Francais, Messages et écrits, 1934–1941* (Lyon: Librarie H. Lardanchet, 1941).

because she contacted Faÿ—she had a direct telephone-contact number to his office (Burns, Dydo, Rice 411)—who intervened to save their lives.[2]

Faÿ was arrested on 19 August 1944, convicted of collaboration in early December 1946, and sentenced to life at hard labor. Probably unaware of the extent of his collaboration, Stein had written a letter to the court defending him. After Stein's death, Toklas wrote to Thomson, "we all owe so much to our friend and Gertrude had this as her only sorrow–she said we would act when the time came to do so–alas alas that she is not here to do so now." She expressed to him her concern for Faÿ, for whom Thomson showed little sympathy (17 December 1946). On 25 January 1947, she wrote:

> I am aghast at your attitude to Bernard and the verdict—you haven't lived in France lately or you couldnt feel as you do—only Bernard's personal enemies believe him capable of such crimes as you believe he committed. And we know with what positive pleasure he collected enemies. No—you have some Frenchmen on your side but they were always his personal enemies—or the French who passed the occupation in New York possibly—Please do not let us ever speak of it again. My memory is not as good as it was so all this wont trouble me as long as it would have in the old days. Didn't you once quote Madame Langlois—how astonishing that such a corrupt person should write such pure music. I'm sure the music for The Mother of Us All is pure if you want it to be pure—and that it is intriguing vital and beautiful. For your music I will make any confession of faith—you want—but for what it is surrounded by—je m'en garde[3]—What do you nourish it on? You may well answer that you are not a pelican.[4] Of course I don't agree with Madame Langlois. Not—It's not the corruption that puts me off—it's the being mistaken—You see so clearly in your music—Perhaps the rest of us see any thing clearly because we havent your gift—Let it go at that.
>
> Would you for Gertrude's sake not mention Bernard's name to a living soul until his situation has changed. I could under that condition easily be
>
> As ever
>
> Alice

However she could, she acted on Faÿ's behalf. Eventually Thomson softened his attitude towards Faÿ, and he and Toklas consulted one

---

2. For a full account of Stein's friendship with Faÿ and her debt to him during the war, see Edward Burns and Ulla Dydo with William Rice, "Gertrude Stein: September 1942 to September 1944," appendix 9 in *The Letters of Gertrude Stein and Thornton Wilder.* 410–12.
3. *je m'en garde*: no way will I do that.
4. In medieval legend, the pelican pierces its own breast to nourish its young with its blood.

another about how to help him. In an effort to advise Mina Curtiss[5] on how to deal with Thomson and apparently with reference to the Hugnet episode, Toklas explained the nature of her friendship with him, "It was only after the reconciliation that followed none too quickly a break in the acquaintanceship caused by Virgil's mistaken judgment that we came to a very real devotion – which doesn't prevent both of us from an easy recital of the other's capital faults. So patience and you'll come through. . . . Virgil is a strange plant one has to give not too assiduous but special care" (Toklas, *Staying* 203).

A good deal of the post-war Thomson-Toklas correspondence concerns favors he does for her, including sending supplies unavailable in post-war France, helping her kitchen "very handsomely to maintain to the French eye the appearance of an American one" (Toklas, 20 April 1947). He ensured that she had all the tea she needed, which became famous in the neighborhood as "Virgil Thomson's tea." He arranged for friends to bring her evaporated milk and California lemon juice in tins as well as a new Hoover vacuum cleaner, the gift of Mildred Rogers. "Gertrude and I," Toklas wrote, "shared an unreasoning faith in new mechanical toys" (9 May 1947). Their correspondence also concerns the work on which he and Stein collaborated, initially their second opera.

Toklas wrote that all "sweetly satisfactory" things he was telling her about the opera "should have been so to Gertrude—you know what it would have meant to her—on the whole no one appreciated you more than she did—but you've always known it of course. It was really from the beginning when you played the whole of Socrates for her—do you remember" (17 December 1946). He scored the music for *The Mother of Us All* between 1 February (according to one manuscript copy) or 6 February (according to another) and 26 March 1947. On 11 April 1947, he wrote about preparations for the performance at Columbia University:

> The opera is finished and its orchestral score is finished, 500 beautiful pages. We are in rehearsal. I have wonderful singers, all of them young people around 30. The Susan B. is a dramatic soprano of sensational quality; I got her from the director of the Metropolitan Opera. Daniel Webster is a bass, 6 feet, 5 inches tall and impressive in every way. Constance Fletcher, John Adams and Joe [sic] the Loiterer, are equally fine. So are Virgil T. and Gertrude S.[6] Even the small roles are handsomely sung. I have not seen the sketches yet for scenery and costumes but they are promised me for tomorrow. The costumes will be slightly larger than the live period pieces and the sets, I am led to hope, comparatively simple. The stage is being directed by a

---

5. Curtiss is a musicologist, and sister of Lincoln Kirstein.
6. In his Prelude to the first published edition of *The Mother*, Thomson lists among the characters: "GERTRUDE S., soprano.—a cheerful stocky woman of middle age wearing a full-cut but plain modern velvet gown of dark color and a brocaded waistcoat" and "VIRGIL T., pleasant and efficient master of ceremonies, in modern morning dress (top hat, cutaway coat, striped trousers, gardenia)."

choreographer from Lincoln Kirstein's Ballet Society. Everything is under control, and I am very happy about it all. Everybody loves the work and believes in it. There will almost certainly be a downtown production next winter. I have a publisher too for both the *Mother of Us All* and *Four Saints*. Also for *Capital, Capitals*.

Maurice has invented some stage action for the only two parts of the opera that are a little obscure. The entire first act will represent a political meeting that ends with a formal debate between Susan B. and Daniel. The final scene represents the inauguration of the statue with U.S. Grant and Lillian Russell, both a bit tipsy and scandalous, as the chief speakers. I do wish you were going to be here for the performance. Perhaps next year, if all goes well, you might be induced to come over and hear it. Constantly I regret that Gertrude cannot hear it. It would make her very happy. Everybody thinks it is going to be very successful and have a long life.

Columbia Broadcasting plans for the 21st of April a performance of *Four Saints*. We have an hour, and will do everything but Act 2.

I shall be arriving in Paris early in June. Please let me know if there are any household objects or other things difficult to acquire in Paris that I can bring you. I shall be travelling with trunks and shall have lots of space.

I am sorry not to have written you more often in the last few months. I have worked literally night and day finishing the opera score and casting the work, all the while keeping up my regular duties; and so I have rather counted on Carl to keep you informed of my progress.... Do let me hear from you. I have worried about you and the Paris heating problem. Francis Rose writes me he has designed a tomb for Gertrude. That is a pretty idea, and I am eager to know what it is like. I should appreciate your telling me what kinds of food would be most useful to you, since I am bringing some along anyway and I can as easily bring you what you want as what you don't.

Love and always devotedly,

Virgil

On 20 April 1947, she wrote that by all accounts he had composed the music for the new opera "beautifully and you know how deeply that satisfies me." She wanted to hear a radio broadcast of *Four Saints*, which he was conducting,

> not that [it] would make up for not hearing The Mother of Us All. How Gertrude would have loved it. Well you'll play it and sing it to me when you come over and I look forward to that and to very little else beside – unless perhaps if you have time youll play Socrate for me the

way you did so touchingly for us up on the rue de Berne. Gertrude and I so often spoke of that evening of introduction.

Toklas was, however, unable to hear the broadcast on her radio (Toklas to Mr. Fassett, 11 June 1947).

On 29 May 1947, Thomson wrote from the Chelsea Hotel at 222 West 23rd Street,

> I have sent you by regular mail a copy of CAPITAL, CAPITALS, which is just off the press. Through some rather absurd errors at the publisher's office, the work got printed before the contract for it was even signed. But that is all right and everything is now being regularized.
>
> Carl and Bill Rogers and others, I am sure, have written you about the performance of *The Mother of Us All*. Their description of it will be more convincing than mine, which is simply that it is very beautiful all the way through from every point of view. The performance of *Four Saints*, which I conducted last Sunday on the radio, was successful also. So much so that I have been invited to record selections from it, amounting to 45 minutes, which is more than half of the whole, for the Victor Company. I shall do this with the same singers and chorus during the last week of June, but the records will not be available commercially for about another year. This is the normal time lag now in the issuing of "serious" music. I must also prepare both the opera scores for the printer, and I have commissions for two orchestral works. All that makes a very busy summer, and so I have reluctantly decided not to go to Paris. I am more regretful than I can say and I am sure you understand how regretful I am that I shall have to delay playing and singing for you the new piece. I shall send a recording of it by the next passenger who seems to have a little baggage space....
>
> Lamont Johnson and his group read Gertrude's resistance play the other night, and it was delightful.[7] We all laughed a great deal and wept a great deal. It is a beautiful play. If New York were not in such a senseless mood these days it would be produced, and it would be successful....
>
> What is your wish about future contracts for publication and performance? (1) Shall I continue to negotiate them with Mrs. Bradley or may I consider Carl's signature as final? (I always submit them to him anyway). (2) Are all moneys invariably to be sent to you through Mrs. Bradley whether or not she has been involved as an agent in the contract?
>
> I am terribly sorry I shall not be seeing you as soon as I had counted on. Always affectionately and yours, Virgil

---

7. *Yes is For a Very Young Man.*

At her husband's death in 1939, Jenny Bradley had taken over the agency and become Stein's agent (see Stein [19 Mar. 1946]). She now represented Toklas. On 2 July 1947, Toklas replied to Thomson,

> About your not coming over I'm more disappointed than I can say. I wanted to see you and to hear the music. Looking forward à ces evenements[8] was so comforting and here you are withdrawing them. Why don't you come in September—which is Paris' nicest month. About contracts naturally anything Carl will do is alright—otherwise it goes through Mrs. Bradley. There must be no loose words for A[llan]. Stein to pick up or unravel because he knows and cares for nothing about anything of Gertrude's works—their publication or production. So be assured Mrs. Bradley will be ready to cooperate with you without any delays. I got Capital Capitals and thank you for that too. . . . Should you hear any rumours that Gertrude and I were Christian Scientists please deny them.

Despite Thomson saying that he would not return to Paris that summer, he did, and several times visited Toklas.

In the autumn of 1947, she learned that Picasso's portrait of Stein, which Stein had willed to the Metropolitan Museum in New York, was being sent, she thought sold, to the Museum of Modern Art. She posted a flurry of letters protesting this flaunting of Stein's wishes. Partly to reassure her, Thomson wrote on 2 November 1947,

> I have finished correcting all the proof of The Mother score and now it will be coming out. The N.Y production is still hanging fire but there will be one in Baltimore anyway. That seems to be certain. . . . The test pressings of 4 *Saints* records are very good from every point of view and sensationally clear as to words. I saw a copy of the letter you received from the Metropolitan. [Alfred] Barr & Lincoln K.[9] & Mrs [Emily Chadbourne] Crane all spoke to me about your letters and Barr said later that he had taken my suggestion and written you a long, complete explanation. It seems there was no sale of the portrait, only a ten-year loan. (The Met does sell, however.) The Met wants the portrait but has no proper place to hang it till they start a 20th century room. They have made a deal to buy 20th century pictures from the Modern Museum and elsewhere and presumably by 1955 or 1960 there will be a 20th century painting in the Met and permanently hung. At present the portrait has been hanging in the main lobby and attracting much favourable comment. I think it also went on tour. Barr thinks that if you insist the Met will keep the portrait though maybe not always hang it. He would like to use it, of course, but not against your

---

8. *à ces evenements*: to these events.
9. Lincoln Kirstein: Harvard graduate, writer, editor, ballet impresario, and friend of Thomson.

wishes. The deal between the two museums (plus the Whitney) seems to be fairly elaborate but all the museum and gallery people approve of it. It is an attempt to make the M.M. a sort of Luxembourg and the Met (with luck) a Louvre. Getting Gertrude and Picasso into such a Louvre, or rather keeping them there, is not impossible, apparently, though the local museum people would all prefer waiting ten years. Don't accept the present arrangement unless you approve of it. Insistence will probably have some effect. Affection always, Virgil.

Toklas replied that she had received "a long pleasant letter from Barr" but was still "furiously angry" though she didn't "know in what direction to break out again." But she was grateful to Thomson, "very grateful indeed" (20 November 1947). She added praise for his book, *The State of Music*, for saying "a lot of important things . . . that belong to what Gertrude used to call the common knowledge which only the wise know - the sage and the old woman in the village. Go on dear Virgil and give us more." Thomson had told her that he is writing a new book, his third, *The Art of Judging Music* (1948).

On 20 November 1947, she asked about *The Mother of Us All*, "Who and how and where are and is the production of Thmoua in Baltimore. I've not given up hope for one in N.Y. though I'm not likely to get over to see it. It would be so perfect if I did." She added, "The Sherry Mangan lunched with me – he's deliciously like the one I used to know in S. Francisco who came back from China – gun running or other wise – romantic rather than adventuresome – sentimental rather than experienced. enfin[10] delicious rather than adorable." Thomson replied on 31 December:

> The Baltimore project blew up because the ladies who found themselves raising money for our opera were unable to make either Gertrude's name or mine unloose the purse strings of that city. So Dr. Lert, the German director of the enterprise, resigned; and now Baltimore has no opera for this season. It is a little like the story of *Four Saints* in Darmstadt.[11] There are other propositions, however, and Mrs. Payne is still saying that she is going to produce the work.
>
> I have made efforts to send you cigarettes. The first one failed. The second is supposed to have succeeded. If it has really succeeded you will receive a carton every week or so. Please let me know the result so that I can take other measures if the present manoeuvre is not satisfactory.
>
> I have written an orchestral piece that is a view of the Seine at night from in front of my house on the Quai Voltaire. The Kansas City orchestra ordered a piece and so I thought it most appropriate that since

---

10. *enfin*: in short.
11. See the letters of Thomson to Stein [4 July 1929], [11 May 1930], and [9 August 1930].

I had written so much music about Kansas City for Paris, I would write about Paris for Kansas City.[12] Now I am about to do a film that deals with Cajuns and the Bayou country. It is a very beautiful film.[13] The opera is now published and you should be receiving your copy. Please tell me everything you think about it as a volume.

My mother has been visiting me for three weeks. She spent Christmas with me and it was all very pleasant indeed. One of the smart aleck friends asked her what she thought of Miss Stein's writing and she replied: "I like it very much when it is intended to be understood. When it is not intended to be understood I do not always understand it."

My new book and Maurice's will both be out on the 16th of February.[14] I was made a member the other day of the National Institute of Arts and Letters. New York is in the middle of a huge snowstorm. I hope you have not been too cold in Paris this winter. If you do get cold please come and visit me. Let me know when the tea runs out, so that I can send you more. There is plenty of everything here and I should be unhappy to think you needed or wanted anything there that I could send you.

I have the test pressings of our *Four Saints* records and they are quite wonderful. I have not heard such good choral diction before on discs. Every word is clear. I am having a busy winter and not an unpleasant one. If the opera is not produced again this year I am sure that it will be done next. Interest in it has neither grown nor diminished. We shall see soon what difference publication makes.

Always devotedly,

Virgil

I miss you.

On 15 January 1948, she wrote, hoping, as Lincoln Kirstein had indicated, that *The Mother* would be performed in New York on election night—"wouldn't Gertrude have liked that." She was eagerly anticipating the resolution of legal tangles that were inhibiting Van Vechten in his distribution of Stein's literary property and looked forward to Thomson's and Grosser's new books, and to receiving the opera, published by Music Press. She wished Thomson well with the music he was writing for the movie, and told him, "Your mother on Gertrude's work is delightful and so right. You know Gertrude said it was the young and the old who understood

---

12. *The Seine at Night*, for orchestra, eight minutes long, completed 31 Dec. 1947, dedicated to the Kansas City Philharmonic Orchestra.
13. *Louisiana Story* (1948), directed by Robert Flaherty.
14. Maurice Grosser, *Painting in Public* (New York: Knopf, 1948).

what she was doing - the young because they were alive and without parti pris[15] and the old because having thrown their prejudice over board on the voyage they once more became alive."

He wrote on 28 January:

> I am terribly sorry the first two efforts to send you cigarettes did not succeed. The third try, now in operation, may. Please let me know within a week or so whether you have them. *The Mother of Us All*, according to Lincoln Kirstein and Mrs. [Barbara] Payne, will be produced next November in New York. Meanwhile, Leland Stanford University will do it in San Francisco in March, Tulane University in New Orleans in April, and probably Syracuse University in May. Lincoln is dickering with Freddy Ashton to direct the New York production. My book and Maurice's have both been sent to you. You should have received the *Mother* score by now. If it is really true that the opera is to be produced in New York for the first of November, I shall not go abroad this summer. I shall have to stay here and get the *Four Saints* score ready for the printer and tend to other unfinished musical work during the first part of the summer. During the last part I shall have to be casting the opera, because we must start rehearsals on October first. That is all the news I have just now.
>
> Always affectionately,
>
> Virgil

She responded a month later:

> Everything has come—it is all beautiful—your book and Maurice's—the opera and the snow—and all cooked in butter as you once said[16]—your book has made [me] so happy—the Harvard lecture—a line or two here and there in the concert articles and then all through the thoughts in season are treasures of aesthetic wisdom—not only applicable to music but so true and deeply felt that they apply to painting perfectly.[17] . . . why not a small volume of nuggets. do think of it—no one can do it any more and the young flounder—so it's up to you to help them—of course you always see clearly but this time you've struck gold—such treasures—. . . . Is the opera going on in November—Is it to be played in S. Francisco. . . . The opera is beautifully presented—the pages are of a delicacy—an exquisiteness not usual in a page of printed music—someone will frame one some day.

15. *parti pris*: prejudice.
16. See Thomson 6 May [1927] and Stein [9 July 1927].
17. "Thoughts in Season" is the title of Part VI, the final section of the book. It contains essays on such topics as "Repertory," "Program Notes," "The Piano," "The Violin," "The Great Tradition," "Radio is Chamber Music," "Surrealism in Music," "French Rhythm," "Americanisms," and "Modernism Today."

A friend agreed to play it for her, she said, "but it wont be your presentation." She sent "a thousand thanks" for cigarettes and urged him to come to Paris (26 February 1948). He replied on 4 March 1948:

> I am delighted you like my book. . . . I have made another effort to send you cigarettes. The aviator who tried a month or so ago was arrested at Orly. Now Madame Lew has gone to Paris and assures me she will communicate with you. Other friends leaving this spring will do what they can, and Mrs Rogers will continue her efforts. It is extraordinary the way everything has missed fire. At present I am not planning to come abroad this summer. I should love to have a visit with you but I know now that I do not get much music written as a travelling reporter. So I say to myself, as I did last year, that I am not going abroad. The opera projects are exactly where they were when I wrote you before. Perhaps I can persuade you to come over next fall if it is really going to be done properly. Beecham, who was here a few weeks ago, assures me that he will do it for the BBC in June. This is all the news I have just now. I am still writing my film score. The piece about Paris was successful in Kansas City and will be played by Stokowski at the Philharmonic in New York two weeks from now. . . . Always devotedly,
>
> Virgil

On 10 April 1948, she wrote to thank him for using as one of his cigarette couriers Mrs. Mina Curtiss, now a regular visitor:

> She is so like her handsome presence—she so completely pleases one's eyes and one's ears—I do thank you for sending her to me. She has even said she would come again. And as for your love and the cigarettes from you—I'm completely protected from all outside annoyances by the comfort of your attentions. You do know how grateful I am to you—how much I count upon you—but really really for the future there must be no materialization of your friendship—To know that you give it is to me enough and so much. . . . She brought me four of your articles which I'm going to read as soon as I've popped this into an envelope—such pleasant proof of attentiveness—touchingly old fashioned. . . .

On 11 April, she wrote of the arrival of further cigarette cartons from him through various channels: "Now that I am surrounded by the largest private collection of Picassos and cigs in Paris—we can call a halt and no matter what the future may produce there'll be no white flag for help from you—a grey one would more than supply the void—So many many thanks to you—dear Virgil." And she told the news from Paris: "the Pavlik—Charles Henri menage has broken up. Can it possibly be true. Bébé [Berard] is threatening a heavy descent upon N.Y.—an illustrated article in Life is prefacing it. I saw Sauget [sic] a moment at the mass for Max

[Jacob]—A new plan for Bernard's release but I've grown pessimistic—alas and alas—. . . Basket has rheumatism. . . . My love and my thanks to you."

Goldwyn Studios in Hollywood proposed to produce *Four Saints* on Broadway again and then to film it. Thomson and Toklas discussed this, but the proposal evaporated. On 21 April, he wrote, "our *Four Saints* records will be issued in October. That means that Music Press will get the score out for that date also. I have finished my movie [*Louisiana Story*] and will record it for the film with the Philadelphia Orchestra the day after tomorrow." On 3 May she replied, "I am so awful glad your music was so successfully recorded. You don't know how very very much I enjoy your success. It seems to be not only my own but Gertrude's too." She also wrote a letter which has not been preserved, to which Thomson replied on 2 June, 1948:

Dear Alice:

It was lovely hearing from you about the sonata, and I am delighted you like Angel.[18] The piece was written in the early part of the summer in Majorca in 1930. Later that summer I stayed with you in Bilignin, where I put Gertrude's film scenario (in French) to music which is also a portrait of Basket. Sylvia's opinion that I am coming abroad this summer is based on the fact that last summer I said I was not going but I did. . . . I do not think I will come, however. I am going to Colorado in July and August. Some lectures will pay my expenses, and I think I should enjoy a little mountain air. I should also enjoy coming to see you, but I don't think I shall be able to, because I have some work for Mrs. [Helen Rogers] Reid[19] which I shall have to do in September and I have to go to Minneapolis in early October. On July 15, Vladimir Golschmann is conducting some of my Portraits with the French National Radio Orchestra. If you are anywhere near an instrument at that time you might enjoy hearing them. "The Mother of Us All" is still hanging fire. Kirstein is active on the subject, and the City Center Opera Company is considering it. I am delighted that you don't like Bartok's music, because I don't either. Your description of it is priceless; I should like to quote it one time if you don't mind.[20] Carl

18. The sonata is Sonata No. 3: On the White Keys, composed for Stein. At the end of the manuscript, Thomson writes "Palma, July 17–18, 1930." "Angel" is probably Angel More, a character in *The Mother of Us All*, the score of which Thomson sent Toklas earlier in the year.
19. Wife of Ogden Reid, owner-publisher of *The Herald Tribune*.
20. She replies, "Too flattered that you should want to quote me on Bartok—so do—but not my name please" (14 June 1948). Toklas's description may have inspired Thomson's review of Bartók, written the following year: "The 'modern music' war was a contest over the right to enjoy discord for its own sake, for its spicy tang and for the joy it used to give by upsetting apple carts. Bartók himself, as a young man, was a spice lover but not at all an upsetter. He was a consolidator of advance rather than a pioneer. As a mature composer he came to lose his taste for paprika . . ." (*Reader* 324). The culinary metaphors suggest Toklas as Thomson's source.

tells me that Rogers's book is very fine. I sent you another small package of tea. Please don't mind, because it gives me so much pleasure. My friends have always spoiled me a little by letting me have my way and I don't like to change my habits. I am preparing *Four Saints* for the engraver now. It will be appearing in October at the same time as the records.

Love always,

Virgil

On 14 June Alice replied that she tried to listen to his portraits on Georges Maratier's radio, but failed to because Maratier was mistaken about the time of the broadcast—"so very disappointing because of my inexperienced opinion that you are the only american among the americans – painters as well as musicians—who know what the modern approach really is—bless you—Love from Alice."

On 3 July, 1948, Thomson wrote that he would be lecturing at the University of Colorado at Denver and seeing what "the Denver Univ. people do with TMOUA on the 22-3-4 of July. . . . No news of TMOUA in New York. . . . I do miss not seeing you this year. I hope that on some pretext you will go away from Paris for a moment. And I do wish you would come next winter and visit me. Always affection Virgil." On 30 July, she wrote that Bernard Faÿ's life sentence had been reduced to twenty years, making him eligible for a general amnesty should one be declared. On 7 October 1948, Thomson wrote:

The Mother of Us All I saw in Denver was just a student performance and not very well sung, except for Susan.[21] It was delightfully and ingeniously directed by one of the instructors. He had movies before the last scene, old news reels of suffragettes picketing the White House and fighting with cops and finally being allowed to vote. That got him over a difficult scene change in a way that I found not at all offensive. There were four performances and everybody in the audience seemed to understand it all perfectly. Stravinsky came and was delighted. You should be receiving a check shortly for the author's rights. If you do not, please let me know. I know nothing about the production last spring in Tulane University in New Orleans except that it was done and seems to have been enjoyed. Leland Stanford [University] changed its mind and did not do the work but says it plans to do it next year. So, I believe, does Western Reserve College in Cleveland, Ohio. My movie is running and being successful. All the press is raves. You will be invited to some kind of private showing in Paris. I have written the proper people telling them that you would probably enjoy seeing it if

---

21. The opera was produced by the Fine Art Department. Thomson saw two of the four performances given (Thomson to Murray D. Morrison, 23 September 1948).

such a showing is given. We did well at the Edinburgh Festival, too, and won a prize in Venice. . . . Jacques Faÿ's son, Michel, gave us all, through his father, the appeal that Bernard's lawyer had made in getting his sentence reduced. I cannot see that for all the foolish things he did, he caused anybody to get hurt. The Sorbonne denunciations like the Masonic business and his handling of the library staff, were unutterably stupid; but the way he managed to appear so consistently in wolf's clothing without causing any harm to anybody makes it clear to me that he was not doing wrong. But O, how he did love seeming to do the wrong thing.

Always affectionately.

Virgil

On 10 January 1949, Toklas wrote:

Dear Virgil

There is so much I have to thank you for and for so long a time that at once I throw myself upon your generosity—perhaps too confidently but with a fair hope that youll understand and forgive. Still under the spell of hearing the records played last night for the first time—of the perfection of the recording—of your masterly conducting—of the beauty of so much of the music that the performances at Chicago had not revealed.[22] I hasten to send you my new appreciation—gratitude felicitations—thinking of you a great deal—talking to Mrs Curtiss who has told me all the beauty of your Louisiana Story—it is only now that the realization of the great importance of your music—always respected is now certain to me. It's quite a possession and I'm proud of you. Bless you Virgil dear—Mrs. Curtiss is so very kind to me. She comes to see me and I enjoy her immensely—her dusky voice—her warmth and abundance—her physical presence. her beautiful ears—how Gertrude would have loved them. Isnt her book an achievement—no sense of translation and her notes are rich.[23] She should publish books and books of notes—such a chronicle as no one else has the love of the material and the self effacement to make. I like your friends. [Edwin] Denby comes to see me when he's in Paris—he wanders about a good deal in a detached way with a most attaching sweetness. There is no news of Bernard but every one is predicting a general amnesty for this year and now that his sentence has been reduced he would be included in it. Can it be possible—The cold dark winter

22. This is the recording of most of *Four Saints* to which Thomson refers above in his letter of 29 May 1947. It was made on 7 June 1947 and has been reissued on CD by BMG, Classics World, RCA Victor, 09026-68163-2.
23. *Letters of Marcel Proust*, trans. and ed. with notes Mina Curtiss (New York: Random House, 1949).

weather makes one less hopeful—spring still four months off . . . Love from Alice

Bernard Faÿ was denied an amnesty. In an undated letter, Toklas wrote that she was "completely upset" at the "verdict . . . it is too horrible." She asked whether it was time for the intervention of Thomson's friend, the powerful French attorney, Suzanne Blum, and added, "I am completely unnerved."

On 10 March 1949, Thomson wrote:

Dear Alice:

I heard *The Mother of Us All* in Cleveland. It was a big stylish opera house with lots of boxes and sixty men in the pit. All that was most elegant. The singers, college students, were a little immature, a little feeble for so grand a format. The whole effort, however, was better than what a university commonly can do. Barbara Payne went out to hear it. She is still thinking she might produce it in New York, if and when she finds the money. So far, that is still if and when. Beecham wrote that he was going to do it at the BBC in May and then that he wasn't. It seems to have been turned down by some music committee, the grounds given being that it is too hard to run up quickly. That is not Beecham's opinion, and he is the one who would have to do the running up.

Picasso was elected lately a corresponding member of the National Institute of Arts and Letters, along with Bernard Shaw, T.S. Eliot and divers other foreign artists. I went to some trouble about this, because some of the older members had political objections to him, thought he was still a Communist.[24] Now, of course, he refuses to answer letters and telegrams asking whether he cares to accept. He probably doesn't know what the outfit is and is waiting for someone to tell him. If you see him, will you please tell him that it is a good outfit and certainly the equal in distinction of the French Académy des Beaux Arts. Also, whether he wants to accept or not, a telegram is easy to answer.

. . . . Love always, Virgil

On 3 May 1949, Toklas wrote to congratulate Thomson on winning the Pulitzer Prize for his music for *Louisiana Story*: "This morning's news of a new honor for you is the nicest thing that has happened to me – if you permit my sharing your pleasure in it – for a long time. Its the greatest satisfaction that recognition of your music should come from so many directions and so continuously – the more the merrier and it must be

---

24. Although a multimillionaire, Picasso had become a member of the French Communist Party in 1944 and certainly was "still a communist."

boring you – please just eat it with a spoon. . . . Love to you always Alice." As a celebratory present, she sent him Stein's cufflinks, and on 18 May, he replied:

> I cannot tell you how touched I am at the gift of Gertrude's cuff links. Also at your sweet letters. Mina [Curtiss] has told me. . . . that Basket is in somewhat better health. Monty Johnson tells me rehearsals are in progress for the play [*Yes is For a Very Young Man*] at the Cherry Lane Theater. Beecham did not do *The Mother*, because the BBC would not let him. If I know Beecham, he will insist and produce it eventually. I have written a sort of funeral piece for band, which I am to conduct in Central Park on June 17 at the opening of the Goldman Band concerts. Now I must do a piano sonata and finish my cello concerto. Otherwise I am deep in Bizet through the wonderful letters and manuscripts that Mina brought me. I spent three weeks in Georgia, driving with Maurice in his new car. He will drive me to the West Coast in August. All that is most agreeable. I do wish you were here and driving with us. The story of Picasso and the Institute is most entertaining and exactly as I thought it would be. If he does not answer by fall, I shall suggest that they write him, reminding that his silence means refusal and expressing regret. I do not think I shall be coming abroad this year, though a brief visit with you in September is tempting. It is a pleasure that Mina is back. She really is a delight to all of us. She is staying in New York awhile because her mother is not well. Mrs. Bradley is here too, but I have not seen her. Avery Claflin and his wife are in Paris and I have suggested you might like to see them. They will be seeing Bernard [Faÿ]'s brother, of course.[25] I hope you will go to the country some. You should not stay in town all year.
>
> Love always,
>
> Virgil

On 21 June, 1949, he wrote about having seen the New York production of Stein's resistance play, *Yes is For a Very Young Man:*

> I presume Carl [Van Vechten] or Lamont [Johnson] has sent you the press on the play, but here it is all over again. It was beautifully presented and very moving. I wept a great deal, and so did many other people, because the story and people are terribly touching. Two of the roles, Denise and Henri, were particularly well played; and Lamont's directing of everything was not at all lacking in subtlety. I am sure the play will be produced constantly. This is all for just now. I shall write you again a little later. I am reading the *Faust* play over and

---

25. The Claflin and Faÿ families were linked since Claflin's father had been friends with Bernard Faÿ during World War I.

over. Mina tells me I shall have to read Goethe in order to understand it. I suppose that wouldn't be a bad idea.

Love, Virgil

He was considering composing music for *Doctor Faustus Lights the Lights*, a libretto that Stein wrote for Lord Berners, who did not set it to music (see note to Stein, 27 June 1938) and has now died. Toklas replied, "No don't take on Goethe's Faust—if you want one Marlowe's would have been Gertrude's choice and certainly more to your taste" (2 August 1949). Later, she added: "Gertrude didn't intend it to be danced—but there is a good deal of ballet introduced—. . . . You cant half fancy what a satisfaction to me that you were thinking of doing the Faustus—dont take the time to think that if anything I could say to make the Faust legend and Gertrude's version more understandingly sympathetic to you it wouldnt have been said long ago—as Carl would say you will probably do it some day. But of course you might do it in my day—this with no hint of teasing or pressure—just with a sigh" (13 August 1950). On 18 June 1949, Toklas wrote that prizes for his music delighted her and mentioned a visit by one of his friends, "a strange old youth" John Cage, whose "not so amiable weaknesses"[26] she forgave, she said, "when he spoke of your music and its influence." Aaron Copland visited, "less approachable than I remembered," and "Freddie" Bowles[27], who "told me what you had been and done for

---

26. On 13 July 1950, she remembered Cage as "very boring—he and his mechanized pianos." His visit to her was facilitated by Thomson, who wrote in a review in the *Herald Tribune* of 22 January 1945:

> Mr. Cage has carried Schönberg's twelve-tone harmonic maneuvers to their logical conclusion. He has produced atonal music not by causing the twelve tones of the chromatic scale to contradict one another consistently but by eliminating, to start with, all sounds of precise pitch. He substitutes for the classical chromatic scale a gamut of pings, plucks, and delicate thuds that is both varied and expressive and that is different in each piece. By thus getting rid, at the beginning, of the constricting element in atonal writing—which is the necessity of taking constant care to avoid making classical harmony with a standardized palette of instrumental sounds and pitches that exists primarily for the purpose of producing such harmony—Mr. Cage has been free to develop the rhythmic element of composition, which is the weakest element in the Schönbergian style, to a point of sophistication unmatched in the technique of any other living composer.
>
> His continuity devices are chiefly those of the Schönberg school. There are themes and sometimes melodies, even, though these are limited, when they have real pitch, to the range of a fourth, thus avoiding the tonal effect of dominant and tonic. All these appear in augmentation, diminution, inversion, fragmentation, and the various kinds of canon. That these procedures do not take over a piece and become its subject, or game, is due to Cage's genius as a musician. He writes music for expressive purposes; and the novelty of his timbres, the logic of his discourse, are used to intensify communication, not as ends in themselves. His work represents, in consequence, not only the most advanced methods now in use anywhere but original musical expression of the very highest poetic quality.

27. Stein dubbed Paul Bowles "Freddy" (his middle name was Frederick) when they met in 1931. In 1947 Bowles composed *Letter to Freddy*, featuring the text of an early Stein letter she sent him.

him and that was a pleasure—Hasn't he satisfactorily become adult—which we used to fear he never might." Mrs. Curtiss had written that Thomson was considering composing a light opera to a play by Georges Feydeau (1862–1921), so Toklas sent him her copy, though his comedies "seemed of inappropriate length for your use. I don't quite see Feydeau and music—unless you have something up your sleeve—which of course you have but does it include music to Feydeau—If it does it only proves me to be wrong in that but not in you." She was not wrong in that.

On 13 October, 1950, she wrote that Yale University Press is agreeing to publish all Stein's unpublished manuscripts, "such overwhelming good news. . . . It's a miracle and I'm endlessly satisfied that I've hung on to know it. The first volume to appear a year from now—What this would have meant to Gertrude you more than anyone can appreciate." On 24 January 1951, he wrote:

Dear Alice:

Mina Curtiss is back and tells me that you love me in spite of my silence of the last few months. I was rather waiting, as a matter of fact, to hear from you whether Suzanne Blum's announced manoeuvre would come to anything. Meanwhile the Harvard petition did not. I had a touching Christmas card from Bernard in prison. Also, Avery loaned me the manuscript Bernard had written. That is the first extended evidence I have had about the state of his mind. I find him a little bitter, as is natural, but not unduly so.

You are angelic to go to hear my music and to write me about it. The Yale Library is having an exhibit of Gertrude's manuscripts next month, and I have promised to make a speech. The director wanted me to talk about Gertrude as I knew her, and he wanted to publish the lecture, along with some others. I replied that I did not wish to use my friendship as subject matter for anything at all but that I would gladly explain our collaboration on two operas, provided it was not to be printed. He accepted my conditions, and so I am speaking on February 27, looking forward to great pleasure in doing so and seeing the collection.

I gave the *Faust* libretto to Freddie Ashton, who immediately invented lovely ways of handling the movement in it, particularly with the dog. His easy approach has simplified the whole matter somewhat in my mind, so that now I think I may be able to make music for it. In any case, I am going to try. I have no very definite plan about going to Europe this summer, but I do want to see you and so I think I probably will. I don't know whether I shall come early in the summer or late. I doubt if I shall stay very long.

. . . Beyond all this, there is no news. I have not written any music all winter. As always happens in such a case, I have imagined myself far busier than if I had been really working. All the same, my love is ever yours, Virgil

Toklas asked for a copy of his Yale talk and said that "The catalogue is like a story to me of those forty happy years" (7 March 1951). That summer, Thomson decided against composing the music for *Doctor Faustus*—a decision that was for Toklas "a constant and increasing disappointment" (9 December 1951). Carl Van Vechten then contracted with Meyer Kupferman to compose the music, as Kupferman eventually did but failed to mount a production. Years later Thomson changed his mind and attempted legally to wrestle from Kupferman rights to compose his own score to Stein's libretto. He again gave up on the idea but largely because of Kupferman's legal insistence on being paid a percentage of Thomson's profits.

After receiving a copy of his latest book, Toklas wrote on 27 March, 1951:

Often I've regretted that it is the N. York Times and not the Herald Tribune that is sent me—for what wouldnt I give to be awakened and enlivened by your articles. But now that Music Right and Left has come and having them concentrated by your choice I'm almost reconciled to having waited. For its an immense pleasure to get such an abundance of your best. It's a shame and pity Gertrude did not know your writing and particularly at this height. She would have delighted in France at its best—Gloomy Masterpiece—Atonality and On Being American[28]—and not because of their subjects. They have a poise of breathlessness that make them clear and convincing—Je vous felicite[29]—Monsieur. And thanks and thanks again for the titles—your sweet dedication and the gift of the book.

On 12 April 1951, he wrote:

I am terribly disappointed about the Presidential rebuff regarding Bernard. According to Avery Claflin, the request for pardon had reached that level when the Grand Rabbi of Paris intervened. I don't know how correct this report is. If so, that is where Suzanne Blum should have been on the job. I am still hoping, or intending, to come and see you. My present plan is for the end of summer. At the beginning, next month in fact, I shall go to the country and start getting some work done. I have travelled like mad this winter; and I have corrected proof on a great many orchestral scores, because all my early works are now coming into print. But I have not written any music. Shortly I shall change all that.

28. Toklas refers to chapters in Thomson's book, ambiguously in her reference to "Atonality," since the book includes "Atonality Today (I)" and "Atonality Today (II)."
29. *Je vous felicite*: I congratulate you.

"Capital, Capitals" is to be given in concert about May 10. I shall rehearse that; and if I have singers that I like, I shall record it for Columbia. I am going to try to use colored people again, because they sing English so very very prettily.[30] Also because they love Gertrude and don't resist her.

Carl has asked me to do a preface for the second volume of Gertrude's miscellaneous writings. That is another reason for coming to see you, because I could not do it without you. I should like to know, as nearly as possible, the date and occasion of the pieces in the book. I do not have ambitions toward "explaining" Gertrude completely, but I could not say anything sensible at all about any writings of hers without knowing when, where and, if possible, why it was written.

My speech at Yale seems to have been successful. The hall was crowded, which means about 800 people, and most enthusiastic. I had not prepared anything, not even an outline. I merely said that I had no intention of giving them a complete picture, but that I was delighted to tell them about the circumstances of our collaboration. Then I recounted how and why I had put to music texts of Gertrude's, what our conversations had been regarding the two operas and what we had said to each other about them. Naturally this procedure gave a more vivid picture of Gertrude than I could have made by attempting a general portrait. I talked rapidly for over an hour and answered questions for about half an hour. The young people asked very intelligent questions. The museum directors seem to consider my speech the most interesting of the three. I am sorry that I did not hear the others. Pavlik, it seems, read his and could not always be heard. Nobody told me what [James] Laughlin was like at all. The exhibition was very pretty, and I was delighted to see some photographs and early portraits of Gertrude that I had not known. I was very happy about the whole occasion, and everybody else seemed to feel that way too. A number of people had come from Hartford and from New York.

On 17 August 1951, Toklas wrote, giving him news of the present whereabouts of Picasso, Hugnet, Cocteau, said she has been taken by friends to the opera but that she would rather have heard "your piano studies played by you—That's what it is to have one's friends three thousand kilometres away away—so far away."

30. Thomson felt entirely vindicated in his first casting of black singers for *Four Saints*. In a review of *Carmen Jones* on 5 December 1943, he writes: "The Negro singers, as always, make opera credible. And, as always, they make music shine. They have physical beauty of movement, natural distinction, and grace. Musically they have rhythm, real resonance, excellent pitch, perfect enunciation, and full understanding of the operatic convention. They never look bored or out of place on a stage or seem inappropriately cast for any musical style. . . . it is a contribution to the repertory of that permanent Negro opera company that is going to provide the solution one day for all our opera problems."

On 24 October, 1951, Thomson wrote to alert her to royalties owed her by the Italian Authors' Society and said:

> It is planned to produce *Four Saints* in Paris in May, probably at the Champs Elysees Theatre. I will conduct, bringing a colored troupe from here. Florine Stettheimer's sets and costumes will be reconstructed by the pious hand of Tchelitcheff, who knew her well and respected her work. I shall know in a few weeks whether Freddie Ashton will be available to do his part. The production is part of a whole festival that is being organized by Nicholas Nabokov for an institution called the International Committee for Cultural Freedom. He is in Paris now, with offices at 41 Avenue Montaigne.
>
> I have just read Sutherland's book on Gertrude.[31] It is full of fine stuff. I think he has come the closest to anyone yet to getting her right from both the inside and the outside. By outside I mean, of course, the outside of the work.
>
> This is all for now. I am busy with lots of notes, including the putting of lots of notes on paper. If you still have influence with Sainte Genevieve, I suggest a candle just to make sure that the *Four Saints* production comes through and works out.
>
> Love ever, Virgil

He also wrote, enigmatically, at the start of this letter, "I am delighted with the news about our friend"—this being Bernard Faÿ. Upset by failure to gain a pardon for him, Toklas had sold two Picassos, a large drawing and a gouache on paper, to raise funds, which she combined with money from another of Faÿ's friends[32] to hire six men who, on 30 September 1951, dressed as nuns, entered a French prison hospital from which they removed Faÿ, who then escaped to Spain and went from there to Switzerland, where he lived in Freiburg and would continue to live until being pardoned, in 1958, by the Minister of Justice, Francois Mitterrand.

On 20 November, Thomson wrote again:

> Your news is always the latest and the best that any of us here receives. You speak of seeing Francis. I suppose that is Francis Rose. If he is in Paris do give him my affectionate greetings. Mina Curtiss has been in the country all fall, is in town now, dining with me tonight. She will come to Paris in March, had planned going end of December, but her mother is not well.

---

31. Donald Sutherland, *Gertrude Stein, a Biography of her Work* (New Haven: Yale University Press, 1951).
32. The friend was a Mme Denise Aimé-Azam, author, editor, Jewish-born Catholic convert, who said that during the war, when she was obliged to wear the yellow star, Faÿ would walk with her in the streets of Paris (Malcolm 73). She had introduced to Toklas the priest who instructed her in the Catholic faith (Edward Burns, letter to Dilworth, 3 March 2007).

The Italian radio fee is being sent here in care of Carl [Van Vechten], who will send it to you. None of it belongs to me, since the broadcast was done without music. None of it would have been mine in any case, since this comes from the Authors' Society and not the musical agency.

The *Four Saints* plans advance in a way that seems favorable. I still think a candle to Ste. Genevieve not a bad investment, if and whenever you have the time. I am delighted that you have changed your housekeeping arrangements. Do please write me about all our friends whenever you see any of them or hear news.

Love ever,

Virgil

On 13 November, she expressed delight with the promise of a Paris production: "nothing as nice will happen to me again," and promised to visit St. Genevieve's shrine.

The saint delivered. So did Ethel Reiner who funded the new production of *Four Saints*, which opened on Broadway on 16 April 1952, running for two weeks to mixed reviews. Again the cast was black, most fresh from music school, including, in her first professional employment, twenty-five-year-old Leontyne Price as St. Cecilia. In June the production opened in Paris in the Champs-Elysées Theatre as part of a Twentieth Century Exposition of the Arts. Thomson conducted. Toklas attended. Reviews were mixed, those who disliked it regretted it not being like Gershwin or considered the music puerile. Toklas was overjoyed. She had the entire cast to a party in her apartment at 5 rue Christine, serving tea, punch, pastry, and four cakes which she made herself (Tommasini 422).

From then on, the correspondence between Thomson and Toklas was sparse, partly because her eyesight was so bad that she needed someone to read and, eventually, to write for her. But Thomson saw her when in Paris, which was often after he quit the *Herald Tribune* in 1954. Nevertheless, they corresponded occasionally until May 1962, when he sent her this necessarily formal letter:

Dear Alice,

Of the texts by Gertrude Stein that I have set to music, those now published as musical works are all copyright in my name and all authorship benefits from their exploitation as musical works are divided equally between her estate and myself.

There are two such pieces still unpublished and uncopyrighted as music. These are the "Film: Deux Soeurs Qui Sont Pas Soeurs" and the "Portrait of F. B."

In order to facilitate the eventual publication of these as musical works, I wonder if you will sign an agreement allowing me to enter into contracts for their musical publication, performance, recording, dramatic usage and all future exploitations as musical works. Also to take out musical copyright in my name at such time as I may see fit. I agree to equal division of all authorship benefits between myself and The Gertrude Stein Estate. Such contracts would reserve all purely literary rights to that estate and all purely musical ones to mine. Individual collections through performing-rights societies would remain, as at present, indivisible.

I should appreciate also your permission to take out copyright renewals on all our joint works in my name and all rights to re-publication under the above terms should they ever go out of print.

All the rights here granted would remain, in case of my death, the property of my estate.

If this agreement is satisfactory to you, please sign one copy of this letter and return it to me, keeping the other for yourself.

Ever devotedly yours,

Virgil Thomson

She signed and returned it.

By the summer of 1965, she was bedridden in a new apartment at 16 rue de la Convention. She had become a Catholic, Thomson thought to ensure that she would see Stein again.[33] The walls of her apartment were bare. Because she sold small Picasso sketches without getting the legal permission, as stipulated in Stein's will, Stein's nephew's widow had sued her, and the remaining pictures were entombed in the Paris Chase National Bank vault.[34] Since the litigation, Thomson had helped to administer a fund organized for her support.

He had received the first draft of the libretto for his opera *Lord Byron*. In Paris in the summer of 1965, he read it to her. She repeatedly commented, "wonderful" but added that "it would be hard to add music to a text so complete in every way."[35] The librettist, Jack Larson, was a poet and playwright who had acted the role of Jimmy Olsen in the *Superman* television series, a role he was reticent about because people tended to

---

33. Virgil Thomson in conversation with Dilworth.
34. Marginal note by Janet Flanner on Jack Larson, "The Keeper of the Rose," a memoir of his visits with Toklas, 1972, typescript, in possession of Larson.
35. Virgil Thomson to Larson, July 1965, quoted by Larson, in possession of Larson, typescript.

identify him with it.[36] He had long admired Stein's writing, so Thomson arranged for him to meet Toklas in October in Paris. Larson phoned and she said, "I'm very old. I'm on my back in bed. Heaven knows what can happen. Tomorrow is Saturday. Can you come at four?" He did, and found her frail but alert and with perfect memory. When he told her how privileged he felt to meet her, she protested, "I'm just a bag of potatoes. They carried me to the hospital like a bag of potatoes, then moved me here like a bag of potatoes. They keep poking me about just so. A bag of potatoes. I've realized that's all I ever was. All I ever did was work to manage the household so that Gertrude didn't have to sell any paintings." She liked Larson. He told her that Thomson was writing his autobiography and said he had read the early chapters and how like its author in tone they were. He visited her twice more. During one of his visits, she confided to him that she and Thomson had not been such good friends when Stein was alive, "But since Gertrude died, he's been one of the best friends to me. I know why too. He's repaying me for what Gertrude did for him."

After his return to New York, Larson received a note from Toklas, in which she enquired of Thomson's autobiography, "How is the book on Gertrude coming along."[37]

She died on 7 March 1967 at the age of eighty-nine and was buried beside Stein in Père Lachaise Cemetery, her name and dates inscribed on the back of Stein's memorial so as not to distract those visiting to pay homage to Stein.

Thomson was inducted into the French Legion of Honor in 1973. He received a Kennedy Honors Award for lifetime achievement in 1983 and a National Music Council Award for distinguished service to American music in 1984. On 18 January 1987, at the age of ninety-one, he died in bed at his apartment in the Chelsea Hotel.

36. *Lord Byron* and Thomson's discovery of Larson had their beginnings in the initial production of *Four Saints*. Immediately after its success, Thomson had considered setting to music Stein's *Byron a Play* (1933), but eventually decided not to. Twenty years later, Gore Vidal suggested he write an opera on Byron. Thomson asked him to write the libretto, but Vidal was unable to. In Los Angeles, John Houseman (theatrical director of *Four Saints*) had seen and liked very much a verse play entitled *The Candied House*, written by Jack Larson and produced at the urging of the New York poet Frank O'Hara. It was a great critical success. Houseman told Thomson about it and its author. Thomson became acquainted with Larson, read his plays, liked them, asked him to write the libretto, and Larson wrote it (Larson in conversation with Dilworth, 15 May, 4 June 2007).

37. The quotations of Toklas here and in the paragraph above are recorded by Larson, typescript, in possession of Larson.

Appendix A
"Virgil Thomson"

by Georges Hugnet
translated by Basil Kingstone

What won our hearts in the negro songs was their purity, simplicity and grandeur, a wonderful new lyricism. What lessons in poetry they give us, which nobody has yet learned from. All those who have tackled negro art (except Picasso and Tristan Tzara) have failed: they've appealed to a taste for exoticism.

I find these qualities: purity, simplicity etc. (not to mention the science of counterpoint which we find in some negro tunes) in the music of Virgil Thomson. I enjoy finding them mingled with the eternal rhythms of popular songs, Sunday hymns, children's songs and dances. Obviously Virgil Thomson doesn't set out to mingle these things. But his mind has these qualities, and his music is clear and cheerful, and makes one's skin feel good. It's a sort of sunshine therapy. His immense purity allowed him to set to music the poems of the Duchesse de Rohan, that Douanier Rousseau of poetry, as well as our *Berceau Gertrude Stein* and those *Four Poems* which a friend of ours so aptly nicknamed the "Gregorian Waltz," a name which gives a very accurate idea of the accompanying music. All the more accurate because Virgil Thomson knows Gregorian chant and all church music extremely well and is consciously or unconsciously inspired by it.

His music accompanies the poems. It remains an independent work, the whole forms a work composed of two distinct contributions and yet is one work. I have never met a musician less given to obscuring the poet's intentions. On the contrary, he highlights them. He puts his magical rose, forever fresh, in the poem's buttonhole. I cannot read the Duchesse de Rohan's poems, or mine, without humming the music, any more than I can imagine children's rhymes like "Malbrouck" or "Maman, les petits bateaux" without music.

As for the influence of Gregorian chant, one can feel it, but always just in the background, especially in certain prose pieces by Gertrude Stein which

Virgil Thomson set to music and in an opera he wrote with her. Gregorian chant is his base and background. On it he indulges in all sorts of fantasies and enchantments. It's a stream which has found its countryside and runs into it with joyful laughter.

I am only speaking here of Virgil Thomson's recent works. In the concert he gave recently, the program combined new works with older ones. Thus one could see his evolution, from the *Church Sonata* whose sure and precise skill I admired, to the *Capital Capitals*, a long rapid musical stream, the flow of a splendidly clear torrent, via the *Song of Solomon*, great and lean, and the *Variations and fugues* in which the organ played virtuoso-style with the luminous, almost childlike choruses of the American popular hymns.

Perhaps I am biased, but I enjoyed less the "modern music," full of dissonances, whose charm is worn out for us. But I respect the wonderful artistic skill it demonstrates. Virgil Thomson has done better things than that. His field is his own and it is an Elysian field, Erik Satie's garden. *Capital Capitals* and all Virgil Thomson's tunes offer us something very new and mark a new way of writing.

Postscript

VIRGIL THOMSON, OR THE DANCING MASTER

Virgil Thomson doesn't *write* music. When he's lying down, the music in his head becomes a bee, a hive, then honey. And here comes music to make us dance and dance, to make angels and negroes dance, poets and firemen, little girls in white dresses and ladies with lorgnettes, to make little boarding school girls dance in the streets and sea anemones, fish, shells and little painted houses dance by the seaside, to make stars and slightly red-faced boys dance, to make big blue flowers dance in an endless uniformly white meadow, and olive trees dance in a valley, and up the trees a whole race of tiny people climb to the edge of the leaves, where the ladybirds fly away, and cry out "Virgil Thomson, Virgil Thomson. . . ."

Pagany, a Native Quarterly, 1 no. 1 (Winter 1930), 37–38.

Appendix B
Miss Gertrude Stein as a Young Girl for Violin Alone
by Virgil Thomson

14 October 1928

5. Manuscript score of Virgil Thomson's portrait, "Miss Gertrude Stein as a Young Girl" (Appendix B)

5. Manuscript score of Virgil Thomson's portrait, "Miss Gertrude Stein as a Young Girl" (Appendix B)

Appendix C
"Virgil Thomson"

by Gertrude Stein

Yes ally. As ally. Yes ally yes as ally. A very easy failure takes place. Yes ally. As ally. As ally yes a very easy failure takes place. Very good. Very easy failure takes place. Yes very easy failure takes place.

When with a sentence of intended they were he was neighbored by a bean.

Hour by hour counts.

How makes a may day.

Our comes back back comes our.

It is with a replica of seen. That he was neighbored by a bean.

Which is a weeding, weeding a walk, walk may do done delight does in welcome. Welcome daily is a home alone and our in glass turned around. Lain him. Power four lower lay lain as in case, of my whether ewe lain or to less. What was obligation furnish furs fur lease release in dear. Dear darken. It never was or with a call. My waiting. Remain remark taper or tapestry stopping stopped with a lain at an angle colored like make it as stray. Did he does he was or will well and dove as entail cut a pursuit purpose demean different dip in descent diphthong advantage about their this thin couple a outer our in glass pay white. What is it he admires. Are used to it. Owned when it has. For in a way. Dumbfounded. A cloud in superior which is awake a satisfy found. What does it matter as it happens. Their much is a nuisance when they gain as well as own. How much do they like why were they anxious. None make wishing a pastime. When it is confidence in offer which they came. How ever they came out. Like it. All a part. With known. But which is mine. They may. Let us need partly in case. They are never selfish.

These quotations determine that demonstration is arithmetic with laying very much their happening that account in distance day main lay coupled in coming joined. Barred harder. Very fitly elephant. How is it that it has come to pass. Whenever they can take into account. More of which that whatever they are later. Then without it be as pleases. In reflection their told. Made mainly violet in a man. Comfort in our meshes. Without any habit to have called Howard louder. That they are talkative. Most of all rendered. In a mine of their distention. Resting without referring. Just as it is. Come for this lain will in might it have taught as a dustless redoubt where it is heavier than a chair. How much can sought be ours. Wide or leant be beatific very preparedly in a covering now. It is always just as lost.

Harden as wean does carry a chair intake of rather with a better coupled just as a ream.

How could they know that it had happened.

If they were in the habit of not liking one day. By the time they were started. For the sake of their wishes. As it is every once in a while. Liking it for their sake made as it is.

Their is no need of liking their home.

Dix Portraits (Paris: Editions de la Montagne, 1930), 27–28.

Appendix D
Life of Gertrude Stein

by Georges Hugnet
translated by Basil Kingstone

Gertrude Stein was born in America, in Allegheny, Pennsylvania. I'd have liked her to be born while her parents were away, or to be born somewhere else, or to be born in Alleghany while her parents were travelling in Austria. Alas, she was born there because her parents were there at that time.

She spent her youth at Radcliffe College (the women's college at Harvard) in Cambridge, Massachusetts and later obtained her doctorate in medicine, counselled by William James, under whom she studied psychology. At John Hopkins University, Baltimore, Maryland, she wrote a thesis on the anatomy of the brain and another thesis on automatic writing. Soon after that she gave up medicine and psychology and at that time, in 1903, came to live in Paris and has never left it since. At once she began to write and in Montmartre she got to know Picasso, Matisse, Apollinaire, Max Jacob and later Juan Gris, In 1926 she lectured at Oxford, Cambridge, London.

I forgot to say that Gertrude Stein owns the finest Picassos in the world.

I also forgot to say that she has a Ford she calls Godiva.

ROSE IS A ROSE

Gertrude Stein was the only person in America to make the effort made in every country and every part of art by many poets and writers, this effort towards a complete and absolute liberation of thoughts and of the words used to express them, and in her are combined names we admire.

Her juvenilia, her early work, are a first step, soon taken and put behind her; other problems concern her and she soon gives up her early style. The language people use to speak, describe, deny and confess seems to her a device from which one can derive something else besides mere thought, something other than more or less musical sounds, namely a multiple thought which branches like a tree, and sounds which have their own independent life and a whole swarming activity of consonants and vowels, which are ordered according to special laws and logic.

After freeing herself from thought, Gertrude Stein wants to get rid of words and their all too ordinary rules. And I was not at all surprised to find out recently that she studied grammar thoroughly and felt that now she knew it well enough to be able to do without it.

Gertrude Stein's effort in English, be it said, is considerably different from what has been attempted in French. I don't think there can be any comparison. I know that all comparisons are senseless, but I would have liked to give some idea of Gertrude Stein's work, which so far has not been translated*, by means of a clever equivalence, defining the unknown by the known. No doubt the result she has achieved is impossible in French and we would have to invent words in order to do what she has done. I am also afraid that with Gertrude Stein more than with other writers, translation would be a betrayal.

There is in her prose a music with a meaning, a life, a thought. It isn't that stupid music we find in French poetry, that sickly-sweet harmony, that short well-balanced rhythm. It's a great river with a continuous current, a force swelling, advancing, cascading, which meets no obstacle, it's a multiple thought which comes towards you and swamps you. Every word is born, lives, a fearsome insect whose mysterious and intense life we know nothing of, which mingles its adventure with the other adventures of the other words.

In French there is a mine yet to be discovered: the simple lyricism of life, everyday sentences, thoughts of innocent people and children, their songs and games . . . But it's a dangerous and difficult game: the idea is not to imitate, or write popular poetry or building superintendent's gossip—the idea is to invent. Gertrude Stein borrows from conversations, proverbs and sayings, songs and games, their surprising true emotion, their dazzling light. She utters precepts respected by innocent people and children, birds and butterflies . . .

I don't think she chooses her thoughts, her rhythms, her words, or puts them in order or arranges them. Everything about her work seems to disprove that. And I can't help admiring the power of her vocabulary and the way she avoids poetic words and thus all facile poetry. Gertrude Stein writes, thinks, mingles irony with drama, the chaste with the obscene, she mixes it all up and it all stays clear and transparent. She describes little girls, flowers and houses, she repeats herself, contradicts herself, denies, affirms, describes. She paints portraits and for that purpose gives complete freedom to little men who come and go and organize the game; the portrait is lifelike, it speaks like a music box.

***

Gertrude Stein writes with several pens and heeds Godiva's advice.

In Spain once, wearing violet and her hands covered with rings, Gertrude Stein was most surprised when people kissed her hand on the street.

*A prose piece by Gertrude Stein, translated by Eugène Jolas, appeared last year in *L'Anthologie de la poésie américaine*.

Appendix E
The Contract for *Four Saints in Three Acts*

Agreement made this day of , 1933, between
 Miss Gertrude STEIN
 27, Rue de Fleurus, Paris VI (hereinafter called the Author)
 and
 Mr. Virgil Thomson
 17, Quai Voltaire, Paris VII (hereinafter called the Composer).

1. It is understood that the Author and the Composer have made an opera in English, entitled FOUR SAINTS IN THREE ACTS, of which the former is the sole author of the text and the latter the sole composer of the music, and that they are the joint and equal proprietors of said work and sole owners of all joint rights therein, except as otherwise herein specified.

   These joint rights shall be the following: operatic, theatrical, concert, radio-diffusion, television, gramophone rights of the combined words and music or any part of same, or any printing or publication of same in any form and in any language whatsoever.

   All rights other than these joint rights shall be reserved to the Author and to the Composer respectively. Such rights are the "literary rights" and the "musical rights".

   a) The literary rights shall be construed as the printing or publication of the text in book, magazine, newspaper, libretto or any other form and in any language whatsoever, by radio-diffusion, elevision, gramophone, etc., provided that no part of the Composer's music is therewith printed or performed.

   b) The musical rights shall be construed as any performance of the work or any part of the work without the words, any arrangement, adaptation, or orchestration of said music, or its printing or publication in any form whatsoever, provided that the Author's words, or any translation or adaptation of said words, are not employed in connection therewith.

c) It is understood between the Author and the composer that neither is privileged to adapt his part of the opera to the work of another author or composer, that is, the Author may not use the libretto with any other composer's music nor may the Composer use the music with the text of any other author.

2. It is understood that, in the event of the said opera being produced or published as a joint work in the United States of America or any other country, the Author and the Composer shall share equally all profits therefrom but they shall not share obligations or expenses, except insofar as hereafter specifically stated.

3. It is understood that no engagements in regard to a production or publication of said joint work, in part or in whole, shall be taken by either Author or Composer without full knowledge and acceptance by the other of the terms on which joint production or publication shall be made, and (* such acceptance not to be unreasonably withheld, V.T. G.S), and no contract shall be valid without the signature of both parties.

4. It is understood that no translation of the author's text shall be adapted to the Composer's music without the consent of both parties and that, in the case of a publication or production in an approved translation, all net profits shall be divided equally between the two parties.

5. In the case either party dies, this agreement may be assigned by his heirs or duly authorized executors but only as a whole and only insofar as the financial profits and obligations are concerned, the right to sanction performance, translation, publication, arrangement, adaptation, etc. remaining entirely the privilege of the surviving party to this agreement.

6. This agreement shall remain in force only so long as the musical part of the opera exists in manuscript only, but, on publication of combined music and text shall be replaced by a contract with the publisher. It is understood, however, that no such contract shall be made by either Author or Composer without full knowledge and acceptance by the other of the terms on which such publication shall be made, and no contract shall be valid without the signature of both parties.

7. The Author authorizes the Composer to take out United States copyright for the said opera, words and music, in his own name, for their joint protection, and agrees to share with the Composer the cost of preparation of a manuscript of the complete score (words and music) for this purpose, such cost not to exceed the total sum of fifty dollars ($50).

8. a) It is understood that all the profits from the production of the opera shall be received by a third party and that said third party shall be

empowered to receive the sums due and divide said sums between the Author and Composer.

b) It is equally understood that at the time of the signing of this agreement and therafter until such time as, for any reason, he shall cease to act, said third party shall be W. A. BRADLEY, of 5, Rue Saint-Louis on l'Ile, Paris IV. At that time, another third party shall be appointed by the Author and Composer to act for them in his place.

c) Nothing in this clause, however, shall be construed as meaning that the third party shall not have the right to instruct the producer to pay directly to the Author or the Composer, with the other's written consent, his share of said profits, but only upon receipt from the producer of a general statement of account showing the amounts due both parties from all sources connected with the production.

9. All matters of controversy, differences or disputes that may arise relating to this agreement shall be submitted to arbitration under the rules and regulations of the Dramatists Guild of the Authors' League of America, Inc.

AS WITNESS the hands of the parties hereto

Signature of the Author
Gertrude Stein

Signature of Witness
A.B. Toklas

Signature of the Composer
Virgil Thomson

Signature of Witness
[Madeleine] Dhermy

Sources Cited

Brousseau, Annie. *Charles Barataud, Criminel ou Martyr?* Limoges: Lucien Souny, 1995.

Bucknell, Bradley. *Literary Modernism and Musical Aesthetics: Pater, Pound, Joyce, Stein.* Cambridge: Cambridge University Press, 2001.

Butts, Mary. *The Journals of Mary Butts.* Ed. Natalie Blondel. New Haven: Yale University Press, 2002.

Cabanne, Pierre. *Pablo Picasso, His Life and Times.* Trans. Harold Salemson. New York, William Morrow, 1977.

Chaucer, Geoffrey. "General Prologue." *The Canterbury Tales. Works of Geoffrey Chaucer.* Ed. F. N. Robinson. Boston: Houghton Mifflin, 1961.

Davidson, Jo. *Between Sittings: An Informal Autobiography of Jo Davidson.* New York: Dial, 1951.

Downes, Olin. "Broadway Greets New Kind of Opera." *New York Times*, 21 Feb. 1934, 22.

Dydo, Ulla. "Picasso and Alice." *Nest* 19 (Winter 2002–2003): 14–20.

———, with William Rice. *Gertrude Stein: The Language that Rises.* Evanston, Ill.: Northwestern University Press, 2003.

Fisher, Clive. *Hart Crane: A Life.* New Haven: Yale University Press, 2002.

Friedmann, Elizabeth. *A Mannered Grace: The Life of Laura (Riding) Jackson.* New York: Persea, 2005.

Gallup, Donald, ed. *The Flowers of Friendship: Letters Written to Gertrude Stein.* New York: Alfred A. Knopf, 1953.

Giroud, Vincent. "George Hugnet at Yale." *Yale University Library Gazette* (April 1999): 131–155.

Grosser, Maurice. "The Story." Program. *Four Saints in Three Acts.* By Gertrude Stein and Virgil Thomson. Dir. John J. D. Sheehan. The Opera Ensemble of New York. Lillie Blake School Theatre, New York. Nov. 1986.

Imbs, Bravig. *Confessions of Another Young Man.* New York: Henkle-Yewdale, 1936.

Katz, Leon. Introduction. *Fernhurst, Q.E.D., and Other Early Writings.* By Gertrude Stein. London: Peter Owen, 1971. i–xxxiv.

Kendall, Alan. *George Gershwin.* New York: Universe, 1987.

Madeline, Laurence. "Picasso and the Calvet affair of 1930." *The Burlington Magazine* 147 no. 1226 (2005): 316–23.

———, ed. *Pablo Picasso Gertrude Stein: Correspondence*. Trans. Lorna Scott Fox. London: Seagull Books, 2005.

Malcolm, Janet. "Gertrude Stein's War." *The New Yorker* (2 June 2003): 58–81.

Mellow, James R. *Charmed Circle: Gertrude Stein & Company*. New York: Avon, 1974.

Moad, Rosalind. *1914–1916: Years of Innovation in Gertrude Stein's Writing*. PhD. diss., York University (United Kingdom), 1993.

Nichol, bp. *The Martyrology Books 1 and 2*. Toronto: Coach House, 1972.

Rascoe, Burton, ed. *Morrow's Almanack for the Year of Our Lord 1928*. New York: William Morrow, 1927.

Ryan, Betsy Alayne. *Gertrude Stein's Theatre of the Absolute*. Ann Arbor: UMI Research Press, 1984.

Stein, Gertrude. *Alphabets and Birthdays*. Vol. 7 of *The Unpublished Works of Gertrude Stein*. New Haven: Yale University Press, 1957.

———. *The Autobiography of Alice B. Toklas*. London: Penguin, 1933.

———. *Capital Capitals*. In *Operas & Plays*, 61–70.

———. "Composition as Explanation." In *A Stein Reader*. Ed. Ulla Dydo. Evanston, Ill.: Northwestern University Press, 493–503.

———. *Daniel Webster. Eighteen in America: A Play*. In *Reflections On the Atomic Bomb*. Los Angeles: Black Sparrow, 1973. 95–117.

———. *Dix Portraits*. Paris: Editions de la Montagne, 1930.

———. *Everybody's Autobiography*. Cambridge, Mass.: Exact Change, 1993.

———. *Film. Deux Soeurs Qui Ne Sont Pas Soeurs*. In *Operas & Plays*, 399–400.

———. *Four in America*. Introduction by Thornton Wilder. New Haven, Conn.: Yale University Press, 1947.

———. *Four Saints in Three Acts*. In *Operas & Plays*, 11–48.

———. *Geography and Plays*. Boston: Four Seas, 1922.

———. *How to Write*. Paris: Plain Edition, 1931; repr., New York: Dover, 1975.

———. *How Writing Is Written*. Ed. with preface by Robert Bartlett Haas. Los Angeles: Black Sparrow Press, 1974. Vol. 2 of the *Previously Uncollected Writings of Gertrude Stein*.

———. *Last Operas and Plays*. New York: Rinehart, 1949.

———. *Lectures in America*. Boston: Beacon, 1935.

———. "Letters and Parcels and Wool." In *As Fine As Melanctha*. Vol. 4 of *The Unpublished Writings of Gertrude Stein*. New Haven: Yale University Press, 1954.

———. *The Letters of Gertrude Stein and Carl Van Vechten*. Ed. Edward Burns. New York: Columbia University Press, 1986.

———. *The Letters of Gertrude Stein and Thornton Wilder*. Ed. Edward Burns, Ulla Dydo, William Rice. New Haven: Yale University Press, 1996.

———. *Lucy Church Amiably*. Paris: Plain Edition, 1930; repr., Normal, Ill.: Dalkey Archive Press, 2000.

———. *Madame Recamier*. In *Operas & Plays*, 355–94.

———. *The Mother of Us All*. In *Last Operas*, 52–88.

———. *Operas & Plays*. Paris: Plain Edition, 1932; repr. Barrytown, N.Y.: Station Hill, 1998.

———. *Painted Lace and Other Pieces [1914–1937]*. Vol. 5 of *The Unpublished Writings of Gertrude Stein*. New Haven: Yale University Press, 1955.

———. *Paris France*. New York: C. Scribner's Sons, 1940; repr. New York: Liveright, 1970.
———. "Plays." In *Lectures*, 93–134.
———. "Poetry and Grammar." In *Lectures*, 209–46.
———. *Portraits and Prayers*. New York: Random House, 1934.
———. *Reflections on the Atomic Bomb*. Los Angeles: Black Sparrow Press, 1973.
———. *A Stein Reader*. Ed. Ulla Dydo. Evanston, Ill.: Northwestern University Press.
———. *They Weighed Weighed-Layed*. In *Operas & Plays*, 231–48.
———. "Three Sitting Here." *Close Up* 3 (Sept. 1927): 17–28, *Close Up* 4 (Oct. 1927): 17–25.
———. "Turkey and Bones and Eating and We Liked It." In *Geography and Plays*. Boston: Four Seas, 1922. 239–53.
———. *Useful Knowledge*. New York: Payson & Clarke, 1928; repr., foreword by Edward Burns and intro. Keith Waldrop. Barrytown, N.Y.: Station Hill, 1988.
Stein, Gertrude, and Virgil Thomson. *The Mother of Us All*. New York: Music Press, 1948.
Stevens, Wallace. *Letters of Wallace Stevens*. Selected and ed. Holly Stevens. Berkeley: University of California Press, 1966.
Thomson, Virgil. *The Art of Judging Music*. New York: Greenwood, 1948.
———. *Four Saints in Three Acts: An Opera by Gertrude Stein and Virgil Thomson*. Complete vocal score. New York: G. Schirmer, 1948.
———. *A Reader: Selected Writings 1924–1984*, ed. Richard Kostelanetz. New York and London: Routledge, 2002.
———. *Virgil Thomson*. New York: Knopf, 1967.
Toklas, Alice B. *Staying on Alone: Letter*. Ed. Edward Burns. New York: Liveright, 1973.
———. *Staying on Alone: Letters of Alice B. Toklas*. Ed. Edward Burns. New York: Columbio University Press, 1986.
Tommasini, Anthony. *Virgil Thomson*. New York: Norton, 1997.
Van Vechten, Carl. *Parties: Scenes from Contemporary New York Life*. New York: Alfred A. Knopf, 1930.
———. *Peter Whiffle: His Life and Works*. New York: Alfred A. Knopf, 1922.
Watson, Steven. *Prepare for Saints*. Berkeley: University of California Press, 1998.
———, director. *Prepare for Saints: The Making of a Modern Opera*. [Hartford]: Connecticut Public Television, 1998. VHS videotape.
Wilson, Robert A., comp., assisted by Arthur Uphill. *Gertrude Stein: A Bibliography*. Rockville, Md.: Quill and Brush, 1994.
Wineapple, Brenda. *Genêt: a Biography of Janet Flanner*. New York: Ticknor & Fields, 1989.

Index

Addis, Louise and Emmet, 111, 112n
Adolphus, Gustavus, King of Sweden, 255n
Aiguy, Diane, Countess d', 88, 88n, 91n, 219, 223, 252n
Aiguy, François, Count d', 88, 88n, 91n, 219, 223
Aiguy, Rose d', 88n
Aimé-Azam, Denise 299, 299n
Aldrich, Mildred, 6, 37, 38n, 72n
  Hilltop on the Marne, 38n
Ames, Winthrop, 109, 110n
Anderson, Sherwood, 6, 24n, 65, 83n, 105n, 172n
Anderson, Thomas, 16, 259, 259n
Angelico, Fra, 197
Antheil, Böske, 31, 31n
Antheil, George, 7, 8, 31, 31n, 122, 123n, 154, 157n
  Ballet mécanique, 31n, 169, 169n
  This Quarter, musical supplement to, 179
  Transatlantic, 154, 155n, 157n
Anthony, Anna O. (Susan B's niece), 18
Anthony, Susan B., (Susan B's grand niece), 18
Anthony, Susan B., 17, 273, 274n
Apollinaire, Guillaume, 309
Aragon, Louis, 95n
Artaud, Antonin, 98n

Arthur, Bea, 276n
Ashton, Frederick, 17, 221, 222n, 230, 237, 253n, 288, 296, 299. See also *Four Saints*, production of
Auntie, Stein's first Ford, 43n
Auric, Georges, 7, 67n
Austin, A. Everett Jr., (Chick) 193, 194n, 195, 196, 197, 198, 202, 203, 210, 212, 217, 228–30, 234, 235, 237, 242. See also *Four Saints*, production of

Baby. See Bérard
Bach, Johann Sabastian, 130, 130n, 155n
Balmain, Pierre, 272n
Barataud, Charles, 119, 119n–120n
Barney, Natalie, 5, 31, 31n, 32, 35n, 37n, 40n, 134, 157, 158, 199
Barr Jr., Alfred, 155n, 157, 157n, 194n, 241n, 285, 286
Barr, Daisy (Mrs Alfred Barr), 157, 157n
Bartok, Béla, 290, 290n
Baskerville, Charles, 69n
Basket I (Stein's poodle), 20, 110n, 113, 113n, 114, 115, 116, 117, 118–9, 120, 120n, 121, 125, 126n, 127, 150, 152, 166, 167, 278, 290

Basket II (Stein's poodle), 294
Batheri, Mme., 64
Baudelaire, Charles, 52n
Beach, Sylvia, 7, 123n, 124, 157, 157n
Bébé. *See* Bérard
Beecham, Thomas, 14, 289, 293, 294
Beethoven, Ludwig van, 61n
Bérard, Christian (Bébé, Baby), 37, 37n, 40, 46, 48, 50, 51, 68, 69, 70n, 82, 84, 85, 89, 91, 94, 94n, 97, 103, 106, 106n, 108, 114, 116, 119, 125, 125n, 132, 133, 134, 151n, 152n, 156, 164, 165n, 168
  Thomson, portrait of, 165n
Berceau de Gertrude Stein . . . sous le titre de Lady Godiva's Waltzes, 62, 62n, 77, 77n, 106, 121n, 175, 176n, 177, 186n, 264, 264n, 303
Berkshire School Musical Association, 247, 248n, 248
Benoist-Méchin, Jacques, 65
Berman, Eugène (Genia), 70n, 85, 87, 89, 103, 119, 120, 123, 127, 129, 132, 133, 150, 152n, 154, 157, 158, 164, 165n
  Hugnet, portrait of, 165n
  self-portrait, 165n
Berman, Léonide, 70n, 152n, 176
Berners, Lord. *See* Tyrwhitt-Wilson
Bernhardt, Sarah, 4, 157
Birchard, C.C., 229
Bird, Bill, 87, 87n
Bizet, Georges, 294
Blackmur, R.P., 29n
Blake, William, 29n
Blanche, Jacques-Émile, 86, 87n
Blues. *See under* Charles Ford
Blum, Suzanne, 272n, 293, 296, 297
Boehm, Karl, 155n, 164n
Bossuet, Jacques-Benigne
  Oraison funèbre d' Henriette de France, 147, 148n
Boulanger, Nadia, 7, 67n, 115n, 122, 123n
Boulez, Pierre, 166n

Bowen, Stella, 33n
Bowles, Paul ('Freddy'), 124n, 171n, 295, 295n
Letter to Freddy, 295n
Bradley, Jenny, 185, 186n, 230, 231, 235, 236, 241, 242, 243, 274, 275n, 284, 285, 294
Bradley, William A., 16, 20, 68, 68n, 185, 186n, 192–220, 221n, 224–44, 250, 275n, 315
Brancusi, Constantin, 165, 166n
Branlière, Alice Woodfin, 63, 63n, 134, 134n
Braque, Georges, 108n, 176n
Breton, André, 65n, 98n, 192
Brewer, Joseph, 119, 119n
Briant, Théophile, 69n
Brillat-Savarin, Jean Anthelme, 44, 45n, 160
Brooks, Romaine, 40, 40n
Brown, Robert Carleton, 137
1450–1950, 137n
Bryher, Winifred, 15, 48n, 224, 225n
Close Up, 48, 48n
Buchanan, Briggs, 28n
Bucher, Jeanne, 187n, 188, 188n
Bucknell, Brad, 15
Burns, Edward, 281n, 299n
Burr, Courtney, 276
Butts, Mary, 28, 29n, 34, 35, 35n, 42, 42n, 46n, 50, 124n, 163
  "Heartbreak House" 163, 163n
Butts, Thomas, 29n
Bynner, Witter, 106, 106n
Byrd, William, 155n

Cady, Carolyn P., 10
Cage, John, 295, 295n
Caldwell, Erskine, 124n
Calvocoressi, M.D., 199, 199n
Capital Capitals, 28, 28n, 30, 31, 32, 33, 33n, 36, 37n, 38, 46n, 54, 66, 67, 67n, 75, 76, 95n, 96, 102, 104, 105n, 106, 107, 109, 109n–110n, 111n, 119n, 140n, 153n, 178, 179, 180, 185n, 200, 203, 211, 212, 213, 231, 232, 233, 235, 263, 264, 283, 284, 285, 298, 304

322 *Index*

Capri, Agnes, 264, 264n
Carson, Kit, 102
Catesby Joneses, 138
Cerf, Bennett, 231, 231n, 234, 238, 253, 254, 258
Cezanne, Paul, 5
Chadbourne, Emily. *See* Crane
Chamber Music Society of Boston, 109
Chaucer, Geoffrey, 266
   Prologue to *Canterbury Tales*, 266n
Chavannes, Puvis de, 176, 176n
Chavez, Carlos, 64, 64n
   Sonata for Piano, 115n, 121n
Chirico, Giorgio de, 119, 119n
Christine, Queen of Sweden, 255n
Church, Georgia, 172n
Church, Ralph Withington, 172, 172n
Cingria, Charles-Albert, 67n, 154, 154n, 172, 172n, 173, 174
   La Civilisation de St. Gall, 172, 172n
Citkowitz, Israel, 115n, 121n
Claflin, Avery, 222, 223n, 223, 224, 225, 226, 228, 294, 296, 297
Clair, René, 265
Claudel, Paul
   Christophe Colombe, 207
Clemenceau, George, 272, 272n
Clermont-Tonnerre, Aimé François Philibert, Duc de, 140n
Clermont-Tonnerre, Elizabeth Gramont, Duchess of, 24n, 37, 37n, 38, 121, 121n, 122, 140, 140n, 156, 157, 158, 175, 177, 179, 181
Cliquet-Pleyel, Henri, 53n, 54, 54n, 55, 65, 80, 83, 83n, 84, 84n, 85, 89, 90, 92n, 101n, 143, 148, 151, 153n, 157, 170, 178n, 226
Cliquet-Pleyel, Mme. *See* Marthe Marthine
Coates, Robert Myron, 55n–56n
   Eater of Darkness, 55–56, 55n–56n
Cochran, Charles, 252, 253n, 254
Cocteau, Jean, 6, 7, 41, 42n, 46, 46n, 48, 67n, 80, 80n, 95n, 124n, 151n, 179n, 226, 298
   La Sang d'un Poète, 80n, 179n
Cody, Buffalo Bill, 4
Colette, 31n
Cone, Etta and Claribel, 39, 39n, 41, 43, 155n
Cook, William, 56–57, 56n
Coolidge, Calvin, 69n
Copland, Aaron, 7, 15, 64n, 94n, 95n, 105n, 115, 268, 295
   on Thomson in *Modern Music*, 119, 119n
   review of *The State of Music*, 263n
   Two Pieces for String Quartet ("Lento molto" and "Rondino,"), 115n, 121n
   Vitebsk, 115n, 121n
Couperin, François, 77n
Covarrubias, Miguel, 37, 38n
Coward, Noel, 253n
Cox, Kenyon, 106, 106n
Crane, Emily Chadbourne, 43, 43n, 45, 46, 46n, 47, 47n, 48, 49, 50, 50n, 53n, 54, 68, 68n, 72, 73, 73n, 81, 163n, 211, 285
Crane, Hart, 29n, 108, 108n, 112, 112n
   The Bridge, 108n
Crane, Josephine Boardman (Mrs Winthrop Murray Crane), 197, 198n, 267
Crane, Winthrop Murray, 198n
Crevel, René, 48, 48n, 53, 54n, 87, 110, 123, 156, 165n
   Paul Klee, 87n
   Les Pieds dans le Plat, 48n
cummings, e.e., 124n, 126n
Cunard, Nancy, 87, 87n
Curtiss, Mina, 282, 282n, 289, 292, 292n, 294, 295, 296, 299
   Letters of Marcel Proust, 292n

Dali, Salvador and Gala, 151n, 265
Damon, S. Foster, 6
Daniels, Jimmy, 197n
Davidson, Jo, 6, 39n, 42, 42n, 43, 45, 46, 47n, 47, 60, 71, 72, 102, 110n, 173
   Between Sittings, 42n
Davidson, Yvonne (Jo's wife), 46, 47n, 63, 102

Davies, Marion, 154, 155n
Delarue-Mardrus, Lucie (Lucy), 112, 113n
De Mille, Agnes, 276, 276n–277n
  Carousel, 277n
  Oklahoma, 277n
  Rodeo, 277n
Dempsey, Jack, 69n
Denby, Edwin, 124n, 163, 164n, 292
Denton, Grace, 246n
de Rohan, Duchess, 72n, 71, 72, 115, 175, 303
Desbordes, Jean, 80, 80n
  J'adore, 80, 80n, 83, 84n
Deutsch, Max, 59n
Diaghilev, Serge, 34n, 66n, 67n, 70n, 91n, 119n, 151n, 155n, 194n
Dial, 7, 72n, 80, 95n, 126, 126n 127n. *See also* Sibley Watson
Dickenson, Anita Thompson, 158, 158n, 159, 170, 176
Dilworth, Thomas, 6, 7, 8, 9, 10, 17, 20, 34n, 46n, 54n, 59n, 79n, 123n, 166n, 245, 251n, 265, 299n, 301n, 302n
Disney, Walt
  Fantasia, 107n
Doolittle, Hilda (H.D.), 48n
  Close Up, 48n
Dos Passos, John, 124n
Dow Dorothy, 18
Downes, Olin, 16
Draper, Muriel, 157
  Music at Midnight, 104, 105n, 107
Duchamp, Marcel, 140n, 165n–166n
  Fountain, 165
  Nude Descending a Staircase, 165
Dumas, Alexandre
  La Dame aux Camélias, 166n
Duncan family, 9
Duncan, Isadora, 31n, 85n
  My Life, 85, 85n
Du Poy (Du Pois), Ellen, 167n, 171, 171n
Durey, Louis, 7
Durham, Paul, 171n
Dydo, Ulla, 53n, 117n, 132n, 143n, 281n

Ebert, Carl, 164n
Elgar, Edward, 77n
Eliot, T.S., 31n, 90, 91n, 126n, 151n, 152n, 293
  "Homage to John Dryden," 91n
Elizabeth, Queen, 34n
Eluard, Paul, 226

Fairbanks, Douglas, 101n
Fassett, Mr., 284
Faure, Etienne, 119n
Faÿ, Bernard, 7, 29n, 53n, 54, 54n, 55, 57, 80n, 85, 85n, 86, 86n, 88, 110, 116, 116n, 117, 118, 122, 123, 129, 134, 138, 142n, 149n, 149, 150, 151, 152, 156, 157, 158, 159, 163, 164n, 174, 186, 193, 239n, 241n, 243, 266, 270, 277n, 280–82, 290, 291, 292, 293, 296, 297, 299
  Franklin, the Apostle of Modern Times, 104, 105n
  "Inquiry . . . into the Spirit of America," 80n
  La Gerbe, 280
  "Modern Music in America," 106, 107n
  Preface to *Making of Americans*, 142n
Faÿ, Emmanuel, 7, 148n
Faÿ, Jacques (Bernard's brother), 294
Faÿ, Michel (Bernard's nephew), 292
Ferry, Marcelle, 108n, 117n, 170, 170n, 183, 187
Feydeau, Georges, 296
Fischer, J., 248, 248n, 249, 249n, 250
Fitzgerald, F. Scott, 6, 31n
Fitzgerald, Zelda, 31n
Flaherty, Robert, 287n
Flanner, Janet, 31, 31n, 35–36, 36n, 87, 92n, 176, 301n
  "Paris Letter," *New Yorker* 8 Dec. 1928, 92n
Ford, Charles Henri, 125n, 220, 221n, 289
  Blues, 125, 125n, 221n
  The Young and Evil, 221n

Ford, Ford Madox, 7, 33, 33n, 35, 137, 157, 262
Forrest, Hamilton, 168
Camille, 166, 166n
Forster, E.M.
  "Anonymity: an enquiry," 91n
Four Saints in Three Acts, 3, 9–17, 19, 37, 240, 241, 245, 246, 252, 253n, 259, 270n, 276, 286
  alteration for production and copyright, 215–20
  appreciation of, 15–6, 19, 34, 54, 57n, 60, 89, 109, 119n, 165n, 185n, 227, 227n–228n, 229, 233
  BBC broadcast of, proposed, 262, 263, 264
  book publication, 181–2, 237, 238, 267–9, 274
  Broadway productions of, 230n, 300
  casting, 167n, 197, 197n–198n, 200, 200n, 208, 209n, 211, 222n, 298, 298n
  contract for, 194–218, 231, 232, 279, 313–5
  Dix Portraits, possible inclusion in, 144n
  German production, possibility of, 124, 124n, 127–30, 130n, 147, 148, 149, 151, 154, 155n, 163, 286
  Hartford production of, 193, 194n, 194–209, 212, 215–6, 221, 224, 226–7, 230
  libretto, writing of, 26–9, 30n, 32–3, 35–6, 37n, 37, 38, 40–1, 48n
  London production, proposed, 255, 256–7, 259, 260, 262n. *See also* Kaufman, Harding
  music of Thomson, book of, possible inclusion, 177, 179
  Paris production, 251–2, 252n, 299, 300
  performed as oratorio, 266, 266n, 267
  performed by Thomson, 85, 87, 94n, 95n, 104, 105–106, 106n, 107n, 109, 111, 112n, 212n. *See also* promotion of
  Philadelphia production, proposed, 253, 258–9
  Pigeons on the Grass Alas, 247, 248n, 249, 257
  promotion of, 94, 97, 100, 105–6, 106n, 152n, 168, 173, 183, 186
  proposed film of, 290
  publication of, 288, 291
  quoted or alluded to, 46n, 53n, 73, 74, 74n, 122, 149, 149n
  radio broadcast of, 283, 284
  recording of, 284, 287, 290, 292
  "Saints' Procession" scene from, 97, 98, 100, 103, 114, 115, 133n
  scenario, 125, 143, 143n, 197n, 215, 229, 231, 232
  score, composition of, 45, 46, 46n, 50, 50n, 60, 62, 68, 72, 74n, 75, 76, 83, 84n, 84, 89, 131, 134, 221
  set, costume, design of, 37, 37n, 77n, 106n, 204, 211, 212, 221, 299
  transition, published in, 114–6, 124, 127
Franciosa, Anthony, 276n
Francis of Assisi, Saint, 10
Friends and Enemies of Modern Music, 194n, 230
Furman, Lee, 142n

Gabrielle (girlfriend of Hugnet), 117, 117n
Galantière, Lewis, 221, 222n, 225
Gallup, Donald, 20
Garden, Mary, 166, 166n, 167n, 167, 168, 170–1, 171n, 172, 172n, 173
Garland, Madge, 61, 61n
Gautier-Vignal, Louis, 157, 157n
Gazzo, Michael, 276n
Genevieve, Saint., 148, 149n, 154, 299, 300
Genia. *See* Eugène Berman
George, Henry, 276
  Progress and Poverty, 277n

Gershwin, George, 15, 300
  Porgy and Bess, 15–16, 252
Ghandi, Mohandas, 148, 149n
Gide, André, 48n, 122
Gilbert, Mark, 161, 161n
Gilbert, W.S., 15, 57n, 254
Giraud, Marthe, 132, 132n, 169n
Glass, Philip
  Einstein on the Beach, 16
Godiva, Stein's Ford, 62n, 98, 98n, 102, 103, 105, 108, 110, 309
Goethe, Johann Wolfgang von, 295
  Faust, 4, 295
Golschmann, Vladimir, 290
Goodspeed, Bobsie (Mrs Charles Godspeed), 241n, 258
Gorer, Geoffrey, 139, 139n
Goya, Francisco, 118, 120
Gramond, Elizabeth de. *See* Clermont-Tonnerre
Grant, Ulysses S., 17, 18, 239n
Graves, Robert, 135, 135n, 137, 163, 163n
  "Future of the Art of Poetry," 91
  Goodbye to All That, 137, 137n
Griggs, Arthur Kingsland, 235, 236n
Grimeu, James, 51
Gris, Juan, 10–11, 176n, 309
Grosser, Maurice, 7, 10, 14, 17, 40n, 114, 122, 125, 128, 129, 134, 137, 138, 139, 140, 142, 143, 143n, 146, 150, 153, 154, 156, 158, 159, 160n, 162, 162n, 167, 170, 171, 172, 173, 174, 178, 182, 183, 183n, 184, 188, 189, 196, 197n, 212, 214–15, 216, 220, 222n, 229, 230n, 231, 232, 236, 237, 239, 241, 242, 254, 258, 283, 294. *See also Four Saints*, scenario.
  Painting in Public, 287n, 288
  review of *Brewsie and Willie*, 276, 276n
Gruenberg, Louis
  The Enchanted Isle, 75n
Guevara, Alvaro, 103, 104n
Guinness, Meraud, 104n

Hall Johnson's Negro Choir, 197
Harcourt, Alfred, 193, 231, 234n, 238, 239n, 240, 241n, 243
Harding, Dolores, 255, 259, 260, 260n, 261–262, 262n
Harris, Roy, 67n, 94n
  Sextet, 115n, 121n
Harvard Glee Club, 7, 97, 98, 99, 100, 111, 112n, 114–115
Harvey, Mrs., 106
Haulleville, Eric de, 50, 50n, 84,
  "Fragments," 93, 93n
Haynes, Camille. *See* Camille Paul
H.D. *See* Hilda Doolittle
Hélène, maid-cook, 108, 108n
Hemingway, Ernest, 6, 7, 87n, 99, 102, 125, 190
Henderson, W.J., in *New York Sun*, 109n
Henri, Catherine, 128
Herrand, Marcel, 64, 65n, 92n
Hitchcock, Henry-Russell, 7, 56n, 94n, 100, 100n, 108, 110, 119, 120, 123, 135, 148, 148n, 152, 154, 155n, 156, 157, 158, 159, 194n, 197n, 265
  The International Style: Architecture Since 1922, 100n
  Modern Architecture, 100n
  In the Nature of Materials 1887–1941: The Buildings of Frank Lloyd Wright, 100n
Honegger, Arthur, 7, 67n
Hoover, Herbert, 86, 86n
Hopwood, Avery, 24, 25n, 25, 26, 27, 74, 74n
Horton, Asadata Dafora, 251n
Horwood, Harry, 150, 151n
Houseman, John, 17, 197n, 221, 222n, 225, 227, 229–30, 231, 234, 237, 242, 251n, 302n. *See also Four Saints*, production of
Hubbell, Lindley, 109, 110, 110n, 111n, 234
  "Letter to Gertrude Stein," 110n, 151n
  letter to *transition* re Stein, 110, 111n
  "Promenade chez Nous," 110n

Hubbs, Nadine
  Queer Composition of America's Sound: Gay Modernists, American Music, and National Identity, 16
Hugnet, Georges, 3, 57n, 61, 62, 62n, 63, 65, 68, 69n, 71, 79–80, 80n, 81, 82, 82n, 83, 84, 85, 86, 87, 89, 92n, 96, 96n, 97, 99, 100, 101n, 103, 107–8, 108n, 110, 111n, 113, 117, 117n, 119, 121n, 122, 127, 128, 129, 141, 141n, 144, 145, 145n, 146n, 147n, 148n, 151, 152, 157, 158, 159, 162, 165, 168, 168n, 170, 170n, 171, 172, 173, 173n, 174, 175, 175n, 176, 176n, 178, 179, 180, 183, 184–5, 187–192, 198, 277, 282, 298
  "L'ami," 69n
  "L'archipel," 153, 153n
  Babylon, 48n
  "Berceau de Gertrude Stein . . . sous le titre de Lady Godiva's Waltzes," 71, 71n, 77n, 178n, 303
  "Berceau de Gertrude . . . ," scored by Thomson. *See under* title
  "Before the Flowers of Friendship Faded Friendship Faded," 192
  "Composition as Explanation" co-translator of, 150
  Dix Portraits, translation, 154, 157
  Enfances, 117n, 161, 161n, 163, 164, 166, 168, 169, 170, 182, 187–8, 189,192. *See also* "Before the Flowers of Friendship Faded"
  40 poésies de Stanislaus Boutemer, 69n
  "Inquiry . . . into the Spirit of America," 79, 80n
  "L'Invention de la rose," 121n, 123
  "Les îles fortunes," 69n
  "Le Journal d'Antoinette," 69n
  Morceaux choisis de La fabrication des Américains, Preface to, 96n, 117n, 123
  opera with Thomson, intended collaboration, 117, 121, 121n, 122
  "Peinture Poesie," 151, 152n
  La Perle, 73n, 104n, 117n, 141n
  "Pléthore et pénurie," 121n
  "Saint in Seven," Introduction to, 85–6, 86n
  Sonate d'Eglise, critique of, 69n
  Thomson's music, planned book of, *See under* Thomson
  Valse Grégorienne, *See under* title
  "La Vie de Gertrude Stein," 86n, 126n, 309–11
  "Virgil Thomson," 79, 81–2, 82n, 124n, 141n, 303–4
Hugnet (Georges's father), 97, 173n
Hugnet, Mme. (Georges's mother), 81n, 151

Ignatius of Loyola, Saint, 10, 13, 25, 25n, 28, 29n, 74, 74n, 127, 127n
  Spiritual Exercises, 25n, 74
Imbs, Bravig, 33n, 61, 62n, 73, 82, 82n, 84, 85, 85n, 86, 88, 89, 90, 92–3, 117, 117n, 122, 129, 134, 150, 150n, 152, 163, 172, 190–2
  The Cats, 173
  Confessions of Another Young Man, 33, 33n
  The Professor's Wife, 72, 73n
Imbs, Jane Maria Louise (daughter of Bravig and Valeska), 150n
Imbs, Valeska, Comtesse Balbarishky (Mme Bravig Imbs), 82n, 85n, 86, 88, 88n, 89, 92–3, 192, 269
Ionian Quartet, 109n
Isaacson, Charles, 110n

Jacob, Max, 65, 69n, 79, 79n, 116, 154n, 176n, 226, 289–90, 309
  "Stabat Mater," 79n

Index 327

Jacott, Nelly, 90, 91n, 99
Jacqueline (Stein's cook), 150, 152, 152n
James, Henry
    The Princess Casamassima, 113n
James, William, 309
Jeanne d'Arc, 153
Jeffrey, Francis, 239n
Jeritza, Maria, 61n
Johnson, Andrew, 17, 272n
Johnson, Lamont, 273, 273n, 284, 294
Johnson, Monty 294
Johnson, Philip, 155n, 194n
Johnson, Richard (also Richard Johns), 80n, 124n
Jolas, Eugene, 132, 133, 158, 311n
    transition, 5, 6, 31n, 62n, 79, 80n, 93n, 101, 102n, 110, 111n, 114, 114n, 117, 124, 127, 133n, 135n, 158, 172n, 181n
Jolas, Maria
    transition, 62n
Jones, Richard, 242
Jouffray, Christine, 169
Jouhandeau, Marcel, 67n
Joyce, James, 7, 12–13, 31n, 83n, 121n, 122, 123n, 244–5
    Chamber Music, 115, 115n, 121n
    "Continuation of a Work in Progress," 80n
    Finnegans Wake, 244–5
    Ulysses, 7, 123n, 244
Judson, Arthur, 246

Kahn, Otto, 60, 173–5, 173n, 174n
Kann, Alphonse, 103, 104n
Kates, George, 154, 155n
Kaufman, Mrs Harry, 255, 256, 257, 259, 261
Khoklova, Olga, see Olga Picasso
Kingstone, Basil 303, 309
Kirkpatrick, John, 94n, 134, 134n
Kirstein, Lincoln, 282n, 283, 285, 285n, 287, 288, 290
Knoblauch, Mary, 61, 62n
Koestenbaum, Wayne, 19
Koussevitsky, Serge, 95n, 97, 97n, 99, 156, 157
Krembourg, Alfred, 183, 183n, 184
Kupferman, Meyer, 297

La Farge SJ, John, 227, 227n–228n
    America, 227, 227n
    Humani Generis Unitas, 228n
Lafayette, Marquis de (Gilbert du Motier), 59, 59n–60n
La Fontaine, Jean de
    Les Contes, 147, 147n
Lalique, René, 95n
Langlois, Louise, 29, 29n–30n, 33, 34, 38, 41, 45, 46, 60, 61, 65, 71, 79, 80, 86n, 89–90, 90n, 94n, 94, 95n, 122, 125, 126, 126n, 127, 128, 129, 132, 148, 148n, 150, 154, 157, 159, 162, 167, 168, 170, 171, 172, 173, 176, 189, 281
Lanvin, Jeanne, 49, 49n, 50, 50n
Larson, Jack 301, 301n, 302, 302n
    The Candied House 302n
    The Keeper of the Rose, 301n
    Lord Byron (libretto), 301, 302n
larus the celestial visitor. *See* Sherry Mangan
Lasell, Chester, 7
Lasell, Hildegarde. *See* Hildegarde Watson
Lasell, Jessie, Mrs Chester Whitin, 7, 39, 39n, 41, 45–46, 47, 47n, 49n, 81, 92, 92n, 96n, 98, 122, 125, 126, 128, 128n, 186
    and family, 157
    patronage of Thomson, 46, 47n, 49n, 73, 96n, 136, 154, 157, 170
Lasell, Jo and Nora, 176, 176n
Lasell, Philip, 7, 28n, 29n, 34, 39n, 41, 53, 104, 115, 116
Latouche, John, 171n
Laughlin, James (Jay), 254, 298
Leigh, W. Colston, 241, 241n, 242–3
Leigh, Walter, 133n, 135n
Leoncavallo, Ruggero, 9
Leroi, Pierre, 70n
Lert, Richard 286
Les Six, 7, 185n
Lew, Mme 289
Lincoln, Abraham, 17
Lindberg, Charles, 68, 69n, 72
Lindsay, Vachel, 65

Lipschitz, Jacques, 6, 56, 56n
Longevialle, Grace-Ives (Yves) de, 149, 149n, 150, 150n
Loy, Mina, 31, 31n, 32
   "Gertrude Stein," 31n
   letter on Stein in *Transatlantic Review*, 31n
Lubochitz, Mme., 77
Luhan, Mabel Dodge, 102, 102n, 104, 105, 105n, 106, 107, 190
Lye, Len, 278n
Lynes, George, 139, 140n

MacCown, Eugene, 148, 148n
MacPherson, Kenneth
   Close Up, 48, 48n
Mangan, John Joseph
   Life, Character and Influence of Desiderius Erasmus of Rotterdam, 88, 88n, 131, 131n
Mangan, Sherry, 7, 24, 24n, 28, 30, 48, 80n, 88n, 124, 124n, 125, 128, 129, 131, 136, 158, 286
   larus, 24n, 28, 29, 29n, 32, 47, 48, 49n, 110n, 110, 124, 124n
   "A Note: on the Somewhat Premature Apotheosis of Thomas Stearns Eliot," 150, 151n, 152n
   Pagany, 80n, 129, 136, 141n, 151n, 151, 152n, 163, 163n, 169, 187, 187n
Maratier, George, 80, 80n, 81n, 81, 82n, 84, 85, 87, 89, 94n, 101n, 104n, 108, 122, 150, 256, 291
Marcoussis, Louis, 176, 176n, 177, 187n, 223
Marinoff, Fania (Mrs. Carl Van Vechten), 37, 38n, 84, 164
Marks, Edward B., 229, 230n
Marlowe, Christopher,
   Doctor Faustus 295
Marsh, Edward, 135n
Marthine, Marthe (Mrs Henri Cliquet-Pleyel), 66, 66n, 81, 83, 83n, 84, 84n, 85, 89, 90, 92n, 101n, 115n, 117, 121, 122, 122n, 143, 148, 151, 157, 170
Martí, Miguel Calvet, 156n

Martin, John, 16
Massine, Leonide, 244, 254, 259
Masson, Andre and Odette, 146, 146n
Massot, Pierre de, 29n, 151n, 163, 183
   Etienne Marcel, 145, 146n
   Preface to *Dix Portraits*, 150, 151n, 154, 156, 164
   Prolégomènes à une Ethique sans Métaphysique, ou Billy Bull-dog et philosophe, 163n, 183, 184n, 187n
Massot, Robbie de, 183, 185
Matisse, Henri, 5, 92n, 236n, 309
Maxwell, Elsa, 39, 39n, 41–2, 42n, 43n
McAlmon, Robert, 29n
McBride, Henry, 16, 71, 72n, 72, 75, 79–80, 109, 110, 116, 127, 159
Mercure, Regis Michaud, 78
   "La Littérature américaine d'Aujourd'huié," 78n
Middleton, George, 43, 43n
Milhaud, Darius, 7, 67n, 185n, 226
   Christophe Colombe, score, 207
Millay, Edna St Vincent, 31n, 207
Mitterrand, Francois, 299
Mock, Alice, 66n
Monnier, Adrienne, 122, 123n, 157, 157n, 244
Monroe, Harriet, 15
Montgomery, Roselle, 142, 142n
Montherlant, Henry de, 29n
Moore, Douglas, 272n, 275
Moore, Marianne, 126n
Morehouse, Ward, 75n
Morgenthau, Henry, 94, 94n
   Ambassador Morgenthau's Story, 94n
Morrison, Murray D., 291n
Mortimer, Raymond, 95, 95n
Moses, Harry, 227, 227n, 228–30, 230n, 234, 235, 237, 238n, 241–2, 249, 254
Mother of Us All, 3, 6, 17–19, 198, 268, 269, 272, 275, 282, 283, 290
   Baltimore production, proposed, 285, 286

Index 329

Mother of Us All (continued)
  broadcast, proposed 294
  Cleveland production 293
  Columbia University production, 274, 275–6, 282–3, 284
  contract for, 277n, 279
  Denver University production 291
  libretto, writing of, 272, 273, 274n, 277n
  New York production, 285, 287, 288, 290, 291, 293
  publication of, 283, 287
  San Francisco production, proposed 288
  scenario, 283
  score, 279, 281, 282, 283, 285, 288
  Syracuse University production, proposed 288
  Thomson's written prelude to, 282n
  Tulane University production, proposed 288

Nabokov, Nicholas, 69n, 299
  Ode, 68, 69n, 70n, 72
Napoleon III, 169n
Neveux, Georges, 101n
Nevin, Ethelbert
  Sketch Book, 178
Newell, Gertrude, 33, 33n, 34, 109, 265
New Yorker, 31n, 36n, 69n, 92n, 176
Nichol bp, 17
  Martyrology, 17
Nicholson, Nancy, 135n
Noailles, Charles, Vicomte de, 73, 73n, 122, 123n, 179, 179n

O'Hara, Frank, 302n
Olivier, Fernande, 11, 147n
Ollendorff, Heinrich Gottfried, 227n
Orbes, 85, 86n, 87n, 117, 126, 126n, 132n, 309–11
Osborne, Herbert, 196, 197n, 212
Osterman, Georg, 4
  Gertrude and Alice: A Likeness to Loving, 4

Pagany, 80n, 110n, 117n, 124n, 136, 141, 141n, 151n, 151, 152n, 163, 163n, 169, 187, 303–4. *See also* under Sherry Mangan
Parker, Dorothy, 16
Pashalinski, Lola, 4
  Gertrude and Alice: A Likeness to Loving, 4
Pasquini, Bernardo, 155n
Patrice
  "Gertrude Stein," *Paris Comet*, 117
Paul, Camille Haynes, 118, 118n, 120, 170, 172
Paul, Elliot, 31, 31n, 62n, 117, 117n, 118, 118n, 120, 122, 125, 133n, 142n, 155, 170
  transition, 31n, 62n
Paul, St., 11, 18, 276
Payne, Barbara, 286, 288, 293
Pazmor, Radiana, 64n
Pecorini, Countess Margherita, 53, 54, 54n, 146, 152, 153
Pegnet, Bertrand, 119n
Pershing, John Joseph, 59n–60n
Pétain, Philippe Marshal, 265, 266, 268n, 280, 280n
Phibbs, Geoffrey, 135n
Picasso, Maria, 156n
Picasso, Olga (née Khoklova, Mme Pablo Picasso), 66n, 163
Picasso, Pablo, 5, 6, 7, 10–11, 37n, 39n, 66, 79n, 92n, 98n, 106, 106n, 108n, 114, 143n, 144, 151n, 155, 156n, 163, 165n, 176n, 187n, 194n, 244, 254, 259, 270, 289, 293, 293n, 294, 298, 299, 301, 303, 309
  portrait of Stein, 279, 285–7
Picasso, Paulo (son of Pablo and Olga), 66, 66n
Pierlot, Baroness Lucy, 76n
Polignac, Princess Edmond de (Singer, Winnaretta), 25n, 39, 39n, 41, 42n, 67n
Polybe (Stein's dog), 161
Porter, Cole, 253n
Poulenc, Francis, 7, 67n
Pound, Ezra, 7, 31n, 87n, 124n, 157

Prahl, Victor, 67n, 186, 186n
Preciosilla, 31, 31n, 32, 35n, 77, 106, 115, 121n, 177, 179
Price, Leontyne, 16, 300
Proust, Marcel, 28n, 37n, 157n
Puccini, Giacomo, 9

Racine, Jean
  Phèdre, 156, 156n
Rascoe, Burton, 56, 56n, 71, 71n, 72
  "Case of Gertrude Stein," 71n
  Morrow's Almanack, 56n, 71, 71n
Ray, Man, 6, 117, 265
Reid, Helen Rogers, 290
Reid, Ogden, 290n
Reiner, Ethel, 300
Renoir, Pierre-Auguste, 5
Reynolds, Mary, 139, 140n, 183, 184, 185
Reynolds, Sir Joshua, 154
Rice, William, 281n
Richardson, Dorothy, 83n
Riding, Laura, 135, 135n, 163, 163n
  Poems, a Joking Word, 135n
Rieti, Vittorio
  Le Bal, 119n
Rilke, Rainer Marie, 31n
Rimsky-Korsakov, Nicolai,
  My Musical Life, 180, 181n
Rivera, Diego, 38n
Robeson, Paul, 255, 255n
Rodakiewicz, Henwar, 97, 102n
Rodker, John, 29n
Rogers, Bill, 284
Rogers, Mildred, 282, 289
Rogers, William, 241n
Rose, Francis, 150, 151n, 153, 165, 199, 256, 258, 283, 299
  Hitchcock, portrait of, 258
  Thomson, portrait of, 258
Rose, Lady Ruth (Francis's mother),153, 153n, 199
Rosenberg, Harold, 124n
Rosenfeld, Paul
  An Hour with American Music, 185, 185n
Ross, Cary, 154, 155n, 157, 158, 159
Ross, Marvin, 241n

Rousseau, Henri (called *Douanier*, the custom's officer), 72n, 108n, 303
Roussel, Gueydan de, 280
Rubinstein, Anton, 77n

Sacks, Walter, 109, 110n
Sade, Marquis de, 89, 90n, 92n
Saks, Gene, 276n
San Francisco Chamber Singers
  Gertrude, Virgil & Four Saints: From Vision to Verity, 4
Satie, Erik, 6–7, 8, 91n, 92n, 151n, 175, 185n, 222n, 223n, 304
  Mercure, 254, 259
  Three Pieces in the Shape of a Pear, 107n
  Socrate, 8, 25n, 92n, 119n, 282, 283
Sauguet, Henri, 65, 67n, 91, 91n, 92, 93, 94n, 144, 148, 168, 169n, 226
  La Chatte, 91n
  La Nuit, 168, 169n
Savarin. *See* Brillat-Savarin
Sawyer, 245
Schumann, Robert, 77n
Schwartz, Lucien, 92n
Scudder, Janet, 53, 54n, 54, 68, 68n, 152
Senabre, Ramón, 153, 153n, 154, 157, 158, 159, 160n, 162
Sessions, Robert, 64n, 69n, 95n, 105n, 115
Shakespeare, William, 4, 137n
  Hamlet, 4, 243
  Macbeth, 251, 251n, 252
Shea, Nora, 246
Shepherd, Arthur
  Horizons, 75n
Sherril, Arthur, 265
Sitwell, Edith, 34, 34n, 104n
Sitwell, Osbert, 34n
Sitwell, Sacheverell, 34, 34n, 109
  Triumph of Neptune, 34n
Smallens, Alexander, 16, 17, 196, 197n, 212, 222n, 227n, 245–6, 247, 255, 266n
Smith, Alfred, 86, 86n
Smith, Peter, 56, 56n, 79, 87, 119
Smith, Sidney, 239, 239n

Soupault, Philippe, 65, 65n
Squire, W.H. Haddon, 148, 149n, 152, 153n, 154
Stanley, Kim, 276n
Stanton, Charles, E., 59n–60n
Stanton, Elizabeth Cady, 274n
Stein, Allan (Gertrude's nephew), 279, 285
Stein, Gertrude
  "Absolutely As Bob Brown Or Bobbed Brown," 137n, 149n
  Américains d'Amérique, see *Making of Americans,* translation of
  "And Now," 239n
  appearance in *Little Review,* 69, 70n
  "Arthur a Grammar," 68n, 82n, 84, 90, 91n
  At Present, 149n
  Autobiography of Alice B. Toklas, 193, 222n, 238, 239n, 240, 241n, 270n–271n
    serial publication in *Atlantic Monthly,* 193, 222n
  "Basket," 120, 120n, 125, 125n, 186
  bibliography in *transition,* 101–102, 102n
  "Bernard Faÿ," 99, 100n, 125, 125n
  A Birthday Book, 126n, 242
  A Bouquet. Their Wills, 76, 76n, 82, 90, 91n
  Brewsie and Willie, 276, 276n
  Byron, a Play, 302n
  Capital Capitals. See under title
  "Carl van Vechten," 56
  "Cezanne," 65
  "Christian Berard," 125, 125n, 154
  "Cocteau," 65
  "Composition as Explanation," 15, 90, 91n, 126n, 133n
    translation of, 150
  Confessions, projected book, 238, 239n, 243
  Contemporaries. See Dix Portraits
  "The D'Aiguys," 88n, 90, 91n
  Daniel Webster. Eighteen in America: A Play, 253, 253n, 254, 255n
  "Descriptions of Literature," 80n
  Deux Soeurs Qui Ne Sont Pas Soeurs. See Film
  Dix Portraits, 100n, 125n, 144, 145, 146, 146n, 147, 147n, 148, 150, 151n, 154,160, 160n, 161, 162, 164n–165n
  Doctor Faustus Lights the Lights, 257, 257n, 294–5, 296, 297
  "Elie Nadelman," 48, 49n
  Emmet Addis the Doughboy, 112n
  Enfances, Stein's "version" of 161, 161n, 163, 164, 166, 169, 170, 182, 187–8, 189
    Hugnet's response to, 168n–169n
    in *Pagany,* 169, 170, 187n
  Everybody's Autobiography, 17, 254, 271n
  Fabrication. See Making of Americans, translation
  "Felicity in Moon-light," 29, 30n, 32
  "Fernhurst," 171n
  Film: Deux Soeurs Qui Ne Sont Pas Soeurs, 120n, 164, 264, 300
  "Finally George A Vocabulary of Thinking" 59n, 155n
  "Five Words In A Line," 120, 120n, 141n
  Four in America, 238, 239n, 240, 243
  Four Saints in Three Acts. See under title
  Geographical History of America, 17
  Geography and Plays, 6, 7, 126n, 178, 236, 240
  "George Hugnet," 88, 88n, 125, 125n
  "He And They, Hemingway," 125, 125n
  How to Write, 59n, 68n, 82n, 100n
  Ida, 17
  "If I told Him: A Completed Portrait of Picasso." *See* "Picasso" (second portrait)
  In A Garden A Tragedy In One Act, 272n

"An instant answer or A hundred prominent men," 80n
"Kristians Tonny," 125, 125n
Lectures, American tour, 238, 239, 239n, 241, 241n, 242, 243, 246
Lectures at Oxford and Cambridge, 34n
"Lend a Hand or Four Religions" 86, 86n
"Letters and Parcels and Wool," 161n
"A Long Gay Book," 126n, 239n
Look and Long, A Play in Three Acts, 272n
"Love a Delight," 29, 30n, 32
Lucy Church Amiably, 38, 38n, 43, 46–7, 47n, 48, 48n, 150, 152, 153, 155, 170, 176, 182
Lyrical Opera Made By Two To Be Sung, 75, 76n, 90, 91n
Madame Recamier: an Opera, 167, 168n, 171, 174n, 178, 182, 183n, 189, 220
Making of Americans, 5, 6, 28, 33n, 96n, 110n, 234n, 238, 240, 243
  abridgement, 142, 142n, 143, 159, 234n
  translation, 96, 96n, 99, 102, 103, 103n, 108, 117, 123, 280
"Melanctha", translation, 149n
Morceaux choises de La fabrication des Américains. See Making of Americans, translation
Mother of Us All. See under title
Operas & Plays, 76n, 216, 218, 222, 236
Painted Lace and other Pieces, 30n, 53n, 186n
Paisieu, 82, 82n, 88, 90, 91n
Paris France, 5, 17, 269, 270, 270n, 271n
"Pavlick Tchelitchef or Adrian Arthur," 125n
"Picasso," 65
"Picasso", second portrait ("If I told Him: A Completed Portrait of Picasso") 65

Pigeons on the Grass Alas. See under Four Saints
"Plays" 12
"Poem Pritten on Pfances of Georges Hugnet," 187n
"Poetry and Grammar," 21
"Politeness," 186n
Portrait of F.B. See under Thomson
Portraits and Prayers, 88n, 100n, 120n, 234n
"Preciosilla." *See under* title
Q.E.D. 5, 62n
Reflections on the Atomic Bomb, 120n
"Relieve," 65
"Saint in Seven," 65, 86n, 123, 131, 132, 132n
  translation of, 126n, 132, 132n
"Sentences" in *How to Write*, 98, 99, 100n, 101, 107, 108n, 114, 120
"Susie Asado." *See under* title
"Talks to Saints Or Stories Of Saint Remy," 132n
Tender Buttons, 6, 82n, 239n
They Weighed Weighed-Layed, 182, 183n
Three Lives, 29, 29n, 32, 39n, 111n, 193, 234n, 238, 240
"Three Sitting Here," 48, 48n
To Do: A Book of Alphabets and Birthdays, 269, 269n–270n
"To Virgil and Eugene," 53n–54n
transition interview, 5–6
"Turkey and Bones and Eating and We Liked It," 161n
Useful Knowledge, 6, 65, 84, 84n, 86, 86n, 111n, 119n, 171n
"Virgil Thomson," 53n, 99, 100n, 102, 103n, 104, 105, 107, 125, 125n, 307–8
Wars I have Seen, 270, 270n–271n
"Water Pipe," 24, 24n, 65
A Wedding Bouquet, 252, 253n
World is Round, 88n
Yes is for a Very Young Man, 272, 273n, 273, 276, 276n, 284, 294–6

Index 333

Stein, Leo, 5, 190
Stein, Michael, 213, 223
Stettheimer, Ettie, 106, 106n
Stettheimer, Florine, 17, 77n, 106n, 194n, 196, 198n, 207, 208, 209n, 212, 221,222n, 230, 232, 237, 250, 255, 259, 299. *See also Four Saints in Three Acts*, sets and costumes
   portrait of Thomson, 209n
Stevens, Wallace, 15
Stoddard, Mrs., 55
Stokowski, Leopold, 195, 197n, 289
Stowe, Harriet Beecher
   Uncle Tom's Cabin, 4
Strauss, Richard, 61, 61n
   Aegyptische Helena, 61n
Stravinsky, Igor, 91n, 155n, 291
Sullivan, Arthur, 15, 57n, 254
Susie Asado, 8, 9, 23, 24n, 31, 31n, 32, 35n, 106, 115, 121n, 176, 225, 233, 235, 237, 242, 251
Sutherland, Donald
   Gertrude Stein, a Biography of her Work, 299
Sylviac, Madame, 130, 130n

Tailleferre, Germaine, 7
Tanner, Allen, 100, 100n, 104n
Tanner, Florence, 101n, 103, 104n
Taylor, Joseph Deems, 106, 107n, 207
Tchelitchev, Pavel (Pavlik), 34n, 52n, 69, 70n, 72, 100n, 103, 119, 125, 125n, 164, 164n, 176, 187n, 190, 289, 298, 299
Teresa of Avila, St., 10, 13, 25, 25n, 26, 28, 29, 29n
   Interior Castle, 25n
   Life of St Teresa of Jesus (autobiography), 25n
   Way of Perfection, 25n
Thomson, Clara May (Virgil's mother), 100, 287
Thomson, Virgil
   Aire de Phèdre, 156, 156n, 157, 165, 175, 176
   Airs divers, 67n

The Art of Judging Music, 286, 287, 288
Le Bains-Bar: waltzes for violin and accordion, 125, 126n
"*Berceau de Gertrude Stein . . . sous le titre de Lady Godiva's Waltzes.*" *See under* title
Book of music, planned, 173, 173n, 175–81,
Bosseut. See Oraison funèbre d'Henriette de France / Bosseut
Capital Capitals, score. *See under* title
Capital Capitals, explanation of, 110, 111n
Christian Bérard: en personne, 125, 126n
Christian Bérard: prisonnier, 114n, 125, 126n
Christian Bérard: soldat, 125, 126n
Church Sonata. *See Sonata da chiesa*
Cliquet-Pleyel in F, 91, 92n, 178n
Commentaire sure Saint Jérome, 89, 90n, 92n, 176
Fable of La Fontaine, 147, 147n, 148, 148n, 150, 175, 176
Film: Deux Soeurs Qui Ne Sont Pas Soeurs (score), 167n, 169, 169n, 175, 264, 264n, 290, 300
Five Phrases from the Song of Solomon 47n, 64n, 66n, 67n, 70n, 92n, 180, 304
Four Saints in Three Acts. *See under* title
Georges Hugnet, poète et home de letters, 91, 92n
Koussevitzsky concert, review of, 95n
Lord Byron. *See* Larson
Louisiana Story, 286–8, 289, 290, 291, 292, 293
Madame Marthe-Marthine, 83, 83n, 84, 92n
Marquis de Sade. *See Commentaire sure Saint Jérome*

Miss Gertrude Stein, 83, 83n, 91n, 91–2, 92n, 305–6
Mother of Us All. See under title
Mrs C.W.L., 92n
Music Right and Left, 297
New York Herald Tribune, 7 Jan. 1946, column in, 6
Oraison funèbre d'Henriette de France / Bossuet, 147, 148n, 148, 150, 151, 153, 154, 155, 156, 178, 180
Piano Sonata No. 3 On the White Keys "for Gertrude Stein," 162, 162n, 167, 169, 171, 177, 273, 290, 290n
Pigeons on the Grass Alas, *See under Four Saints Portrait of F.B.* (score), 125, 126n, 300
Portraits of Ladies: Exercise in Composition: for 4 Clarinets, 100, 101n, 103, 125, 126n
Portrait of Señorita Juanita de Medina Accompanied by Her Mother, 77, 77n, 92n
Preciosilla (score). *See under* title
review of *Carmen Jones*, 298n
review of John Cage, 295, 295n
River, 254
Russell Hitchcock, reading, 148, 148n, 157, 157n
Sauguet, from Life, 92, 92n, 93
The Seine at Night, 287, 287n, 289
La Seine, Duchess of Rohan, 71, 72n, 115, 121n, 175, 185n
Singe et la Lèopard, 148, 148n
Les Soirées bangolaises, 92n
Sonata da Chiesa, 67n, 69n, 70n, 98, 99n, 101, 104, 107, 112n, 177, 185n, 304
Sonata d'Eglise. See Sonata da Chiesa
Sonata No. 3. *See* Piano Sonata No. 3
Song of Solomon. See Five Phrases for the Song of Solomon
Stabat Mater, 79n*The State of Music*, 263, 263n, 265, 286

Susie Asado, score. *See under* title
Symphony on a Hymn Tune, 76, 77n, 79, 79n, 81, 84n, 84, 86, 89, 95n, 97, 97n, 98, 99, 100, 101, 104, 107, 112n
Valse Grégorienne. See under title
Variations and Fugues on Sunday School Hymns, 33, 33n, 67n, 304
Violin Sonata No. 1 (1930), 152, 153n, 162, 162n, 174, 186, 186n
Wars I have Seen, review of, 270–1
Todd, Dorothy, 61, 61n
Toklas, Alice Babette
    The Alice B. Toklas Cook Book, 170n, 267n
Tommasini, Anthony, 7
Tonny, Kristians, 70n, 80, 80n, 81, 81n, 84, 84n, 85, 87, 89, 94n, 97, 99–100, 101n, 101, 103, 106, 108, 116, 118, 119, 122, 125, 134, 138, 147n, 150, 152, 152n, 158, 158n, 159, 164, 164n, 170, 176, 177, 187n, 188
    Faÿ, portrait of, 164n
    self-portrait, 164n
Toscanini, Arturo, 16
Tourel, Jennie, 67n
Transatlantic Review, 31n, 33n
transition, 5–6, 31n, 62n, 79–80, 80n, 93, 93n, 101, 102n, 110, 111n, 114, 114n, 117, 124, 127, 133n, 135n, 158, 172n, 181n. *See also* Paul Jolas
Tunney, Gene, 68, 69n, 72
Tyrwhitt-Wison, Gerald (Lord Berners), 257n, 295
A Wedding Bouquet, 252, 253n
Tzara, Tristan, 6, 48n, 57n, 59, 59n, 95n, 303
    "Inquiry . . . into the Spirit of America," 80n

Ursel, Comtesse de, 72, 73n
Ursel, Henri, Comte de, 72, 73n, 103, 104n

Index   335

Valéry, Paul, 86
Valse Grégorienne, 67n, 121n, 175, 177, 178, 179, 180, 185n, 264, 264n, 303
Vanity Fair, 7, 38n, 42n
Van Vechten, Carl, 25n, 38n, 56n, 82, 82n–83n, 84, 99, 101, 104, 105n, 105–6, 106n, 107, 113, 113n, 114, 117, 118, 119, 120, 122, 123, 127, 129, 136, 148, 148n, 154, 156, 158, 162, 163, 164, 165n, 166, 167, 168, 170–1, 172, 173–4, 222n, 226n, 236, 251, 253, 266, 274, 277n, 279, 283, 284, 285, 287, 294, 295, 297, 298, 300
  book of Thomson's music, planned preface, 176, 177, 180–1, 181n
  book publication of opera, preface, 181, 181n
  Parties: Scenes from Contemporary New York Life, 164, 165n
  Peter Whiffle, His Life and Works, 136, 136n
Verdi, Giuseppe
  La Dame aux Camélias, 166n
Verdi, Nancy Clare, 39n, 41, 125
Victoria, Queen, 239n
Vidal, Gore, 302n
Villemorin, Pierre Louis François Lévêque de, 149, 150n
Viot, Jacques, 165, 165n
Vitrac, Roger, 97, 98n, 100, 101n, 103
  Les Mystères de l'amour, 98n
  Victor, ou Les enfants au pouvoir, 98n
Volti (The San Francisco Chamber Singers)
  "Gertrude, Virgil & Four Saints: From Vision to Verity," 4
Voorhies, Rousseau, 238, 239n

Wagner, Richard, 9, 52n
  Lohengrin, 4

Walska, Ganna, 109, 110n
Washington, George, 9, 60n, 239n
Watson, James Sibley, 126, 127n
Watson, Hildegarde (Mrs Sibley), 7, 47, 47n, 95n, 107n
Watson, Sibley, 99, 107n
Watson, Steven
  Prepare for Saints: The Making of a Modern Opera (video), 4
  Prepare for Saints: Gertrude Stein, Virgil Thomson, and the Mainstreaming of American Modernism, 4
Wayne, Beatrice Robinson, 259, 259n
Webster, Daniel, 17, 173, 253, 253n
Weissberger, Arnold, 276, 276n, 279
Wells, Orson, 251n
Wertheim, Alma Morgenthau, 93–4, 94n, 106, 183, 226n
Wharton, Edith
  Glimpse of the Moon, 58–9, 59n
Whittemore, Thomas, 236, 236n
Wilde, Oscar, 52n
Wilder, Thornton, 248, 248n
  The Bridge over San Luis Rey, 248n
Williams, William Carlos, 31n, 87n, 124n
  "Improvisations," 80n
  "The Work of Gertrude Stein," 141n
Wilson, Robert, 16
  Einstein on the Beach, 16
Wilson, Woodrow, 171, 171n
Winters, Yvor, 29n
Woolf, Leonard, 91n
Woolf, Virginia, 91n
  "Mark on the Wall," translation, 150n
  "Mr. Bennett and Mrs. Brown," 91n

Young, Stark, 16
Yvonne (girlfriend of Hugnet), 117n